Alamein

Also by the Same Authors:

Fire in the Night – Wingate of Burma, Ethiopia and Zion

PREVIOUS BOOKS BY JOHN BIERMAN:

Dark Safari: The Life Behind the Legend of
Henry Morton Stanley

Napoleon III and His Carnival Empire

Odyssey

Righteous Gentile: The Story of Raul Wallenberg,
Missing Hero of the Holocaust

PREVIOUS BOOKS BY COLIN SMITH:

The Last Crusade (novel)

The Cut-Out (novel)

Carlos – Portrait of a Terrorist

Alamein

War Without Hate

JOHN BIERMAN AND
COLIN SMITH

VIKING
an imprint of
PENGUIN BOOKS

VIKING

Published by the Penguin Group
Penguin Books Ltd, 80 Strand, London WC2R ORL, England
Penguin Putnam Inc., 375 Hudson Street, New York, New York 10014, USA
Penguin Books Australia Ltd, 250 Camberwell Road,
Camberwell, Victoria 3124, Australia
Penguin Books Canada Ltd, 10 Alcorn Avenue, Toronto, Ontario, Canada M4V 3B2
Penguin Books India (P) Ltd, 11 Community Centre,
Panchsheel Park, New Delhi – 110 017, India
Penguin Books (NZ) Ltd, Cnr Rosedale and Airborne Roads,
Albany, Auckland, New Zealand
Penguin Books (South Africa) (Pty) Ltd, 24 Sturdee Avenue,
Rosebank 2196, South Africa

Penguin Books Ltd, Registered Offices: 80 Strand, London WC2R ORL, England

www.penguin.com

First published 2002
I

Copyright © John Bierman and Colin Smith, 2002
The moral right of the authors has been asserted

Set in 11.5/14pt Monotype Bembo
Typeset by Rowland Phototypesetting Ltd,
Bury St Edmunds, Suffolk
Printed in Great Britain by Clays Ltd, St Ives plc

A CIP catalogue record for this book is available from the British Library

ISBN 0-670-91109-7

In gratitude, to those who turned the tide

Now this is not the end. It is not even the beginning of the end. But it is, perhaps, the end of the beginning.

Winston Churchill

Sixty years! He's old and out of sorts
But still he smiles to see them on the screen,
The lads they were, tin hats, enormous shorts
As big as bivouacs. Full magazine,
One up the spout, going in at the high-port
Through smoke, a newsreel shot in black and white;
A fake for civvies, so he'd always thought,
It wasn't cameras shooting that first night.

And then live interviews – well, just about –
Old men, false teeth and medals, pretty toys
Dangling from their ribbons. Gaunt or stout
They wheeze or croak. Fade out. He hears the noise
Of bugle's rhetoric; then words: Lest we forget.
He snorts, then wonders why his face is wet.

Vernon Scannell, private soldier,
51st Highland Infantry Division

Contents

List of Illustrations

List of Illustrations

Section Three

52. The End. On a Tunisian beach, an Italian soldier lies dead beside a boat

The authors and publisher are grateful to the following for permission to reproduce photographs: Imperial War Museum for Nos. 1, 3–17, 20, 26–29, 31–34, 36–38, 40–42 and 44–52; Ariye Shai for Nos. 18–19; Associated Press for No. 21; Alex Berger-Almasy for No. 22; US Library of Congress for No. 23; Bundesarchiv (Koblenz) for Nos. 25, 35 and 43; Robert Hunt Library for No. 30; Revista Militar/ Brigadier Cerba for Nos. 2 and 24.

List of Maps

OVERVIEW OF NORTH AFRICA
FROM TUNIS TO CAIRO

SICILY

Algiers

ALGERIA

35°N

TUNISIA

Tunis
Cape Bon
Efidaville
Sousse
Valletta
MALTA

Tebessa
Kasserine

Gafsa
Sfax
Chott el Fejaj
Gabes
Chott
Djerid
Tebaga Gap
Mareth
Medenine
Wilder's Gap
Tripoli

M E D I T E R

Gulf of Sirte

30°N

GRAND ERG ORIENTAL

Arco dei Fileni
(Marble Arch)
marked border
between Cyrenaica
and Tripolitania

TRIPOLITANIA
PROVINCE

Hamran Sand Sea

ALGERIA

L I B

25°N

Murzuk Oasis

Murzuk
Sand Sea

FRENCH WEST AFRICA
(NIGER)

FRENC

20°N

0   100   200   300 miles
0   100   200   300   400   500 km

5°E

10°E

15°E

Fort Lamy
(N'Djamena)

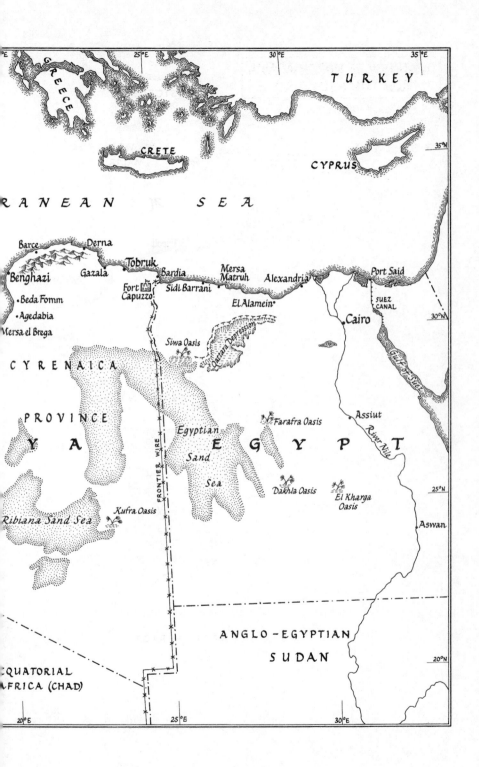

Reunion

Rommel Barracks, Germany, November 1999

You have to keep reminding yourself that in their youth these convivial old men were doing their utmost to kill each other. You have to keep reminding yourself, too, that for all the beery bonhomie of this Eighth Army–Afrika Korps reunion, the desert war it commemorates was no contest of moral equivalents. It was part of a life-or-death struggle of flawed democracy against brute dictatorship, and the fact that these veterans are now so comfortable in each other's company must not be allowed to imply that the struggle was pointless. Nor should it be allowed to legitimize the easy evasion that time inevitably heals all wounds.

What it does signify is the extent to which shared experience, common hardship and mutual respect can create a bizarre comradeship of antagonists. These old soldiers know something about themselves, and each other, that can only be guessed at by those who have not tasted the chaos, terror, confusion – and the manic adrenalin high – of battle.

Whatever barrier exists between erstwhile Tommy and quondam Fritz six decades after the events that bring them together now, it is one more of language than of sentiment. And that's a barrier that crumbles without too much difficulty as British, German and a handful of Italian veterans meet in the barracks named after Germany's legendary desert commander, Field Marshal Erwin Rommel. A few words of pidgin, remembered smatterings of each other's soldier slang, memories of mutual privations and a song they loved in common, these are enough to close the culture gap.

None of these men is younger than his late seventies, and most are well into their eighties. As youngsters they went to war – some as volunteers, others as conscripts – with callow notions of King and Country on the one side, Volk und Führer on the other. The desert rapidly rendered them older, sadder and wiser. Many bear the visible legacy of the wounds they received in North Africa. All bear the subtler ravages of advancing age and harrowing recall. Theirs was a bitter and implacable war in which death came in many terrible ways.

Yet men on both sides like to say that it was a war without hate –
Krieg ohne Hass, as Rommel himself is said to have described it.

However that may be, it was a war virtually without atrocities,
which makes it remarkable enough. Conducted across a largely un-
populated terrain, it provided no scope for the slaughter of non-
combatants, intended or inadvertent. And, soldier on soldier, it was
fought with a regard for the rules of war unmatched on any other
Second World War battle front. Rommel must take a lot of the credit
for this: he was a stickler for the Geneva Conventions and saw to it
that British prisoners were treated humanely, receiving the same
medical attention if wounded as his own men. The British recipro-
cated, of course, and there are those on both sides who are not ashamed
to use the term 'chivalry' to describe the spirit of the campaign. That
may be putting altogether too much of a gloss on the mechanized
mass-slaughter that occurred in the North African desert between 1940
and 1943, but it's these old men's recollection and their justification for
whatever their duty required them to do in the heat of battle. If that's
self-deception, surely they've earned the right to it.

There's an enormous paradox at the heart of Rommel. For all his
insistence on the Geneva Conventions and the extraordinary respect
– even veneration – his dash and brilliance inspired among subordinates
and opponents alike, he was nevertheless a fervent admirer of Hitler
and would remain so until it became clear to him that his Führer was
losing the war. An unquestioning patriot and hard-core militarist, but
otherwise profoundly apolitical, Rommel was a professional soldier,
pure and simple. War to him was an exhilarating game, and he was
able to play it with no more hatred for his opponent than, say, the
captain of a rugby football team might feel for his opposite number.
In his limited way, he may be counted an honourable man – albeit in
a deeply dishonourable cause.

But if Rommel is the one authentic Second World War hero of
whom a democratic post-war Germany has no need to feel ashamed
– and, so to speak, the ghostly master of ceremonies at this reunion –
there's a far less savoury spectre sniffing at the edges of the feast.
The Panzerarmee Afrika was, after all, a significant part of Hitler's
instrument for world domination. And while it may be the one branch
of the Wehrmacht whose veterans least deserve to be considered
'criminals and murderers', the powers-that-be within the German
Ministry of Defence are clearly uneasy about this reunion. Their fears,

that it may appear to be a glorification of Hitler's war-machine and an implicit endorsement of the militaristic traditions which, together with racist dogma and unbridled nationalism, were an essential ingredient of National Socialism, are not unreasonable.

As a front-page article in the widely respected *Suddeutscher Zeitung* points out, although the Afrika Korps was never involved in war crimes and enjoys a high reputation abroad, 'the Wehrmacht as such, and any part of it, does not belong to the tradition of the present-day German forces'. Consequently, says the newspaper, Defence Ministry officials 'pushed the alarm button' when they learned belatedly that the pending reunion was to be held on ministry property. With 200 guests coming from abroad – some from as far away as Australia – it would not have been possible to call the reunion off at short notice, but the Defence Ministry has done its best to tone things down. On the first night of this three-day event, for example, the army bandsmen playing 'oompah' music as the veterans swigged beer and swapped reminiscences had to appear in Bavarian peasant garb instead of uniform. On the second night (misgivings at the ministry having been partially allayed), they were permitted to play in uniform. But, perhaps as a quid pro quo, their selections were less martial in tone, even including the Israeli folksong 'Hava Nagila'. You have to wonder what six million Jewish ghosts might make of that.

A further concession to political correctness has turned a Grosser Zapfenstreich into a mere Serenade. A Zapfenstreich, with its alarming onomatopoeia, is a nocturnal martial ceremony dating back to the seventeenth century, a sort of tattoo, originally devised to register that all ranks had left the taverns and brothels and had returned to camp before 'Lights out'. The version presented for this occasion had been shortened and lightened. But even in this guise it seemed disturbingly reminiscent of the kind of ceremonial associated with the Nazi era.

It is a moonless night and the only illumination comes from flaming torches held aloft by shadowy markers as uniformed men perform intricate drill-movements to the wail and thump of fife and drum. In daylight or under floodlights – as, for instance, at the Edinburgh Tattoo – this kind of display might seem innocuous enough, if stirring. Here, the flaming torches and the encircling dark lend it a sinister cast. And when the band plays the tune (the original words of which have been abandoned) of the old national anthem, 'Deutschland über Alles', and, the twenty-minute ceremony over, the shadowy column stalks off into the night, flanked by the torch-bearers as side drums mark the step, you find yourself reflecting that the sight and sound of uniformed Germans on the march can still make you feel uneasy. Yet later, up close and in the full glare of the barrack hall lights, the bandsmen and soldiers are revealed to be harmless amateurs – adolescent girls and boys and well-padded middle-aged burghers, belonging to a local folkloric music society. Their muskets are theatrical props and their uniforms a threadbare kind of Ruritanian motley.

Sam Bradshaw, leader of the Eighth Army Old Comrades' Association, bears his eight decades and three war-wounds lightly. He went through the entire North African campaign, and then on until the end of the fighting in Italy, and had seven tanks destroyed under him in the process. Starting as a private soldier, he earned the hard-come-by honour of a battlefield commission and ended the war with the rank of major.

As chairman of the Eighth Army Veterans' Association, Bradshaw has made the maintenance and strengthening of links between his organization and the Deutsche Afrika Korps Verband something of a personal crusade. If anything, he seems more exercised than his phlegmatic opposite number, Karl-Heinz Tesch, over the German government's ambivalent attitude towards its desert war veterans.

Bradshaw's record of service, and his youthful lack of political perspective beyond the conventional patriotism of the day, is typical of his wartime generation. He joined the Territorial Army in 1938 when it began to seem that war was inevitable. 'I was young and enthusiastic,' he recalls, 'and didn't quite realize what I was getting into. To me, we were there because we were there. We were in it and we had to win it. We were just doing our job.'

Such unreflective stoicism is hardly the style of today's youth, and some may think that this is just as well. Still, Bradshaw is no proto-Rambo; he makes no pretence that the traumatic experiences of war in the desert left him unmarked. 'It affected me later in life,' he says. 'I had a breakdown just after the war and another in 1966 . . . You can only take so much and as you get older your memories get stronger. At these get-togethers with old comrades, of course, you screen out the bad stuff and concentrate on the good times.

'But when you're alone . . .'

He trails off. Sam Bradshaw is not of a type or a generation that likes to display its hurts. The nightmares, hinted at, go undescribed. 'All of us feel the war was a terrible waste of human life and it should never happen again,' he says. 'But if there has to be war, the desert war was a wonderful example of how it should be fought, because it was based on deep respect of men at the sharp end for each other.'

Lean and spare, wearing an embroidered Loden coat, a Tyrolean trilby and string tie, and sporting a limp and a walking stick, Hans-Gunther Stark, the Afrika Korps veterans' archivist and editor of their magazine *Oase*, is the very picture of a retired member of the German military caste. Descended, as he tells you proudly, from several generations of army officers, he helped to set up the supply logistics of the Afrika Korps, then he transferred to the Eastern front, where he served as an artilleryman and was badly wounded. 'That was an entirely different war,' he says. 'The hatred on both sides was intense. This was never so in the desert. The Mediterranean was a barrier the SS never crossed.'

Karl-Heinz Boettger, a one-time tank commander who became West German military attaché in London after the war, comes to the hotel where a twenty-strong Australian contingent are staying and insists on buying beer for all of them. He is voluble and passionate about friendship between old enemies and is perturbed by the image of Wehrmacht culpability in the Nazi extermination campaign. 'That crime against the Jews cannot be eradicated,' he says, quite un-prompted. 'I am ashamed, but I cannot take the blame. Nevertheless, here in Germany we are regarded as murderers.'

Like many German veterans and their families, Boettger is particu-larly exercised about the controversial photographic exhibition, 'The Germany Army and Genocide', that has been travelling the country under government sponsorship to drive home the uncomfortable lesson of the German soldiery's participation in Nazi-era crimes. Although this is not a charge that can be laid against Rommel's men, they feel they are being tarred with the same brush.

In evidence of the respect each side felt for the other in the desert war, Boettger displays a glowing obituary he wrote for *Oase* on the recent death of the New Zealand double-VC, Captain Charles Upham, whose company took him prisoner during a battle on Ruweisat Ridge, near El Alamein, in July 1942. Boettger remembers especially the New Zealand platoon sergeant to whom he surrendered after being severely wounded. He was 'a fine soldier and a sensitive human being – he brewed a cup of tea that revived me and I still consider that cup of tea the best and most welcome drink I have had in my life'.

In advance of the reunion, Hans–Gunther Stark and Willi Utz, now a wealthy industrialist, then a junior officer on Rommel's staff, drive a few kilometres to lay a wreath on the simple memorial that stands a few yards from the spot where Rommel died exactly fifty-five years previously. Suspected (falsely, as it happens) of complicity in the failed July 1944 bomb plot to assassinate Hitler, but an outstanding national hero to the German public at the time, Rommel had been given a choice by Hitler through two generals sent to his house by the High Command: swallow poison and safeguard your reputation, your wife and your young son, or face trial with the other conspirators and die a traitor's death. The generals left him in a staff car parked on a dirt road at the edge of a forest while he took the pill they had given him. They returned a few minutes later to find him dead, his lips a tell-tale cyanide blue. He was given a state funeral with full military honours.

Rommel's widow Lucie was permitted, with their young son Manfred, to go on living on the small country estate at nearby Herr-lingen that a grateful Führer had bestowed upon his once-favourite field marshal. Today, a plaque at the entrance to the estate, now the property of an architect, reveals a piquant history: between 1933 and 1939 when it was confiscated by the Nazis, the house and grounds were a holiday camp for Jewish children. So does the stain of Nazi racial crimes besmirch even those who may have had no direct part in them.

Back at Rommel Barracks where the reunion is in full swing, there's a good deal of drinking, but no obvious drunkenness. A table full of Royal Tank Regiment veterans from Wales, among them four Chelsea Pensioners resplendent in their knee-length scarlet coats, give a sub-dued rendering of 'Land of my Fathers'. The really raucous singing comes from a table occupied by veterans of Italy's Young Fascists Regiment – 'the heroes of Bir el Gubi', as they choose to describe themselves. Periodically they burst into bombastic blackshirt song of the kind that Germans are forbidden by law to sing. For whatever reason, veterans of the less ideological Italian units – and you think especially of the Ariete and the paras of the Folgore Division, who acquitted themselves so well at Alamein – do not bother to attend these reunions. Perhaps, unlike the old 'Young Fascists', they do not want to be reminded of the dishonorable cause for which they fought. Benito Mussolini used to praise those of his followers who were with him from the start in 1922 as 'Fascists of the First Hour'. The die-hard 'heroes of Bir el Gubi' may be termed Fascists of the Last Hour. Some wear Bersaglieri hats, melodramatically adorned with black cockerel plumes, an incongruous accompaniment to their civilian lounge suits and sports jackets. Others wear the black felt fez of their regiment. Many sport beards, Garibaldi-style. Some have brought along their wives, alarmingly pugnacious women wearing grey fascisti berets.

Are these bellicose old men still wedded to the blackshirt credo? 'Sempre!' insists their leader and archivist, Antonio Ciocci. And Mussolini? 'A great man betrayed by weaklings,' says Ciocci. Not everyone, it seems, has learned the lessons of the Second World War.

You can't help noticing during the four days of this reunion how much nostalgic talk there is of Rommel and how little of his nemesis, the Eighth Army commander, Bernard Montgomery. Among the men of both sides Germany's most dashing commander of the Second World War continues to enjoy a degree of respect and affection that is denied to the methodical, businesslike 'Monty'.

In the field and in his day, the British commander was a tremendous morale-raiser, communicating to the troops his own conviction that at last they had a leader who could beat the vaunted Desert Fox at his own game. But, for all his perky self-confidence, 'Monty' lacked the charisma that creates an enduring legend. While Rommel's lustre endures beyond the grave, Monty's has been somewhat clouded by his subsequent feuds with Eisenhower and the other American generals and by his living on into a cranky, egocentric and increasingly querulous old age. As Churchill put it: 'In defeat unbeatable: in victory unbearable.' The poison pill Hitler sent to Rommel via his two tame generals was perhaps a gift of an unintended kind to the reputation of his once favourite field commander.

The final act of this reunion is a ceremonial wreath-laying at the evangelical cemetery in Herrlingen where Rommel is buried. The morning is bright and brisk and the veterans, many of them leaning heavily on sticks, are kept waiting without audible complaint for an

hour and a quarter for the arrival of Rommel's son Manfred, formerly
mayor of Stuttgart and an icon of democratic, post-Hitler Germany.
He is not to blame for the delay: he is suffering from Parkinson's
Disease.

After the wreaths have been laid, a politically correct (in the best
sense) speech is delivered – in German and faultless, accentless English
– by a youngish Colonel Jakobson of the politically correct (in the
best sense) Bundeswehr. No serving officer of more senior rank has
been allowed to undertake the task, for the Ministry of Defence
remains uneasy to the last about the reunion.

The ceremony ends with a plangent solo trumpet playing a verse
of the traditional lament for a fallen comrade, 'Der Gute Kamerad'.
Pre-dating Hitler as it does by several generations, the song has no
jarring ideological connotations. It expresses no triumphalism, no
overblown patriotism, simply a soldier's grief at the death of a friend.
All can relate to that, and for Tommy, as for Fritz, it is a lament not
only for the charismatic Rommel but for all the fallen of that long-ago
desert war.

PART ONE

The Italians

This land was made for War. As glass
Resists the bite of vitriol, so this hard
And calcined earth rejects
The battle's hot, corrosive impact.

– Jocelyn Brooke,
Royal Army Medical Corps

For nine months Benito Mussolini dithered and agonized, changing his mind almost daily about whether or not to take his country into the war that began with the German invasion of Poland on 1 September 1939. General Sir Archibald Wavell, commander of British forces in the Middle East, compared the Italian dictator to a man who has ostentatiously climbed to the top of a high diving-board and then lost his nerve. 'I think he must do something,' Wavell, an unusually thoughtful professional soldier, wrote to a colleague. 'If he cannot make a graceful dive he will at least have to jump in somehow; he can hardly put on his dressing-gown and walk down the stairs again.'

As C-in-C Middle East, Wavell had a very direct interest in whether Mussolini would take the leap and when. Il Duce's new Roman Empire spread out on either side of Wavell's bailiwick – to the southeast encompassing most of the Horn of Africa, including recently conquered Abyssinia, and to the west, along the Mediterranean coast, taking in Cyrenaica and Tripolitania, today's Libya. If Mussolini did go to war, one of his aims would doubtless be to link up the two halves of his African empire by driving the British out of Egypt, Palestine and Sudan, in the process taking over the Suez Canal, the short route to India and the Far East.

Although as a young revolutionary socialist he had inveighed passionately against Italy's seizure of Libya from the decaying Ottoman Empire, Mussolini now revelled in his possession of what he liked to call Italy's Fourth Shore. The indigenous Senussi tribesmen of Libya had been comprehensively crushed and 100,000 Italian settlers had taken root in white, flat-roofed houses in burgeoning towns such as Benghazi, Derna and Tobruk, spread out along the Mediterranean littoral.

There had been tension along the border between Libya and Egypt in the mid-1930s. But when Rex King-Clark, a young British Army officer with a private income and a taste for aviation, flew into Benghazi at the controls of his single-engined Miles Whitney Straight in March 1937, he was made welcome enough. King-Clark, on his

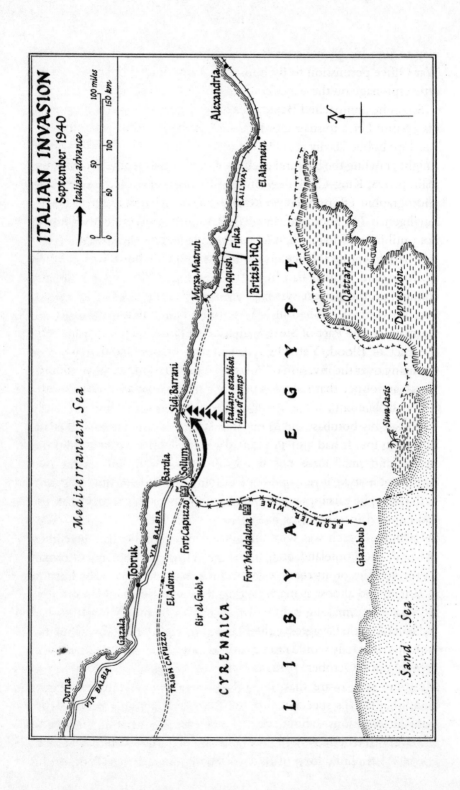

ITALIAN INVASION
September 1940

→ Italian advance

100 miles
150 km

0   50   50   100

Mediterranean Sea

Alexandria

El Alamein

Fuka   RAILWAY

Marsa Matruh

Baqqush   British HQ

Sidi Barrani

Italians establish
line of camps

Sollum

Bardia

Fort Capuzzo

Fort Maddalena

FRONTIER WIRE

Giarabub

Tobruk

VIA BALBIA

El Adem

Bir el Gubi

TRIGH CAPUZZO

Gazala

VIA BALBIA

Derna

CYRENAICA

L I B Y A   E G Y P T

Qattara

Depression

Siwa Oasis

Sand

Sea

way to join his Manchester Regiment in Palestine, had been given War Office permission to fly himself there, provided he undertook a little espionage on the way: flying combined with spying.

So, as he approached Benghazi's little airport at 200 feet he aimed his 35-mm Leica to snap shot after shot of the harbour, where Italian warships bobbed lazily at anchor, and its environs. The next day, after a night crawling the bars and eyeing the settler girls around Benghazi's main piazza, King-Clark flew on to Alexandria and Cairo, where his photographic efforts were gratefully received by Royal Air Force intelligence. His photos of Benghazi harbour would prove useful, but not until June of 1940 when Mussolini finally took the plunge.

Up to that point Il Duce's performance had been bewildering. After all, Mussolini himself had been the first to use the word 'Axis' to conjure up the perfect synergy between Fascist Italy and National Socialist Germany. Then in May 1939 he had drawn even closer to Germany in the Pact of Steel, which he had originally wanted to call the Pact of Blood. Yet when Britain and France declared war on Germany over the invasion of Poland, Mussolini's immediate response was to announce that Italy was neither a neutral nor a combatant, but a 'non-belligerent'.

For all his bombast, he knew that Italy was not ready to fight a European foe. It had a small industrial base. It made some good cars, aircraft and small arms but not enough of them. And despite its considerable style, it remained one of the poorest countries in Europe with per capita earnings no more than the average American or Briton had enjoyed in 1800. Nor had Fascism done much to correct social inequalities, which was why the middle classes tended to support it. In 1939, the homeland of Fiat and Alfa Romeo had only 372,000 motor vehicles on its roads, compared to over two and a half million in Britain and almost as many in France. The shortage of drivers and mechanics was making it difficult for the Italian army to mechanize.

General Carlo Favagrossa, the Under-Secretary for War Production, estimated that Italy would not be ready for hostilities against the Anglo-French until October 1942 at the earliest. In his saner moments Mussolini was aware that, far from the eight million bayonets he brandished in his speeches, his army could field no more than ten front-line divisions – about 200,000 men – and those poorly equipped and over-stretched following the annexation of Albania in April 1939. For all Mussolini's love of a good parade, his armed forces barely matched those of the British, who had been reluctantly rearming for only three years. Compared with their German Axis Pact partners, the Italians were, militarily, barely on the same planet.

Italian tanks were good for crowd control and frightening Ethiopian horsemen but not much else. They were lightly armoured, under-gunned and difficult to see out of. Radio communication was rare, which made the movements of even small formations difficult to co-ordinate. A squadron commander might have to relay his orders by flying various coloured pennants or even flashing Morse signals. The Italian artillery was little better. A lot of it dated from before 1918 and had never been properly refurbished. Nevertheless it would turn out that, of all the Italian army, the gunners often proved the bravest, sometimes serving their guns until they were literally overrun by enemy tanks. Still, with the best will in the world Italian gunners could not be expected to match, in accuracy or rates of fire, the British Army's new 25-pounder field-gun.

It was the same story with the other two services. Out of the vaunted Regia Aeronautica's 1,760 aircraft, only 900 could really be described as front-line machines. True, Italian aircraft frequently won international air races and held speed records, but the best planes were not always the ones the air force got. By the summer of 1940, when British and German fighter pilots were duelling over the south of England in Spitfires, Hurricanes and Messerschmitts – low-wing monoplanes with closed cockpits and retractable undercarriages – Italy's front-line fighter was the Fiat CR-42 biplane, a pretty aircraft but at least 100 mph slower.

The navy was in a similar plight. There were no aircraft carriers because the Italians believed that air superiority over the Mediter-ranean could be maintained from bases in southern Italy and North Africa. They had a few good ships, but gunnery was poor and the latest advances in radio communications, electronic warfare and counter-measures had been ignored. What the Italian navy did have was the Tenth Light Flotilla, pioneering frogmen with human tor-pedoes, midget submarines, and high-speed launches packed with explosives – brave men with clever and innovative equipment but a tiny élite who could not hope to make up for the navy's other deficiencies.

Came the traumatic spring of 1940, and the mesmerized Italians watched their invincible ally introduce the 'effete' democracies to

Blitzkrieg. Unbelievably, the five-million-strong French army – considered by Stalin, among others, to be the most formidable in the world – began to crumble. On 10 June 1940 Mussolini, with what the *New York Times* memorably called 'the courage of a jackal at the heels of a bolder beast of prey', found the nerve to dive from his high board.

On the same day, Erwin Rommel reached the English Channel with the first German tanks. This stocky figure, at the time virtually unknown outside the Wehrmacht, was already a favourite of Hitler by virtue of his tactical daring, his insistence on leading from the front and his adroit handling of personal publicity. Now Rommel handed one of his officers the Leica he always carried with him, a personal gift from Propaganda Minister Josef Goebbels, and clambered on to the turret of a tank to pose for a picture.

As for Mussolini, he thought the war was as good as over. 'I only need a few thousand dead so that I can sit at the peace conference as a man who has fought,' he confided to Marshal Pietro Badoglio, his Army Chief of Staff. A few days later, France surrendered and Britain stood alone, weakened and seemingly in danger of imminent invasion. There would surely never be a better chance for Mussolini to grab some glittering prizes from the tottering British Empire. Hitler had just seized most of continental Europe in less than three months; why could not Mussolini create an enormous Italian colony, stretching from Libya in the west to Palestine in the east and from Egypt in the north to Kenya in the south?

Meanwhile the British in the Middle East were trying to maintain the illusion that they were spoiling for a fight and were thick on the ground. As soon as Mussolini declared war, the British 11th Hussars started to raid Italian roads and smaller outposts. Known as the Cherry Pickers for a Peninsular War incident in which they were ambushed while raiding an orchard, the 11th Hussars were simultaneously all that was right and all that was wrong with the British army. The regiment had charged with the Light Brigade at Balaclava, and almost a century later its Crimean War officers would have felt quite at home at a 1940 mess night.

Almost to a man the officers were tall, upper-class young Englishmen who came to a formal dinner wearing the same skin-tight crimson trews that had seen service in the Crimea. They had almost all attended the same top six English public schools – Eton, Harrow, Winchester, Wellington, Rugby and Charterhouse – and were almost all interested in polo, gambling and women, not always in that order. Most of them were addicted to some kind of dangerous sport – hunting, point-to-point, the Cresta Run – and if they were not always terribly bright they were generally very brave. Now they began to cross into Libya in their elderly and rather stately-looking Rolls-Royce armoured cars to find out what was happening and, when they could, to raise hell.

It soon became apparent that, despite their numerical superiority, the Italians' morale was not always good. Years of fighting the recalcitrant Senussi tribesmen of Cyrenaica seemed to have left them with an ingrained fear of leaving their splendid coastal highway, whereas the British almost immediately took to hit-and-run raiding in the desert.

Not that they could invariably hit as hard as they might. Rea Leakey, a Kenyan-born subaltern* commanding a light reconnaissance tank of the 1st Royal Tank Regiment, joined with the Hussars in an attack on the Italians' Beau Geste-style Fort Capuzzo. Once within range, Leakey found himself forced to fire his service revolver at the fort through the gaping port in his turret that should have been filled by a Vickers machine-gun. His gunner had to fire a rifle through the port that was intended for the other Vickers. Leakey's tank had only recently arrived from England, and somewhere along the way someone had removed its armament, rendering it about as lethal as a tractor.

In the first week of hostilities Capuzzo was briefly captured and prisoners taken. The Hussars, who at least had machine-guns, ventured east of Bardia almost as far as Tobruk itself, and ambushed a column of vehicles. Their captives included General Lastucci, the Tenth Army's Engineer-in-Chief, and his mistress, whom he was trying to evacuate. A high-spirited female, she demanded to be returned to Bardia but the general insisted that she remain with him and apparently got his way.

The British campaigned, as they always would, with the minimum of creature comforts. Day after day they wore the same clothes until they all smelled as bad as each other. At night, when the desert lost all its daytime heat, they shivered under a couple of blankets in the lee of their vehicles. They ate bully beef and hard biscuits for days on end and kept their morale up with frequent brews of hot, sweet, milky tea

---

* And first cousin of the famed anthropologist Louis Leakey.

made with water boiled on flames from petrol-soaked sand in a cut-down fuel can. An officer might eke out the occasional bottle of whisky, but generally speaking there was no alcohol unless it had been decided to issue a rum ration; the British Army had no scruples about fuelling a little Dutch courage.

As the weather moved into the hottest weeks of the year, it began to weed out the unfit. Port-faced majors and beer-bloated sergeants, men in early middle age who had grown soft on convivial nights in the mess, simply could not cope. In particular, some of the old sweats soon lost their appetite for the claustrophobic world of tank warfare and began to pull strings for the cushy jobs back at headquarters, or even further down the line, if they played their cards right. A few took more desperate measures.

Sergeant (later Major) Patrick Cleere, a seven-year veteran of the 7th Queen's Own Hussars who was also involved in the skirmishing around Capuzzo, had to put down a mini-mutiny. Like Leakey, Cleere commanded a troop of three speedy but lightly armoured Vickers reconnaissance tanks (though his, at least, had the benefit of its machine-guns) and after taking a direct hit he had bailed out and commandeered another vehicle. But when Cleere's wireless operator realized they were going into action again, he pulled out a revolver and ordered the sergeant to turn back. Cleere managed to disarm the mutineer and took him back to squadron headquarters, where he was placed under close arrest. Not long after this a medical officer declared that the second member of Cleere's crew, the gunner who operated the heavy machine-gun, was suffering from 'shell shock', and he too was evacuated. Cleere seemed quite unfazed by this but collected a fresh crew and, like the vast majority, soldiered on.

All this was small-scale stuff, however. Mussolini, determined to show the Germans that his army knew how to fight, ordered General Rodolfo Graziani, his supremo in Libya, to invade Egypt immediately. At first Graziani demurred; skirmishing with Arab guerrillas armed with muzzle-loaders was one thing, taking on the British Empire something else. The Italian army was still not mechanized enough for a desert campaign and most of his infantry, it seemed, were expected to get to Cairo in the same manner as Napoleon's regiments – on their feet. Mussolini insisted that the British had never been weaker. If Graziani would not do as ordered, he would find somebody who would. By 13 September 1940, Italian engineers had finished cutting several wide gaps in the layers of concertina barbed wire along the border. Through them poured the best part of the Italian Tenth Army, about 100,000 men.

The full-scale desert war that erupted with Mussolini's invasion of Egypt was to be waged almost entirely along a firm-surfaced coastal strip and a limestone plateau rearing up behind it atop a 500-foot escarpment. The entire arena was rarely more than forty miles deep and mostly a lot less – open country and ideal for heavy armour, which was able to manoeuvre as freely as warships at sea. South of the coastal strip and its adjoining plateau, the terrain was a very different matter. Beneath the most crucial sector of the arena, extending some 300 miles along the seashore from El Alamein to Tobruk, lies the Qattara Depression, a bottomless salt marsh, impassable to tanks and extremely difficult for most other kinds of heavy military vehicle.

But the Qattara sink-hole is only a small part of the Great Libyan Desert, which is itself an eastward extension of the Sahara and by far the world's largest true desert. The Great Libyan Desert extends 1,100 miles from east to west and over 1,000 from north to south, covering an area roughly equivalent to the entire Indian subcontinent. Perhaps a quarter of this forbidding, waterless expanse – a realm in which only sand vipers, scorpions and a handful of amazingly durable Senussi tribesmen and their camels and goats survive – is taken up by three dramatic features, rising out of a boulder-strewn gravel plain, where desert winds have created wave upon wave of parallel sand-dunes 300–400 feet high. These are the great sand seas – the Egyptian Sand Sea, the Kalansho Sand Sea and the Ribiana Sand Sea – and to the high command on both sides at the outbreak of war these seemed to constitute an impassable barrier, covering their mutual southern flank and therefore of only negative strategic significance. But one apparently over-the-hill British officer had the expertise and experience to understand that this was not the case.

Major Ralph Bagnold of the Royal Signals, a gentleman-adventurer in the classic mould, had pioneered desert exploration in the 1930s and, although middle-aged at the outbreak of the Second World War, he was to conceive, found and for a while lead the Long Range Desert Group – arguably the most dashing and successful irregular formation

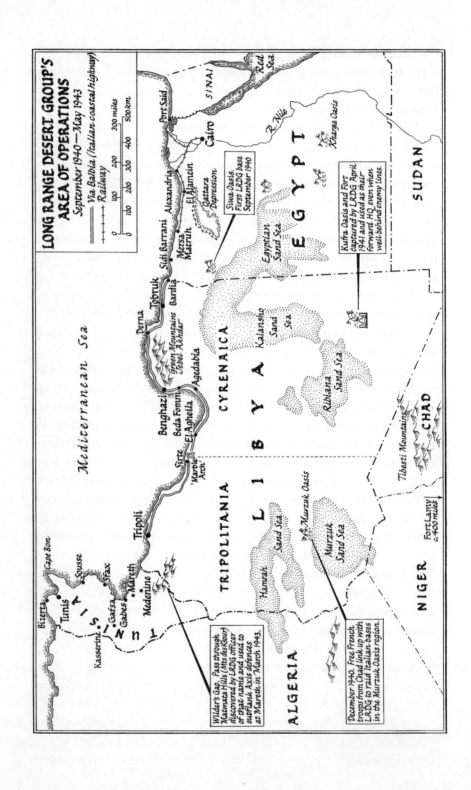

LONG RANGE DESERT GROUP'S AREA OF OPERATIONS

September 1940 – May 1943

Via Balbia (Italian-coastal highway)
Railway

0 100 200 300 400 500 km.
0 100 200 300 miles

Mediterranean Sea

Red Sea

SINAI

Port Said

R. Nile

Cairo

Alexandria

El Alamein

Mersa Matruh

Qattara Depression

Siwa Oasis. First LRDG base September 1940

E G Y P T

Kharga Oasis

Egyptian Sand Sea

Kalansho Sand Sea

Ribiana Sand Sea

Kufra Oasis and Fort captured by LRDG April 1941 and used as their forward HQ even when well behind enemy lines.

SUDAN

Sidi Barrani

Bardia

Tobruk

Derna

Green Mountains
Jebel Akhdar

Agedabia

Benghazi

Beda Fomm

El Agheila

Sirte

Marble Arch

C Y R E N A I C A

L I B Y A

TRIPOLITANIA

Tripoli

Hamrah Sand Sea

Murzuk Oasis

Murzuk Sand Sea

December 1940. Free French troops from Chad link up with LRDG to raid Italian bases in the Murzuk Oasis region.

Tibesti Mountains

CHAD

Fort Lamy c.400 miles

NIGER

ALGERIA

Cape Bon

Bizerta

Tunis

Sousse

Gafsa

Sfax

Kasserine

Gabes

Mareth

Medenine

T U N I S I A

Wilder's Gap. Pass through Matmata Hills (Mts des Ksour) discovered by LRDG officer of that name and used to outflank Axis defences at Mareth in March 1943.

on either side for the entire war. And yet Bagnold's achievements were to remain unsung and his very existence little known to any but a handful of surviving North African war veterans and desert exploration specialists.

A First World War veteran and professional soldier,* Bagnold was called out of retirement as a reservist in August 1939 and the following month found himself on a troopship in the Mediterranean, heading for a routine posting in Kenya. En route, his ship was involved in a collision with another in the same convoy and had to put into Port Said for repairs. Finding himself unexpectedly back in Egypt, where he had been stationed during the 1920s and 1930s, Bagnold caught a train to Cairo to look up old friends. Wavell heard he was in town and sent for him. He knew that Bagnold and a number of like-minded fellow officers had performed some extraordinary feats of desert exploration in their pre-war off-duty time. Initially at the wheel of Model-T Fords, and later in modified trucks, and navigating by dead reckoning and the stars, Bagnold and his friends had driven far out into the unmapped desert and found that quick wits, grit and mechanical inventiveness could get them across huge distances without getting bogged down, getting lost or dying of thirst as their more cautious comrades predicted they would. Bagnold, for example, developed an accurate sun compass, allowing him to dispense with the conventional magnetic compass that was rendered unreliable by the steel of his vehicles. He and his comrades learned to conserve the water in their radiators by the simple expedient of leading the overflow pipe into a can on the outside of the vehicle where, as the engine cooled, it would condense and be returned. They learned to reduce tyre pressure from 90 to 15 pounds per square inch when driving over loose sand and then to reinflate for hard surfaces – a commonplace nowadays, but somebody had to think of it first. They learned to carry metal channels to put under the back wheels for traction when vehicles bogged down. They learned where the water-holes were and where to cache fuel supplies. Above all, Bagnold discovered that the huge dunes of the sand seas could be mounted with surprising ease if one drove at them full tilt.

---

* And brother of the 1930s popular novelist and playwright Enid Bagnold, author of *National Velvet*.

I increased speed to forty miles an hour, feeling like a small boy on a horse about to take his first big fence . . . A huge glaring wall of yellow shot up high into the sky a yard in front of us. The lorry tipped violently backwards – and we rose as in a lift, smoothly without vibration. We floated up on a yellow cloud. All the accustomed car movements had ceased; only the speedometer told us we were still moving fast. It was incredible . . .

It wasn't quite that simple. As the spy, soldier and author Fitzroy Maclean discovered as an officer in the Special Air Service, 'too much dash had its penalties. Many of the sand dunes fell away sharply at the far side and if you arrived at the top at full speed, you were likely to plunge headlong over the precipice on the far side before you could stop yourself and end up with your truck upside down on top of you forty or fifty feet below.'

Bagnold, who made the first east–west crossing of the Libyan Desert in 1932, had no formal training, except in engineering. But he was solidly self-educated in hydrology, geophysics, oceanography and geography, and was the author of what was to become the standard textbook on sand dunes,★ a classic work which is used to this day by the US National Aeronautics and Space Administration to interpret Mars data.

In sending for this adventurous polymath as soon as he heard he was in Cairo, and then getting his posting to Kenya rescinded, Wavell demonstrated the far-sightedness for which he was to become legendary. Yet Bagnold himself had little idea initially of the ultimate military value of his pre-war explorations.

Never in our peacetime travels had we imagined that war could ever reach the enormous empty solitudes of the inner desert, walled off by sheer distance, lack of water and impassable seas of sand dunes. Little did we dream that any of the special equipment and techniques we had evolved for very long-distance travel, and for navigation, would ever be put to serious use.

When the Italians entered the war, Bagnold began to think differently. He sent Wavell a note asking for an interview and, thanks to an old friend from army college days who was now Wavell's ADC, he was facing the C-in-C across his desk within an hour. Boldly, Bagnold

★ *The Physics of Blown Sand*, Morrow, New York, 1941.

urged Wavell to authorize a small mobile scouting force to find out what the Italians were up to in the high desert. When Wavell asked what they would do if they found that the Italians were not up to anything there, Bagnold suggested that they might perpetrate some acts of desert 'piracy'. The normally austere Wavell liked that idea and permitted himself an unaccustomed smile. Giving Bagnold six weeks to get his unit organized and ready for action, Wavell also dictated an order to heads of department and branches that any request Bagnold might make for personnel and equipment 'should be met instantly and without question'. Bagnold came away astounded. 'What a man! In an instant decision he had given me absolute *carte blanche* to do anything I thought best.'

With six weeks to recruit, equip and train the little raiding force authorized by Wavell, Bagnold lost no time in sending for two of his pre-war desert companions: Bill Shaw, who was in Jerusalem as curator of the Palestine Museum, and Pat Clayton, who was a government surveyor in Tanganyika. They were hurriedly commissioned and kitted out as army captains. None of the founding triumvirate was young; Bagnold was forty-four, Shaw was the same age but looked older, and Clayton really was older and had prematurely white hair.

For his rank-and-file, Bagnold was given permission to recruit 150 volunteers from the newly arrived New Zealand division. This suited him well because he felt that, being mainly farm boys, the New Zealanders would be more adept with machinery and more used to maintaining vehicles than the average British Tommy.

To transport his nascent long-range group, Bagnold acquired a fleet of thirty new and used 30-cwt Chevrolet trucks – ten for each of three forty-man patrol groups – plus three 15-cwt command cars. Each patrol was to carry ten Lewis machine-guns, four Boyes anti-tank rifles, and a 37-mm Bofors light anti-aircraft gun, plus the Brens, rifles and Thompson sub-machine-guns all British infantry carried.

Shaw taught the young New Zealanders how to use a sun compass and other navigational skills, assisted by a lance corporal who had been a mate in the merchant navy, while Bagnold took personal charge of signals training, using Army No. 11 wireless sets which, although officially with a range of only seventy miles, could be made to transmit Morse messages for more than 1,000 miles across the desert at certain times of day.

Bagnold established his first operational base at Siwa, an oasis

sandwiched between the escarpment of the Qattara Depression and
the Egyptian Sand Sea, close to the frontier of Italian-occupied Libya
and 350 miles from Cairo. His men arrived there by the unprecedented
feat of bringing their trucks in convoy 150 miles across the supposedly
impassable Egyptian Sand Sea, having 'taken to the strange new life
like ducks to water, quickly learning the tricky art of driving over
dunes, spotting and avoiding the worst of the dry quicksands'.

It was 13 September 1940 when they reached Siwa – where they
had previously cached stocks of petrol, food and water – to commence
operations. Two days later, the Italians invaded in force across the
Libya–Egypt frontier, pushing east along the hard-surfaced coastal
strip towards the Nile Delta. Far to the south, two of Bagnold's patrols
mounted a mini counter-invasion.

Bagnold's pre-war expeditions had all been carried out during
the winter months; now, in mid-September, the daytime heat was
paralysing – 'we could not travel at mid-day at all but lay under our
trucks and gasped' – and there were a number of cases of heat-stroke.
After dark, though, the mercury plunged below freezing point.
Despite these extremes of temperature and frequent choking sandstorms, one patrol, commanded by the New Zealander Captain Teddy
Mitford, went through the Kalansho Sand Sea and successfully attacked
Italian petrol dumps and emergency landing fields along the 'Palificata',
the signposted, hard-surfaced route to an isolated Italian stronghold at
the Kufra Oasis. The other patrol, commanded by Clayton, passed
through Italian-occupied territory to make contact with French forces
in Chad. The French at that time were undecided whether to join de
Gaulle's Free French or to remain loyal to the Vichy collaborationist
regime. Clayton's unexpected visit was instrumental in encouraging
them eventually to link up with the Allies.

First missions accomplished, the two patrols rendezvoused at the
southern tip of the Gilf Kebir, where a pre-positioned supply dump
awaited them, before returning to Cairo via the Kharga Oasis. They
had covered 4,000 miles – half of it through enemy territory – and
demonstrated convincingly how effective small armed groups of dedicated desert pirates could be. Wavell was delighted, promoted Bagnold
to lieutenant-colonel and gave the green light for three new patrols
to be formed, drawing volunteers from the Brigade of Guards, a
Rhodesian brigade and an Indian division, and British Yeomanry
regiments. Thus, Bagnold's little private army proved itself and became

officially designated the Long Range Desert Group. As Bagnold would recall:

During the next few months, raids were made on a number of enemy-held oases. For greater effect, isolated little garrisons were shot up, when possible on the same day. To the Italians, the raiders seemed to appear from nowhere, as if from a fourth dimension, and to disappear just as rapidly . . . Graziani was beginning to doubt his intelligence reports of [British] weakness. The invading Italian army halted for vital months.

In December 1940 the irrepressible Bagnold flew to Fort Lamy in Chad to follow up on the contacts Clayton had previously made there with the French. He proved himself as able a diplomat as a desert traveller: Chad came in openly on the Allied side, the only French colony to do so, and French troops immediately linked up with the LRDG to raid Italian bases in the Murzuk Oasis region, 600 miles west and 400 miles south of the Italian front line on the Mediterranean. This was followed by a successful joint assault on the Italian fortress at Kufra, made possible by the use of French artillery weapons too heavy for the LRDG to carry. French shells holed the stout walls of the fort and the garrison surrendered.

With Kufra in Allied hands, the LRDG set up its headquarters there in April 1941. 'During our move,' Bagnold would recall, 'temperatures exceeding 50° Centigrade [120°F] were found to be tolerable, even on a restricted water ration, owing to the dryness. The worst discomfort came from severe sandstorms, which lasted several days. They made eating very difficult.'

At Kufra, Bagnold became in effect military governor of an occupied enemy territory the size of northern Europe where the last rain had fallen seventy years before. In deference to de Gaulle's demands, he flew the French tricolour alongside the Union Jack. While there, Bagnold managed to get another of his pre-war travelling companions, Guy Prendergast, flown out from Britain to become his second in command, and on 1 July 1941 Bagnold handed over to him and went to Cairo to join headquarters staff* as a full colonel, conscious that 'at

---

* Known derisively as the Short Range Shepheard's Group, for the tendency of its members to spend much of their free time in the veranda and bar of Shepheard's Hotel, Cairo's most fashionable watering-hole.

forty-five, after prolonged rough living in intense heat, I was no longer feeling at my best'.

Under Bagnold, 'the mosquito army', as Wavell would admiringly call the LRDG, quickly achieved legendary status, although its origin-ator remained largely unknown. Under Prendergast, it was to go on harrying the enemy throughout the North African campaign, not only as a raiding force in its own right but as the 'Libyan Desert Taxi Service' that would guide Lieutenant-Colonel David Stirling's Special Air Service units through the desert on their spectacular forays behind enemy lines.

The Italian invasion of Egypt started reasonably well. Wavell had been complaining for some time that he just did not have the men to stop a determined strike across the border. His Western Desert Force, commanded by Major-General Sir Richard O'Connor, consisted of just two divisions: the 7th Armoured Division and the 4th Indian and they were both seriously under strength. Seventh Armoured had fewer than half the tanks they were supposed to have, 65 instead of 220.

Nor could Wavell expect any help from the small Egyptian army which manned its frontier forts. Although under British tutelage, the Cairo government had been allowed to declare that Egypt was a 'non-belligerent'. This was a popular move with his subjects, for many young Egyptian officers – among them the future presidents Gamal Abdel Nasser and Anwar el Sadat – loathed their British occupiers so much that they were almost openly sympathetic to the Axis cause, despite the Italians' ill-treatment of their fellow Arabs, the Senussi.

O'Connor was well towards the top of Wavell's short list of assets. A wiry scrum-half of a man, he was energetic but with the diffident and preoccupied air of the academic he might have been.* He had already decided that in the event of an Italian offensive he would not try to meet it at the frontier. Instead, he would leave a mobile screen of light tanks and armoured cars supported by a small amount of artillery to harass and delay them. This force was to be commanded by Brigadier William Gott,† a charming and affable six-footer and former army boxing champion, known to his contemporaries as 'Strafer' Gott in ironic echo of the First World War German battle slogan '*Gott straf England*' ('God punish England'). The rest of Western Desert Force would fall back on Mersa Matruh where, just east of that little port, O'Connor had established a strong defensive position that he called the Baggush Box after the nearby hamlet of Maarten Baggush.

---

* Among his medal ribbons was the Italian Silver Star for Valour he had won in Italy in 1918 when the Italians were Britain's allies.
† Despite its Germanic sound, Gott was an old Yorkshire name of Viking origin.

Mersa Matruh was about 150 miles west of Alexandria, and one of the reasons why it was such a good defensive position was that it was easy to supply. It was the terminus of a single-track railway which went through the little town of El Alamein and gave its hot and sticky military passengers a tantalizing glimpse of white sand and blue water as it followed the coast towards the sound of the guns.

As the Italian offensive gathered impetus, the 1st Blackshirt Division recaptured Fort Capuzzo, learned to put up with the hit-and-run attacks of Gott's rearguard, and eventually came to a halt at the village of Sidi Barrani, about sixty miles inside Egypt. Count Ciano, Mussolini's son-in-law and Foreign Minister, noted in his diary: 'Il Duce is radiant with joy.'

Not for long. Although all that stood between a quarter of a million Italian soldiers and the Suez Canal were O'Connor's 30,000 men, Italian intelligence did not know exactly how weak the British were. Mussolini urged Graziani to press on. Instead, Graziani ordered his troops to dig in. His procrastination was partly to do with the problem that would come to bedevil all desert commanders when things were going well for them: the better you did, the longer your lines of communication became and the more acute your problems of supply. Before Graziani advanced again he wanted to stockpile dumps of fuel and ammunition. But this was easier said than done.

What Mussolini chose to call his 'Fourth Shore' bordered what was still a British lake. The Royal Navy continued to dominate the Mediterranean, especially the eastern end of it, where they had home ports at Alexandria, Port Said and Haifa, and airfields to give them cover. This made it difficult for the Italians to use Tobruk, the best port in Libya and only 150 miles west of their front line at Sidi Barrani.

Logistical problems were not the only reason Graziani was reluctant to attack. He knew that his numerical supremacy might not make him as strong as he appeared to Mussolini. So did some of his more thoughtful young officers. 'We're trying to fight this war as though it were a colonial war in Africa,' one wrote in a letter that was never to reach home. 'But this is a European war in Africa fought with European weapons against a European enemy. We take too little account of this in building our stone forts and equipping ourselves with such luxury. We are not fighting the Abyssinians now.'

In the main, Mussolini's conscripts were confronted by British professional soldiers, albeit underpaid and poorly equipped members of a neglected peacetime army being hurriedly inflated to a size considered compatible with total war. The 7th Armoured Division had been in the Middle East since the 1938 Munich crisis. They would shortly adopt as their insignia a native rodent known as the jerboa, the Desert Rat, and stencil its silhouette in red paint on their vehicles. Towards the end of 1939, they had been brought up to their proper strength by reservists and Territorials called up on the outbreak of war. There were also a few conscripts, but most of O'Connor's troops were not the citizens in uniform who would soon make up the bulk of the British Army.

The Other Ranks were mainly still the men of Kipling's Barrack-room Ballads, a secret tribe shunned by most honest taxpayers until the guns began to shoot. Like gypsies, they spoke an almost impenetrable argot, English studded with elements of Urdu and Arabic, acquired, like their tattoos, in the back rooms of Empire. At that stage one of the rare conscripts was R. L. Crimp, a bemused City of London clerk transformed into a rifleman in the 7th Armoured Division's truck-borne infantry. In the diary he kept throughout the campaign, he noted this impressive example of rifleman argot: 'Taro, chinas, just shufti this. The coolos zift. Duff scoff peachy if Ombasha can't buddly 'em.' And gives the translation: 'One moment, pals, just look at this. The whole lot's bad. Rotten meal soon if the corporal can't change them.'

Most of these regulars had already been away from Britain for over two years. Mail was tremendously important for morale. Airmail letters, 'aerograms' as they were called, had recently been introduced, but they usually came out by ship and could take as long as three months to arrive. Sometimes a successful U-boat attack meant that they did not arrive at all. Really urgent messages came as telegrams via overseas cable. All communications, to or from Britain, were read by military censors.

Nevertheless, in the summer of 1940 morale tended to be good and had actually improved since Italy's declaration of war. Like most professional soldiers who have not experienced battle or have been long out of it, many of the 7th Armoured Division hankered to put years of training into practice. They felt humiliated at the thought that there were civilians at home who had experienced more high explosive than they had and might yet face a German invasion.

'The Germans are bombing London and other cities at home

night after night. It takes courage to even read the news,' Hermione
Ranfurly confided to her diary the day the Italians had reached Sidi
Barrani. In defiance of the War Office, Lady Ranfurly had followed
her young husband, the Earl of Ranfurly, otherwise 2nd Lieutenant
Dan Ranfurly, aged twenty-six, out to the Middle East, travelling
alone with a small revolver concealed in her girdle.

The Earl had been posted to British-ruled Palestine with his Yeomanry regiment, part of the last British cavalry division in the process
of being turned into tank crews or gunners. Officered mainly by the
landed gentry (Ranfurly had brought his valet Whitaker as well as
his horse), the Yeomanry regiments were part-time soldiers of the
Territorial Army and typified the reluctance of all cavalry regiments
to mechanize.

For a while, until the casualty lists got too long, their commanding
officers and adjutants tended to be regulars. Below them were the
sons of the fox-hunting squirearchy, not a few of them amateur
steeplechasers who knew every racecourse in the land and had broken
bones on most of them. Those who did not come from this background soon learned to act as though they had, determinedly amateur
with a hint of *noblesse oblige*.

Yeomanry summer camps, where for two weeks 'Northland' fought
'Southland' using tactics that had been polished in the Boer War, were
generally regarded by officers and men alike as an excuse for hard
riding and even harder drinking, the officers dining under canvas with
the regimental band playing and they in dress uniform of blue patrols
with chain-mail on the epaulettes.

Not surprisingly, the Yeomanry sometimes had difficulty adapting
to the concept of total war. The Nottingham-based Sherwood
Rangers under the Earl of Yarborough had even tried to take with
them to Palestine a pack of foxhounds belonging to the Brocklesby
Hunt. They were eventually thwarted by French transport officers
(while proceeding by train to Marseilles where a troopship awaited)
who objected to the trouble these ridiculous *Anglais* were putting
them to. Obliged to dip a reluctant toe into the twentieth century,
most of the Yeomanry regiments would eventually become part of an
effective armoured division, though often at a terrible cost to those
who officered much of it.

The social divide between officers and men was even wider in
O'Connor's infantry division, the 4th Indian. But, unlike much of the

Yeomanry at this stage, the professionalism of the Indian rank-and-file was undisputed. Well led, they were undoubtedly as capable as their British counterparts. Only when bad leadership landed them in prison camps did the allegiance of some of these colonial troops begin to waver. Even then the majority refused to break their oath to the King Emperor and join the Indian Legion of Subhas Chandra Bose, the brilliant Bengali nationalist who had rejected Gandhi's pacifism and fled to Germany at the outbreak of war.

Among the peasants who make up the martial races of the sub-continent, soldiering was (and often still is) considered an honourable and lucrative calling, offering an immediate improvement in one's standard of living. There was intense competition to get into the various regiments of the old British Indian Army and, once in, a man hoped to stay in, occupational hazards excepted, until he was in early middle age. Indian Army soldiers such as the Sikhs and the Gurkhas could be very tough indeed, and their officers had to match them.

Nor, any longer, were these officers all British. Since the end of the First World War, when Indian troops had fought for Britain in France and the Middle East, attempts had been made to 'Indianize' the Indian Army by taking the radical step of giving it Indian officers – or at least officers who were of undeniably Indian extraction, though in every other way indistinguishable from British officers – so 'Brindians' became the catchword, or 'Brown Sahibs' to the less reverent.

It had started very slowly, for Sandhurst and Woolwich quickly weeded out those heartbroken Indian cadets judged unable to cope with the cultural and language difficulties. How many good soldiers were wasted because they could not hold their unaccustomed drink is impossible to say. Still, by 1940 Indian majors and captains were becoming slightly less exotic. By the end of the war they would be commanding battalions and even brigades.*

In the summer of 1940, then, the 7th Armoured Division and the infantry of the 4th Indian Division waiting to meet Graziani's Blackshirts in the desert were, regardless of race, highly drilled professionals, skilled at handling their weapons and capable of enduring considerable hardship. Like the Tenth Italian Army they lacked the tactical training, the close air support, or the armoured strength of the

---

* And after the war, two of them – Ayub Khan and Yahya Khan – would become presidents of Pakistan.

German army whose meticulous logistics and hair-trigger reactions had just introduced Europe to the concept of Blitzkrieg. But in these opening weeks of the desert war, the British could display an old-fashioned élan and doggedness that Graziani might have taken more seriously if he had not been misled by thoughts of his numerical superiority.

As it was, it appeared that Wavell was content to allow O'Connor to hold the line in the Western Desert while British forces concentrated on driving the Italians out of Abyssinia and, with Graziani pausing at Sidi Barrani, the war in the Western Desert became something of a sideshow. Still, Gott's rearguard continued to harass the enemy when they could. Small mobile columns of armoured cars, artillery and truck-borne infantry named 'Jock columns' after their inventor, Lieutenant-Colonel Jock Campbell, would start set-piece battles with the Italians, preferably from ambush, then disappear and pop up elsewhere. Some Blackshirt officers seemed to regard these will-o'-the-wisp tactics as evidence of British decadence. In another letter that never got to Italy one wrote:

But for the cowardice of the English who flee from even our lightest shelling and smallest patrols, we would have committed the wildest folly in coming to this appalling desert. The flies plague us in millions from the first hour in the morning. The sand always seems to be in our mouths, in our hair and in our clothes, and it is impossible to get cool. Only troops of the highest morale and courage would endure privations like these, and even prepare to press the advance to still greater triumphs in the cause of Fascism and the Duce.

Mussolini was unimpressed. While he fretted about his army's lack of progress, the first troops from Australia and New Zealand began arriving in the Middle East. These two self-governing British Dominions of the southern hemisphere, together with the Union of South Africa, would eventually contribute large numbers of men and vast reservoirs of courage to the desert campaign. In Australia and New Zealand the call to arms had gone up within hours of the declaration of war. Only in South Africa was there any foot dragging. Many Afrikaans-speaking Boers whose grandfathers and fathers had fought the British, with German support, at the beginning of the century wanted to remain neutral. Some, including the future President and champion of apartheid John Vorster, were openly pro-Nazi. But Prime Minister Jan Smuts, the veteran Boer commando turned imperial visionary and an admirer of Churchill, overcame internal opposition and brought the Union of South Africa into the war on 6 September.

Despite divisions between South Africa's two white tribes, Afrikaans-speakers contributed generously to the fund Ouma ('Grannie') Smuts set up to see that every South African serviceman in the Western Desert got a daily tot of Commando brandy and a packet of Springbok cigarettes. Not surprisingly, some of the biggest donations came from South African veterans of 1914–18.

In the war that had ended only twenty-one years before, Australia and New Zealand had also suffered grievous losses and by the 1930s both countries seemed to have lost their taste for more twentieth-century bloodletting. New Zealand, for all its male-dominated, rugby-playing, rural beeriness, was nevertheless where women had first been allowed to vote and where socialist and anti-militarist views thrived. Indeed, in the 1920s and '30s it had not been uncommon for members of New Zealand's tiny regular army to avoid boarding public transport in uniform for fear of insult. In Australia, where there was high unemployment and, as in Britain, considerable support for Chamberlain's policy of appeasing Hitler, there was no relish for another war.

And yet, when war came, these egalitarian-minded, cricket-loving democracies at the bottom of the globe, more than 10,000 miles away from 'the old country' and its perennial problems with the more assertive parts of continental Europe, followed Britain as unhesitatingly as they had twenty-five years before. They may not have embraced the war with the almost carnival spirit of 1914, but only outright pacifists, Communists or Irish republican sympathizers felt they had any choice. 'Where [Britain] goes, we go,' announced Michael Savage, New Zealand's first Labour prime minister. 'Where she stands, we stand.'

In 1939 New Zealand had a population of just over 1.6 million; it was one of the smallest independent countries in the world. Yet it continued with plans to raise and send one infantry division to serve with the British Expeditionary Force in France. Per head of population, this was the equivalent of Britain raising twenty-five divisions – a division consisting of about 15,000 men.

Australia was not to be outdone. By April 1940 part of the Australian

6th Division, the first of four divisions Australia would send overseas, was under Wavell's command in Palestine. When the rest of the division arrived and word got about that it was about to be sent to Egypt, the Cairo government protested; Cairo had not quite overcome the trauma caused by the Australian Light Horse's riotous 1918 victory party. The British authorities relented and kept the Australians in the Palestine that their fathers and uncles had helped liberate from the Ottoman Empire. Only the better-behaved New Zealanders were posted to Egypt.

Neither of the divisions from Down Under was fully trained or equipped; even the basics were lacking. Yet during the next two years they would collect seven Victoria Crosses, while New Zealander Lieutenant Charles Upham would become the third man in history to win the VC twice. The Australian and New Zealand formations were almost entirely amateur. Battalion commanders and above tended to be lawyers, architects and engineers who had served with some distinction as young officers in the Anzacs, the Australia New Zealand Army Corps, of 1914–18.

Officers and men alike had volunteered for the usual reasons: out of a kind of patriotism that is now almost extinct; because their mates had; because, just like their backpacking grandchildren yet unborn, they wanted to have adventures and see the world. Some enlisted because they were out of work, and a few joined up for ideological reasons.

But by the winter of 1940 the only fighting the 6th Australian Division had seen was with the Palestine Police, mostly British ex-soldiers and as partial to beer and fisticuffs as the Aussies were. In the Western Desert the Italian front line had not advanced an inch, Graziani having built a series of little forts around Sidi Barrani but showing no inclination to move out of them.

By now Mussolini's attention was elsewhere. For some time he had been picking a fight with neutral Greece. The Germans, already planning to attack Russia and not wanting trouble in the Balkans, told Mussolini that this was not the right moment to attack Greece, but Il Duce was not listening. He was jealous of Hitler and yearned for conquests of his own to put Italy on an equal footing with Nazi Germany.

On 28 October 1940 the Greek dictator General Yiannis Metaxas was handed an ultimatum. Greece must immediately concede all territorial demands or consider itself at war with Italy. Metaxas refused to be intimidated and answered Rome with a resounding 'no'. Even as he did so, Italian troops were crossing the Albanian border into Greece. But within three weeks the Greeks had chased the invaders off their soil, inflicted heavy casualties, and pursued them back into Albania itself.

In London, where the Luftwaffe's nightly bombing was now at its height and people needed something to cheer them up, a new popular song went:

> What a surprise for the Duce, the Duce,
> He can't put it over the Greeks!
> What a surprise for the Duce, they do say
> He's had no spaghetti for weeks!

This was only the start of Mussolini's humiliation. Churchill wanted a prompt demonstration of support for Greece, the only country to side voluntarily with Britain when she stood alone. The Royal Navy responded immediately with a daring raid on the southern Italian port of Taranto by a squadron of carrier-borne Fairey Swordfish, elderly, open-cockpit biplanes, in which three major battleships were sunk or crippled for the loss of two aircraft. British naval ascendancy in the Mediterranean was thus assured for some time to come.

Meanwhile Wavell had given O'Connor the go-ahead to launch Operation 'Compass', a large-scale raid in the Western Desert that might be developed into a full-scale offensive. Churchill was delighted but continued to insist that Metaxas be given British air support. Eventually, about half Wavell's available air power, some seventy-four aircraft, went to Greece. This significantly reduced the bombing of Italian logistics, particularly the ports of Tobruk and Benghazi. Nevertheless, preparations went ahead for Compass and, to overcome transport difficulties, O'Connor secretly established dumps of fuel and ammunition well forward of his own lines.

The island of Malta, lying alongside Axis shipping routes to North Africa, was to play a crucial role in the developing desert war. Yet the British had left it woefully unprepared for the task. At the outbreak of hostilities the colony was virtually defenceless and was moreover governed by a religious fanatic who tended to entrust important decisions to the whims of the Almighty rather than deal with them himself.

Because of its uncomfortable proximity to Italian air bases, the British War Office had decided by the mid-1930s that the island was an expendable pawn on the Mediterranean chessboard. Over Winston Churchill's lonely objections, the Royal Navy moved its Mediterranean Fleet headquarters from Valletta to Alexandria, 1,000 miles to the east. And by the time Il Duce entered the lists in June 1940 Malta found itself with a garrison of fewer than 4,000 troops and barely five weeks of food stocks for a military and civilian population of 300,000.

Crucially, its anti-aircraft defences consisted of no more than forty-two guns and four ageing Gloster Gladiator fighters to pit against the 200 Italian fighters and bombers based on Sicily, ten minutes' flying time away. The Gladiator was the last of Britain's biplane fighters before the advent of the monoplane Hurricanes and Spitfires and fortunately more or less a match for the similar-looking CR-42 biplane that was the mainstay of the Italian fighter fleet. The Italian plane's slight edge over the Gladiator in climb and acceleration was offset by the heavier punch of the Gladiator's four .303 Browning machine-guns, but the Gladiator was not fast enough to catch Mussolini's three-engined Savoia-Marchetti SM-79 bombers. 'Even when it had a height advantage and was correctly positioned it could usually achieve at best only one close pass at the SM-79,' fighter pilot John Lapsley recalled, some forty years later.

That Malta had even those four Gladiator interceptors to guard it was something of a miracle. Air Commodore F. H. 'Sammy' Maynard, an irreverent New Zealander who had recently been appointed the island's Air Officer Commanding, found the four aircraft in a dockyard warehouse, inside crates marked 'Boxed Spares – Property of the Royal Navy'. They had been left behind by the aircraft carrier *Glorious* before sailing to her doom in Norwegian waters in April 1940. Boldly disregarding a convention relegating the air force to a decidedly inferior hierarchical position relative to the Senior Service, Maynard appropriated the four crates and had their contents assembled.

Hardly had the Gladiators been put together before the Director of Naval Supplies, getting wind of this impertinence, demanded the Navy's property back. Over Maynard's protests, the planes were dismantled and the parts re-crated. They were about to be sent back to Plymouth when the Navy had a change of heart and said that they could stay in Malta after all. Maynard had the four planes put together once again and, flown by members of his personal office staff, none of whom had been trained as a fighter pilot, they became operational by 5 May 1940 – just one month and six days before the Italians launched their first air raid on the island.

The Gladiators did not manage to engage the enemy on that first day, during which the Italians came over six times; owing to the unfinished state of the Luqa airfield where they were based, they were unable to get airborne in time. But, as one Maltese eyewitness put it, during subsequent raids the Gladiators and their pilots 'worked miracles and must have frightened the Italians with their sheer impudence'.

Although the islanders' first experience of aerial bombardment was terrifying, they soon learned to live with it and, in the words of a woman who lived through the ensuing aerial siege, 'in a few weeks the raiders were treated [by the populace] with contempt'. During those early weeks the Gladiators – three of them operational at any one time while the fourth remained in reserve – achieved world fame as Faith, Hope and Charity as, with their top speed of barely 250 miles an hour, they took on the might of Mussolini's Regia Aeronautica. But the fierce barrages put up by Malta's thirty-four heavy and eight light anti-aircraft guns (subsequently increased to a total of 112 heavy and sixty light guns) were the main deterrent.

As one British gunner would recall, the raiders first came in – generally at dawn, midday and late afternoon – at about 18,000 feet then, growing bolder, came down to 10,000. After that 'we bagged one or two every other day so they started coming in at 20,000 feet'. Major R. I. K. Paine, Royal Artillery, was equally dismissive of the Italians' performance: 'Their bombing was never very accurate. As they flew higher it became quite indiscriminate.' Mabel Strickland, editor of the *Times of Malta* (of which her father, Lord Strickland, was the proprietor), was even more contemptuous: 'The Italians decided they didn't like [the Gladiators and the anti-aircraft fire] so they dropped their bombs twenty miles off Malta and went back.'

By the end of August, Faith, Hope and Charity had been joined by a squadron of twelve Hawker Hurricane interceptors, spared from a crucial role in the Battle of Britain which was then raging, and flown in from the deck of HMS *Argus*, a merchantman converted into an aircraft carrier.

And that was it for the time being. In the first five months of hostilities, Faith, Hope and Charity and the Hurricanes intercepted seventy-two enemy formations and damaged or destroyed thirty-seven enemy planes, causing Francesco Cavalera, an Italian fighter pilot escorting the three-engined Savoia-Marchetti bombers, to concede after the war that during that period 'Malta was really a big problem for us – very well defended.'

For all their caution, the high-flying Italian raiders took 330 lives and caused 297 serious casualties in the early months of the war, inflicting considerable destruction on Valletta and other Maltese towns. But this was only a foretaste: the island's real ordeal was to begin in January 1941, when Hitler's Fliegerkorps X arrived in Sicily, along with the Afrika Korps' arrival in Libya.

The British were the latest in a long line of rulers of the tiny, three-island archipelago known as Malta – the eponymous main island plus minuscule Gozo and microscopic Comino – in all 122 square miles (316 square kilometres) of coralline limestone, rearing out of a then-limpid Mediterranean and located a mere sixty miles from Sicily and 200 from the North African coast. Racially, its people were a unique mixture* of Phoenician, Arab, Italian and British, devoutly Roman Catholic and speaking an Arabic dialect, written (though a long way from phonetically) in the Latin alphabet and with distinct Italian undertones.

During their long and turbulent history, the most remote and authoritarian of their rulers had been the Knights of the Order of

---

* Some Maltese civilians evacuated from the island to South Africa were outraged to be classified as 'non-European' when they were landed at Durban.

St John, who held off a lengthy siege by the Turks in 1565. The knights held sway from 1530 until 1798, when Napoleon banished them, having briefly occupied Malta on his way to defeat at the Battle of the Nile. In 1814, under the Treaty of Paris and at the request of the Maltese people, the island was ceded to Great Britain, the only proviso being that the Protestant English would respect and maintain the primacy of the Catholic Church.

By April of 1940 Malta was being ruled by a British military governor who was just about as Protestant as it was possible to be: Lieutenant-General Sir William Dobbie was a member of the Plymouth Brethren, a dour and puritanical sect which dispensed entirely with ritual, robes, music and any recognizable form of priesthood. However, despite the yawning theological chasm between them, the Maltese respected him as a sincere and devout Christian.

A veteran of the Boer War and the First World War, and a former Commandant of the School of Military Engineering, Dobbie had been called out of retirement to become the island's Governor and Commander-in-Chief – a post which he felt sure 'God had in mind for me'. 'Prayer and penance' would become his prescription for the island under siege. Others would have preferred a more down-to-earth approach and faulted him for his delay in setting up an effective civil defence system, ordering the digging of air-raid shelters or introducing an efficient food-rationing system.

King George VI's cousin, Lord Louis Mountbatten, who came to Malta in the spring of 1941 in command of the destroyer HMS *Kelly*, was not alone in considering Dobbie to be little more than 'a religious maniac'. To a friend in England, Mountbatten wrote: 'He prays aloud after dinner, invoking the aid of God in destroying our enemies. This is highly approved of by the Maltese, who have the same idea about God, but I would prefer an efficient Air Force here.' The redoubtable Mabel Strickland felt likewise:

At San Anton [the Governor's residence] every night about seven, everyone would be summoned for prayer . . . Dobbie would stand against the mantelpiece and he would pray out loud and we would stand as reverently as we could and he would ask the Almighty to bless the convoy [bringing supplies to the island] . . . but he never prayed to stop the bombing, as that was God's will . . . but actually God helps those that help themselves . . . [and] the trouble was that God's will was interpreted to him by Lady Dobbie.

Churchill, although a sceptic in matters of religious faith,* and by temperament more Cavalier than Roundhead, had an exaggerated respect for the Puritan tradition of 'Sword and Bible' and failed to perceive the 'Cromwellian' Dobbie's shortcomings. He considered him 'a Governor of outstanding character who inspired all ranks and classes, military and civil, with his own determination' and 'a soldier who in fighting leadership and religious zeal recalled memories of General Gordon and, looking further back, of the Ironsides and Covenanters of the past'. Not until May 1942 would Churchill change his mind about Dobbie.

While the Maltese were being bombed and British and Commonwealth troops were enduring the dangers and privations of the desert stalemate, upper-crust Cairo was enjoying a life of ease and plenty, as if in luxurious denial of the war in its backyard. European capitals might lie in ruins and London suffer the day and night assaults of the Luftwaffe, but, insouciant in a world at war, the cosmopolitan Cairo élite – and members of the British military, diplomatic and business hierarchy headquartered in the Egyptian capital – feasted lavishly, drunk copiously, coupled freely and partied endlessly. The bon vivant diplomat Henry ('Chips') Channon, arriving from a bomb-scarred and blacked-out Britain on New Year's Day 1941 to spend a few days with the British ambassador, Sir Miles Lampson, and his Italian-born wife, found Cairo 'just my affair – easy, elegant, pleasure-loving, trivial, worldly'.

At the upper levels of Cairo's kaleidoscopic social scene, where senior officers of GHQ Middle East mixed easily with foreign diplomats, wealthy locals and their womenfolk and the sprigs and appendages of Egyptian royalty, there was no hint of wartime austerity and, despite a few half-hearted raids by the Italian air force, scarcely a whiff of danger. For those who could afford them and who carried the right social credentials, Cairo offered an abundance of distractions. You could visit the river-front terrace of Shepheard's Hotel for cocktails, the awning-covered Lido of the Gezira Sporting Club for lunch, the garden at Groppi's pâtisserie for coffee and profiteroles at any time during the day and, at night, such spots as the Kit-Kat Club, afloat on

---

* He liked to describe himself as 'a flying buttress, supporting the Church of England from the outside'.

the Nile, or Madame Badia's by the Pont des Anglais, to view the belly-dancers. More intimate pleasures were of course freely – or, should one say, expensively – available in both Cairo and Alexandria, 120 miles to the north on the Mediterranean.

As Noël Coward, no ascetic himself, commented after visiting Cairo a little later, 'Somewhere in the vague outside world there might be a war of some sort going on . . . All the fripperies of pre-war luxury are still in existence here, rich people, idle people, cocktail parties, dinner parties, jewels and evening dress'. It was 'enjoyable, of course . . . but almost lacking in taste'. Another high-living visiting celebrity, the society photographer Cecil Beaton, found that at first sight Cairo 'seemed French in spirit – somewhat like Nice'. He felt that 'Blimpism' plus the Cairo climate 'plays upon a man's moral fibre as relentlessly as on his physique' and that 'the second rate thrives in Cairo'.

This was the more salubrious face of Cairo, of course. The novelist Lawrence Durrell, arriving as a refugee from Greece and presumably seeing less of the high life than Coward or Beaton, saw something quite different. He was appalled by 'this copper-pan of a blazing town with its pullulating, stinking inhabitants . . . its cripples, deformities, opthalmia, goitre, amputations, lice and fleas'.

Among the Allied military, the better-smelling fleshpots of Cairo and Alexandria were not the exclusive preserve of headquarters staff. A field officer taking a well-earned break from the desert could share facilities with 'the gabardene swine' of GHQ,★ as many front-line soldiers called them, and, if so inclined, pick up one of the attractive Nicoles and Babettes – Frenchified daughters of the Greek, Armenian, Jewish or Coptic middle classes – who, for the price of a meal, a few drinks and a box of chocolates, were often willing to offer the lonely warrior an hour or two of sweet consolation.

★ A satirical rhyme of the time went:

> We never went west of Gezira,
> We never went north of the Nile,
> We never went past the pyramids,
> Out of sight of the Sphinx's smile.
> We fought the war in Shepheard's and the Continental Bar,
> We reserved our punch for the Turf Club Lunch
> And they gave us the Africa Star.

For Other Ranks, the attractions offered by Cairo were more basic. The rancid bars, live shows and urine-and-carbolic-reeking brothels of the Wagh el Birket red light district did a roaring trade, as did the official VD Centres★ that were set up by GHQ to ensure that pox and clap did not produce more casualties than enemy fire. In The Berka, as the quarter was called, the street tout would offer Tommy Atkins his 'sister' – 'all white inside, like Queen Victoria' – or hustle him into a bar to watch a fat lady do unspeakable things with a donkey. If sufficiently aroused, Tommy might then take his pick of the girls who sat on display outside tatty street-booths. Later in the war, the military authorities would set up authorized brothels in dismal tenements where the Medical Corps handed out condoms and ointments to the clientele, who then waited in line to be serviced.

Cairo enjoyed the unique distinction of being at one and the same time a neutral capital and a major base for a nation at war – a paradox that made a nonsense of the government's May 1940 declaration of Cairo as an Open City and thereby supposedly immune to attack. Formally, Egypt was an independent country, with a constitutional monarch, a representative parliament, an appointed prime minister and a seat at the League of Nations. But it was bound by a 1936 treaty that gave Britain the right to station troops on Egyptian soil to safeguard the Suez Canal and the short route to India. So, in virtually all but name, the country was a British protectorate, its true status signalled by the fact that, alone among the diplomatic corps, Lampson held the rank of ambassador; the rest were all either consuls or ministers. Had it suited the British, they could have pressured the Egyptian government to declare war on the Axis powers, but they seemed satisfied that Egypt had broken off diplomatic relations with the enemy, interning adult German and Italian males and sequestering all Axis property. After all, the British felt no need of Egypt's puny army and, given control of its railways, airports and seaports, and censorship powers over its news media, they were content so long as the pro-Axis inclinations of certain Egyptian politicians were suppressed.

That many among the Egyptian political class resented the British enough to be pro-Axis was hardly surprising. The British had been a dominating presence for generations, turning the largest of Arab

★ There were seven of them at the height of the desert war when 140,000 British and Commonwealth soldiers were stationed in and around Cairo.

countries into a quasi-colony, and, while the wealthy élite of the cities might rub along well enough with the representatives of empire, to the vast majority – especially the Islamists and the new generation of middle-class Egyptian Army officers – they were an unwanted intrusion, and all the more so since the outbreak of war had brought the working-class soldiery of Britain and the white Commonwealth to their shores.

There was also, or had been, a substantial Italian presence in Cairo. In the 1930s a large and predominantly pro-Fascist Italian community had encompassed all classes from garage mechanics and chambermaids to wealthy architects, builders and bankers. There were thriving Italian sporting and social clubs and a magnificent Leonardo da Vinci Art Institute. When Mussolini declared war, all Italian property was sequestered and all Italian men interned, leaving their womenfolk to fend for themselves, many of the younger finding recourse in prostitution.

Among the officers of the British military and administrative services and the business community, there were many with a genuine attachment to Egypt and its people, and the educated officer class as a whole had the grace to hide a certain amiable contempt for the host nation under a cloak of public school *politesse*. But Tommy Atkins, by and large, made little attempt to disguise his disdain for the Wog, an acronym for 'worthy oriental gentleman', freely used as either a noun or an adjective: wog food, wog women, wog soldier, and so forth. The small trader or taxi driver who had most contact with the British and Commonwealth Other Ranks had learned to tolerate a certain amount of abuse and occasional violence. But when the soldiery, at the close of a movie show, stood and insulted the Egyptian king and queen with a crude parody of the national anthem – 'King Farouk, King Farouk/Hang your bollocks on a hook . . .' ★ – his sense of self was outraged.

This was the Cairo in which, on the evening of Saturday, 7 December 1940, General Wavell hosted a party for senior officers at the Turf Club, having spent the afternoon attending a race meeting at Gezira together with Lady Wavell and their two daughters. The wealthy Egyptian punters attending the races could be excused for thinking that Britain's Commander-in-Chief Middle East had as relaxed an approach to the war as their hedonistic young monarch.

★ This was the least obscene version. All versions cast highly improper aspersions, too, on the character of Queen Farida, daughter of the Shah of Iran.

Farouk had riled the British by refusing to allow his retinue of Italian servants to be interned. 'I'll get rid of my Italians when you get rid of yours,' he is supposed to have told Lampson in a barbed reference to the ambassador's Italian wife. True or false, the sophisticated Cairenes to be found in the French-speaking salons of Zamalek loved to repeat the anecdote, and even some British officers had to admit that, for a wog, Farouk had a sense of humour. Less amusing were the strong lights shining from His Majesty's summer palace in Alexandria which mocked the black-out of a city frequently subjected to night raids by Italian bombers trying to hit the British warships in its harbour.

As Christmas approached, so the party pace increased. As far as prestige was concerned, the best parties to attend were hosted by either Lampson or Wavell. Among those at the Turf Club that evening, exactly a year before the Japanese attack on Pearl Harbor ended United States neutrality, was Colonel Bonner Fellers, the US military attaché in Cairo, a man to whom Wavell and his staff were extravagantly well disposed. Before Fellers left, Wavell invited him to attend some pre-Christmas 'manoeuvres' in the Western Desert.

Two days later, Lieutenant-Colonel Vittorio Revetra, commander of the Regia Aeronautica's fighter forces in Libya, flew a CR-42 on a dawn patrol across no man's land and spotted dozens of trails of slow-moving vehicle dust approaching from the south-east. They made no attempt to attack the nearest Italian positions but drove straight through a gap the Italians had left between two groups of fortified camps, south of Sidi Barrani. Once through, they turned north and started following the track through a minefield made by Italian transport. This was the beginning of Operation Compass.

Infiltrating the Italian lines and then attacking their camps from the rear was a brilliant start to O'Connor's campaign. Surprise was complete, and not only for the Italians. The American Fellers exulted: 'General Wavell told me they were going to do manoeuvres, so up I went as an observer, and God dammit – it was the works.' Likewise, until almost the last moment most of the British rank and file were under the impression that they were training for an attack to be mounted after Christmas.

It had been a cold night in the desert, the temperature close to freezing, and O'Connor's men were glad of their greatcoats and an issue of rum. Now they advanced behind the shellfire of their

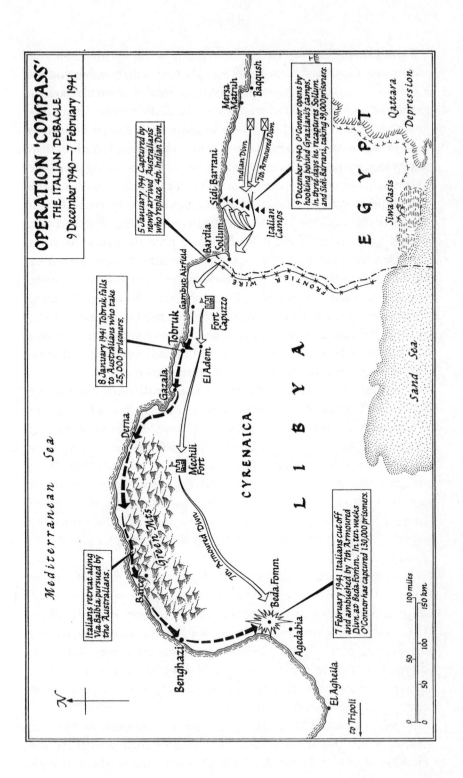

OPERATION 'COMPASS'
THE ITALIAN DEBACLE
9 December 1940—7 February 1941

5 January 1941 Captured by newly arrived Australians who replace 4th Indian Divn.

9 December 1940 O'Connor opens by hooking behind Graziani's camps. In three days he recaptures Sollum and Sidi Barrani, taking 39,000 prisoners.

8 January 1941 Tobruk falls to Australians who take 25,000 prisoners.

7 February 1941 Italians cut off and ambushed by 7th Armoured Divn. at Beda Fomm. In ten weeks O'Connor has captured 130,000 prisoners.

Italians retreat along Via Balbia pursued by the Australians.

Mediterranean Sea

Mersa Matruh
Baqqush
Indian Divn
7th Armoured Divn.
Sidi Barrani
Italian Camps
Sollum
Bardia
Gambut Airfield
WIRE
FRONTIER
Tobruk
Fort Capuzzo
Gazala
El Adem
Derna
Mechili Fort
Green Mts
Barce
7th Armoured Divn
CYRENAICA
LIBYA
Beda Fomm
Benghazi
Agedabia
El Agheila
to Tripoli

EGYPT
Siwa Oasis
Qattara Depression
Sand Sea

100 miles
150 km.
50   100
0   50
0

N

25-pounder artillery and the occasional scatter of bombs from a low-flying RAF Blenheim bomber. As the barrage lifted, the Italians crouched in the bunkers gradually became aware of a new sound.

At first it was a faint humming and scraping, somewhat like a distant mechanical digger. Gradually it worked up into a dreadful crescendo, somewhere between a whine and a roar. It heralded the approach of the heaviest tanks the British army possessed, the Mark-Two Matildas. Named after a popular feathered cartoon character of the time because its twenty-seven tons moved about as elegantly as an overweight duck, the Matilda averaged no more than six miles an hour over rough desert. Like all British tanks at that time, its main armament was a two-pounder cannon whose range and penetrating power left a lot to be desired; but what the Matilda did have was three inches of armour plate, a hide impenetrable to almost anything the Italians had to offer.

General Pietro Maletti seized a machine-gun and tried to rally his men, but his gallantry soon cost him his life. Within an hour the camp had surrendered and the British had captured 4,000 prisoners, together with their tanks and artillery. It was the beginning of a rout.

O'Connor's elated troops seemed unstoppable. One infantry battalion went into the attack kicking a soccer ball in front of them. Another battalion, poised to attack one of the Italian camps, fired a couple of bursts of machine-gun fire and was astonished to be greeted by white flags. Within three days the Italian army been bundled out of Egypt, leaving behind 237 intact artillery pieces, 73 tanks and 38,300 prisoners – more men than O'Connor's entire force. 'We have about five acres of officers and 200 acres of other ranks', was the famous report of one of the landed gentry who officered the Coldstream Guards.

The British pursued the Italians along the Via della Vittoria, the sixty miles of fine new road Mussolini's engineers had spent the last six months building from Sidi Barrani to the Libyan border. Now O'Connor's vanguard churned the Victory Way's freshly rolled surface to dust and stormed on through Halfaya Pass – 'Hellfire Pass' to his troops – and established a toehold in Libya by capturing Fort Capuzzo.

This extraordinary victory had been the brain-child of Brigadier Eric ('Chink') Dorman-Smith, Commandant of the Middle East Staff College, who had been sent to O'Connor as a 'special adviser' by Wavell. Described by the influential military historian Basil Liddell-Hart as 'the outstanding soldier of his generation', Dorman-Smith was also a practised seducer of other men's wives.* It was he who spotted the gap in the Italian defences and saw the opportunity to launch a surprise attack in their rear.

His and O'Connor's joint triumph was followed by a lull and a loss of momentum. They had hoped to pursue the Italians along the coast to Benghazi itself, but Wavell had decided to send the desert-wise and highly effective 4th Indian Division to join the British offensive against the Italians in Abyssinia. Their replacement would be the eager but green young Australians, fresh from their training camps in Palestine. To O'Connor this 'came as a complete and very unpleasant surprise . . . It put paid to the question of immediate exploitation . . .'

There was no opportunity for the Australians to gently 'work up' to their first combat role. They were to be blooded at Bardia, the first port in Italian Libya past the Egyptian frontier, strongly fortified and a hard nut to crack. Its garrison was commanded by Lieutenant-General Annibale Bergonzoli, called 'Electric Whiskers' by his troops for his spiky white beard, parted in the middle. The British started the battle with an attack at dawn when the temperature was still so low that a man's breath lingered like cigarette smoke. Two days later the Australians and their various Pommy attachments had captured Bardia, together with almost 40,000 prisoners, 120 tanks, 400 artillery pieces and 650 trucks.

Yet it had not been entirely one-sided. British Commonwealth dead and wounded numbered about 500. Many who survived learned the real horror of tank warfare in ways that would haunt them for life. When one of Captain Rea Leakey's light Cruiser tanks took a hit, its radio remained on 'send' and the entire squadron could hear what was going on inside.

The driver was killed by the first shot and the commander, our newest young officer, had one of his hands shattered. The driver's foot still rested on the accelerator and the tank continued . . . Suddenly [the commander] yelled, 'The tank's on fire' . . . Before the two in the turret could bale out they had to open the hatches . . . [They] were stuck fast. Then all we heard were the most terrible screams of agony; they were being burned alive while their tomb of fire still went on towards the enemy.

* He also happened to be a close friend of the author Ernest Hemingway and godfather to one of his sons.

The Royal Navy came close inshore and began to shell the fortress. Sergeant Cleere of the 7th Hussars, watching the bombardment through field glasses, spotted a herd of gazelle fleeing from an unexploded naval shell that was rolling down an escarpment 'like a small beer barrel'.

Gunner Leonard Tutt of the Essex Yeomanry came across the corpse of an Australian and was struck by the pristine state of his equipment. 'A gas mask haversack [was] strapped in position on his chest. A veteran of a few weeks' active service would have discarded that. I noticed that his rifle was new too: the stock honey colour unlike our oil-blackened relics of World War One . . .' But the majority of the Australians emerged from their initiation intact and with the confidence of men who have discovered that almost everything they had been taught actually worked.

Thanks largely to their own propaganda, many Italians were terrified of the Australians before ever meeting them in battle. Rome Radio had talked of the British 'unleashing the Australian barbarians in the desert'. The Melbourne-born British war correspondent Alan Moorehead seems to have been as awed as the Italians by these 'men from the dockside of Sydney and the sheep-stations of the Riverini [who] presented such a picture of downright toughness with their gaunt dirty faces, huge boots, revolvers stuffed in their pockets, gripping their rifles with huge shapeless hands, shouting and grinning – always grinning . . .'

Most of O'Connor's troops were filthy, their crumpled uniforms unwashed, their pores blocked with sand and their bowels with bully beef and biscuits. They were amazed to discover how well fed the enemy was. There was a cornucopia: chocolates, jams and cheeses, imaginatively prepared dried vegetables which boiling water transformed into wonderful stews and minestrone soups, and plenty of Frascati and Chianti wine and the best Italian mineral water to wash it all down.

Front-line dugouts came fully furnished with the kind of luxuries most British troops had not seen for months – and some had never seen at all. Moorehead, knowing his readers were struggling to make do in a Britain where practically all luxuries had disappeared, described 'Officers' beds laid out with clean sheets, chests of drawers filled with linen and an abundance of fine clothing of every kind. Uniforms heavy with gold lace and decked with the medals and colours of the parade ground . . . pale blue sashes and belts finished with great tassels and feathered and embroidered hats and caps . . . great blue cavalry cloaks that swathed a man to the ankles, and dressing tables . . . strewn with scents and silver-mounted brushes.'

On and on went the Australians, sweeping along the splendid Via Balbia which the engineers in the Italians rearguard had the heartbreaking task of dynamiting and mining to keep this horde of latter-day Visigoths at bay. Overhead flew the Desert Air Force, some in the newly delivered Hurricane fighters that had established air superiority over the Regia Aeronautica's biplanes. Once they were sure they were over Italian lines, the Hurricanes strafed anything that moved – though usually with more enthusiasm than accuracy.

Tobruk, one of the best fortified towns in the colony, fell in two days. Tom Bird, a lieutenant in the Rifle Brigade who took part in its capture, expressed the feelings of most of the British and Commonwealth troops towards the enemy when he wrote home saying: 'This is a good war to be in out here, because hardly anyone gets hurt on either side. The Italians give in before we have time to do them any harm and before they have much of a chance of doing us any harm.'

The Royal Navy immediately began to clear Tobruk's harbour of wrecks so that O'Connor would no longer have to bring all his supplies up overland from the Nile Delta. Among the port's considerable booty was a fleet of Lancia and Fiat trucks which the Australians commandeered to replace their own vehicles, which were beginning to fall apart. On they rushed in their new transport. Gazala and Derna fell. 'The Tel Aviv police gave us a better fight,' said one Australian officer.

Lieutenant Bird, in another letter home, said: 'I couldn't help feeling sorry for the enormous number of prisoners that we seemed to collect almost everywhere.' Feeding them was a considerable problem and 'it was really most inconsiderate of them to get captured in such large bodies'. And, writing three weeks later from the Turf Club in Cairo, where he was enjoying a rest out of the line: 'One can't help feeling that it is a great bit of luck to have been able to have a practice over or two, so to speak, with the Italians. What more delightful people to fight could there be?'

The Italian Tenth Army was running, partly out of panic and partly due to Graziani's desire to preserve it as a formation by getting behind a line they could hold. O'Connor, like most British officers a fox-hunting man, was determined to corner his quarry before it went to earth.

Immediately south of the coast road between Derna and Benghazi rose what the Senussi call the Jebel Akhdar – the Green Mountains – verdant highlands with the occasional brook meandering down wooded slopes. O'Connor decided to send the 7th Armoured Division behind these mountains on a 200-mile hook that would cut off the Italians' retreat by bringing the British armour to the coast road south of Benghazi, at the hamlet of Beda Fomm. It was a daring plan. The heavy tanks, shedding their tracks with maddening frequency, could barely average ten miles an hour over the rough terrain, so a brigade group consisting of armoured cars, towed artillery and infantry was sent on ahead. Racing through rain and sandstorms, this advance guard took thirty hours to get to Beda Fomm, just in time to amaze and horrify the first units of the Italian Tenth Army on their way west to Tripoli.

The advance guard beat back repeated Italian attempts to break through their line until the Desert Rats' tanks and artillery arrived, some hours later. The Italian column, tailing back along the road for ten miles, was trapped between the 7th Armoured and the Australians, pushing them west along the coastal highway. In the late afternoon Leakey saw the first white flags appear and guessed that the end was near: 'By last light prisoners were coming in by the hundreds.' O'Connor's gamble had paid off, Mussolini's Tenth Army was finished and, after almost sixteen months at war, the British had achieved their first land victory.

True, it could not be compared to the German conquest of most of Western Europe, but victory it undoubtedly was. 'If I may debase a golden phrase,' an exultant Anthony Eden told Churchill. 'Never before has so much been surrendered by so many to so few.' In ten weeks' campaigning O'Connor's 30,000 men had advanced over 500 miles, destroying 400 tanks and 1,292 artillery pieces, routing an army five times their number and taking 130,000 prisoners. All this was at the cost of 476 dead and 1,225 wounded. Using a hunting metaphor he knew his commander-in-chief would appreciate, O'Connor signalled Wavell: 'Fox killed in open.'

Five days later, Erwin Rommel, a different kind of fox altogether, arrived in North Africa.

PART TWO
Enter Rommel

Heiss über Afrikas Boden die Sonne Gluht.
Unser Panzermotoren singen ihr Lied!
Deutsche Panzer im Sonnenbrand
Stehen zur Schlacht gegen Engeland.

– Afrika Korps marching song, anonymous

It is not at all clear how or when Rommel became known as 'the Desert Fox'. He was already a legendary figure to the German public, having been the first Panzer commander to reach the English Channel in the six-week Blitzkrieg that conquered France in 1940. But it was as the Desert Fox that he would become known to the British, and to the world at large.

In all probability the sobriquet was the invention of a sub-editor on one of London's popular dailies at some time in the spring of 1942, after Rommel had been in the desert for about a year. It had the necessary ambivalence about it: the murderer in the chicken coop, grudgingly admired for the skills that got him there in the first place. Perhaps, locked in the grinding tedium of total war, the ever-sporting British public relished the opportunity to recognize a dashing foe. Churchill himself would not be able to resist bestowing a generous accolade in the House of Commons: 'We have a very daring and skilful opponent against us, and, may I say across the havoc of war, a great general.'

Yet an abiding myth needs to be dispelled: Rommel was never an anti-Nazi. On the contrary, like so many German officers, he was a great admirer of Hitler as long as Germany seemed to be winning. And Hitler was a great admirer of Rommel. For some time theirs was one of those relationships of boss and subordinate which is the envy of colleagues who cannot wait to see the spoiled favourite take a fall.

In Rommel's case, perhaps, disillusion with Hitler set in a little earlier than with some of his brother officers; even so, it happened slowly and was by no means a Damascene conversion. Until a few weeks before his death, he was still putting his considerable talents entirely at the service of Führer and Fatherland.

Rommel was born on 15 November 1891 at Heidenheim, a Black Forest market town about thirty miles north of the cathedral city of Ulm. There was no military tradition in the family. Rommel's father, also named Erwin, was a Protestant schoolteacher, like his father before him. A harsh and overbearing man, he nevertheless must have sensed his son's true vocation, for it was he who urged young Erwin to join the army as an officer cadet in 1910.

As a junior infantry officer, Rommel distinguished himself early in the First World War, winning the Iron Cross, both first and second class, fighting the French. 'Where Rommel is, there is the front,' said the men of the 164th Württembergers, his local regiment.

But the honour that really set him apart was the ribbon he wore at his throat: the Pour le Mérite, an old Prussian order that, until the arrival of the Nazis, was Germany's highest award for bravery. Rommel won this in October 1917, when Germany went to the aid of its Austro-Hungarian allies against the Italians in the mountains of north-east Italy. It was there, aged twenty-six, that Rommel first displayed what a complete warrior he was, an acute tactical sense matching his courage and a compelling power of leadership. 'Anybody who once came under the spell of his personality turned into a real soldier,' recalled Theodor Werner, one of Rommel's junior officers at the time. 'He seemed to know just what the enemy were like and how they would react.'

Leading a battle group of 300 men, Rommel captured an entire gun battery at bayonet point, part of the way up the 5,400-foot Mount Mataiur, the Italians' Alpine stronghold. With an extra four companies of Württembergers under his command, he went on to surround and capture 2,000 reputedly crack mountain troops. The following morning, with two other officers and only a few of his highly trained Alpine infantry, he burst into a camp of the Salerno Brigade and took another 1,500 prisoners by sheer bluff. Without pausing for sleep, in the next twelve hours he drove his unit, among them heavy machine-gunners, ever upwards towards the summit and to within point-blank range of the last defenders. In all this, Rommel lost only one man killed, amply proving the maxim he had drilled into his troops: 'Sweat saves blood.'

More than that, he demonstrated a rare gift for bluff and for persuading an enemy that, in certain circumstances, surrender was an honourable course; also that if a frontal assault were necessary, it should be launched with the strongest possible force against the narrowest possible front. Once a hole had been made, one should press on regardless, leaving a minimum of men behind to keep the gap open, and proceed to create mayhem within the enemy's vulnerable rear echelon. These were exactly the tactics he would employ twenty-five years later in the desert.

Having cleared the enemy off the strategic peaks, Rommel barrelled on, snapping at the heels of the fleeing Italians. By dint of forced marches across deep snow, frozen heights or icy torrents, he would get behind the enemy, then panic him into surrender or further headlong flight. On other occasions he might stun the Italians with the sheer élan of a frontal assault against desperate odds.

As he approached the Italian headquarters town of Longarone, packed with enemy troops, Rommel led his men in a dash across the last bridge before the town, ripping out demolition fuses as they went. Longarone was the high-water mark of Rommel's Italian campaign. In one day he took 8,000 prisoners, the best part of division, and it was here that he captured the coveted Pour le Mérite.

Eventually several British and French divisions were transferred to Italy from the Western Front and the Austro-German offensive petered out. At this stage, the hero of Longarone was turned into a staff officer and spent the rest of the war, apparently reluctantly, at various rear headquarters.

In the anarchy of the immediate post-war years Rommel remained in uniform, one of an élite cadre of middle-ranking officers who had survived not only the war but also the Allied-imposed shrinking of the German military. Cocooned from the poverty and political angst that would eventually doom the Weimar Republic, Rommel spent the next few years moving with his wife Lucie from one garrison town to another.

Rommel had been an officer cadet in Danzig when in 1911 he met Lucie at a formal ball. They married in 1916 when Rommel had already been wounded twice and infantry subalterns were a poor prospect. Like Rommel, Lucie's father was a schoolmaster, but temperamentally they appeared poles apart. The port of Danzig (now Gdansk) was a cosmopolitan place. Lucie had Italian and Polish blood and was slim, dark-haired and vivacious – she had won tango competitions. At first she looked unpromising material for a garrison *Hausfrau* and they remained childless for twelve years. Not until the end of 1928 did Lucie bear Rommel their only child, their son Manfred. It was some years before Manfred discovered that he did have a half-sibling, his illegitimate sister Gertrud.

Trudel, as Rommel called her, was the product of an affair he had in 1912 with Walburga Stemmer, the daughter of a seamstress. Walburga was still in her teens and perhaps a bit plumper than the elegant and slightly older Lucie, with whom he had 'an understanding'. He met Walburga while on manoeuvres near the small town of Weingarten in south-west Germany, some hundreds of miles away from his betrothed in Danzig. Their daughter was born the following year, and for a while Rommel seems to have considered breaking off his engagement to Lucie and setting up home with the mother of his first born. He called her 'his little mouse' and wrote, 'It's got to be perfect, this little nest of ours.'

It never happened, though Rommel supported his daughter and remained in touch while Walburga, in a Germany full of war widows bringing up children on their own, clung to the hope that one day Erwin would return to her. Then, in the year of Gertrud's fifteenth birthday, Manfred was born. Shortly afterwards Walburga died, officially of pneumonia, though some years later the family doctor revealed to Gertrud that her mother had taken an overdose. Lucie knew about her husband's daughter and throughout her life Gertrud was in contact with her father. But though they were in regular correspondence, his letters were always signed 'Uncle Erwin' just as Manfred knew his half-sister as 'Cousin Gertrud'.*

While Hitler ranted against the Jews and wooed the Ruhr industrialists, Rommel steadily climbed the promotion ladder. The scars of his three First World War wounds were well healed. Nor did he show any sign that the war had inflicted other, less visible scars. Like most of the survivors among Europe's professional officer caste, he came through the nightmare, rationalized his experiences and spent the next twenty years trying to make sure that his side would fare better next time. As did many of his contemporaries, he subscribed fully to the belief that Germany had not been defeated in the Great War but had been 'stabbed in the back' by Jews and Communists.

By early middle age the Rommels were regarded by their contemporaries as a fairly staid couple, pleasant, but boring. Rommel scarcely drank, nor did he have much small talk. Inside and outside the mess he talked shop. His sports were entirely predictable: shooting, fishing and skiing. He was good with machinery and had a head for mathematics – for mental exercise he memorized the complete table of

---

* By 1942 Gertrud was married to a man named Pan and Rommel had a three-year-old grandson called Josef. At the time of writing Josef Pan, Rommel's only grandchild, is a fruit and vegetable wholesaler in Kempten.

logarithms. But he showed no interest in the arts and rarely picked up a book that did not have a military theme. He collected postage stamps and learned to fly light aircraft. Only his musical tastes were eccentric, inflicting on Lucie his tortured attempts to learn the violin.

In 1934, a year after Hitler came to power, all German officers were required to take an oath of loyalty to the Führer. For Rommel, as for most of them, this was not difficult. Tearing up the Treaty of Versailles and restoring Germany's military muscle was high on Hitler's agenda. As the son of a provincial schoolmaster, Rommel shared the Nazis' contempt for the aristocracy, especially the patrician Junkers who still dominated the General Staff. He spoke with a broad Schwabian accent and distrusted those, like the Junkers, who spoke *Hochdeutsch*, the German equivalent of Oxford English.

All in all, like most German officers, he thought the Nazis' virtues far outweighed their vices. Returning from a lecture tour in Switzerland, he commented that the younger Swiss officers often expressed their admiration for 'our new Germany', some of them showing 'remarkable understanding of our Jewish problem'.

In 1937 Rommel edited some of the lectures he had been giving at the War School in Potsdam and got a local publisher to bring them out as a book called *The Infantry Attacks*. Surprisingly, it became enough of a best-seller for Rommel to arrange with his publisher to have the royalties paid annually in order to avoid tax.

The book brought Rommel to Hitler's attention and before long he found himself attached to the Führer's headquarters as a staff officer. Hitler was impressed, frequently inviting him to parties with senior Nazi officials and, as Rommel would recall, 'seemed to think I was a bright fellow'.

Among Hitler's inner circle, Rommel got on to friendly terms with Josef Goebbels, the club-footed Nazi propaganda minister, and with Heinrich Himmler, head of the SS and future architect of the Holocaust. One photograph shows Rommel seated at a table and laughing uproariously, apparently at something Himmler has just said.

In August 1939 Rommel was promoted to major-general and put in charge of the Führer's personal protection, with a 380-strong bodyguard unit equipped with anti-tank and anti-aircraft batteries. As Hitler's mobile headquarters followed the advance into Poland, this ring of steel went with it. Rommel found himself admiring Hitler's physical courage, frequently having to pull 'German Soldier Number

One', as Hitler liked to call himself, away from incoming fire. Most German generals found it easy to believe that the 'Austrian Corporal' was probably brave enough – in the First World War he had been decorated for running messages through gauntlets of fire. Now those who had had doubts as to their leader's grasp of grand strategy shed their reservations as one splendid victory followed another.

And nothing was more splendid than the victory that came the following spring, when Rommel's division was in the vanguard of the German Blitzkrieg across France. For the price of 42 tanks lost in action, mostly to a British counter-attack – the first time in his career that Rommel found himself up against British troops – his division took 97,000 prisoners, nearly all French but including 10,000 Scots Territorials of the 51st Highland Division. Soon afterwards, Rommel took part in the Nazi victory parade through Paris. Like his Führer, he was walking on air.

Even before Rommel's arrival in North Africa with his Afrika Korps, the Luftwaffe's Fliegerkorps X had descended on Sicily with 450 dive-bombers and fighter escorts. Malta was to be their chief target for, despite the island's woeful state of ill-preparedness, it was already proving a thorn in the flesh of the Axis powers. Aircraft based on the island had given the Royal Navy the information it needed to sink or cripple three Italian battleships at anchor in the Gulf of Taranto on 11 November 1940, Armistice Day.

This crushing blow to Mussolini's fleet, and his dwindling prestige, was accomplished by a squadron of elderly British Swordfish torpedo-bombers, open-cockpit biplanes with a maximum speed of only 100 mph, flying from the aircraft carrier, HMS *Illustrious*. Aerial photographs taken by Malta-based reconnaissance planes and flown immediately to *Illustrious* had made the operation possible, and the Mediterranean Fleet commander, Admiral Sir Andrew Cunningham, acknowledged this in a thank-you letter to the RAF's 'Sammy' Maynard.

In the few weeks following the Taranto raid, a small, Malta-based aerial strike force of twelve Swordfish – affectionately dubbed 'Stringbags' by their Fleet Air Arm two-man crews – and sixteen more up-to-date, twin-engined Wellington bombers launched dozens of raids on Axis shipping. The Mediterranean was demonstrably not the 'Italian lake' Mussolini had proclaimed it to be.

But revenge for the losses at Taranto was soon to be exacted – not by the Italians but by Fliegerkorps X, who announced their arrival in the region with a devastating attack on a convoy of British merchant ships as it approached Malta from the west. The convoy was escorted by a powerful naval force including *Illustrious*, which the German Stukas chose as their prime target. Within minutes they had scored half a dozen direct hits on her with armour-piercing 500- and 1,000-pound bombs, leaving the carrier a smoking, red-hot ruin. 'There was no doubt we were watching experts,' conceded Cunningham, who witnessed the attack from his flagship, HMS *Warspite*. '. . . We could not but admire the skill and precision of it all.'

As the Stukas turned their attention to Malta itself, the islanders were soon recalling the high-level Italian raids of earlier days with feelings almost of nostalgia. In contrast to their allies, the Stuka pilots dived low, sirens screaming, to deliver their bombs, ignoring the formidable screen of flak thrown up by the island's artillery defences. 'There was no feeling of contempt for the German squadrons,' recalled Queenie Lee, a Red Cross nurse who served throughout the siege. 'That was then a struggle for existence . . .' Echoing Admiral Cunningham, the Royal Artillery's Major Paine commented: 'To give them their due, they really meant business.'

Under a merciless hail of Nazi bombs, the island's civilian population now took to a troglodytic existence, sheltering in the ancient catacombs, carved up to sixty feet deep in the island's soft limestone rock.*

While the Germans hoped to terrorize the civil population into revolt and surrender, their principal military target, apart from the airfields, was the giant naval dockyard and any British warships they could catch undergoing repairs inside Valletta's magnificent Grand Harbour. When the grievously damaged *Illustrious* limped in on 10 January, with 126 dead and 91 wounded, the Luftwaffe made an all-out effort to finish her off.

For seven days they attacked the carrier almost non-stop as it lay berthed in French Creek, while the crew and an army of Maltese 'dockyard mateys' worked feverishly to make her seaworthy again. Almost miraculously – and partially protected by a ferocious defensive box-barrage put up by the island's overworked anti-aircraft gunners – *Illustrious* was sufficiently patched up to slip out under her own steam on the night of 23 January. Little more than an empty shell, she made her way successfully to Alexandria and a major re-fit.

If the Luftwaffe failed to finish off *Illustrious*, they certainly wreaked havoc in the densely populated urban areas all around the harbour.

---

* If the friable limestone was a lifesaver below ground, it was a menace above. Surgeon Captain E. Heffernan of the Royal Navy found that the traditional use of thick layers of powdered rock as insulation and weatherproofing meant that 'although the victims [of air raids] may be untouched by stones and other falling weights, they are asphyxiated almost invariably by the dust from the walls and roofs . . .'

Lieutenant-Commander M. S. Blois-Brooke, whose destroyer *Imperial* also put into Valletta for battle repairs in early 1941, divided his time between the defence of his ship and rescue work ashore. He found the task of digging out casualties from bombed buildings 'both sad and disgusting. Sad because there were invariably relatives waiting about . . . and all the time [they] kept up a sort of dirge in Maltese . . . Nothing would stop this frightful noise, not even a request to keep quiet because we wanted to listen for a cry or some noise that would lead us in the right direction.'

Blois-Brooke also entertained suspicions that not all Maltese were loyal to the Allied cause. As *Imperial*, her repairs completed, prepared to leave Grand Harbour, she was pinpointed by enemy planes and came under concentrated attack. 'How did the enemy know where to find us?' he speculated. 'They didn't attack anyone else that night. They knew exactly where we were. We put it down to the very efficient spy system they had in Malta. It was widely believed that many of the priests were spies . . .'

His suspicions were almost certainly exaggerated, if not entirely un-founded. True, there was a pro-Italian element in Maltese society, and some of its members were interned for the duration of the war, but no evidence has ever surfaced of an active Axis spy ring on the island. Nor can there be any doubt about the courage and tenacity of Maltese civilians under what would become the most sustained and intense aerial bombardment of any target area in the Second World War.

Blois-Brooke, for one, was not ashamed to admit his own fear: 'Anybody who says he is not afraid when being bombed is either brainless or a damned liar!!!' His candour was echoed by, among others, Gunner H. Fleming, a telephonist plotting the approach of enemy aircraft at Royal Artillery headquarters. He owned up to 'the paralysis of fear'.

When the alert went my hands grew cold and numb; every nerve in my body became painfully cramped and if I was on duty I was never able to concentrate during the raid . . . The medical authorities termed this fear 'anxiety neurosis' and it was surprising what a great number of men suffered from this complaint.

Indeed. The Malta Command psychiatrist would find that at least 25 per cent of the garrison displayed a response to aerial attack that bordered on the pathological. Nevertheless, 'anxiety neurosis' was a dirty word so far as the military authorities were concerned – 'a misnomer which makes "cold feet" appear respectable,' as one propaganda poster put it.

The Nazi blitz on Malta was four months old when Mountbatten arrived aboard HMS *Kelly*. After dining at the Governor's mansion he became convinced that the pious General Dobbie was close to capitulating. Mabel Strickland would recall that, one morning in April, Mountbatten 'came striding into my office and said, "Now I know how the silly old fool feels and that he will surrender the island".' But if Mountbatten intended to pass on his misgivings to higher authority, he soon had more immediate and pressing matters on his mind. His destroyer was ordered to Crete the next day to meet the German invasion of the island. Within forty-eight hours he was swimming for his life as the *Kelly* sank under Stuka attack.

Already, through her newspaper, the *Times of Malta*, Miss Strickland had braved wartime restrictions and Dobbie's personal displeasure to denounce the 'haphazard and slipshod' way in which the colonial administration was handling its civil defence obligations. 'There can be little excuse for this lack of imagination after seven months of war,' said a *Times* editorial. Through highly placed connections in Britain, and a confidential letter sent by the hand of a returning RAF officer, Miss Strickland tried to alert Downing Street to Dobbie's shortcomings. But if her views did reach Churchill, the Prime Minister did not respond.

And for a while the matter of Dobbie's leadership qualities would remain moot, for in May 1941 Malta was given an unexpected respite when Fliegerkorps X was withdrawn from Sicily to take part in the battle for Crete. This left the targeting of the island once again to the Italians, whose high-flying bombers – usually coming over at night – were greeted by the Maltese almost as old friends. 'It was a comforting sight to look up and see the black crows, as we called them,' one civilian recalled. 'They often dropped their bombs in the sea,' said the artillery officer, Major Paine. 'In each raid the first one to be shot down was the signal for cheering all over the island and the other planes immediately jettisoned their bombs and made off for home as quickly as they could. If one got caught in a searchlight it dropped everything.'

The respite was not to last. By the end of 1941, with Crete captured and Greece subdued, the Luftwaffe would return to Sicily in even greater strength and Malta would enter into its most intense period of aerial bombardment. 'I've given up counting the number of air raids we're getting,' Vice-Admiral Wilbraham Ford, naval commander on Malta, would report at the beginning of January 1942. 'The enemy is definitely trying to neutralize Malta's efforts and, I hate to say, is gradually doing so.'

Rommel's pride and pleasure at being given command of the Afrika Korps might have been severely tempered had he realized the extent to which Hitler regarded North Africa as a sideshow. The Führer's plans for Barbarossa, the invasion of Russia, were already well advanced and the date set.

Churchill, too, was about to downgrade the desert war. Knowing how important it was to demonstrate, particularly to the Americans, that Britain did not abandon its allies, he told Wavell to ready an expeditionary force to be sent to help the Greeks who, having hurled back the Italian incursion, now faced a far greater threat from the Wehrmacht.

This new obligation dashed O'Connor's hopes of completing the conquest of Libya, which was well within his grasp. Rommel himself would say later that if O'Connor had been allowed to push on into Tripolitania, 'no resistance worthy of the name could be mounted against him'. But it was useless to demur when, to comply with Churchill's instructions, Wavell reluctantly reduced the Cyrenaica garrison to a mere frontier force, just big enough to deter the Italians, and sent off the Australian 6th Division, jaunty conquerors of Bardia and Tobruk, to eventual defeat in Greece. With them went the as yet untested New Zealand Division, as keen as only soldiers who have not seen battle can be. The Antipodeans were supported by the Crusader tanks of a brigade of the 2nd Armoured Division, newly arrived from Britain.

Another brigade from that division was sent to replace the Desert Rats of the 7th Armoured who, after six gruelling months of campaigning, had been pulled back to the Nile Delta to rest and re-fit. Supporting the two tank regiments of the 2nd Armoured with its artillery, engineers, signals and various logistical units was an infantry battalion from the East End of London, the Tower Hamlets Rifles. These Cockneys were mostly Territorials – weekend soldiers, called to the colours on the outbreak of war – many of them worried sick about the fate of their families in the Blitz.

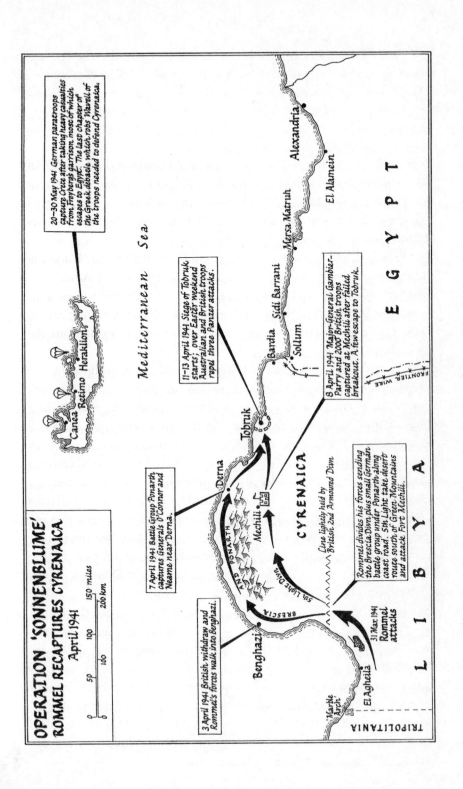

OPERATION 'SONNENBLUME'
ROMMEL RECAPTURES CYRENAICA

April 1941

0 50 100 150 miles
0 100 200 km

20–30 May 1941 German paratroops capture Crete after taking heavy casualties from Freyberg's garrison, most of which escapes to Egypt. The last chapter of the Greek debacle which robs Wavell of the troops needed to defend Cyrenaica.

Canea Retimo Heraklion

Mediterranean Sea

11–13 April 1941 Siege of Tobruk starts; over Easter weekend Australian and British troops repel three Panzer attacks.

8 April 1941 Major-General Gambier-Parry and 2000 British troops captured at Mechili after failed breakout. A few escape to Tobruk.

Alexandria

Mersa Matruh

Sidi Barrani

Bardia

Sollum

El Alamein

FRONTIER WIRE

E G Y P T

7 April 1941 Battle Group Ponarth captures Generals O'Connor and Neame near Derna.

Tobruk

Derna

Mechili

CYRENAICA

5th Light Divn and Ponarth

BRESCIA

Line lightly held by British 2nd Armoured Divn

Rommel divides his forces sending the Brescia Divn plus small German battle group under Ponarth along coast road. 5th Light take desert route south of Green Mountains and attack Fort Mechili.

3 April 1941 British withdraw and Rommel's forces walk into Benghazi.

Benghazi

31 Mar. 1941 Rommel attacks

Marble Arch

El Agheila

TRIPOLITANIA

L I B Y A

Their officers, also weekend soldiers, mainly worked in the City and campaigned in a style that would not have gone amiss in Wellington's Army of the Peninsula. Lance-Corporal Ken Bowden would recall one officer who travelled with a bell-tent, a carpet and a tin bath. Water was in short supply so, when they were camped near Benghazi, this officer would send his batman down to the sea with a bucket to fill it.

Such eccentricities apart, the armoured brigade was miserably ill-equipped to cope with the coming showdown with Rommel. Its light Crusader tanks were worn out, most of them having clocked up between 10,000 and 15,000 miles on anti-invasion exercises before leaving Britain. And though they were fast they were delicate, highly-strung machines, their engines and gearboxes constantly giving out and their tracks prone to snapping and slipping off their bogies.

The British had no tank transporters in the Middle East at this time. The Crusaders were unloaded at Tobruk, from where they had to drive 400 miles to the front. Behind them crawled the trucks carrying the overworked fitters, putting the breakdowns back on the road where they could and towing them to workshops where they could not.

The rest of the brigade's tanks – the heavier Valentines and Matildas – had not yet arrived from Britain and their crews were temporarily equipped with captured Italian M13 tanks, the most despised fighting vehicles in the desert. Every dozen miles or so they tended to come to a halt as their engines boiled over; to cool them down without wasting precious water, their crews had to resort to urinating into the radiators.

Alongside the armoured brigade was the Australian 9th Infantry Division under General Leslie Morshead, veteran of Gallipoli, known to his irreverent troops as Ming the Merciless because of his habit of scrunching up his face and narrowing his eyes when confronted with a difficult problem. One such problem was the rowdy off-duty behaviour of his troops who, as Britain's new desert force commander, Lieutenant-General Sir Philip Neame,★ complained, were responsible for 'numerous disgraceful incidents'. These included 'drunkenness, resisting military police, shooting in the street, breaking into officers' messes and shooting at officers' servants'.

Though only recently enlisted, little trained, and clearly somewhat

★ Neame, a First World War VC, had replaced the victorious O'Connor, who was convalescing from a stomach ulcer in Egypt.

wild, these Aussies were to prove themselves in battle. They were somewhat better off than the British in both pay and equipment. The captured Italian mortars, anti-tank guns and light anti-aircraft guns they had been issued were of far better quality than the M13 tanks. But the Australians were handicapped by a shortage of wheeled transport.

Not so the other Commonwealth formation in the Western Desert Force, the 3rd Indian Motor Brigade. This formation was composed of cavalry regiments with names out of a roll-call of the Raj – Gardner's Horse, King Edward VII's Own and Prince Albert Victor's Own – now mounted on 200 trucks of various shapes and sizes, with scout cars for brigade headquarters. In weaponry they were less well served. Each regiment had only half its allotment of Bren light machine-guns and, of the forty-two Boyes anti-tank rifles★ they should have had, the brigade had only three.

Notwithstanding the failure of the Raj to equip them with basic firepower, the *esprit de corps* of these Indian regular soldiers, some from families which had been serving the British for 200 years, was high. Most of their white officers also had long family connections with their regiments, they and their men inhabiting a military cocoon from which the less pleasant facts of twentieth-century life were excluded. There was probably not a man among them who would have found the notion that the Raj was six years from extinction any less fantastic than flight to the moon. The only sign that times might be changing was to be found in the spruce and martial form of Major Rajendra Sinjhi, second in command of Gardner's Horse and that rarity, a Sandhurst-trained Indian officer.

This was the sparse – not to say skeletal – force that was to face Rommel's Panzers and their Italian allies. His 5th Light Division, the first German formation to arrive, had 150 tanks. More than half of them were Mark III and Mark IV Panzers armed with 50-mm and 75-mm cannons. Both types could fire high-explosive as well as armour-piercing shells, making them more effective against artillery and infantry than the British armour.

The Panzers were well supported by anti-tank guns, including the dual-purpose 88-mm anti-aircraft guns that had proved so effective in

★ Immensely long-barrelled, shoulder-held weapons that fired a 0.55-inch solid shot, effective enough against Italian tanks but, as would later prove, almost incapable of penetrating German armour.

France in an anti-tank role. Superbly accurate, they could stop a tank over a mile away and would become, to the British, the most feared weapon in North Africa. Its reconnaissance battalion was equipped with eight-wheeled armoured cars, much more suited to rough terrain than the South African Marmon-Harringtons with which most of their British equivalents were equipped. Rommel also had at his disposal five depleted Italian divisions, whose armour included about eighty of the sub-standard M13 tanks.

The British facing him had only forty-seven tanks, including captured M13s, some of which mounted only machine-guns.

But, for the time being, Rommel seemingly had no idea how weak the British were – nor how slow their response time could be. Accordingly, he wasted a lot of effort on unnecessary deception measures. When the Afrika Korps began to disembark on 14 February he ordered the Italian harbourmaster at Tripoli to ignore black-out regulations and unload the vessels around the clock, and under arc-lights after dark. He got Italian engineers to manufacture fake tank bodies out of canvas and wood, mount them on Volkswagen cars and park them where they could be seen by Allied reconaissance planes.

He held a parade in Tripoli at which real Panzers were driven around in circles, giving the impression of much greater numbers to anyone who might be watching. A junior staff officer, Leutnant Heinz-Werner Schmidt, soon spotted the trick. 'After a quarter of an hour I noticed a fault in one of the chains of a heavy Mark IV Panzer, which somehow looked familiar to me . . . Only then did the penny drop . . .'

Libya remained Italian territory and Rommel was nominally subordinate to the new Italian commander-in-chief, General Italo Gariboldi. Like the German high command, Gariboldi did not want to mount an offensive yet. Rommel had his own ideas about that. His pending Operation Sonnenblume ('Sunflower') was ostensibly to be no more than a blocking operation, to prevent a British drive on Tripoli, but he had much more ambitious plans: the re-conquest of all Libya and the occupation of Egypt and the Suez Canal.

Contrary to the predictions of the British staff, he had his forces ready for action within days of arrival – tank crews, Panzer Grenadiers, reconnaissance units on their BMW motorcycles and assault pioneers with their flame-throwers and explosive charges – led by junior officers and NCOs who had learned the unstoppable craft of Blitzkrieg in Poland, Norway, Holland, Belgium and France.

When these forces struck on 24 March at the westernmost British outpost, El Agheila, Churchill sent an anxious message to Wavell: 'I presume you are only waiting for the tortoise to stick his head out far enough before chopping it off.' To adapt a famous later phrase of Churchill's: Some tortoise, some head. Anything less tortoise-like than Rommel in the desert would be hard to imagine: he was throwing his men into battle as soon as they stepped off their ships.

Gunner Len Tutt of the Essex Yeomanry, standing by his 25-pounder howitzer near El Agheila, heard the whine and rumble of approaching armour and saw German tanks coming over a facing hill, 'wireless aerials with pennants atop, like a field full of lancers. They assumed hull-down positions and blasted the thin screen of recovered tanks . . . Men of the Tower Hamlets went forward to face them in Bren carriers and were virtually destroyed in a matter of minutes; their bravery was unquestioned but they never should have been asked to face such odds.'

The Germans had close air support, a concept the British had not yet mastered. Lance-Corporal Ken Bowden of the Ordnance Corps watched as the Cockney infantrymen sprayed Bren gun fire at the dive-bombing Stukas, shouting the kind of imprecation beloved of British war film scriptwriters: 'Take this for London, you bastards!' To Bowden, the Stuka was 'the very embodiment of Blitzkrieg, terrifying with its fitted siren that shrieked your doom as it fell out of the sky in a near-vertical dive. The main German thrust was hooking around us into the desert, then heading up the coast road . . . so we were left holding the road in a rearguard action. It was a bravely fought but losing battle that obviously couldn't last long. We suddenly had orders to pack up what we could and scarper'.

As the Germans advanced through Cyrenaica, Rommel did what O'Connor had done going the other way. He divided his forces, sending a formation of the Italian Brescia Division along the coastal Via Balbia and the German 5th Light Division deep into the Cyrenaican hump, south of the Jebel Akhdar, the Green Mountains. Behind the Panzers came lines of trucks deliberately raising as much dust as possible in the hope that they might be mistaken for one huge tank column.

As usual, Rommel led from the front or, to be more precise, from above the front. Many of his daylight hours were spent in his single-engined Fiesler Storch spotter-plane with its NCO pilot, though he often took over the controls himself. Flying low to avoid RAF fighters, Rommel searched out his men and, when he saw that a column had stopped, landed as close as possible to demand why the sweating, dust-caked commander in question was resting. The most frequent reply given was that they were out of fuel – a full tank in a Mark III Panzer gave it a range of about 100 miles. For the hard-driving Rommel this was no excuse. Could they not siphon it out of some of their trucks? What were they waiting for? Let the Panzers go ahead, while some heavy trucks went back to Tripoli to load up with drums of tank diesel and return instantly, a round trip of almost 2,000 miles.

When the Italians urged Rommel not to send his men on a certain route because they had heavily mined it during their retreat, he insisted that General Johannes Streich's 5th Light Division continue regardless. Streich, an amiable character when not being asked to perform the impossible, was no great admirer of Rommel and relations between the two became tense. His men were driving at night without headlights. Their first casualty was the truck carrying the combat pioneers' demolition charges. They swerved past its flaming carcass and drove on until they got bogged down in soft sand, staying there till daylight, when they could safely start digging themselves out.

Within hours, Streich's lead Panzers again ran out of fuel. Rommel got two of the Luftwaffe's versatile Junkers-52 tri-motor transports to land on a nearby salt lake, laden with 40-gallon drums of diesel. Soon Streich's Panzers were moving on, the setting sun behind them.

On the coast meanwhile, the British evacuated Benghazi so hurriedly that the Arabs took advantage of the hiatus between British departure and German arrival to rape, murder and pillage the Italian settlers who had clung to their homesteads. Wavell had impressed on Neame that it was much more important to keep his force intact than to defend useless territory. Benghazi might have prestige value but was 'of little military importance'.

Since Neame was unable to share Wavell's thoughts with his men, their morale sank. They did not understand why they were constantly being ordered to pull out of good defensive positions. Were the Germans so good, so powerful, so invincible? One panicky withdrawal after another, and the remorseless air attacks on vulnerable lines of transport, suggested that they were. Retreat was turning rapidly into rout.

Gunner Tutt's 25-pounder battery held up some Panzers for a while with a barrage of indirect fire. Then, after dark, the order came to fall back.

. . . the rot seemed to set in. We dropped into action a little way down the road but had hardly surveyed the position before we were ordered to withdraw again. There seemed to be no overall direction. Too many units were on the move at the same time, a mistake which contributed to a growing panic . . . we soon saw the danger signs of men abandoning a stalled truck and running to get on another vehicle, when possibly a few seconds under the bonnet would have kept it going. Others were abandoned because they had run out of petrol, and yet there were three-tonners loaded down with the stuff passing on either side.

The Tower Hamlets Rifles were caught up in the same rearguard action at the Mersa el Brega defile along the coast road. Their opponents were newly landed Panzer Grenadiers of 8th Machine Gun Regiment. All morning on 1 April the Cockney Territorials held them back with their mortars and Brens. In the afternoon the Germans sensed that the British were yielding and began to advance on either side of the road. By dusk they were twenty-two miles east of Mersa el Brega and the British were in full flight. Lance-Corporal Bowden recalled that 'some of the lorries broke down or ran out of petrol, and so as to deny their use to the enemy, they were put out of action by destroying the distributor cap, or putting an axe or a pick-axe through the engine, or if all else failed by setting them on fire . . .'

The first tank battle between British and German forces in North Africa took place at dusk the next day in the area of Chor el Bidan. The Germans won. Forty-five minutes after the first shots were fired, those British tanks still able to move were retreating eastwards, leaving behind seven smouldering wrecks – 'a ghostly sight in the rapidly falling dusk,' one Panzer Grenadier noted. His account of the battle, in a regimental history published privately after the war, attributed the Germans' success to 'our better tactics, the self-reliance of our commanders and our greater mobility . . .'

Shortly afterwards the German armour were to use a tactic that would succeed against the British time and again. The Panzers made contact with British tanks, then appeared to think better of it and went back, luring their pursuers on to a screen of anti-tank guns. Some of these were the deadly, long-barrelled 'eighty-eights'. At this point, though, most of the British tank losses were through mechanical breakdowns, some of which might have been repaired on the spot were it not for the growing panic. Lieutenant-General Michael Gambier-Parry, commander of the depleted 2nd Armoured Division, would later estimate that he lost one Cruiser tank through mechanical problems for every ten miles his squadrons travelled.

Sensing the British confusion, Rommel did his best to cut off their retreat by hooking behind them and cutting the coast road, the Via Balbia. Ahead of his tanks he sent a fast-moving battle group, about 250 strong, led by Oberleutnant Gustav Ponarth, commander of the 8th Machine Gun Regiment. His instructions were to cut the coast road in a defile, just east of Derna, where it descended then snaked up again into the Green Mountains.

Ponarth's men soon began scooping up astonished British and Commonwealth soldiers from the jumble of weary troops crawling eastwards in a perpetual traffic-jam. Most of those who fell into Ponarth's net believed they were well behind British lines and were too shocked to offer resistance.

On the night of 6 April Neame decided to move his operational headquarters back from Marura, a hamlet along the Via Balbia, well east of Derna, to Timini, about sixty miles west of Tobruk. At this point he had been joined by the convalescing O'Connor, whom Wavell had sent back to 'assist' Neame, probably as a prelude to replacing him. He and O'Connor set off in Neame's car. With them was Brigadier John Combe, who had been commanding the armoured cars of the 11th Hussars which had first reached Beda Fomm. Behind them in a Ford Mercury van with the generals' batmen and baggage came 2nd Lieutenant Lord Ranfurly, Neame's ADC. Before long they had been stopped by traffic-jams, and military police directed them on to a side track into the desert, from which they could rejoin the coast road further east. They drove by moonlight, Neame at the wheel, his vision further obscured by dust. After a while, O'Connor began to suspect they were off-course. 'I felt from the position of the moon that we were going too far to the north and on three different occasions I said so, and on the last occasion persuaded Neame to stop.'

Neame was persuaded to relinquish the wheel and let his driver take over. The two generals dozed off as the car bumped along the potholed track. Behind them came Ranfurly and the batmen. There was another halt. Combe and Ranfurly got out to confer. As they met, Ranfurly heard somebody shouting. 'It was very dark and we could see nothing. Suddenly a figure loomed out of the blackness and the next thing I knew he had stuck a tommy gun in my middle. He shouted something incomprehensible and then more figures appeared. They were Germans.'

Neame and O'Connor surreptitiously ripped off their badges of rank, but the Germans realized at once that they had captured a couple of high-ranking officers. O'Connor managed to conceal a flat little .32 Beretta automatic, booty from happier times, down his trousers and a few days later plotted to use it to hijack the aircraft taking him and Neame to Italy. But this came to nothing, and the generals were to remain prisoners until the Italian armistice in 1943.

A convoy carrying the remnants of the Tower Hamlets Rifles was also caught in one of Ponarth's ambushes. Lance-Corporal Bowden was bringing up the rear with the quartermaster's section when he heard automatic fire raking their officers' cars ahead. Bowden got out to see what was going on, then 'jumped into a scout car and rushed off, followed closely by our own lorry. We were chased by some Germans in a half-track tank, but we managed to shake them off.'

They made their way to Mechili, an old Ottoman fort about fifty miles due south of Derna and the sea, at a crossroads of old caravan routes. The approaches to the fort were defended by trenches that etched out an oval-shaped perimeter roughly 1,200 by 800 yards, within which the British had cached big dumps of petrol, food and ammunition. Rommel was determined to have it.

Gambier-Parry, who reached the fort on the evening of 6 April, intended to hold Mechili until help came, unaware that the remainder of his tanks were fleeing east along the coast road. Gambier-Parry had brought with him an anti-tank battery of the Royal Horse Artillery and the thin-skinned Marmon-Harrington armoured cars of the King's Dragoon Guards. Otherwise, all he could contribute to Mechili's defence was one Cruiser tank and the signallers and clerks of his divisional headquarters.

The mainstay of the Mechili defence was the Indian motorized cavalry, supported by an Australian anti-tank regiment from New South Wales, equipped with two-pounders. Attached to them and the Indians were various stragglers such as Bowden's group of fifty or so

Tower Hamlets Rifles and some gunners who had brought with them one Bofors anti-aircraft gun and one 25-pounder – Mechili's total artillery.

Bowden soon found himself digging trenches, priming grenades and generally preparing for a siege. The food they had brought with them was pooled and the inevitable bully beef stew taken out to the trenches in steaming dixies as the enemy began regular shell-fire on their positions.

At Streich's mobile headquarters, fifteen miles distant, they were hoping for an easy victory. Even before Gambier-Parry's arrival they had three times approached the trenches under a white flag to demand surrender. This had been curtly rejected.

The seasonal khamsin winds whipped up a sandstorm that turned the desert into a choking fog, filled trenches, ruined food and frayed tempers – especially in the German camp, where Rommel had arrived in his Storch. He and Streich had never got on, and now Rommel was furious at Streich's insistence on waiting for his tanks to catch up with him before attacking Mechili. At one point he even accused Streich of cowardice – an insult he grudgingly withdrew only after Streich threatened to throw his Knight's Cross at Rommel's feet.

When the first eight Panzers did turn up the next day, their turret rings were so jammed by dust that they would not turn properly. There was further delay while the turrets were removed and cleaned. Rommel promised Streich Italian artillery support and ordered him to attack at dawn on 8 April. Before he could do so, the British, realizing that their position was untenable and no rescue operation likely, attempted a mass breakout.

A sandstorm added to the chaos and confusion of the battle that began at first light when the Germans realized what the enemy was attempting. At one point General Streich grabbed a rifle to defend his headquarters vehicle from attack by Dragoon Guards' armoured cars. Rommel watched the start of the battle from his Storch, dodging machine-gun and rifle fire from both British and Italian troops; his allies failed to recognize his aircraft.

Lance-Corporal Bowden, in a lorry close behind Gambier-Parry's command vehicle, an armour-plated Dorchester the size of a bus, watched the last act unfold. 'As we gathered speed we were fired on by enemy tanks. A sergeant of the Tower Hamlets slashed through the tarpaulin roof of the lorry he was riding in and with his Bren gun returned their fire enthusiastically. He certainly had a go but his brave opposition was in vain.'

Gambier-Parry had decided the game was up. His command vehicle came to a halt and he waved a white handkerchief through a hatch in the roof. An open-topped Kübelwagen drove up and a German officer holding a sub-machine-gun called out in English: 'All Englishmen, hands up and come this way.'

A few of the British – about 300 in all – refused to accept surrender and managed to break out to the west, firing as they went. Among them was the squadron commanded by Major Rajendra Sinjhi of the Indian motorized cavalry. They eventually reached British lines. The remaining 2,000 survivors, including Gambier-Parry, were taken prisoner. With others, Bowden was taken to a PoW cage near Benghazi. There he encountered two Italian soldiers he had befriended only a few weeks before when, as prisoners of the British, they had been part of a working party Bowden commanded: 'Whom should I find staring at me through the barbed wire, but Paolo the Barber and Roberto the Chef . . . They had tears in their eyes . . . They alerted the rest of the team and furtively every evening passed over the wire presents of white bread, eggs, cheese, jam and wine.'

The fall of Mechili was the climax of Rommel's first desert offensive, but he was not there to witness it. After flying above the battlefield he had landed some miles away to speak to the crew of an idle 88-mm gun. On touching down the undercarriage of his Storch had hit a boulder and he had been forced to commandeer a truck to get to Mechili. By the time he got there, the contents of Gambier-Parry's command vehicle were being cleared out. Rommel walked over and spotted a pair of plastic sand-goggles with an elasticated strap. He tried them on, then pushed them up so that they rested rakishly just below the eagle on the crown of his flat cap. 'Booty, permissible even for a general,' he said. A German war photographer then took the first pictures of the Desert Fox as the world would remember him.

Gambier-Parry's Dorchester was booty of an even more substantial kind. Rommel requisitioned it, and another like it, one for himself and one for Streich. Instead of Dorchesters they were now to be called 'Mammoths' on account of their bulk, with the names 'Max' and 'Moritz', after the characters in a popular German children's story.

Rommel had created his legend. In a mere fortnight he had swept the British out of Cyrenaica, undone all of O'Connor's victories and put new heart into the Italians, who felt they had chosen the right ally after all.

The capture of Tobruk, the best harbour between Tripoli and Alexandria, was Rommel's next objective. Intoxicated by the success of his Blitzkrieg tactics so far, he expected the port to fall almost as a matter of course, solving his increasingly urgent supply problems at a stroke. Spurred on by his Panzers' critical fuel shortages and his anxiety to destroy or capture the British in Tobruk before they could escape by sea, he was however in an even greater hurry than usual.

In his haste, he arranged with the Luftwaffe to fly 3,500 men of the 15th Panzer Division to Tripoli, accompanied by their commanding officer, Major-General Heinrich von Prittwitz, while their heavy equipment and the rest of the division followed by sea. Massive airborne troop-movements in those days were rare. The men of the 15th made the crossing in a fleet of 208 corrugated-sided, tri-motored Junkers-52 transports, part of an aerial armada being assembled for the forthcoming parachute assault on the island of Crete.

Twenty-one-year-old Panzer Grenadier Rolf-Werner Völker found the 180-mile trip from the toe of Italy to Tripoli eventful, to say the least. Like most of his comrades, he had never flown before and the briefing they received before take-off was daunting. Life-jackets were to be worn at all times, though not inflated. For added buoyancy and to help keep their heads up, should they find themselves in the Mediterranean they were told to remove their gas masks from their chest packs. The non-swimmers began to look somewhat pale. There were no seats on the aircraft. The eighteen Panzer Grenadiers aboard each plane arranged themselves on the floor amid a jumble of kitbags and weapons and a tied-down BMW motorcycle. They circled Sicily for an hour until the entire fleet of Ju-52s had assembled and then headed south for Tripoli with an escort of twin-engined Messerschmitt-110 fighters.

To evade detection by enemy radar, they flew low in groups of three, a mere eighty or ninety feet above the waves, and it was a bumpy flight. One after another Völker and his fellow passengers threw up. Then, soon after the Messerschmitt escort had left them to return to Sicily, the worst happened. Over the drone of the Junkers' engines they heard machine-gun fire and realized they were being attacked by British aircraft. Völker recalled:

It was pandemonium as our pilot flew even lower and jinked from side to side. Men and kit were sliding about in all directions. We were scared and we were angry. We knew there was only one turret gunner on the plane to defend it, but there was a Spandau [machine-gun] stored in the fuselage and we smashed one of the windows with a fire-axe and got the Spandau up to it. I started firing it at the British planes. A lot of men in other Junkers were doing the same and I could see their tracer, and my own, streaming towards the enemy. I don't know if we hit any of them but it was good for morale to be able to shoot back and they seemed to be backing off. Then our pilot suddenly banked and before I could stop firing I had put several holes in our own wing. Luckily, I didn't hit an engine or anything important.

Back on terra firma at Tripoli, Völker and his comrades had little time to brood on events during the crossing. Quite possibly the panic was caused not by British fighters but by RAF reconnaissance aircraft from Malta at the edge of their range; Ju-52 transports would have been easy targets for even the most cautious fighter pilot.

Within hours, Italian trucks were taking them east towards Tobruk, 1,000 miles away. Their commanding officer, the patrician young Major-General Prittwitz, had even less time to draw breath. Rommel sent for him to come immediately to the Tobruk sector with only his personal staff. There Rommel ordered Prittwitz, entirely new though he was to the desert, to prepare to lead an attack on Tobruk's defences by a 1,500-man battle group, spearheaded by Ponarth's machine-gun battalion. This assault was to be launched from the east while elements of Streich's 5th Panzer lunged up from the south.

Prittwitz had no choice but to obey this peremptory order. But he was fated never to get as far as Tobruk's outer perimeter. Leading a reconnaissance group of armoured cars, and ignoring warnings from German forward units, he ran into a wall of artillery and anti-tank fire just beyond Kilometre Stone 13 and eight miles short of Tobruk itself. Together with his driver and staff, Prittwitz was killed – the first, but not the last, German general to die in North Africa.

Learning of Prittwitz's death shortly after the event, a furious Streich chased after Rommel's Mammut to tell him the dire news. Rommel had already heard it and he laid into Streich for chasing after him in a captured British vehicle. 'I was about to have the gun open fire on you,' he said.

'In that case,' Streich retorted, 'you would have managed to kill both your Panzer Division commanders in one day.'

Contrary to Rommel's belief, the British were decidedly not planning to abandon Tobruk as they had Benghazi. Churchill had insisted that the town should be 'held to the death without thought of retirement', not only to deny Rommel its port facilities but also to maintain a base from which to threaten his land supply lines south of the perimeter.

Shrugging off the death of Prittwitz, Rommel ordered a new attack on the perimeter the following day, Good Friday, 11 April. When that failed, he ordered another on the 12th and yet another on Easter Sunday, the 13th. Although there were more than 30,000 British and Commonwealth troops within the thirty-mile perimeter, out-numbering his own force by ten to one, they were spread out, and Rommel believed that by concentrating 3,000 infantrymen and forty tanks at one vulnerable spot he could blast his way through and drive on to seize the town itself.

But the spot was not at all vulnerable. The Italians had given Tobruk a formidable network of strongpoints, interconnected by concealed passageways and fronted by a deep anti-tank ditch, and the predomi-nantly Australian defenders were extremely pugnacious. On Easter Sunday, a platoon of Australian infantry was locked in hand-to-hand combat with Ponarth's men, who were trying to bridge the anti-tank ditch. When the Aussies charged with fixed bayonets, Corporal Jack Edmondson, in civilian life a sheep farmer from Wagga Wagga, was shot in the neck and stomach. 'Still he ran on,' recalled his platoon commander, Lieutenant Frank Mackell, 'and we were into them. In spite of his wounds, Edmondson was magnificent. As the Germans scattered he chased them and killed at least two. By this time I was having difficulties★ wrestling with one German on the ground while

---

★ These 'difficulties' were of a particularly macabre kind. Mackell was unable to withdraw his rifle and bayonet from a prostrate German soldier he had impaled. The dying German held his legs in a fierce embrace while another German approached with a pistol.

another was coming straight at me with a pistol. I called out "Jack" and from about fifteen yards away Edmondson ran to help me and bayoneted both Germans. He then went on and bayoneted at least one more.' Edmondson died of his wounds and was posthumously awarded Australia's first Victoria Cross of the Second World War. Ponarth was killed during the day's fighting and, their spirit broken, 250 of his men were taken prisoner as they sheltered in the anti-tank ditch. His machine-gun battalion, which had started out so gloriously, had ceased to exist.

Front-line soldiers are rarely aware of the larger strategic implications of the actions they take part in, but the men of 425 Battery, 107 Regiment, Royal Horse Artillery, were left in no doubt by their commanding officer, Captain Graham Slinn, what was at stake at Tobruk. Slinn – 'a quiet, courageous English gentleman', as Bombardier Ray Ellis remembered him – told his men that if the port fell the Germans would conquer Egypt and get their hands on Middle East oil. He quoted the final passage of Henry V's speech before Agincourt – 'You know your places; go to them and God be with you' – and said the fate of England and the free world was in their hands. Ellis recalled: 'The guns glowed red as we put down a defensive barrage.'

At what Rommel termed the *Schwerpunkt* – the point of maximum pressure – the RHA's 25-pounder howitzers were employed in an anti-tank role, firing over open sights from shallow pits. They had no armour-piercing solid shot and fired high explosive which had to make a direct hit to stop an oncoming Panzer. Despite this handicap and the fact that it was still quite dark, 'the first shot from Number One gun set the lead tank on fire [and] Number Two gun's first round lifted the turret clean off another . . .'

Retaliation was swift, as at least fifteen tanks opened up on the British gunners with both cannon and machine-gun fire. Soon two officers and four men were down, 'but we were getting hit after hit . . . and every time a tank was hit a cheer went up'. Amid the dust and smoke, there was confusion among the German tank commanders. Some who were advancing towards the gap that had been punched into the defence line found their way blocked by others who had turned around to retreat. One who found himself in this predicament was Leutnant Joachim Schorm of the 5th Panzer Regiment. Quite apart from enemy fire, his Mark III Panzer had problems with brakes, gears and engine. 'Some of our tanks are already on fire. The crews call for doctors, who dismount to help in this witches' cauldron. Enemy anti-tank units fall on us with their machine-guns firing into our midst . . . Our own anti-tank guns and 88s are almost deserted, the crews lying silent beside them . . .'

All the German assaults of that terrible Easter weekend were repulsed with heavy losses to the attackers. Over the next three weeks Rommel made several fresh attempts to break through the perimeter, but the most he could achieve was a small and costly salient in its south-west corner. Having suffered his – and the German army's – first reverse of the war, he deployed mainly Italian troops, stiffened by a few of his own, to continue the land siege while the bulk of his forces enlarged and consolidated their positions at the Egyptian frontier. German dive-bombers and artillery continued a relentless pounding of the perimeter positions and the town itself.

As Tobruk settled down to a prolonged siege, Morshead's Australians began catching up on what they had yet to learn about the desert and tank warfare. They learned fast. Lieutenant (later Major) A. O. McGinley of the 7th Royal Tank Regiment, recalled:

We wanted to prove to the Aussies that it was quite safe to lie low in a ditch or trench and let a tank drive straight over them. As each brigade came into reserve . . . we had them dig slit trenches, lie in them and ran over them . . . This training paid off and when Jerry broke in about the end of May the infantry just laid low while the Mark IV Jerry tanks rolled over them, then came up, wiping out the German infantry following. This left the Jerry tanks completely cut off from their support and both the artillery . . . and our tanks . . . had a field day, knocking all of them out.

John Youden, then an eighteen-year-old private in the 2/13th Australian Infantry, gave the authors a graphic account of trench life on the perimeter, enduring temperatures ranging between 40°C by day and 0° at night and frequent dust storms, each lasting three or four days.

We all had dysentery and that was worse than the enemy fire. During daylight you couldn't leave your hole to relieve yourself. Still, when the Germans dropped 'surrender' leaflets★ they made good toilet paper. Your tin hat came in handy, too. You could use it as a shovel, a cooking pot, a toilet and a wash basin. Two boots made a good pillow. We had two litres of water a man a day and little except bully beef to eat; we ate it at night when it was cold and not too greasy. But there was always plenty of tea – a great morale-booster, with Carnation milk and lots of sugar.

Boredom, rather than danger, was the major threat to morale. The Australians went out on fighting patrol every night, partly to harass the enemy, partly to give themselves something to do – 'you looked forward to [the patrols], even if they were dangerous,' explained Youden. The British and enemy positions could often be over a mile apart, and night patrols, ranging between them, had to navigate by the stars in the absence of recognizable landmarks. By daylight the defenders were frequently dive-bombed as many as eight or ten times a day, and 'after they dropped their bombs they came back and strafed you'.

What kept the garrison going through these unremitting hardships was 'mateship', recalled Howard Lockwood, a private with the 2nd/17th Australians during the siege of Tobruk. 'You couldn't let your mates down. That's what it was all about – not Democracy, King and Country or any of that stuff.'

Even after the bloodiest encounters around the perimeter, both sides managed to maintain a rough-hewn regard for the other's casualties. Sergeant Bill Tuitt, a timber-mill foreman from South Australia who had been put in charge of his battalion's stretcher-bearers, made frequent forays into no man's land, under a flag of truce, to recover the dead and wounded. On one occasion he and his party were given a shouted warning by a German that they were approaching a minefield.

We could see the bodies of thirteen of our chaps lying there. A couple of Jerries came out with a mine-detector and guided a lieutenant and a doctor out to us . . . They brought out four wounded and let the truck come up to

---

★ These read, in part, 'Single soldiers waving white handkerchiefs are not fired on. Strong German forces have already surrounded Tobruk and it is useless to try and escape . . . Our dive-bombers and Stukas are awaiting your ships . . .'

take them away. Then they carried out the bodies of fifteen dead and helped us with those still on the minefield. When the last of our dead had been brought to us, the lieutenant . . . lowered his flag and I lowered mine. I saluted him and he saluted back, but he gave me the salute of the Reichwehr [*sic*], not of the Nazis.

Boredom was a particular problem for British tank crews who, without fuel, were largely unable to use their vehicles. Thirsting for action, Tank Regiment officer Rea Leakey, now an acting major, attached himself to an Australian infantry battalion as an acting corporal and went out one night with two privates to man a concealed artillery observation post, over a mile into no man's land. For much of the next day, by field telephone, Leakey called down 25-pounder fire on to the Germans' forward positions. Late in the afternoon, the spotters were themselves spotted and the Germans sent out a party of infantry to deal with them.

Leakey and the two privates – a clerk and a dairy farmer – held the Germans off for a while with Bren gun fire and grenades. One German, with fixed bayonet, got close and, the Bren having jammed, Leakey shot him with his revolver: 'I hit him between the eyes and he fell back dead.' Under protective artillery fire, Leakey and his two companions then managed to escape back across no man's land to their own lines.

Lieutenant McGinley of the 7th RTR found a less dramatic way to deal with boredom. 'Being a bit musical', he made a guitar out of a pick-handle, signal wire and 'bits of enemy lorries'. Seven or eight such instruments took shape and McGinley taught the men of his troop to tune and play them. Then they 'had a bit of a concert in the officers' mess [which] went down very well. The squadron leader was so tickled that he got on the field telephone to brigade HQ and said "Listen to this," holding out the phone. Brigade were equally amused and plugged in Division, who in turn plugged in several others. Just as well Rommel did not choose that moment to attack.'

It was during the long siege of Tobruk, with men of the two sides deployed in relatively static positions around the defensive perimeter, that the song destined to become the veritable signature-tune of the war in North Africa was first heard.

Broadcast to the German troops but heard across the desert silence at night by the British and Australians too, the smoky voice of a Bremerhaven-born nightclub singer named Lale Andersen evoked an immediate response. She sang a ballad of longing and separation entitled 'Lili Marleen', about a young woman waiting under a street light outside a barracks for her soldier lover. '*Wenn sich die späten Nebel drehn/Werd ich bei der Laterne stehn/Wie einst Lili Marleen/ Wie einst Lili Marleen.*' ('Your sweet face seems/To haunt my dreams/My Lilli of the lamplight/My own Lilli Marlene', in the subsequent English version.) In their foxholes, the grimy front-line defenders of Tobruk pricked up their ears and called out, 'Louder, please, louder!' And a twentieth-century musical legend was born.

Not only the sweaty rank-and-file were enchanted by Lilli. She made an enduring impression, for instance, on the Oxford-educated SAS officer and author Fitzroy Maclean when, deep behind the lines and on his way to a commando raid on Axis-occupied Benghazi, he heard Lale Andersen's voice come drifting across the night from the radio at a nearby enemy command post. 'Husky, sensuous, nostalgic, sugar-sweet', it 'seemed to reach out across the desert,' he would later recall.

Another British officer, Captain C. F. Milner of the Rifle Brigade, felt impelled to write to the BBC in September 1941, only one month after the song was first broadcast, to declare 'Lilli Marlene' (the subsequent English spelling) 'the most bewitching, haunting, sentimental song of the war' and Lale Andersen's voice 'at once seductive and soothing, husky, intimate but mysteriously unattainable'. More pragmatically, Squadron Leader R. A. Foggin of the Desert Air Force urged the BBC to find a rival to Lilli, warning that the original might 'possibly create a feeling that the Germans who can produce such good music etc. cannot be such bad chaps after all'.

Perhaps it was Lilli Marlene's calculated ambiguity that created so powerful and universal an appeal. She was at once the girl that Tommy or Fritz might hope to marry and the tramp they would go to for illicit sex, for surely no 'nice girl' would be found standing underneath a street light in front of a barrack gate. Lilli Marlene was, in short, that archetypal if clichéd male fantasy figure: Virgin and Whore.

Lilli Marlene's road to universal stardom had not been an easy one. She started life as a poem in 1917 by an infantryman named Hans Leip. The poem languished unnoticed until it was set to music in 1938 by a composer of popular songs named Norbert Schultze. Later that year it was recorded by Lale Andersen, a then little-known nightclub chanteuse. On disc, the song sold only 700 copies and might have died, unmourned, but for the pure chance of its finding its way to *Soldatensender Belgrad*, the radio station set up in occupied Belgrade in 1941 to beam morale-building programmes to the Afrika Korps. The station was short of recorded material and a corporal was sent to Vienna to bring back whatever he could find. From a pile of records gathering dust in the cellar of a studio he dug up Leip and Schultze's unconsidered opus. Back in Belgrade, the officer in charge of the forces' station thought that 'Lili Marleen' might just do as close-down music – and a legend was born.

Hitler's twisted little propaganda chief, Josef Goebbels, was not pleased by the song's instantaneous popularity among the Nazi soldiery. He thought it 'unheroic' and not at all in the martial spirit of the Third Reich – but even in the Third Reich the will of the common man could not be completely ignored, especially when the common man happened to be also the front-line soldier.

Meanwhile, in London, the BBC was getting letters demanding to know why its forces' programme wasn't able to put out anything half as good. British propaganda chiefs and the BBC's programme directors took the message on board. In an internal memo, a BBC executive named Morris Gilbert posed the question: should they 'crush' Lilli or 'adopt' her? As Gilbert observed, 'one school of policy makers held that the song should be resolutely barred, on the score that it could not help but attract and seduce and . . . enervate the war effort. Anything so warm, so simple, so appealing could not but arouse sympathy and kindred softer feelings towards its German creators . . .' But banning the song would involve the necessity of 'producing a song of greater lilt and seduction which would overwhelm it – a tall order'. On the other hand, 'adopting it would involve producing a suitable lyric in English and plugging it with terrific emphasis and tenacity until it should simply be identified as a British product and its enemy origins forgotten'.

After consultation with the War Office and the Home Office (which had set up a Dance Music Policy Committee to weed out 'unhelpful' items of popular entertainment), the BBC plumped for 'adoption'. A popular songwriter named Tommy Connor – progenitor of 'I Saw Mummy Kissing Santa Claus', 'It's My Mother's Birthday Today' and similar Tin Pan Alley gems – was commissioned to anglicize and sanitize Lili. 'I knew about the German version, but I couldn't use that,' he would say in a post-war interview. 'Wasn't it all about a young prostitute who wanted to give as much for her country as the soldiers so she gave her body? Can you imagine that in English? I had to write a song imagining the girl as a daughter, a mother, a sister or a sweetheart – a song that wouldn't offend the hearts and morals of people.'

Connor's cleaned-up version, lushly orchestrated, was handed over to Ambrose and his Orchestra and his star female singer, Anne Shelton, and broadcast on the forces' programme 'Ask Anne'. They never stopped asking and the rest, as they say, is showbiz history. But surely a little more than that: an inscrutable fragment, perhaps of universal social history. For 'Lilli Marlene's appeal was not restricted to the fighting men. It would become a wildfire favourite among civilian populations on both sides of the war – even among the civilians of Nazi-occupied Europe – and was to be translated into French, Spanish, Italian, Dutch, Norwegian, Danish and Swedish.*

As the siege wore on, Wavell made two attempts to dislodge the Germans from their positions along the Libyan-Egyptian frontier. Operation 'Brevity' in May 1941 and Operation 'Battleaxe' in mid-June were costly failures. In the latter, almost 100 British tanks, including the heavily armoured Matildas, were lost in a massive frontal attack. Many of these fell victim to the deadly German 88s but others, which were not fatally damaged and could have been recovered, were left on the battlefield because, unlike the Germans, the British had not yet developed tank recovery units.

After the failure of 'Battleaxe', Churchill sacked Wavell by sending him as C-in-C to India, an unjust reward, many thought, for a man who had done so much against the Italians and might have done better against Rommel if Churchill's adventure in Greece had not squandered so many of his best troops. Wavell's replacement was General Sir Claude Auchinleck, aged fifty-seven, a tall, lean, broad-

---

* One Nazi-occupied country where it was definitely not appreciated, though, was Yugoslavia where, according to the BBC's Deputy Director of Music, there was 'evidence of intense resentment, leading even to demonstrations, by Yugoslav patriots on hearing "Marlene" included in BBC transmissions'.

shouldered scion of the Anglo-Irish Ascendancy. Arriving in Cairo, Auchinleck found awaiting him a confidential letter from the CIGS, Sir John Dill, warning him not to give in to pressure from Churchill by launching an offensive before he was good and ready. On a subsequent flying visit to London, Auchinleck extracted from Churchill an agreement that no new attack should take place before November.

Meanwhile, political pressure from the Australian Government, who felt their men had done enough, made it necessary to withdraw most of Morshead's division by sea from Tobruk and replace them with British troops of the newly formed 70th Division. Getting the Australians out of Tobruk and their replacements in under the constant threat of air strikes and submarine attacks was a high-risk operation for the Royal Navy. Under protest from Admiral Cunningham, they carried it out in three moonless periods of nine nights each, between mid-August and the end of October. When the Navy called it off, only one Australian battalion remained within the perimeter.

Along with the British infantry, the ships had also brought an armoured brigade with more than sixty tanks, most of them the heavy if under-gunned Matildas. They were there to spearhead part of the forthcoming offensive, in which it was planned that the beleaguered Tobruk garrison would break out and meet up with British troops advancing from the east. It was to be codenamed 'Crusader'.

PART THREE
Crusader

Peter was unfortunately killed by an 88:
It took his leg away – he died in the ambulance.
When I saw him crawling he said:
'It's most unfair – they've shot my foot off.'

How can I live among this gentle
Obsolescent breed of heroes, and not weep?

– Keith Douglas,
Sherwood Rangers Yeomanry

Auchinleck's 'Crusader' offensive was prefaced by two daring and imaginative commando raids, one intended to kill Rommel in his headquarters, the other to destroy part of his Luftwaffe support on the ground. Both were led by patrician young Scots. Both were unmitigated disasters.

The British Army's youngest lieutenant-colonel, Geoffrey Keyes, MC, aged twenty-four – Eton, Sandhurst, the Royal Scots Greys, and son of Admiral of the Fleet Sir Roger Keyes, Head of Combined Operations – led the No. 11 (Scottish) Commando attack on what was thought to be Rommel's headquarters, 250 miles behind the front line. The concurrent raid by the nascent Special Air Service, that was intended to cripple enemy tactical air capabilities, on Axis airfields equally far behind the lines was led by twenty-six-year-old Captain David Stirling.*

The former Italian prefecture at Beda Littoria had been pinpointed as Rommel's HQ by a combination of seemingly infallible signals and human intelligence, SIGINT and HUMINT in military jargon. The original information came from an analysis of 'Ultra' intercepts, by which the British had access to the Germans' supposedly undecipherable 'Enigma' code. Unwilling to act on the basis of signals intelligence alone, Middle East headquarters sent in Captain (later Lieutenant-Colonel) 'Jock' Haselden to provide first-hand human intelligence. Haselden was uniquely well qualified for the mission. A seasoned Arabist who in civilian life had been a Cairo cotton broker, he was friendly with the Senussi tribesmen of Cyrenaica and thoroughly familiar with their dialect, habits and customs.

One night in mid-October 1941 he was dropped by parachute in the vicinity of the ancient city of Cyrene, Hannibal's birthplace, and, disguised as a Senussi, took up watch from an escarpment overlooking

---

* Stirling, Ampleforth, Cambridge and the Scots Guards, was first cousin to the Highland chieftain Lord Lovat, one of the founders of the British commandos on whose head Hitler personally settled a reward of 100,000 marks.

Beda Littoria, an Italian administrative centre. Parked around the stuccoed building that had been the Prefettura, Haselden noted a number of Afrika Korps vehicles and, entering and leaving the building, a steady stream of German personnel. Finally, he spotted a figure he identified through his field glasses as Rommel himself, coming down the steps and driving off in his personal command vehicle, the unmistakable Mammut. Two nights later, Haselden rendezvoused with an LRDG patrol and returned to Cairo with the apparently clinching eyewitness evidence.

A few days later, Keyes' commando unit, part of 'Layforce' – after its overall commander, Colonel Robert Laycock⋆ – was given the go-ahead for Operation 'Flipper'. And on the night of 13 November 1941, four days before the scheduled start of Crusader, the raiding party arrived by submarine at a designated point off a small cove, twelve miles from Beda Littoria.

The weather was terrible. A sudden storm whipped up waves that capsized a number of the lightweight, collapsible canvas-covered folboats that were to take Keyes and his men ashore. Of the original raiding force, only Keyes, Captain Robin Campbell, Lieutenant Robin Cook and seventeen Other Ranks were able to disembark successfully. Together with Laycock, leading a three-man headquarters unit, they came ashore, soaking and exhausted, to be met by Haselden and a Senussi guide. Haselden led them to a cave where they lit a fire and dried off.

Keyes and his reduced force spent the next day revising their plan of attack. Keyes' No. 1 Detachment was to make the attempt to kill or capture Rommel, while a No. 2 Detachment, led by Cook with six Other Ranks, made their way to a crossroads south of Cyrene to blow up a communications facility. They set off to their objectives after dark and in heavy rain, leaving Laycock's group behind to maintain contact with the submarines. The storm that had affected their plans so badly continued all that night, and Keyes and his men were once again soaked and thoroughly chilled by the time they reached the shelter of a cave, about a mile from their objective. There they laid up, recovering their strength and refining their plans for the assault.

⋆ Laycock, who ultimately became Head of Combined Operations, was the model for 'Brigadier Ritchie-Hook', dauntless 'biffer' of the enemy in Evelyn Waugh's *Men at Arms*.

The attack began next night at midnight. Campbell and a Sergeant Terry followed Keyes up the steps to the front door of the target house while the rest of the force were deployed around the grounds. 'Just inside,' Campbell would report later, 'we were confronted by a German in steel helmet and overcoat. Geoffrey at once closed with him, covering him with his tommy-gun. The man seized the muzzle of Geoffrey's gun and tried to wrest it from his grasp. Before I or Terry could get round behind him he retreated, still holding on to Geoffrey . . . Geoffrey could not draw a knife and neither I nor Terry could get round Geoffrey as the doors were in the way, so I shot the man with my .38 revolver . . .' The thunderstorm raging outside cloaked the sound of Campbell's shot and he, Keyes and Terry raced up a flight of stairs and threw open the door of a lighted room, surprising a group of enemy officers. Campbell pulled the pin of a grenade and threw it into the room. 'Before Geoffrey could shut the door the Germans fired. A bullet struck Geoffrey just over the heart and he fell unconscious . . . I shut the door and immediately afterwards the grenade burst with a shattering explosion. This was followed by complete silence . . . Sergeant Terry and I carried [Keyes] outside and laid him on the grass verge by the side of the steps leading up to the front door. He must have died as we were carrying him outside, for when I felt his heart it had ceased to beat.'

Moments later, Campbell was crippled by one of his own men when he went to the rear of the building and was mistaken for a German. The bullet smashed his shin bone. Terry, finding himself on his own in a building full of thoroughly alerted German troops, beat a retreat, shooting an enemy soldier dead as he went. Other members of the raiding party had been unable to get into the building by the back door. Had it merely been locked, they could have broken it down easily enough, but a middle-aged and nervous German quartermaster corporal named Barth was in the habit of barricading it at night from the inside with a heavy canister of water and a big filing cabinet.

When the men deployed outside heard the heavy exchanges of fire at the front of the house, they suspected that they had walked into a trap. And when Terry appeared, gasping out the news that Keyes had been killed and Campbell wounded, the raiders made off into the dark, aided by the chaos and clamour of the thunderstorm.

All the mayhem and heroics had been in vain. Rommel was not in the building. He was not even in North Africa. Some two months previously the German commander had moved his headquarters far closer to the front line, and it was pure mischance that Haselden had seen him leaving the prefecture in October after a brief visit to what had become his Quartermaster General's headquarters. And two weeks prior to the raid, Rommel had flown to Italy to rest and celebrate his fiftieth birthday in Rome with his wife Lucie.

Notwithstanding all this, Operation Flipper might still have given Crusader a kick start. To have wiped out the Germans' quartermaster's headquarters five hours before the opening of a major British offensive would have been no small matter. In the event, the sum total achieved was two German officers and two enlisted men dead, for the loss of Keyes and the capture of Campbell.* Sergeant Terry and two others escaped and managed to make their way back to the British lines after an epic forty-one-day trek. Finding water to drink was never a problem for them: it rained virtually non-stop.

As for Lieutenant Cook and his No. 2 Detachment, their sabotage mission failed totally and all were either killed or captured. Laycock and his three headquarters men were evacuated from the shore by submarine, and on his return to Cairo he had harsh words to say about the planning and preparations for Operation Flipper, which revealed an alarming degree of what could only be termed amateurishness. 'The demolitions attempted were for the most part ineffective since those responsible for carrying them out had only undergone an elementary and inadequate course in the use of explosives . . . Touch with the submarines was extremely difficult to maintain, since I was the only person ashore with a knowledge of Morse Code and such messages as I sent were made with a torch which had no proper key, but a switch which had to be pushed off and on.'

On his return from Italy, Rommel was amazed that the British should imagine he would maintain an HQ as far behind the front line as Beda Littoria. But he must have considered it a backhanded compliment that they should take the unusual step of trying to assassinate an enemy commander. Ever concerned to appear chivalrous, he ordered that Keyes' body should be buried with full honours in the

---

* Campbell survived, thanks to the unstinting skill of a German army surgeon, Dr Werner Junge, who amputated his leg. Campbell spent the rest of the war in a PoW camp.

military cemetery at Benghazi, alongside the four Germans he and his men had killed.

Seven months later, after due deliberation in Cairo and Whitehall, Keyes was awarded a posthumous Victoria Cross. Britain was in dire need of heroes at the time, and official propaganda depicted the raid not as an ill-planned fiasco but as a deed of outstanding derring-do.*

David Stirling, the leader of Crusader's other disastrous preliminary raid, had taken up parachuting on what can only be described as a self-taught and unofficial basis. Shortly after being posted to the Middle East as a Scots Guards lieutenant attached to Layforce, he began begging rides from RAF friends and jumping with standard aircrew parachutes. He enthused others with his ideas, somehow managed to 'borrow' an old RAF Valencia transport for an afternoon in April 1941, and did a practice jump with Welsh Guards Lieutenant 'Jock' Lewes and six Other Ranks volunteers. At 6 feet 6 inches, Stirling was rather bulky for such activities and injured his legs and back severely enough to spend the next two months in hospital.

That might well have been the end of his parachuting career but, undaunted, he spent his time in hospital drawing up plans for an airborne raiding force to attack enemy facilities, in particular airfields, far behind the lines. As he told a female visitor to his bedside at Heliopolis Hospital, 'When I have got my legs to function again I have a scheme to put to Headquarters – it may be difficult to get them to accept it, but it is vital they do.'

In the event it was surprisingly easy. Carrying a briefcase full of plans, and still limping, the softly spoken Stirling talked his way into GHQ and the office of Auchinleck's Deputy Chief of Staff, Major-General Neil Methuen Ritchie of the Black Watch, a fellow Scot and an old family friend. Stirling's idea was disarmingly simple: infiltrated silently by land, sea or parachute, a small force of five men, properly selected, trained, motivated and equipped, could raid an enemy airfield more

---

* Forty-five years after the black farce at Beda Littoria, there was an ignominious postscript when Keyes' brother, the second Baron Keyes, underwent a 'financial reversal' and sold Geoffrey's Victoria Cross to an American collector. In 1995 the new owner in turn sold it on, through Spinks, the medal and military memorabilia auctioneers, to an anonymous telephone buyer. The winning bid was £121,000. Britain's Imperial War Museum had dropped out of the bidding at £105,000, of which Keyes' sister, Kathleen Williams-Powlett, had pledged £70,000.

effectively than a force of 200. And a force of 200 could raid thirty to forty different airfields on any one night.

Impressed by the sheer boldness of this proposal, Ritchie took Stirling to see the Commander-in-Chief who, equally impressed, promoted Stirling to captain on the spot and promised him all the men and resources he required. Stirling was gratified but insistent on one major condition. Leery of interference by hidebound GHQ staff officers, he insisted that his force should be responsible to Auchinleck himself. 'The Auk' agreed, and by the end of July 1941, Captain Stirling – with Lieutenant Lewes in charge of training★ – was in command of the seven officers and sixty Other Ranks of a formation designated as 'L' Detachment, Special Service Brigade. Thus was born the Special Air Service.

The pre-Crusader raid which was its first major operation was doomed from the outset, not by faulty intelligence or poor planning but by the same violent storm that made it so difficult to disembark Keyes' commandos. As gales blew inland across the Western Desert, kicking up blinding sandstorms, the RAF, three of whose Bristol Bombay transports were to take Stirling and fifty-four of his men to their drop zones near Axis airfields at Timini and Gazala, wanted to call the whole thing off. But Stirling was determined to carry on, and Auchinleck, anxious to give Crusader maximum support, let him have his way.

It was a turbulent ride and deeply disorientating to the RAF pilots and navigators, who quite simply lost their way and dropped Stirling and his men miles off-target, scattering them like dandelion seeds. As Captain Malcolm Pleydell, 'L' Detachment's medical officer, recalled: 'In the stormy blackness of that night, broken only by an occasional flash of lightning, the men jumped out of the planes into a wind that was blowing at half-gale strength. They drifted down fast, striking the ground heavily . . . dragged hard along the stony surface before they had an opportunity to find their feet.'

That was the fate of Stirling's plane-load. Another of the three Bombays was lured by bogus radio signals, and in zero visibility, to land on a German airfield, where all aboard were promptly taken prisoner. The third Bombay dropped its passengers over the Great

---

★ Lewes was killed while taking part in an airfield raid in early 1942. Stirling once said that Lewes 'could far more genuinely claim to be the founder of the SAS than I'.

Sand Sea, where they perished among the dunes. Stirling himself was knocked unconscious on landing. When he came to, he began signalling with a flashlight to rally his men to him in the dark. After an hour only a handful were with him while their containers (with explosives, time fuses and other sabotage equipment) were nowhere to be found. They had little idea of their exact position except that they were far behind enemy lines and without even basic infantry weapons.

They had no option but to make their way as best they could to a prearranged pick-up point, where they were met by a patrol of the LRDG. Of the fifty-four who had started out, only twenty-one were picked up. As Pleydell reported, the raid was 'a most complete and utter failure'. Still, Stirling had learned an unforgettable lesson: for the rest of the desert war the Special Air Service, belying its name, would travel by land, either in its own vehicles or escorted by the LRDG – the Libyan Desert Taxi Service as it became known – to the target area and back.

Despite its unpropitious start, the SAS would go on to perform a number of daring operations, including a risky reconnaissance into Axis-occupied Benghazi in the spring of 1942, in which Stirling was accompanied by the Prime Minister's son, Captain Randolph Churchill, anxious to prove his mettle.* Auchinleck was enormously impressed by Stirling, quickly promoting him to major and then lieutenant-colonel. In the course of the North African campaign, the infant SAS managed to destroy over 250 German and Italian warplanes, to blow up vehicle parks, ammunition and petrol dumps and to derail trains, hijack trucks, mine roads and generally wreak havoc behind the lines.†

* Later in the war, Randolph Churchill was to become a member of Fitzroy Maclean's mission to the Yugoslav partisans in Nazi-occupied Yugoslavia.
† Stirling's wartime career came to an abrupt end in January 1943 when he was taken prisoner while leading a raiding party near Sfax in Tunisia. He spent the rest of the war 'in the bag', as contemporary Eighth Army slang had it. He died in 1990 but six decades after its birth his brain-child, the SAS, remains very much alive and arguably the most dashing, admired and effective of all the world's special forces.

As Rommel returned from his Roman holiday to his field head-quarters, thirty miles east of Tobruk, British armour was already crossing the Egyptian border in strength to begin Crusader. But for almost forty-eight hours after his return, Rommel failed to behave like the brilliant general he had abundantly proved himself to be and, instead of responding to the British incursion, demonstrated an inflexibility worthy of his opponents at their worst.

Despite the pleadings of his staff, he refused to believe that a major British offensive was under way, dismissing it as a reconnaissance in force. On no account, he insisted, should this British sortie be allowed to interfere with his plans for a final assault on Tobruk, scheduled for 20 November.

The over-confidence that had cost him so dear in the Easter battles for Tobruk had been replaced by dogged, painstaking rehearsal. Nothing had been left to chance. Rommel's infantry had been practising clearing bunkers for weeks, his artillery had been studying firing plans and stockpiling ammunition, and his engineers surveying where best to clear lanes through British minefields for the Panzers. Only when the BBC announced that a major British offensive had begun did Rommel admit the obvious, put aside his own plans and begin to react. This delay should have proved fatal. As it turned out, it was exactly the right thing to do.

Since Hitler's attack on Russia in June had removed the threat of an invasion of Britain, Churchill had been generous with *matériel* and reinforcements for North Africa. In armour alone, the new commander of the newly named Eighth Army, Lieutenant-General Sir Alan Cunningham (younger brother of Britain's Mediterranean Fleet commander, Admiral Sir Andrew Cunningham) outnumbered Rommel by about 700 tanks to 350.

His plan was to mass those tanks at a point where he thought Rommel would be obliged to come out and do battle and then to crush the Germans with superior numbers. The site Cunningham chose for this showdown was Gabr Saleh, a dot on the map along an

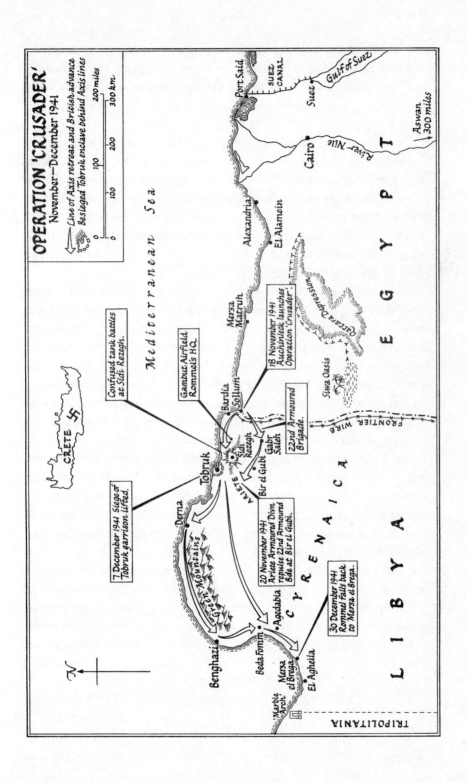

OPERATION 'CRUSADER'
November–December 1941

→ Line of Axis retreat and British advance
∿∿∿ Besieged Tobruk enclave behind Axis lines

0   100   200   300 km
0   100   200 miles

CRETE

Mediterranean Sea

Confused tank battles at Sidi Rezegh.

7 December 1941 Siege of Tobruk garrison lifted.

Gambut Airfield Rommel's HQ.

18 November 1941 Auchinleck launches Operation 'Crusader'.

22nd Armoured Brigade.

20 November 1941 Ariete Armoured Div. repulse 22nd Armoured Bde at Bir el Gubi.

30 December 1941 Rommel falls back to Mersa el Brega.

Port Said
SUEZ CANAL
Gulf of Suez
Suez
Cairo
River Nile
Aswan, 300 miles

E G Y P T

Alexandria
El Alamein
Mersa Matruh

Qattara Depression

Siwa Oasis

FRONTIER WIRE

Bardia
Sollum
Sidi Rezegh
Gabr Saleh
Bir el Gubi
ARIETE
Tobruk
Derna
Green Mountains

C Y R E N A I C A

Benghazi
Beda Fomm
Agedabia
Mersa el Brega
El Agheila

Marble Arch

L I B Y A

TRIPOLITANIA

N

old camel-caravan track called the Trigh el Abd. While the planned-for tank battle raged, Cunningham's two infantry divisions, mainly Indians and New Zealanders, were to attack further north along the coast to relieve Tobruk by meeting a sortie staged by its garrison towards the El Duda ridge.

Lieutenant-General Willoughby Norrie, commander of XXX Corps, whose 7th Armoured Division contained most of the Cruiser tanks intended to destroy Rommel's armour, had been against massing at Gabr Saleh, arguing that it was not far enough west to threaten Rommel and provoke the desired counter-attack. The best place for the showdown, Norrie suggested, was the Axis airfield at Sidi Rezegh, another ancient caravan stop, on the Trigh Capuzzo, about twelve miles south-east of the Tobruk perimeter.

Norrie had far more experience of tank warfare than Cunningham, who had only recently arrived in North Africa after waging what was virtually a nineteenth-century colonial campaign against the Italians in Ethiopia. Cunningham had never before commanded large armoured formations with their enormous logistical tail of vehicles bearing the fuel, water and ammunition needed to keep the tanks going. When he arrived in the Western Desert he even had to be shown how to operate a radio telephone. East Africa, with its camels and mules and its spirit of make-do, had been nothing like this.*

But Cunningham rejected Norrie's advice. To get his new command up to scratch and plan an offensive, he had been working eighteen-hour days, seven days a week, for two months and, like Rommel, he found it hard to contemplate a change in his carefully laid plans. Nor could he bring himself to accept that he was now playing in a bigger league: he had proved his ability in East Africa† and would surely do so again. What he missed most was the comfort of his pipe, which an army doctor had recently urged him to give up, and sleep. By the time the battle started, Cunningham, determined to prove himself worthy of his East African reputation, had already overworked himself to the edge of physical and nervous exhaustion.

* The British historian Correlli Barnett has cruelly but accurately compared Cunningham to 'the successful owner of a village shop suddenly put in charge of a London department store'.

† With the assistance of a brilliant guerrilla-type campaign, headed by the future Chindit leader, Orde Wingate, who personally restored Emperor Haile Selassie to the throne.

Norrie accepted his commander's decision and did not make an issue of going to Sidi Rezegh. Fortunately for Rommel, as it turned out, his immediate subordinate, General-leutnant Ludwig Crüwell, was less pliable than Norrie. He had arrived a few weeks previously and, like Rommel himself, he was bad at taking orders: he took it on his own initiative to send his Panzers to meet the British armour at Gabr Saleh.

During the summer lull, both sides had reorganized their armies in a way that reflected how they were being sucked into what a later generation of military planners would call 'mission creep'. While O'Connor's Western Desert Force (which Churchill, ever the romantic, preferred to call 'the Army of the Nile') had been restyled the Eighth Army, Rommel's augmented force was now 'Panzer Group Africa'. This group consisted of his old Afrika Korps, now commanded by Crüwell, to which a new division, the 90th Light, would soon be added to the tanks of 15th and 21st* Panzer Divisions. In addition there were five Italian infantry divisions with some supporting artillery, though without adequate transport.

In theory, Rommel did not control the best Italian desert formations. These were the Ariete armoured division, newly equipped with an improved version of the M13 tank, and the Trieste motorized division, which was mostly infantry but also had a few tanks and artillery. Both divisions had plenty of Italy's 47-mm anti-tank guns which, though they did not have the range of the German 88s, were lower, easier to dig in and often detectable only when it was too late to avoid their fire. Designated the Corpo d'Armati di Manovra XX, officially they came under the direct command of Field Marshal Ettore Bastico, the Italian officer supposedly commanding all Axis forces in North Africa and nominally Rommel's boss. Bastico was mindful of his dignity and, like most senior Italian officers of the day, had adopted a style of speech that might best be described as Mussolini Florid. 'General Bombastico' was Rommel's private name for him, and he undermined Bastico's authority by giving direct orders to the Ariete and Trieste Divisions whenever he felt like it. While things were going well, this suited these above-average Italian divisions who, after

---

* The 21st was the re-named and expanded 5th Light, the first German formation to arrive in North Africa.

their humiliation at the hands of O'Connor, reckoned that German military genius was better than no genius at all.

On the whole, relations between the Italians and their overwhelming allies were seldom better than tepid. The average Italian soldier was never as taken in by Mussolini's braggadocio about a 'new Roman Empire' as the average German soldier was about Hitler's 'thousand-year Reich' and – inferior equipment, discipline and training apart – this lack of motivation showed in their tendency to surrender or retreat when the going got really tough. The Germans, as much as the British, liked to joke about the number of reverse gears in Mussolini's tanks.★ After one Italian retreat which left the flank of a German unit dangerously exposed, Wilfried Armbruster, Rommel's interpreter, described his allies in a furious diary note as 'a race of shits'.

For their part, the Italians resented the arrogance and condescension of their allies. Further, many of them harboured bitter memories of the First World War, when Germany and Austria had been the enemy. The recollections of Colonel Paolo Caccia-Dominioni, commanding a battalion of combat sappers and the outstanding chronicler of the Italian army's part in North Africa, spoke eloquently of the resentments under which the Italians laboured vis-à-vis their German allies. The Germans, he said, enjoyed 'undreamed-of advantages', such as 'rest periods, leave, reinforcements and above all the open or tacit approval of commanders on the spot and the general public at home'. As for the Italians, 'Weary from their years of service in Africa, they were sick of promises never kept, degraded by arms and equipment which were farcically inadequate, stranded in their front-line paradise with no guardian angels to take care of them. However . . . often enough the ragged and ill-nourished Latins set an example of courage to the haughty grenadiers of Prussia.'

The mutual antipathy between the Italians and their German allies contrasts strangely with the growing mutual respect between the Germans and the British. The young Rifle Brigade officer Tom Bird, now a captain and with a Military Cross to his credit, had a chance to read some British newspapers while recovering from a leg wound in Cairo. The papers were 'swearing to take vengeance on our enemies when we beat them' and Bird was horribly shocked. 'I wonder if

---

★ The Germans had a song that went: '*Kennst du den Avanti Schritt?/Ein Schritt vor und zehn züruck.*'

everyone in England has grown so bitter,' he wrote in a letter home. 'I'm glad to say it is certainly not so out here. I, and I think most of those with whom I have talked, have a certain admiration for the German enemy . . . The Germans certainly behaved very well towards the prisoners that they captured and behaved well when they themselves were captured . . . In a year or so when we have won the war we shall have to live peacefully with the enemies.'

In charge of most of the British armour in the coming battle was the popular 'Strafer' Gott, who had recently been elevated to command of the 7th Armoured Division. This veteran formation – the original Desert Rats – had never been so powerful. Supported by truck-borne infantry and artillery, it now consisted of three armoured brigades: the 22nd, an untested Yeomanry formation equipped with the latest Cruiser tank, the Crusader; the old sweats of the 7th,★ with some Crusaders but mostly early-model Cruisers; and – the envy of the division – the 4th Armoured Brigade, the first formation in the Western Desert to be equipped with American tanks. This was the M3 light tank, known to the British, who preferred names to numbers, as the Stuart† or, less formally, as the Honey because of the sweetness and reliability of its Pratt & Whitney aero-engine, which gave it a top speed of almost 40 mph and made it the fastest tracked vehicle in the desert if not the world. Its main armament was a 37-mm cannon which had a little more penetrating power than the two-pounder on the British-made tanks – though, like them, it could only fire armour-piercing rounds and not the shrapnel-producing high explosive that could cut down enemy anti-tank crews.

The Stuart's most serious defects were its thin armour (for which its speed was supposed to compensate) and the aviation fuel its radial engine drank, which detonated all too easily and with a terrible whumph. But the men taking the Honey to its first battle had yet to discover this frequently fatal shortcoming. And as they got to know their new tanks, they were generally grateful to the workers of the Detroit Tank Arsenal, whose folded notes urging them to 'give that guy Hitler hell' would sometimes surface like messages in a bottle.

★ The 7th Armoured Brigade was deliberately given the same number as the division to confuse German signals intelligence.
† After Jeb Stuart, a dashing Confederate cavalry commander of the American Civil War.

The 4th were commanded by Brigadier Alec Gatehouse, a hard-driving Royal Tank Regiment officer who thoroughly understood armoured warfare and whose mind was uncluttered by the equestrian foppery often flaunted by his equivalents in the recently mechanized cavalry.

In desert war – then and subsequently – the tank is the primary weapon, an armour-plated monster spewing fire and destruction as it plunges straight ahead to its objective. Or so it seems to the 'poor bloody infantry' as they deploy, naked and horribly exposed, across an unforgiving landscape of rock, grit and thorns. To the men inside the tanks, the advantages of speed, armour plate and fire-power seem not nearly so clear-cut. When the hatch is closed for action and the engine reaches its optimum heat, it becomes stiflingly hot and the combined stench of fear, fuel, sweat, cordite and machine oil can be overpowering. The outside world is visible only through slits in the armour, and what little can be seen is often obscured by swirling clouds of dust.

The crew characteristically consists of a driver, a gunner, a radio operator and a commander. They cannot see each other's faces and must communicate by intercom. The charge may be exhilarating but there is always the fear of being trapped inside a metal tomb if one's machine is disabled by a thrown track or, even worse, hit by armour-piercing enemy fire, causing its ammunition to explode and its fuel tanks to ignite. This was known as 'brewing up',* an experience never to be forgotten by those fortunate enough to survive it.

For the British tank crews the odds against survival were alarmingly shortened by the range and accuracy of the German 88s, and there was considerable resentment within the Eighth Army at the failure of their superiors to give them a comparable weapon, which many believed was already at hand if only the general staff had the wit to adapt it and press it into service. This was the British 3.7-inch (94-mm) anti-aircraft gun, and Lieutenant (later Major) David Parry of the 57th Light Anti-Aircraft Regiment, Royal Artillery, for one, felt there was 'no excuse for the sheer stupidity of the General Staff' in not allowing it to be used in an anti-tank role.

---

* Curiously, the same phrase was used by the British to describe the far more congenial business of making tea, then – as now – the mainstay of the British fighting man.

He recalled in a post-war memoir: 'During all this time over a thousand 3.7-inch AA guns stood idle in the Middle East . . . Many never fired a shot in anger during the whole of the war.'

Cunningham's divisions crossed the frontier into Libya in long, dust-billowing lines of vehicles often twenty or more miles in length. They bypassed the Axis border garrisons at Bardia, Sollum and the Halfaya Pass and concentrated at Gabr Saleh. When Rommel failed to respond, Cunningham's plan began to unravel and the first cracks to appear in the façade of confidence he had tried so hard to maintain. In response to Norrie's and Gott's entreaties to be allowed to seek out the enemy, the enormous concentration of British armour around Gabr Saleh began to disperse.

The process began when one of Gott's armoured-car reconnaissance patrols located the Ariete division at Bir el Gubi, another bump in the desert a few miles north-west of Gabr Saleh. While the eager 'new boys' of 22nd Armoured Brigade dashed off to deal with the Ariete, the 7th Armoured Brigade were sent further north to capture the Italian airfield at Gambut, where Rommel had his headquarters. Once this was accomplished, they were to move on about ten miles west to the larger airfield at Sidi Rezegh – the very place where Norrie had wanted to concentrate the entire division. This left Gatehouse's 4th brigade in their pristine Honeys to hold Gabr Saleh.

Gambut was lightly held – Rommel was away – and the airstrip was soon in British hands. But after this initial success, Brigadier Jock Campbell, who commanded the brigade and its supporting infantry and artillery, was ordered to stay put and await the arrival of the rest of 7th Armoured Division before moving on Sidi Rezegh.

This did not happen as quickly as it should have. The 22nd Armoured Brigade had already suffered a setback. Never in action before as a unit, the Territorials of the County of London Yeomanry and the Royal Gloucester Hussars had charged the Ariete with considerable élan. Judging by all they had heard about the Italians, this should have been enough to send them flying; instead, the 22nd were shot to pieces.

The Italian tank crews had dug their inferior M13s in hull-down positions and were well covered by their anti-tank guns. By nightfall, when the Yeomanry limped away, they had lost more than forty of their brand-new Crusaders, which the veterans of 7th Brigade had always said should have gone to those who knew how to use them.*

Unlike Rommel, Crüwell, the clever and arrogant son of a wealthy hymn-book publisher, had always believed that this was a full-scale British attack. Without waiting for Rommel's approval, he ordered his 15th Panzer Division to do what Cunningham had been longing for: to take on the British tanks gathered at Gabr Saleh. But now, rather than being outnumbered by an overwhelming concentration of British armour, the Panzers were faced by a significantly smaller force: the 123 Honeys of 4th Armoured Brigade.

It was the battle début of the American light tanks, and Gatehouse used them well. Rather like fighter pilots, their commanders had learned how to exploit the Honey's speed and manoeuvrability to get behind their opponents and put a solid shot into their engines. Nevertheless, outnumbered by heavier tanks and startled by the sudden 'flamers' in their midst as wounded Honeys 'brewed up', the brigade started to fall back towards the south. The 22nd Brigade, still in the vicinity of Bir el Gubi after its humiliating encounter with the Ariete Division, was told to go to the 4th Brigade's rescue in the hundred-or-so Crusaders it could still muster. But shortly after the arrival of these reinforcements, the 15th Panzer Division, now cremating the stylish Honeys with sickening frequency, withdrew towards Tobruk.

Rommel, at last resigned to shelving his attack on Tobruk, was beginning to play a much more active part in the proceedings. He personally pulled together a battle group which blocked the Tobruk garrison's attempted breakout and link-up with the relieving force, confining the British to a narrow salient up to El Duda ridge. There, murderous infantry fighting ensued in which Captain James Jackman of the Northumberland Fusiliers won a posthumous VC.

Sergeant (later Captain) Ken Hall, commanding a platoon of the 2nd/13th Australian Infantry Battalion which had remained behind when the bulk of the Australian division was withdrawn, recalls that during the breakout fighting 'friendly fire' was often as damaging as the enemy's.

---

* The Desert Rats had not only missed out on the Honeys, but had been at the end of the queue when the Crusaders came in. Consequently only half of their battered old Mark IV Cruisers – like their crews, veterans of Beda Fomm – had been replaced.

We were moving up to the scarp line for a bayonet charge in three lines abreast, with 25-pounder supporting fire. One of our guns was firing short and a shell fell behind my platoon, killing twenty out of twenty-eight men. Those of us who were left joined other platoons and took part in the charge . . . [Later in this engagement] one of the supporting British tanks slewed and fired down our lines, killing five . . . By contrast, five German tanks came within yards of us as we crouched in sangars [stone barricades] and inexplicably didn't open fire. I can't explain it. They could have killed us all.

Elsewhere, Rommel decided to concentrate both his Panzer Divisions, the 21st as well as the 15th, against Jock Campbell's tanks, guns and motorized infantry, which had at last been allowed to advance on Sidi Rezegh from Gambut. For the British, this turn of events started a gruesome comedy of errors. Cunningham and Norrie became convinced that the Afrika Korps were in full retreat. Their ill-used 22nd and 4th Armoured Brigades, tails back in the air and a few of their damaged tanks recovered and repaired, were promptly ordered to pursue the 'retreating' 15th Panzer Division and cut it off. It was rather like the old lady who thinks the mugger who has just snatched her handbag is running away because he is frightened of her umbrella.

Eventually, almost all the German, British and Italian tanks clashed on a hideously level stretch of gravel for the biggest tank-battle of the North African campaign to date. It was a wild, confusing, exhausting affair, fought on both sides by unslept, unfed, red-eyed men. It was a struggle that was particularly chaotic on the British side, whose senior commanders had not yet become as proficient as the Germans at orchestrating tanks, artillery, infantry and air power into co-ordinated fighting units, each arm supporting the other. Rather, they encouraged the spirit of the charge and then every man for himself. 'This will be a tank commander's battle,' Strafer Gott told his 7th Armoured Division. 'No tank-commander will go far wrong if he places his gun within hitting range of an enemy.' After eighteen months of desert warfare, this was about as far as British tank tactics had evolved.

In very little time, the battle grew into such a layered, complex thing that it rapidly spun out of control. On both sides, the soldiers required to do the killing and the dying had even less comprehension than usual of the big picture and scant idea of whether they were winning or losing. Space, mobility, dust, poor navigation and even poorer radio communications all added to the chaos.

Apart from Tobruk, there were few fixed positions. Axis and British tanks blundered unintentionally and unannounced into the concentrations of parked, aerial-bedecked vehicles that made up the headquarters of various enemy major formations and took them prisoner. To Bill Close, a Royal Tank Regiment regular and senior NCO with Gatehouse's thin-skinned Honeys, it felt like being caught up in a whirlpool: 'We all went round in ever decreasing circles until we were sucked on to the rocks at Sidi Rezegh.'

The epicentre of this whirlpool was the airfield itself with its shattered aircraft and almost total lack of cover. To Close it looked like 'nothing more than a sordid cemetery, covered with open graves and funeral pyres. Dead gunners and infantry sprawled everywhere beside smashed weapons.'

Tank and gunner regiments, in the words of the Henry Newbolt poem that most of the British officers had learned at school, were 'blinded by dust and smoke', while the sands of the desert were not so much 'sodden red' as sodden black by oil weeping from scorched tanks. On all sides these lay broken and abandoned, yet often oddly intact-looking until the lethal, small hole through their armour was spotted. Sometimes the only indication of something amiss would be the grilled and naked body of a crew member sprawled alongside.

Sergeant (later Major) Sam Bradshaw, a twenty-one-year-old ex-Territorial commanding one of 7th Armoured Brigade's rare Crusaders, recalls not only the devastation wrought by the German 88s – 'nine of them took out most of my regiment of 52 tanks in a matter of 25 minutes' – but the superiority of the enemy tank guns. 'A Panzer Mark IV could knock us out at about 2,000 yards,' he said. 'We called our [two-pounder] gun the pea-shooter and we had to get within 600 yards of a target to hit it.'

As British tank casualties mounted and the 7th were down to fewer than thirty 'runners', they were rallied and led back into action by the extraordinary figure of Brigadier Jock Campbell.* He had just turned fifty, older than a lot of officers back at GHQ Cairo who were only too happy to admit that their days of front-line soldiering were over. Now he seemed to be everywhere at once on the battlefield. One

---

* Holder of a First World War DSO with Second World War bar (and an MC) and originator of the so-called 'Jock columns' – mixed battle groups of guns, armoured cars and motorized infantry that he led on expeditions behind the lines.

moment he was seen to be helping to load and fire 25-pounders whose crews, as they had at Tobruk, were taking on the Panzers over open sights despite fearful casualties. The next he was doing something even Rommel had never tried: leading tank charges in his staff car, a sedate Humber saloon hardly intended for such off-piste activity.

Bradshaw recalls that Campbell 'wasn't actually in the car, but sitting on its roof with his long legs dangling over the windscreen, shouting directions to his driver then waving us to follow. There were nine tanks behind him, all the runners that were left in my regiment. It was a tremendous example of leadership. How could you not follow someone like that?'*

A mile from the airfield, a company of the Rifle Brigade was in reserve, among its duties that of guarding a group of 300 German and Italian prisoners in a wadi that provided reasonable cover from stray shells from the distant tank-battle. One of the Italian PoWs had with him a frisky little white dog named Moshka which ran about, making friends with men of both sides. Among them was the now veteran Rifleman Crimp, who was 'appalled' when his company commander, concerned that Moshka's barking might give away their position to an enemy foot patrol, ordered the dog to be shot.

Nobody relishes the job much as it's a friendly little tyke. Besides, shooting it is easier said than done . . . on the ground it frisks continually. A chap from one of the other sections takes a pot and misses. His next shot hits it, somewhere near the base of the spine, so that the poor little beast can only drag its hind quarters and yelp in agony. The expression of reproach in its eyes upsets everyone . . . 'For God's sake shoot it through the head at once,' shouts Mr R. [the officer] vehemently. A couple more rounds do the trick. Then some Italians dig a hole and bury the carcass.

Crimp and his comrades had further misgivings when, following the arrival of a truck bearing rations and water, they were ordered not to give any to the prisoners, who were 'already getting clamorous for

* Campbell, who refused to be evacuated after receiving a nasty flesh wound, won one of three VCs awarded for gallantry at Sidi Rezegh. From captivity later, General von Ravenstein sent him a letter of congratulations 'with warm heart'. The other two Sidi Rezegh VCs were posthumous: a rifleman who silenced a German anti-tank position by charging it with a Bren gun, and a subaltern who kept firing after all the men of his anti-tank troop had been killed.

food and drink'. Crimp and his comrades felt 'awkward' about eating and drinking in the sight of these prisoners. Was the order not to feed them intended to soften the PoWs up prior to interrogation? The Germans discovered a written order to that effect among a batch of captured documents and, at Rommel's furious behest, made an open radio broadcast threatening reciprocal action. Shortly afterwards, the British let it be known that the order had been 'a mistake'.

The battle of Sidi Rezegh reached its climax on 23 November, the last Sunday before Advent and the day the Germans call *Totensonntag*, the Sunday of the Dead. By then, one after the other instead of concurrently, so that their strength was never as concentrated as it should have been, the British armoured brigades had all done battle with the Panzers. Tanks blundered into both defeat and triumph. The vehicles and personnel of Crüwell's Afrika Korps headquarters and the HQ of Gatehouse's 4th Brigade were both captured – though their respective commanders were absent at the time.

Gatehouse, deprived of his staff and communications, found himself trying to put his brigade back together from an armchair tied to the top of his tank, with a tartan rug across his lap. It was bitterly cold after dark and, with the beginning of the winter rains, not much better in the first few hours of daylight.

By now there seemed so little discernible order to the battlefield that in places Germans and British became inextricably mixed. Bradshaw's was the only Crusader that was still a runner in his troop of three and he was searching for the rest of his squadron, weaving his way between burning tanks and 'people who were dying or dead', when he saw 'a fellow walking along, limping'.

I drew alongside and called out, 'Are you Italian?' He replied, in very good English, 'No, I'm not a bloody Italian, I'm a German,' obviously annoyed at the suggestion. He was wounded, so I gave him a lift on the tank. He sat on it under the gun. I gave him a drink of water and he gave me a [British] Capstan cigarette. 'We got one of your supply columns,' he said. We saw some German armoured cars about 1,000 yards away and he rolled off the tank, though wounded, and hobbled towards them. My gunner traversed on to him and I shouted on the intercom 'Don't fire – let him go.' And he turned round and saluted and called out cheekily, 'I'll see you in London.' I called back, 'Make it Berlin.'

1. British troops in Wavell's counter-attack. Here infantry with 17-inch bayonets fixed charge an Axis position. In the foreground lies a dead Italian soldier, probably killed by artillery – he has a head wound. Judging by the absence of cover and the presence of a photographer, the British were not expecting much opposition.

2. Instantly identifiable as Bersaglieri by the black, fighting cock's feathers in their headgear, a heavy machine-gun team fire at some distant British transport, possibly Bren-gun carriers. Note the spent rounds being ejected from the breech.

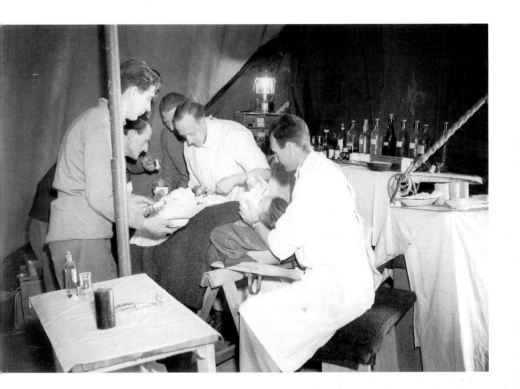

3. *Top left:* A long column of Italian prisoners, some of them clutching suit-cases, being escorted to the rear after the first phase of O'Connor's offensive in December 1940.

4. *Bottom left:* Captured Italian General 'Electric Whiskers' Berganzoli lands on Egyptian soil, accompanied by one of his aides and escorted by a British officer sporting a large fly-whisk.

5. *Above:* Surgery by oil lamp in a tented British dressing-station in Libya. The anaesthetist is holding a chloro-form pad to the nose and mouth of the patient, who lies on the stretcher he was brought in on.

6. *Right:* General Sir Bernard Freyberg (later Lord Freyberg), a First World War VC whose New Zealanders were con-sidered by Rommel to be among the cream of the Imperial forces.

7. British commander-in-chief Sir Archibald Wavell, who lost an eye in the First World War. Wavell might have finished the desert campaign in 1941 had Churchill not insisted that he send some of his best troops on an ill-fated expedition to Greece.

8. 'Ming the Merciless'. Lieutenant-General Sir Leslie Morshead, whose 9th Australian Division stopped Rommel at Tobruk.

9. Australian troops advancing on Bardia and wearing greatcoats against the early-morning chill. Troops soon discovered that the desert could be much colder than they had ever imagined.

10. The delicate moment of surrender. In the half-light of dawn, some anxious-looking Italians give themselves up to the Australians.

11. Fort Capuzzo, the Italians' *Beau Geste* frontier post, its mud brick no match for high explosive. It changed hands several times.

12. *Left to right:* Newly captured British generals O'Connor and Neame and Brigadier Combe still find something to smile about, though their plan to hijack the aircraft taking them to Italy failed. But two years later, after Mussolini was deposed, all three escaped to Allied lines south of Rome.

13. 'The Auk'. Every inch a fighting soldier, the sun-tanned General Sir Claude Auchinleck, who held Rommel at El Alamein but lost Tobruk and with it Churchill's confidence.

14. The Desert Fox. 'Don't worry about your flanks.' Erwin Rommel, his trademark captured British goggles on his service cap, explains his next move to an incredulous-looking young officer while an amused aide listens in.

15. General Sir William Dobbie, the religious zealot and Governor of Malta who praised the Lord but failed to unload the ammunition.

16. 'The most bombed place on earth'. A street in Valletta during the Axis bombing of Malta from airfields in Sicily only sixty miles away.

17. 'Faith'. One of the Gladiator biplane fighters that were Malta's only air defence against the initial attacks from Mussolini's Regia Aeronautica.

Next day, Bradshaw was himself wounded and at the mercy of a German soldier with a rifle. The circumstances are a good indication of just how confused the fighting at Sidi Rezegh became. Badly wounded in the buttocks, he had baled out of his Crusader after it received a direct hit. Lying in some scrub, he watched with horror as the tank bumped and lurched towards a German position, its trapped and dying driver still at the controls.

Shortly afterwards, hardly able to walk, Bradshaw was picked up by another British tank and strapped into a device called the Campbell stretcher, a cocoon of canvas and bamboo struts in which a casualty was wrapped and then slung outside the armoured hull. Packaged like this, with only his head showing, Bradshaw was carried back towards the nearest field-hospital. Their route took them over a ridge through which the British armour had advanced earlier in the day, bypassing a German infantry position. The Germans had not yet, to use that most masking of military euphemisms, been 'mopped up'.

For some reason, the tank carrying Bradshaw stopped briefly in the middle of these marooned members of the Afrika Korps. Suspended helplessly from its side, Bradshaw made eye-contact with an enemy rifleman in a slit trench, no more than a yard away. But 'there was nothing I could do, I was trussed up like a chicken. I smiled at him, he smiled back at me and then we were on our way.'

Slowly, the 7th Armoured were being worn down. Cunningham's superior tank strength had been squandered by his doing just what he planned not to do: introducing them into the battle piecemeal, so that Rommel was able to deal with each of the division's three brigades separately. At times it was the British who were outnumbered. And even in those places where they were not, the Germans often outwitted them with the well-tried tactic of luring them on to their anti-tank guns, which the British had not yet learned to neutralize with their artillery. In any case, the 25-pounders were often too busy taking on the Panzers to deal with the 88s.

By the eve of Totensonntag the 7th and 22nd Armoured Brigades had hardly any runners left at all and the 4th, lacking its captured headquarters, was scattered about the desert, over which Gatehouse bumped in his armchair, trying to gather up his lost lambs. Under the cover of darkness the British withdrew from the airfield itself and went a little way eastwards towards Gambut. For the men who had been following Brigadier Campbell it was particularly hard to take; despite their losses, they had often thought themselves at the edge of victory. Among the last to leave were the gunners, who always impressed the Germans as the most professional branch of the British army. Behind them the flat land around Sidi Rezegh was dotted with fires from blazing vehicles and abandoned ammunition and fuel dumps.

Rommel then did something so bold, so outrageous, so quintessentially Rommel-esque that, by all the lucky stars he ever followed and all the bluffs of Blitzkrieg he ever perpetrated, it should have led to his greatest triumph. Had his opponents been a little more demoralized it might have done; instead, it lost him the battle.

While the British were still trying to work out what had gone wrong at Sidi Rezegh, and Cunningham, realizing the enormity of his tank losses, teetered on the edge of a nervous breakdown, Rommel decided to do precisely what the commander of the Eighth Army dreaded most. On the morning of 24 November 1941, leaving 90th Light and the Italian divisions to keep the New Zealanders from breaking through to besieged Tobruk, he put himself at the head of his remaining Panzers and led them east towards the Egyptian frontier, about 100 miles away. It became known as the 'dash for the wire' – the entanglements originally laid by the Italians to mark the Libyan-Egyptian border.

By this action, Rommel hoped to stampede Cunningham's soft rear echelons – all those drivers and technicians who had a rifle somewhere but never expected to have to use it – back into the Delta. In the wake of this confused and fearful rabble would come his Panzers, who would join up with the three Axis garrisons Cunningham had bypassed on the frontier and 'liberate' the eager Egyptians just as Napoleon had (briefly) freed them from the Ottoman yoke. The North African campaign would be over and a grateful Führer would surely send reinforcements for the subsequent invasions of Palestine and Syria and the oilfields of Iraq and Persia.

Rommel was in no doubt about it. 'You have the chance of ending this campaign tonight,' he reportedly told General Johannes von Ravenstein, commander of the 21st Panzer Division, before they set off. This sublime optimism was not shared by Ravenstein and even less by the insubordinate Crüwell; but Rommel had so often proved his critics wrong that it was difficult to argue with him.

As far as Rommel was concerned, it was the kind of mixture of decisive action and sheer bluff that had worked so well against the Italians in 1917 and against the French only eighteen months before. And to a limited extent, in November 1941, it did work against the British. As part of Rommel's broad column, at times forty miles in length, struck a glancing blow at the headquarters of Norrie's XXX Corps then ploughed on through several divisional and brigade HQs, it did create panic or, in the word the Eighth Army would bequeath to the language, a 'flap'.

Norrie's headquarters was made up of about fifty vehicles parked in a shallow depression, fringed with camel thorn and protected by a squadron of armoured cars. When the flap started, shortly after dawn, a party of war correspondents, not long up, were trying to wash, shave and make tea with the least possible amount of water. Among them was Alan Moorehead of the *Daily Express*, who would recall that the entire camp fled 'like a shoal of mackerel before a shark' as the Panzers approached and enemy shells began to fall among them.

The churned-up dust . . . blotted out the sun and visibility became reduced to two hundred yards or less . . . Men and vehicles of entirely different units travelled along together . . . My party stuck to the Signals vehicle . . . Twice we stopped and while men ran from one vehicle to another asking for orders . . . more shells came over the horizon. We were being followed – and fast. So the hue and cry went on again. Occasionally vehicles around us ran on to mines or were hit by shells or were simply fired by their bewildered drivers who believed the enemy to be upon them . . . All day for nine hours we ran. It was the contagion of fear and bewilderment.

Most of the rear echelon troops did not stop running until they were back across the Egyptian border. Most of the front-line troops, however, kept their nerve, as did senior officers such as Norrie, Gott and Gatehouse, the last still commanding from the armchair on top of his tank. Apart from a South African infantry brigade that was badly mauled by Rommel's thrust, the forward troops remained in position, hardly aware of what was going on behind them. Along the coast they were doing rather well, particularly the New Zealanders. Despite stubborn resistance by the Afrika Korps' 90th Light Division, they had practically joined up with the Tobruk garrison on the El Duda ridge.

But Cunningham despaired and wanted to call off the offensive.

Auchinleck sacked him. It was a hard decision to make, partly because the tank losses at Sidi Rezegh suggested that Cunningham might well be right and partly because Auchinleck had himself picked Cunningham to command the Eighth Army and was famously loyal to his subordinates.

Not wishing, at this vital juncture, to disrupt the command system by replacing Cunningham with one of the Corps commanders, Auchinleck chose as his successor Major-General Neil Ritchie, Deputy Chief of the General Staff in Cairo. Ritchie had never commanded anything bigger than a battalion in the field, and that had been in 1938. But he was considered solid and competent enough for the job and, when it came to balancing risk with gain, Auchinleck's orders left him in no doubt about what he was supposed to do: 'Attack the enemy relentlessly, using all your resources, even to the last tank.'

Auchinleck's cool was admirable. By now the battle-map was one of the most complicated in the history of warfare. The journalist Moorehead likened it to 'an eight-decker rainbow cake'. In the past, with the exception of the enclave at Tobruk, Axis troops had always been west of the front line and British imperial troops to the east. But if satellite images had been available in 1941, an overview of the North African battlefield at midday on Tuesday, 25 November, would have revealed several alternate layers of British troops and Axis troops, starting at Tobruk and ending at the Halfaya Pass over 100 miles away. Within this vast frame – in which, according to one estimate, some 30,000 armoured and soft-skinned vehicles, British, German and Italian, were wheeling about in an area of 3,000 square miles – the fortunes of war changed with bewildering speed.

Sidi Rezegh was an untidy and abnormally treacherous battlefield. Friends and foes were often impossible to identify until it was too late. Captives became jailers when rescuers blundered across them, entire formations 'disappeared' because their signals trucks had been captured and the next link in the chain of command had no idea where they were. All three armies were using each other's transport. Nobody could be sure a vehicle was what it appeared to be until he had had some conversation with its occupants.

Field hospitals were shared to the point where it was hard to tell whose hands they were in. According to Brigadier Desmond Young, Rommel's first biographer, a British surgeon showed Rommel himself around a casualty clearing station under the impression that he was a visiting Polish general and quite failed to notice the way the German wounded were trying to arrange their broken bodies to attention.

On the first night of the 'dash for the wire', both Rommel and Crüwell stood a very good chance of being captured. In one of the Mammuts, the British Dorchester armoured command vehicles the Germans had captured at Mechili seven months before, they had ventured deep into Egyptian territory. But when they tried to find their way back through the wire, they were unable to locate a gap. As darkness fell and they were still unable to locate an exit, Rommel decided to rest for the night.

They pulled their Mammut off the dirt track a little way – though not too far, for fear of becoming bogged down in soft sand – and, as it happened, on the main supply route of the 4th Indian Division that was busy tightening its hold around the German garrison at Halfaya Pass. Throughout the night, British trucks rumbled by, some containing infantry who might well have offered to help the poor general (for Dorchesters were used mainly by generals) so inconveniently stranded by the side of the road. None did so. Brigadier Young, serving with the 4th Indian Division, put it down to a soldierly preference to 'let sleeping generals lie'.

Yet even Rommel's luck was not immutable. Ravenstein's Panzers came within sight of two huge British supply dumps, each six miles square. If the British had lost them, most of the Eighth Army's forward troops would have been without fuel or water. Instead, after a cursory examination through his field glasses, Ravenstein decided they were not worth further investigation and pressed on: every diversion had to be balanced against its likely cost in precious fuel. As it happened, though, Ravenstein had been looking at enough fuel to take his 21st Panzers to Baghdad.

Meanwhile, conscious perhaps that the head of an army group should stay a little closer to his headquarters, Rommel went back to the Libyan port of Bardia, east of Tobruk, to await developments. Much to his fury, he was joined there the following day by Ravenstein and what was left of his Panzers. Rommel accused Ravenstein of allowing himself to be duped into pulling back by a false radio message planted by the British. But in fact the orders to withdraw had come from Lieutenant-Colonel Siegfried Westphal at Panzer Group HQ, who had issued them without reference to Rommel because he could not find him. It took considerable moral courage for this bright, thirty-nine-year-old operations officer to do what he did – further evidence, if any were needed, of how far the Allied propaganda myth of the Prussian automaton was at variance with reality.

While Rommel had been 'at the wire', the situation at the front he had left behind him had altered radically. The British had taken advantage of the Panzers' absence to renew their attacks on Sidi Rezegh. Gott's shattered armoured brigades had managed to recover and repair dozens of tanks that had been left, abandoned, on the battlefield; and, in Westphal's opinion, the situation at Tobruk and Sidi Rezegh had become critical: it could be saved only by the return of the Panzers. Had he been wrong, a court martial would not have been out of the question. But Rommel, in sullen mood, reluctantly accepted that Westphal had made the right decision in calling the armour back.

As it turned out, it was already too late. The Panzers did return to Sidi Rezegh and they did push the British off those blood-soaked flat lands again. But it was, at best, a pyrrhic victory. When it was over, the Afrika Korps had only some forty tanks left. Shortly afterwards, the Italians admitted that British successes against their shipping were such that it would be several weeks before tank losses could be made good. For the first time in his life, Rommel had to concede defeat. He knew that if he was to save what was left of his command he must withdraw. Simply by refusing to give up, Auchinleck's faith in his superior numbers and the sheer resilience of some of his soldiers had won the day.

By 7 December 1941, most of the Axis forces had pulled back west of Tobruk, thus ending a siege of 242 days – the longest in the history of the British army. The defenders had made Tobruk a household word in the English-speaking world, but news of its relief was eclipsed by the Japanese attack on Pearl Harbor the same day, stealing the headlines and bringing America into the war.

Now it was the turn of the Axis forces to be besieged in the Libyan-Egyptian border garrisons of Bardia, Sollum and the Halfaya Pass. Luftwaffe transport squadrons from Crete were doing their best to drop them supplies, but were taking heavy casualties. With the airfields of Gambut and Sidi Rezegh in British hands, the Messerschmitt-109s no longer had the range to fly escort, and it was obvious that the border garrisons would not last long.

Rommel originally intended to hold on to most of Cyrenaica, with

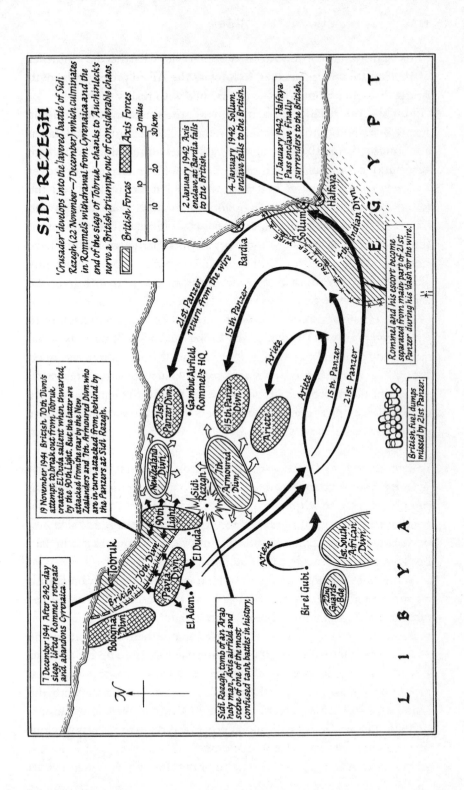

SIDI REZEGH

'Crusader' develops into the 'layered battle' of Sidi Rezegh (22 November–7 December) which culminates in Rommel's withdrawal from Cyrenaica and the end of the siege of Tobruk – thanks to Auchinleck's nerve a British triumph out of considerable chaos.

British Forces   Axis Forces

0 10 20 20 miles
0 10 20 30km

19 November 1941. After 242-day siege, British, 70th Divn's attempt to break out from Tobruk creates El Duda salient when, thwarted, by the 90th Light. But the latter are attacked from the rear by the New Zealanders and 7th Armoured Divn who are in turn attacked from behind by the Panzers at Sidi Rezegh.

7 December 1941. After 242-day siege, lifted Rommel retreats and abandons Cyrenaica.

Sidi Rezegh, tomb of an Arab holy man, Axis airfield and scene of one of the most confused tank battles in history.

2 January 1942. Axis enclave at Bardia falls to the British.

4 January 1942. Sollum enclave falls to the British.

17 January 1942. Halfaya Pass enclave finally surrenders to the British.

Rommel and his escort become separated from main part of 21st Panzer during his 'dash for the wire'.

British fuel dumps missed by 21st Panzer.

21st Panzer return from the wire

15th Panzer

Ariete

Ariete

Ariete

Ariete

15th Panzer

21st Panzer

15th Panzer Divn

Gambut Airfield • Rommel's HQ

21st Panzer Divn

New Zealand Divn

7th Armoured Divn

•Sidi Rezegh

90th Light

British, 70th Divn

Pavia Divn

El Duda

Bologna Divn

Tobruk

El Adem•

4th Indian Divn

Halfaya

Sollum

FRONTIER WIRE

Bardia

E G Y P T

1st South African Divn

22nd Guards Bde.

Bir el Gubi.

L I B Y A

a line starting south into the desert from Gazala, some fifty miles west of Tobruk. Then he realized that Gott's 7th Armoured Division was threatening to outflank him. To the disgust of the Italian High Command, he decided to give up the province and fall back to a strong position in the salt pans of Mersa el Brega, giving up Benghazi and almost all the other territory he had won back for the Italians after O'Connor's romp through it.

A few days before Christmas 1941, the correspondent Moorehead found himself, in heavy rain, following the British vanguard through the wreckage of the Italian settlements west of Derna, that rare part of the North African battleground where civilian life intruded.

This lush valley was once a thriving dairy settlement and its white homesteads and creameries were among the finest in Africa . . . Four armies – Graziani's, Wavell's, Rommel's and Auchinleck's – had crossed the valley [and] left a curse upon the place. The fences were broken and doors of the homesteads flapped and admitted the wind and the rain . . . A few settlers lingered on and they stood in their doorways staring vacantly and without comprehension . . . This final catastrophe in the valley was too much. Nothing here was able to struggle against the war any more . . . Under our eyes the land was returning to its old sterility.

The Honeys of Gatehouse's 4th Brigade got in among the withdrawing Axis soft transport once or twice, burning vehicles and killing those who were not quick to surrender. But in the main Rommel conducted a masterful retreat over 300 miles and rarely allowed any of the tired British armour, still smarting from the mauling they had received at Sidi Rezegh, to get behind him.

Sometimes the armoured cars, which generally headed the British pursuit, found out the hard way that the Germans still had to be treated with caution. Leutnant Heinz-Werner Schmidt, who at his own request had left Rommel's staff to get back into the field, commanded an anti-tank unit that was part of the German rearguard. On Christmas Eve they engaged some British and South African armoured cars and captured a British officer and three Other Ranks. All prisoners were supposed to be immediately transported to divisional headquarters, but Schmidt was in festive mood. When the British officer promised not to escape, he invited the 'Tommies' to spend the night. 'Since it was Christmas Eve, I saw to it that the Englishmen were each given a bottle of beer, chocolates, and cigarettes . . . "You have pretty generous Christmas fare," [the British officer] remarked. I did not tell him that we only had these luxuries because we had salvaged them from a dump which was being burned . . .'

Four days later, the Afrika Korps gave the British 22nd Armoured Brigade a particularly severe mauling on the outskirts of Agedabia, a scruffy village at the south-western edge of the Cyrenaican bulge. An armoured car squadron of the 12th Lancers, out ahead of the cautiously advancing brigade, was first to feel the weight of Crüwell's vicious counter-attack. Corporal Stan Doughty, aged twenty-one, just arrived in the desert and not yet used to his newly issued South African-made Marmon-Harrington armoured car, scarcely knew what hit him. 'There was an almighty bang. The interior of the car was full of smoke and the gunner and myself got out as quickly as we could, as the whole thing was going up in flames . . . I shall always remember the screams of the driver who was trapped . . . It would have been hopeless to try and help him, but I must admit we didn't, a fact which has burned my conscience ever since.'

Having disposed of the armoured car screen, Crüwell's Panzers tore into the 22nd Brigade's Honeys and Crusaders, destroying sixty-five of them for the loss of sixteen of their own, before resuming their withdrawal to the west.

Three days later, despite orders to conserve ammunition, the Afrika Korps greeted New Year's Day 1942 with a tremendous *feu de joie*. For three minutes they fired hundreds of the Wehrmacht's distinctive green Very lights into the air, together with thousands of rounds of tracer from their machine-guns while even the artillery joined in with a shell or blank charge and, in lieu of fireworks, grenades were tossed recklessly into the night. Then, Leutnant Schmidt, recalled 'from the dark distance where we knew the screen of British tanks lay, a counter-display of yellow Very flares also went up to greet the New Year'.

For the British, the Afrika Korps' celebrations were another worrying indication that enemy morale was much higher than it ought to be. According to the military ledger, Operation Crusader had undoubtedly ended in defeat for the Axis. They had been obliged to abandon Cyrenaica and Rommel had lost about a third of his command, most of them among the 36,000 prisoners taken. Total British casualties were 18,000 – the majority killed or wounded.

All the Afrika Korps divisional commanders were among the casualties. Neumann-Silkow of 15th Panzer (who had a Scottish mother) was killed by shell fire. Sümmermann, commander of 90th Light, was mortally wounded by a strafing RAF Hurricane. Ravenstein, who had dashed to the wire and back, was captured when he ran into a New Zealand road-block while hurrying to a conference with Crüwell.* Shortly afterwards, Crüwell himself was hospitalized with a severe attack of jaundice.

Yet Rommel had saved the best part of the Afrika Korps and dug them in at Mersa el Brega. Their spirits were as high as ever, for losing territory did not bother them overmuch. They knew they had done well against considerable odds and, given the chance, would so again. Whatever his senior officers might think (and Crüwell, on his sickbed, was particularly scathing about the 'cavalry charge' into Egypt), Rommel's magic had not faded among the rank-and-file. They called him 'Erwin' and told each other he was one of them, a soldier's soldier.

Nor did Hitler's confidence falter. 'I know I can rely on my Panzer Gruppe,' he said in a New Year message. Rommel would soon prove that his confidence was not misplaced.

---

* At this point Ravenstein was the only German general in captivity anywhere in the world. He narrowly escaped drowning when the ship in which he was being sent from Tobruk to Alexandria was sunk by the Luftwaffe. While in detention in Alexandria he sent a letter of congratulation to Jock Campbell on his VC. From Alexandria, Ravenstein was shipped to captivity in Canada. En route, through the Mediterranean, he led a PoWs' plot to take over the ship and sail it to Vichy French West Africa. It failed, and he remained in captivity in Canada until 1948.

During the next four months, Malta would achieve the distinction of becoming the most heavily bombed place on earth. In March 1942 alone, the main island – one-sixth the size of Greater London – would receive within its ninety-five square miles a greater weight of bombs than had been dropped on the whole of England during the 1940 Battle of Britain. April was even worse: in thirty days Malta received thirteen times the tonnage of bombs inflicted on the city of Coventry during the Luftwaffe's notorious saturation raid of November 1940. Altogether, between the beginning of January and the end of April, the island endured 154 days and nights of bombing, compared with London's fifty-seven.

On 10 May Field Marshal Albert Kesselring, Hitler's C-in-C South, reported to Berlin from his headquarters in Rome that 'Malta has been completely eliminated as a base of the enemy's navy and air force.' He scarcely exaggerated. Quite apart from the wholesale loss of life and the destruction of houses, schools, hospitals, churches and other public buildings, all but one of Malta's reservoirs had been destroyed, along with food stores, telephone exchanges, fuel dumps and power stations. The naval dockyards were a shambles, the harbours were blocked by air-dropped mines that were replaced faster than they could be swept up, and the five remaining submarines of the Royal Navy's 10th Flotilla, which had wreaked great havoc among Rommel's supply ships, had been forced to abandon their base for Alexandria. 'There was very little defence against enemy aircraft,' recalled Chief Petty Officer Joe Brighton of HMS *Porpoise*, a submarine that had been pressed into service as an underwater supply vessel.★ 'Three [submarines] were sunk at their base and when we ran in with supplies we

★ External ballast tanks were converted to carry kerosene and petrol and a battery section removed so that the battery tank could be filled with supplies. Bales of dried cabbage were carried on the torpedo stowage compartment deck. Five Thames-class submarines made a total of sixteen supply runs in an operation codenamed 'Magic Carpet'. In one month they brought in 84,000 gallons of petrol, 83,000 gallons of kerosene, twelve tons of mail, thirty tons of general stores, six tons of ammunition and 100 passengers.

had to enter harbour submerged, lie on the bottom during the day and surface at night to disembark stores. To show ourselves during the day was almost certain to be fatal.'

Grace Bates, a British nurse, kept a diary of the dark days of Malta's cruellest month:

Monday, 6 April – Constant raids as before . . . Every ship in the harbour has been hit with the exception of HMS *Penelope*, which has had many near-misses.

Wednesday, 8 April – The dockyard, they say, is just about 'written off'. King George V Hospital is razed to the ground. The seat of government has moved to Crendi. We get at least three bad raids a day . . .

Thursday, 9 April [arranging a party for the next night] – Are we all crazy to think of dancing and merry-making in these very serious times? I don't think so . . . we must continue to live as normally as possible . . . Piling up all the pleasant memories we can will help fortify us if worse things should come.

Saturday, 18 April – At the beginning of the day we had six serviceable fighters, but by nightfall they were all out of commission.

In truth, Air Vice-Marshal Hugh Lloyd, responsible for the island's air defences, had hardly a fighter plane left. One Rhodesian Spitfire pilot remembered the day 'when only five of us were airborne and we encountered over 200 enemy aircraft – 40 [Messerschmitt] 109s escorting bombers – but the Spitfires shot down four bombers over Grand Harbour. Time after time as my wheels touched the ground I had to go up again to avoid being shot to pieces on the ground . . . One chap actually landed, taxied 50 yards and ran out of petrol.'

There was a desperate need for more Spitfires, the fastest, most manoeuvrable and most lethally armed interceptors the RAF had to offer, and flying fighters in penny packets off the ageing HMS *Argus*★ was no answer. Nor could the British use HMS *Eagle*, a more up-to-date carrier, because it was laid up with defects to its steering gear, or HMS *Victorious*, whose lifts were too small for Spitfires.

★ In November 1940, twelve Hurricanes had been brought by HMS *Argus* to within 420 miles of Malta. With tailwinds they could comfortably reach the island, but half way there the wind veered around 180 degrees and all but three of the squadron ran out of fuel and plunged into the sea.

Churchill, the 'Former Naval Person'★ as he styled himself, sent an urgent message to President Roosevelt: 'Would you be willing to allow your carrier *Wasp* to do one of these trips? . . . With her broad lifts, capacity and length we estimate that *Wasp* could take fifty or more Spitfires.' Roosevelt agreed immediately. On 20 April, forty-seven of the RAF's latest Spitfire 5-Cs took off from *Wasp* and landed safely at Malta's Luqa and Takali airfields, both still under dust clouds from a German raid. But the Spitfires were not ready for action; their guns were imperfectly synchronized, their radios unreliable and their carburettors in need of cleaning. While they were on the ground, being made serviceable for combat, the Luftwaffe destroyed all but three of them.

In early May, at Churchill's urgent request, *Wasp* was pressed into service again. Sixty-two more Spitfires arrived on 9 May – this time in fighting condition. Rapidly refuelled, and their pilots relieved by Malta-based colleagues, they took to the air again within fifteen minutes to do battle with an incoming wave of enemy aircraft.

It was just one big mass dogfight. There were probably well over 100 fighters in the air at the same time. The ack-ack gunners put up a terrific barrage, but the boys in the Spitfires were so keen to get at the Hun that they couldn't resist the temptation of rushing through our own barrage . . . [Stukas] were dropping everywhere in flames . . . More than twenty enemy planes went down into the sea. We gave the Hun such a hiding that he didn't dare show his face again for a whole week.

For Queenie Lee, watching from the ground like hundreds of her fellow Maltese, this was 'our red letter day. The sky was an absolute circus . . . Machines fell out of it like flies . . . The sea front was lined with cheering crowds who forgot the falling shrapnel and splinters in the sheer thrill of witnessing a battle where we at last held our own and were superior.'

Though many trials and hardships lay ahead, the Luftwaffe were never again able to bomb Malta with impunity. In the next few days they lost sixty planes. And a jubilant Churchill cabled the American carrier that had brought the Spitfires to the beleaguered island: 'Who says a Wasp can't sting twice?'

★

★ Churchill ran the Admiralty for part of the First World War.

In Libya, behind his defensive line at Mersa el Brega, Rommel had been far from downhearted as 1942 dawned. His lines of communication were no longer dangerously extended and fresh supplies of tanks, troops, fuel and ammunition were reaching him in quantity as the Luftwaffe resumed its aerial pounding of Malta, interdicting British action against his supply convoys. And if time was on Rommel's side, so – albeit inadvertently – was Colonel Bonner F. Fellers, the US military attaché in Cairo.

As one of Rommel's staff officers would say after the war, the stream of intelligence unwittingly provided by Fellers over the next several months, by way of code messages intercepted on their way to Washington, was 'stupefying in its openness' and 'contributed decisively to our victories in North Africa'. Even before America's entry into the war, the gregarious Colonel Fellers – West Point Class of 1918 and a recent graduate of the US Army War College – had access to the highest levels of GHQ, Middle East. After the US entered the fray, he became privy to many of GHQ's closest secrets.

But the supposedly impenetrable 'Black Code' in which he transmitted his top-secret information nightly to Washington was far from secure. The Italians had extracted the code book from a safe in the US Embassy in Rome one night in September 1941, three months before the Japanese attack on Pearl Harbor brought America into the war. The pilfering of the Black Code was a masterstroke of the otherwise little-remembered General Cesare Ame, head of Mussolini's military intelligence branch. He had duplicate keys to the embassy and two agents inside it. One of them, Loris Gherardi, opened the ambassador's safe and, carefully noting the positions of all the documents inside, gingerly extracted the Black Code book. Two of his colleagues, waiting in a car outside, rushed it to military intelligence headquarters, where it was photographed page by page before being returned and replaced by Gherardi, exactly as he had found it. The Americans never realized anything untoward had occurred and the Italians were thenceforth able to intercept and read the secret military attaché traffic to Washington from every US mission in Europe, the Middle East and North Africa.*

* In a similar security disaster, the Americans' diplomatic code had been breached by a massive leak at their London embassy earlier that summer when a code clerk there named Tyler Kent gave copies of some 1,500 coded telegrams, together with duplicate keys to the code and index rooms, to a spy ring run by the Italians. Unlike

Mussolini, puffed up with pride at having acquired an asset his overpowering German allies lacked, refused to let them have a copy of the pilfered Black Code book. He did, however, authorize Ame to let them have decodes of early messages from Fellers to Washington. Armed with these, and assisted by Fellers' invariable habit of starting and ending his messages the same way, the German cryptographers soon figured out how to break the code for themselves.

When America entered the war in December 1941, Fellers graduated from trusted friend to indispensable ally with privileged access to the most sensitive information. In a dispatch dated 23 January 1942, for example, he was able to inform Washington (and thus the Germans) that the British were withdrawing 270 warplanes from North Africa and sending them to the Far East. Six days later, he was able to telegraph a complete run-down on British armoured strength, including the number of tanks in working order, the number undergoing repair, the number available for action and their whereabouts. And so forth, right into mid-summer 1942, when he would give the Pentagon and Rommel full details of British tank losses – '70 per cent were put out of action and at least 50 per cent permanently destroyed' – in crucial battles which would see the fall of Tobruk and Mersa Matruh. He would also tip the Germans off to pending British commando raids on Axis airfields.*

As Dr Herbert Schaedel, chief of the Germans' main radio intercept station at Lauf, near Nuremberg, would recall after the war: 'They went crazy at Supreme Headquarters to get all the telegrams from Cairo.' Within hours, Fellers' messages were decoded, translated and on their way back to Rommel's field headquarters, where they kept the Desert Fox informed of British losses and often the exact whereabouts of British forces the night before. He gleefully called these intercepts 'my little Fellers' and it seems possible that, at this point, they were of more use to Rommel than the 'Ultra Secret' (Britain's ability to crack the Germans' 'Enigma' encryption device) was to his enemies.

---

the case of the Black Code, however, the leakage was quickly discovered and Kent – acting, he claimed, out of a desire to keep America out of the war – was tried and given a lengthy jail sentence.

* The full texts of Fellers' messages to Washington are to be found in the 'office diary' of General George C. Marshall – chairman of the joint US chiefs of staff at the time – in the National Archives in Washington, DC.

True, since the end of June 1941 the British decryption centre at Bletchley Park, near London, had been able to intercept, decode and translate German naval codes, providing a wealth of detailed information about Axis shipping in the Mediterranean and making it possible to disrupt Rommel's vital supplies of fuel and ammunition. True, in September 1941 Ultra notched up another advance when Bletchley finally solved the Enigma keys used by Rommel's head-quarters in their communications with Rome and Berlin.

But the fact that the British had cracked Enigma had to remain a very closely guarded secret, and strenuous efforts had to be made to cloak any action that might give evidence of that to the enemy. This occasionally meant giving the Axis a tactical victory rather than revealing that the British had advance warning of their plans. Where this was not feasible, mythical agents such as 'Boniface' were invented as cover, while totally unnecessary reconnaissance flights were made over the Mediterranean, for example, to explain away Britain's successes in locating Africa-bound convoys.

The Ultra Secret, then, did enable the British for a while to sink a large number of Axis supply ships and forestall the movements of Rommel's armoured formations during Auchinleck's 'Crusader' offensive. But these advantages were temporarily lost in December 1941 when, while boosting their U-boat resources and air power in the Mediterranean sufficiently to cut their shipping losses, the Germans also varied their army codes. Bletchley's boffins could no longer decipher Rommel's signals to OKW (the German High Command), and it would not be until mid-1942 that they would succeed, allowing Britain's Ultra Secret once more to pay substantial dividends in North Africa.

Yet even though the Ultra Secret was in many ways the answer to an intelligence officer's prayers, its possession had its drawbacks. As a Top Secret War Office minute pointed out, 'instead of being the best it tended to become the only source. There was a tendency . . . to be fascinated by the authenticity of the information into failing to think whether it was significant at the particular level at which it was being considered . . . Probably essential wood was ignored because of the variety of interesting trees on view. The information purveyed was so remarkable that it tended, particularly if one were tired or over-busy, to engulf not only all other sources but that very commonsense which forms the basis of intelligence.'

In the desert war, the Ultra Secret was undoubtedly a blessing to the British, but a mixed blessing. No such drawback seems to have applied to the 'little Fellers', which substantially enhanced Rommel's reputation for an uncanny ability to fathom what the British were up to. Hitler himself was aware of Fellers' inadvertent contributions to the Axis cause. In one of his rambling after-dinner monologues, the Führer expressed the hope that the US attaché would 'continue to inform us so well over the English military planning through his badly enciphered cables'. For his part, Fellers would boast to his superiors in Washington that 'many times friendship has produced the information rather than the fact of my official position'.

The British society beauty, Countess (Hermione) Ranfurly, was one of Fellers' many valuable early contacts in social and intelligence circles. Besides being the wife of General O'Connor's captured ADC, Lieutenant Lord Ranfurly, she was secretary to George Pollock, the chief of Britain's Special Operations Executive (SOE) in Cairo. Lady Ranfurly found Fellers 'an original and delightful person who seems to say exactly what he thinks to everyone regardless of nationality or rank'. His candour may not entirely have pleased the Pentagon. In January of 1942 he complained to Lady Ranfurly over lunch that he was 'getting unpopular' in Washington because 'they think that I'm a defeatist. The trouble is your top brass are overconfident which they've no right to be: your gear is still inferior to the enemy's, and you are less well led – too many senior officers are sitting on their arses at GHQ.' This was true enough, but Fellers himself was surely guilty of an equal complacency, if not downright slackness, in failing to safe-guard the integrity of his messages. Had he been more security-conscious and varied the way he prefaced and signed off his dispatches to Washington, they would not have been so easy to pick out from the hundreds of messages going through the Germans' main radio intercept station every day, and not so easy to decode quickly.

Code Black (so named from the colour of its binder) was a fairly complicated two-part encryption system whose groups were re-enciphered every so often by adding a new number to each group of the message. But the Germans had noted that Fellers began each dispatch with the words 'Milidwash' (Military Intelligence Division Washington) or 'Agwarwash' (Adjutant General War Office) so that when a new number was added to the group it was a matter of simple arithmetic to decipher it. He also signed off in the same way every time. Thus, as Dr Schaedel disclosed in a post-war conversation with the British author Bruce Norman, 'Rommel, each day at lunch, knew exactly where the Allied troops were standing the evening before.'

During all this, Fellers was engaged in a savage little turf battle with General Maxwell, who had been sent to Cairo as head of the US military liaison office there after America came into the war. Clearly, the two men did not hit it off. Within a few days of Maxwell's arrival, Fellers cabled Washington complaining that the newcomer was trying to sideline him. Maxwell had 'placed members of his staff in close relation with British GHQ, Middle East, including some officers with intelligence,' Fellers reported, and this 'operates against my gathering information here'. To serve the best interests of the US Army, Fellers urged, 'my position should be made clear by appointing me the War Department's official liaison officer for intelligence activities' at GHQ, Middle East.

For his part, Maxwell was out to restrict Fellers' activities to 'Egyptian affairs only', excluding him from the big picture. In a message to the Pentagon, Maxwell proposed that 'to avoid conflicting activities between my staff and the office of the Military Attaché, and to preclude possibility of presenting divergent views, I shall provide the War Department Military Intelligence Service with my personal estimates of the situation and enemy activity from time to time'.

This did not wash with Major-General George V. Strong, head of the Pentagon's G-2 intelligence branch. 'We have received a wealth of valuable military information from Fellers and none whatever from Maxwell,' he observed in a memo to the US Army Chief of Staff, General George C. Marshall. Maxwell was 'not a trained observer, has no military intelligence background, and has no combat troops training,' said Strong, adding: 'I am disposed to question the value of his "personal estimates of the situation and enemy activities".' That was enough for Marshall, who curtly cabled Maxwell that his plan to confine Fellers to Egyptian affairs was 'not repeat not desired'.

But Fellers' victory was short-lived. At the end of June 1942, the British, conscious of a serious and persistent security leak, began checking all possible sources. Officers from MI8, the signals intelligence service, turned up at Fellers' office to review his security measures. 'They seemed satisfied,' Fellers told Norman, somewhat disingenuously, after the war. 'They didn't say anything about the code being broken, but it made me wonder why they were doing it.'

Soon the British were in no doubt that Fellers' office was the source of the steady intelligence leakage, and Strong suddenly found it 'highly desirable that [Fellers] should come home for consultations'. No reason was given – at least, not in writing – other than the flimsy one that 'with the reorganization of the Middle East Command it appears that Colonel Fellers' usefulness . . . has ceased'. At the same time, the Black Code was scrapped. And in Berlin an official memo lamented the loss of the Fellers intercepts which had 'told us all we needed to know, immediately, about virtually every enemy action'.

Exactly how the British discovered that Fellers was Rommel's 'Good Source' remains unclear. One version has it that a German domestic radio broadcast gave the game away in a propaganda item poking fun at the Americans by revealing how easy it was to tap into their communications from Cairo. If correct, some heads must have rolled for that indiscretion. A perhaps more likely explanation is that analysis of the Enigma decrypts cumulatively made it apparent that the US legation had to be the source of the leaks.

However that may be, the Black Code affair was acutely embarrassing for a while to Anglo-US relations in the Middle East. But the British could not make a public fuss; they were deeply beholden to the Americans for all kinds of arms assistance, in particular tanks. And even in confidential internal memos, the American top brass would continue to fudge the reasons for Fellers' abrupt removal from Cairo to a non-job in Washington. There is no record, for example, that General Marshall was officially informed of the real reason for Fellers' recall, though it seems likely that he was told verbally.

Nevertheless, Fellers' career did not suffer. He was awarded the Distinguished Service Medal in recognition of his 'uncanny ability to foresee military developments' in the Middle East and for the 'clarity, brevity and accuracy' of his dispatches. He was subsequently promoted to Brigadier-General and transferred to the Pacific theatre as military secretary to General Douglas MacArthur, whom he greatly admired.*

Although the US War Department did not commit to paper the true reason for Fellers' removal from Cairo, word must have filtered down to a select few from the Chief of Staff's office. Lady Ranfurly

---

* One officer who served with him on MacArthur's staff described Fellers as a strident Anglophobe. After his retirement from the army he became a prominent and active member of the hard-right John Birch Society.

recalls that when she mentioned Fellers' name approvingly to General Dwight D. Eisenhower at a Cairo dinner party in November 1943, he cut her dead. 'Any friend of Bonner Fellers is no friend of mine,' he said, and turned his back to resume a conversation with Kay Summersby, his driver and reputed paramour.

As Rommel gathered strength for a counter-offensive from his position at Mersa el Brega, a chapter of dismal recent history was about to repeat itself on the British side. Only a year after Wavell had been robbed of the chance to complete the conquest of all Libya by having to send some of his best troops to Greece, the same thing was happening to Auchinleck as Japan's entry into the war drew seasoned desert troops and aircrews to the Far East.

The 7th Armoured Brigade was sent to Burma with 150 Honeys and Crusaders. The 70th Division, whose breakout from Tobruk had contributed so much to the Sidi Rezegh battle, was sent to India to cope with famine and civil unrest.* Two of the three Australian infantry divisions were sent home to fight the Japanese in the tropical slush of New Guinea and Bougainville. And if Morshead's 9th Division was allowed to remain in the Middle East, it was partly because there was not enough shipping available to take them home.

In addition to the drain on the Eighth Army, four RAF squadrons were sent to the Far East, while Britain's ability to supply Malta was made even more difficult by the withdrawal of half a dozen Australian warships from the Mediterranean. Thanks to his 'little Fellers', Rommel was kept informed of all this.

Auchinleck could no more prevent this withering away of men and *matériel* than had Wavell before him. But to compound the problem, he betrayed an extraordinary ambivalence, hoping for the best – an advance all the way to Tripoli – but preparing for the worst – a retreat all the way to the Egyptian frontier and beyond.

The British commander had been categorically assured by GHQ Intelligence that Rommel was not being reinforced with fresh supplies of men and *matériel*. In fact, the Germans had received substantial tank replacements by way of two convoys which, escorted by Italian warships, arrived in Tripoli harbour following the destruction of the

---

* Later they would see action again as the main element of Orde Wingate's second Chindit expedition behind Japanese lines in Burma.

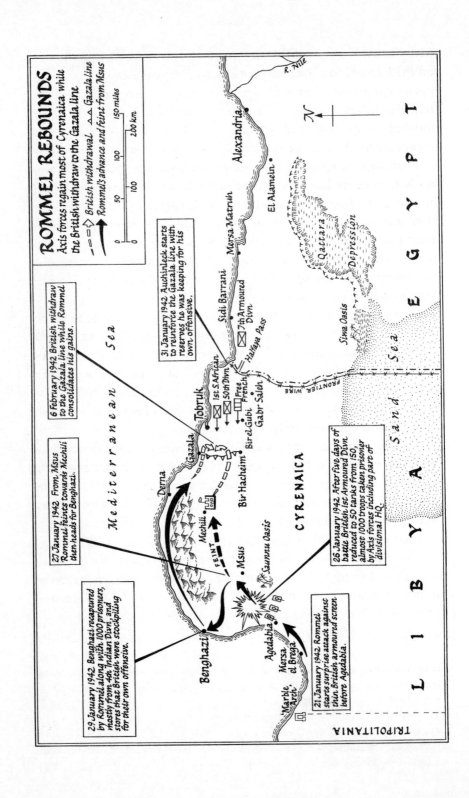

ROMMEL REBOUNDS

Axis forces regain most of Cyrenaica while the British withdraw to the Gazala line

- - - ⊳ British withdrawal   ⌒⌒ Gazala line
━━▶ Rommel's advance and feint from Msus

0   50   100   150 miles
0   100   200 km

27 January 1942. From Msus Rommel feints towards Mechili then heads for Benghazi.

6 February 1942 British withdraw to the Gazala line while Rommel consolidates his gains.

31 January 1942 Auchinleck starts to reinforce the Gazala line with reserves he was keeping for his own offensive.

29 January 1942 Benghazi recaptured by Rommel along with 1000 prisoners, mostly from 4th Indian Divn, and stores that British were stockpiling for their own offensive.

26 January 1942 After five days of battle British 1st Armoured Divn reduced to 50 tanks from 150, almost 1000 troops taken prisoner by Axis forces including part of divisional HQ.

21 January 1942 Rommel starts surprise attack against thin British armoured screen before Agedabia.

Mediterranean Sea

Derna

Gazala
Tobruk

1st S.African
50th Divn
Free French
Bir el Gubi
Gabr Saleh

Mechili

Bir Hacheim

FEINT

Saunnu Oasis

Msus

Benghazi

Agedabia

Mersa el Brega

Marble Arch

CYRENAICA

L I B Y A

TRIPOLITANIA

Halfaya Pass
Sidi Barrani
7th Armoured Divn

FRONTIER WIRE

Mersa Matruh

El Alamein

Alexandria

R. Nile

E G Y P T

Qattara Depression

Siwa Oasis

Sand Sea

Malta-based K Force of British cruisers and destroyers in a minefield off the Libyan coast. Lieutenant-General Sir Frank Messervy, in temporary command of 1st Armoured Division, was incensed at GHQ's refusal to believe the Panzers had been reinforced. This 'infuriated the forward troops who had actually seen them,' said Messervy, and consequently 'we were on the wrong foot when [Rommel] advanced'.

Even though ignorant of the German build-up, Auchinleck was ready to contemplate a worst-case scenario. In a 'Most Secret' operational instruction, he notified Ritchie that while his 'present intention' was to continue the advance into Libya and capture Tripoli, 'we must face the prospect . . . of having to pass to the defensive . . .' In that eventuality, said Auchinleck, 'it is NOT [Auchinleck's emphasis] my intention to try to hold, permanently, Tobruk, or any other locality west of the Frontier'.

Indeed, Auchinleck was even able to contemplate having to withdraw to a position well behind the Egyptian frontier. 'Work will be continued in accordance with the original plans on the EL ALAMEIN position,' he instructed Ritchie. This, some seven months before it started to feature in the news bulletins, appears to be the first mention in any important official document of El Alamein, a scruffy little railhead only sixty miles from Alexandria.

It was probably first earmarked during pre-war exercises which envisaged a rather more determined Italian invasion of Egypt than the one that transpired. If the worse came to the worst, here was a marvellous defensive position: a front line starting at the coast and ending about forty miles due south among the wind-sculpted buttes and mesas of the Qattara Depression, impassable to armour and thus impossible to outflank.

That Auchinleck, having just pushed Rommel right out of Cyrenaica, should even be thinking of pulling back beyond the Egyptian frontier – and of surrendering the glittering propaganda and logistical prize of Tobruk★ – presents a stark contrast to the mind-set of

★ Auchinleck may have been at least partly influenced by Admiral Cunningham's objections to the prospect of future naval losses if a besieged Tobruk had once again to be supplied by sea. During the siege of April to December 1941, the Royal Navy and Merchant Navy had brought in seventy-two tanks, ninety-two artillery pieces and 33,946 tons of stores and had also brought in 32,677 men and taken out 34,115. The cost of all this had been twenty-seven warships and six merchantmen sunk and 539 lives lost – one life for every fifty tons of supplies and one warship for every 1,000 tons, as Cunningham estimated (Winston, *Cunningham, the Greatest Admiral Since Nelson*, pp. 235–6).

Rommel, who thought only of smashing his way through to the Nile. Even as Auchinleck dictated his instruction to Ritchie, Rommel was completing his plans for the devastating assault he was about to launch. 'Dearest Lu,' he wrote to his wife on 21 January, 'two hours from now the army will launch its counter-attack. After thoroughly weighing all the pros and cons I have decided to risk it.'

Rommel had gone to considerable lengths to ensure surprise. Encouraged by his 'little Fellers' disclosure of British weakness and daringly disregarding the military maxim that 'time spent on reconnaissance is never wasted', he forbade any stepping up of recce patrols. He would simply advance until he met an enemy whom he knew he outnumbered and then do what he usually did: make it up as he went along. He also kept movement behind his own lines to a minimum to avoid any massing of vehicles that might be spotted by the RAF. Not even his divisional commanders were told of the offensive until two days before it began. By contrast, and Ultra intercepts notwithstanding, British tactical intelligence was abysmal.

The result was that the inexperienced 2nd Armoured Brigade fell victim to the kind of perfect Blitzkrieg Rommel and every other Panzer commander loved to deliver. It was a cruel baptism of fire: outnumbered and outfought, their tanks picked off before they were properly sure where the enemy fire was coming from, what the 2nd Armoured had learned during training went out of the window. Who had time to rally into a box formation now? The sight of trucks full of the wounded, accompanied by grim-faced men who had managed to get out of their burning tanks alive, panicked some of the support troops and they bolted. An officer in the Royal Dragoon Guards reached for the usual, rather tired, equestrian metaphor, beloved of the cavalry regiments. It was 'like a hunting field,' he said as the rear echelons galloped by in their field kitchens, petrol bowsers, workshops and signals vans.* It was worse than that: the fox had turned and was chasing the horses and hounds.

On and on rolled the Panzers. One column took the Via Balbia along the coast, passing Beda Fomm where, in another age, the 7th Armoured Division had closed O'Connor's trap on the Italians. Sixty

---

* The initials of the Royal Army Service Corps, RASC, whose supply columns followed the front-line troops, were caustically rendered by some as standing for 'Run Away Someone's Coming'.

miles inland, the Germans surprised the largest part of the British tank force while it was trying to sort itself out, a few miles north of the oasis of Saunnu. Part of the divisional staff was captured, and 1st Armoured reduced to about fifty of its original 150 tanks.

Among the spoils was a tank park containing thirty battle-worthy Valentines, the heavy infantry tank quite admired by the Germans for the thickness of its hide. The Germans found it hard to believe how completely their fortunes had been reversed. 'The pursuit attained a speed of 15 mph, and the British fled madly over the desert in one of the most extraordinary routs of the war,' reported Rommel's astounded chief intelligence officer, Colonel Friedrich Wilhelm von Mellenthin. For Leutnant Heinz-Werner Schmidt and his anti-tank gunners it was a first experience of working in close support of the Panzers, using tactics that the British, with their rigid separation of different arms, only mastered after one painful lesson after another:

We leapfrogged from one vantage point to another, while our Panzers, stationary and hull down if possible, provided protective fire. Then we would establish ourselves to give them protective fire while they swept on again. The tactics worked well and, despite the liveliness of his fire, the enemy's tanks were not able to hold up our advance . . . We could not help feeling that we weren't up against the tough and experienced opponents who had harassed us so hard on the Trigh Capuzzo.

As they advanced, the Germans increasingly found themselves replacing broken-down vehicles with captured British transport, dining on much-prized British rations, and donning scraps of British uniform. Judging by some contemporary photographs, British webbing belts appear to have enjoyed something of a vogue. Wolfgang Everth, whose reconnaissance company had added a British water tanker and ration truck to its strength, noted:

We obtain further things from Tommy's supply dump and slowly make ourselves become Tommies – our vehicles, petrol, rations and clothing were all English. I . . . breakfasted off two tins of milk, a tin of pineapple, biscuits and Ceylon tea. Unfortunately, the reality of war soon returned again. The English made a low-level air attack [and] four men were killed and several wounded.

Despite its recent drain of men and machines to the war against Japan, the Desert Air Force was one of Auchinleck's best assets. By the beginning of 1942, it more or less equalled the Axis air forces in North Africa in numbers, though not yet in quality. The Messerschmitt-109F fighter had established air superiority for the Axis and would retain it until the arrival of the first Spitfires, much later in the year. Until then the Desert Air Force had to rely on its Hurricanes and American-built P40s and P41s which the British, preferring names to numbers, called Tomahawks and Kittyhawks.

Except at very low altitudes, the Tomahawks and Kittyhawks were hopelessly outclassed by the Messerschmitts. But their sturdy airframes could take a lot of punishment and they were perfectly adequate for ground strafing, giving point to the art work of a New Zealand squadron leader who started the vogue for decorating the Tomahawks' noses with shark's teeth.*

Unfortunately for the Eighth Army, the Desert Air Force was no longer going to make much difference to the struggle for western Cyrenaica. As the Afrika Korps continued to advance, the British had to send their short-range fighter-bomber squadrons back to the Egyptian border. Behind them, part of the growing easterly stampede, came truckloads of RAF mechanics and spare parts.

Auchinleck believed in delegating and was most reluctant to interfere with subordinates. Nevertheless, he was beginning to have his doubts about Ritchie: the man he had chosen to replace the broken Cunningham might be better at hiding his emotions but was just as much out of his depth.

In London, Churchill, already trying to put a brave face on serial calamity in the Far East, was stunned by the fresh reverses in North Africa and made his disappointment with British generals obvious by

---

* On the first day of Rommel's offensive, the Luftwaffe made an enterprising bid to interfere with British fighter replacements. A Heinkel long-range bomber, stripped of its upper and belly turret guns and all other excess weight, flew 800 miles to Fort Lamy (now N'Djamena), the capital of Free French Chad, to bomb the RAF airfield there. Fort Lamy was an important staging-post on the 4,000-mile Takoradi Trail, starting in what is now Ghana and ending in Egypt via Sudan. The British used this route as a fast and comparatively safe way to bring in aircraft from Britain. The defences there no more expected an air raid than snow, and eight new Hurricanes were wrecked on the ground. More importantly, 80,000 gallons of aviation fuel went up in flames.

becoming almost as fulsome as Hitler about Rommel. Replying to a question in the House of Commons on 27 January, he electrified the nation with his reference to Rommel as 'a very daring and skilful opponent . . . and, may I say across the havoc of war, a great general'.

In Cairo, where adjectives like daring and skilful had not been applied to a British general since O'Connor smote the Italians, Auchinleck had already flown to Eighth Army headquarters to take over from Ritchie. He was caught flat-footed by Rommel's next move.

The Germans had reached the caravan stop of Msus, in the middle of the Cyrenaica bulge. From there Rommel had the choice of going east towards Mechili so as to threaten the Eighth Army's main supply route, or north through the Green Mountains to Benghazi and the coast. He chose to feint towards Mechili while personally taking charge of the real thrust, to Benghazi.

A few armoured vehicles, accompanied by enough trucks to kick up a sizeable column of dust, headed towards Mechili. Auchinleck and Ritchie took the bait and ordered what remained of 1st Division's armour to block Rommel's feint. Benghazi was captured on 29 January, the eighth day of the German offensive, and with it much of the petrol and ammunition Auchinleck had been stockpiling for the attack he had told Churchill he hoped to deliver no later than 15 February. Rommel had reduced Auchinleck's 'Crusader' gains to little more than the relief of Tobruk.

A lull ensued along a line stretching from Gazala on the coast, southward to Bir Hacheim, a fortress garrisoned by a Free French brigade. Although he had captured petrol and plenty of soft transport at Benghazi, Rommel did not immediately have the wherewithal to pursue the British any further. Instead, he went home to be fêted and applauded by a grateful nation. Hitler made him the Wehrmacht's youngest colonel-general and upgraded his Panzer Group to a Panzer Army. But, obsessed with the Russian front, the Führer would not give Rommel the extra men he wanted. Rommel was understandably frustrated: 'Before us a lay a land rich in raw materials – Africa and the Middle East could have spared us further worries about oil shortages. The strengthening of my army by just a few more divisions and adequate supplies would have been enough to ensure the complete defeat of the British armed forces in the Near East.' Instead, a trickle of reinforcements brought his three existing divisions up to something like full strength – about 36,000 men in all. Apart from battle casualties, their ranks were constantly being thinned by jaundice and dysentery. Rommel himself, who rarely slept for five consecutive hours and lived mainly on adrenalin, was not in good health. He needed to wait before resuming the attack.

Meanwhile, the almond blossom in the looted Italian settlements along the coast, and in the homesteads on the slopes of the Green Mountains, heralded the arrival of the African spring. Soon desert wadis would briefly become a garish carpet of wild flowers. Rommel himself was spotted filming them with an 8-mm cine-camera.

While the opposing armies faced each other, motionless, along the Gazala line, a small and highly unconventional unit was in training under conditions of the tightest security at Mersa Matruh, 320 miles to the east. Its members wore German army uniform, carried German weapons and German identification papers, drilled in German and gave and received orders in German. Even off duty they addressed each other only in German; yet all were members of the British army and, except for their two officers and two instructors, were Palestinian Jews of either German or Austrian origin.

The unit to which these men belonged was styled the Special Interrogation Group (SIG), a formation whose very existence was so nebulous that it was sometimes incorrectly referred to as the Special Intelligence Group or the Special Investigation Group. Its progenitor and commander was Captain Herbert Cecil Buck, MC, a fluent German-speaker, born in British-ruled India into a military family and educated in post-First World War Germany, where his father was serving in the army of occupation on the Rhine.

The SIG's purpose was to raid behind the lines disguised as German troops. This was a triply dangerous business. To operate behind the lines was risky enough; to do so wearing the enemy's uniform and in violation of the Geneva Conventions carried the risk of summary execution in the event of capture;* to be so captured and identified as a Jew could only compound the offence. Among the very few British special forces officers who knew of the SIG's existence it was known as Bertie Buck's Suicide Squad.

The idea of raising such a unit began to germinate in Buck's mind while his battalion of Punjabi Muslims, part of the 4th Indian Division, was training in British-mandated Palestine before deploying to the Western Desert. With a Punjabi driver and a platoon of his men in

---

* When German commandos, wearing American uniforms, were captured during the Battle of the Bulge in December 1944, they were indeed court-martialled and executed by firing squad.

the back of the truck, he was heading along the coast road from Tel Aviv to Haifa one day in the summer of 1941 when he stopped to pick up two young female hitchhikers. One was Leah Schlossberg, the thirteen-year-old daughter of well-to-do and cultivated German Jews who had emigrated to Palestine as refugees from the Nazis. Many years later, she was to become known to the world as Leah Rabin, widow of the assassinated Israeli Prime Minister, Yitzhak Rabin.*

On the way to Haifa, as they chatted in German, Buck mentioned how much he missed classical music and the opera. She told him that there was plenty of both to be had in Tel Aviv and invited him to meet her parents. 'One Saturday afternoon the front doorbell rang and there he was,' Mrs Rabin recalls. 'He and my parents struck up an immediate rapport. He was a very impressive person – quiet, intellectual and absolutely brilliant. He spoke eight or nine languages.'

Buck was already beginning to think about raising his special unit and asked the Schlossbergs to help him get in touch with members of a German-speaking unit of the Palmach, the permanent cadre of Haganah, the illegal but officially tolerated Jewish underground army. He talked about transferring from his Punjab Regiment to the commandos and, somewhat mysteriously, asked Leah's older sister to visit some specialist bookstores to find him volumes containing the words and music of traditional German army songs.

Soon after that, Buck went with his regiment to the Western Desert where, as a company commander, he was taken prisoner near Gazala towards the end of 1941. It was then that his big idea began to take concrete shape. Eluding his captors in the confusion surrounding the 'Crusader' battles, he stripped the uniform from the corpse of a German officer and bluffed his way past enemy positions until he met up with a British patrol.

Emboldened by the experience, Buck submitted to GHQ in Cairo his plan for a clandestine force of German-speaking Jews. This received a positive reception from Colonel Terence Airey, a senior officer in the Special Operations Executive, formed to wage (in Churchill's words) 'ungentlemanly warfare' in enemy-occupied territories. Buck's

---

* Her older sister, Aviva, would also become the wife of a noted Israeli military commander, Major-General Avraham Yoffe.

idea was 'ungentlemanly' enough, being in direct contravention of the rules of war as widely observed by both sides in North Africa.

Airey gave Buck's brainchild its cover name and minuted: 'It is intended that this sub-unit should be used for infiltration behind the German lines . . . They will frequently be dressed in German uniform and will operate under the command of a British officer who has already proved himself to be an expert in the German language.'

And in a message to 'Jock' Haselden, now lieutenant-colonel commanding the Special Air Service's D Squadron, headquartered at Siwa, Airey described the kind of operation he had in mind for the SIG. They could 'use a captured German lorry with machine-guns and a two-pounder [anti-tank gun] inside it as a sort of Q-ship.* It would go out and time its arrival on the main road before dusk and shoot up small convoys and particularly staff cars and then make off into the desert at dark.'

Buck began his search for personnel at a prisoner-of-war camp near Cairo. There he found two German NCOs who had been captured near Tobruk in November 1941 – a Sergeant Walter Essner and a Corporal Heinrich Bruckner. Both had served in the French Foreign Legion before being conscripted into the Wehrmacht and managed to convince British intelligence that they were committed anti-Nazis by passing on useful information they gleaned from fellow PoWs. Their role in the SIG would be to instruct Buck's Palestine-Jewish volunteers in everything they would need to know about the Afrika Korps – kit, rations, weapons, training, drill movements, disciplinary procedures, right down to current army slang, songs, taboos and grouses.

Buck found his Jewish volunteers within the ranks of the Palmach and the 51st Middle East Commando, the latter a formation (60 per cent Jewish and 40 per cent Arab) that, under the command of Lieutenant-Colonel 'Kid' Cator of the Royal Scots Greys, had seen action in the campaign which drove the Italians out of Ethiopia, providing a remarkable example of Arab-Jewish comradeship in battle that was, alas, never to recur.

---

* British First World War merchant vessels carrying Royal Navy crews. Looking decrepit and hardly worth a torpedo, they would lure unsuspecting U-boats to surface in order to shell them, and come within range of the Q-ship's concealed guns.

Senior in rank among the volunteers, and acting as unofficial liaison between Haganah and the British Army, was Company Sergeant-Major Israel Carmi, born Weinmann in Danzig in 1918. Carmi had served in the Palestine Police and later in the Special Night Squads, a counter-terrorist unit set up by the pro-Zionist British officer, Captain Orde Wingate,* during the 1936–8 Arab Revolt in Palestine. Another typical volunteer for the SIG was Ariye Shai, born Adolf Scheinik in 1922, near Leipzig. He had come to Palestine aged sixteen and joined the British army in December 1940, serving first in the Pioneer Corps before transferring to 51 Commando. Also an ex-member of 51 Commando was Maurice ('Monju') Tiefenbrunner, born in 1915 in Wiesbaden, who had arrived in Palestine as an illegal immigrant, only days before the outbreak of war in September 1939, and had joined the British army within weeks.† Like Shai, Tiefenbrunner had seen action against the Italians in East Africa, but his enemy of choice was the Germans. So Buck's offer in March 1942 of direct action against Hitler's Afrika Korps seemed providential, if extremely risky. 'He said "Don't answer now but take a few days to think it over," ' Shai recalled. 'But I said "Yes" right away.'

Buck took his new recruits to Mersa Matruh for three months of intensive training in such subjects as desert navigation, motor vehicle maintenance, unarmed combat, demolition – but, above all, how to pass as German soldiers. They were housed in a group of huts at the far end of an isolated desert encampment, well away from other units in order to maintain secrecy. On arrival they were issued with captured German uniforms, which they wore at all times, captured German infantry weapons such as Luger pistols and Schmeisser sub-machine-guns, and captured Wehrmacht paybooks, doctored to contain details of their new 'identities'. Shai became 'Corporal Adolf Schubert'.

To augment their cover, Shai and his comrades carried photographs of supposedly German 'wives' and 'sweethearts' (in fact, British army ATS girls, dressed up for the camera without being told why) and 'love letters' and kitschy souvenirs from home. Inside their compound they were allowed to speak only German, from '*Kompagnie aufstehen*'

---

* See the authors' *Fire in the Night*, Macmillan, London; Random House, New York.
† All three are still alive at the time of writing – Carmi in Haifa, Shai in Bat Yam and Tiefenbrunner in Jerusalem. No other survivors of the SIG could be traced.

at daybreak to '*Lichten ausstellen*' at night. Essner and Bruckner were good teachers. 'They kept putting us to the test with sudden questions – sometimes waking us in the middle of the night – to see if we would betray ourselves,' Shai recalled. But he never quite trusted the two German NCOs, and neither did Carmi. Buck told the Jews that the Germans had been cleared and could be trusted. 'He was a brilliant man, but a little naïve,' Carmi remembers.

Indeed, at one point Buck made a duty visit to Palestine with Essner in tow. Leah Rabin well recalls meeting Buck with 'this tall, handsome, very blond, very German-looking German who he said was working with him in the commandos. They were on their way to Jerusalem and as I wanted to see a friend there Captain Buck gave me a lift in his car.' That evening Leah, Buck and Essner had dinner together in a Jerusalem restaurant, where they were joined by Aubrey Eban – then a major in British military intelligence and, after the war, as Abba Eban, to become Israeli Foreign Minister and UN ambassador.

Buck's second in command, Lieutenant David Russell, was equally unconventional. A Scots Guards lieutenant and, like Buck, a fluent German-speaker, he had the engagingly extravagant habit of bathing his feet in cognac after training marches in the desert. Asked by Shai why he didn't drink the cognac instead, 'he laughed and replied "I've got plenty left for drinking."'

The SIG's earliest operations involved the setting-up of roadblocks behind German lines where, dressed as *Feldpolizei*, they would stop enemy vehicles to acquire intelligence on Axis troop movements by asking the kind of questions only military policemen can get away with: What is your unit? Where have you come from? Where are you going? Other exploits included small-scale sabotage raids and forays to obtain enemy vehicles, uniforms and weapons for future use.

It was in June 1942 that the SIG were given their first major assignment. Two vital Allied sea-convoys – one from the east, one from the west – were heading for beleaguered Malta and orders went out from GHQ to launch commando strikes against Axis airfields in order to reduce the threat of enemy air attack. David Stirling of the SAS, the 'phantom major' now promoted to lieutenant-colonel, drew up the plans under which sabotage teams were to blow up enemy aircraft on the ground at Benghazi, Derna, Martuba and Barce in Cyrenaica and Heraklion in Crete. Thirty Free French paratroopers belonging to a unit that had defected from Vichy-controlled Syria and been absorbed into the SAS were assigned to carry out the attacks at Derna and Martuba. Posing as prisoners of war, they would travel to the target airfields in the back of two captured Afrika Korps trucks, driven and guarded by Buck and nine SIG men in Wehrmacht uniform.

These co-ordinated attacks were to be carried out on the night of 13–14 June, starting out from the oasis at Siwa, on the edge of the Egyptian Sand Sea, where the Long Range Desert Group had its operational headquarters. With an LRDG escort, the SIG men, in two Opel trucks and accompanied by a Volkswagen command car, then headed north and west towards Derna, 300 miles away. 'Corporal Schubert' was driving an Opel adorned with the palm tree and swastika symbol of the Afrika Korps, and with fifteen French commandos in the back, ostensibly prisoners on their way to a holding camp.

Bruckner drove the second truck, also with fifteen 'prisoners', while Buck was in the command car, wearing the uniform of a German private, with Essner beside him. After four days' driving, as they began to near German and Italian positions, the LRDG escort left them to finish the journey on their own, arranging to rendezvous at a remote pick-up point after the operation.

As night was falling Buck's party came to a roadblock on the outskirts of a sprawling Axis transit camp. An overweight German corporal ran towards the command car with a panted warning: 'Your convoy should park here for the night. There are British commandos about and it's not safe after dark.' He was so excited that he forgot to demand the password. Buck thanked him for the good advice and led the trucks into the camp, where they refuelled, the French paras lying low in the back.

They parked, and the SIG men piled out. Some bought cigarettes and chatted easily with unsuspecting enemy soldiers. Shai and some others went to a field kitchen, where they stood in line with their mess tins. 'I was sick and tired of the British army bully beef,' he recalled, 'and the idea of some good German grub was irresistible.' While standing in line, Shai conversed with genuine Germans in the queue: the war would soon be over and they'd all go home, *nicht war?* 'Looking back, it seems strange but I felt quite calm and unafraid,' Shai recalled. 'At twenty you think you're immortal.'

No guard post questioned them as they drove out of the transit camp, later that evening. Five miles short of Derna they reached their jump-off point and split up. Shai, with the turncoat German sergeant Essner and two other SIG men, headed for Martuba with a fifteen-man French demolition squad in the back of their truck. The second truck, with the German corporal Bruckner in the front with SIG men Eliyahu Gottlieb and Peter Haas, and its contingent of French saboteurs, headed for Derna. Buck waited with Sergeant Tiefenbrunner at the jump-off point to liaise by walkie-talkie between the two groups, who were to reassemble there after the night's work.

At Martuba, where a squadron of Messerschmitt-109 fighters stood on the ground, the Free Frenchmen deployed silently, clearing the low barbed-wire fence to attach their time-fused 'sticky bombs' without attracting the attention of sentries in a nearby guardhouse. Shai and his two SIG comrades crouched near by, ready to give covering fire if necessary. They had scarcely finished their task when a ball of fire lit up the night sky from the direction of Derna. Shai and his party raced to their vehicle and drove off.

At the reassembly point, they found Buck pacing anxiously. Clearly, something had gone horribly wrong. The time-fused charges of the Derna party should not have gone off until well after both teams had rendezvoused and vanished into the desert. Buck glanced anxiously at his watch. It was past 3 a.m. and they had to move off well before first light. He was about to give the order to leave when they heard a cry and out of the dark staggered Lieutenant Augustin Jourdain, commander of the Free French contingent, supported by two of his men. He was able to gasp, 'Get away, get away fast' before losing consciousness.

As Jourdain was given first aid, his two compatriots told Buck what had happened. They had driven openly into Derna where, approaching a German guardroom, Bruckner had stopped the truck, claiming that it was overheating. He went into the guardroom, ostensibly to get assistance – and came out minutes later with a dozen German soldiers, who surrounded the truck and ordered its occupants out at gunpoint. The Free French commandos began climbing out of the back as if to surrender. Haas and Gottlieb, dressed as they were in German uniforms, knew they were as good as dead and came out shooting.

In the savage exchange of fire that followed, one of the SIG men pulled the pin out of a grenade and tossed it into the back of the truck, where it landed among the explosive charges. It was in the confusion

following the enormous blast that resulted that Lieutenant Jourdain*
and two of his men managed to escape in the dark.

Deciding that there was no point in waiting any longer for stragglers,
Buck ordered, 'Let's go.' The SIG men buried their German uniforms,
changed into British khaki drill, and sped off into the desert with the
remaining French commandos. As dawn broke, they found cover and
lay up during the hours of daylight to avoid detection by patrolling
enemy aircraft. Tiefenbrunner 'felt ill with shame and anger' at the
thought that Bruckner had betrayed 'some of our best comrades' at
Derna. 'I made myself stay alert all the time,' Tiefenbrunner recalled
in a privately published post-war memoir, 'ready to kill [Essner] should
he make a wrong move.'

Shai could see that Buck was 'very upset, feeling it was his fault for
having trusted Bruckner'. Essner remained silent; no one spoke to
him, but his fellow German's treachery clearly left him more than ever
open to suspicion. Had Buck given the order, he would have been
shot on the spot. But retribution would have to wait; the priority now
was to get back safely to British lines.

They travelled on for four days, moving by night and lying up by
day, always on the look-out for enemy air patrols, when they saw a
column of dust coming towards them from the south-east. There was
nowhere to take cover, only open desert all around. Buck and his men
waited apprehensively, hoping against hope that it was a search-and-
rescue patrol from the LRDG. Then through the dust they identified
the outlines of a Ford truck that did indeed belong to the 'Libyan
Desert Taxi Service'. Buck walked forward and was recognized. 'They
gave us food and water, which by then we needed very badly, and led
us back, a long day's drive, to Siwa,' said Shai.

When Buck and his men reached Siwa, he reported that the French
sticky-bombers might have destroyed between fifteen and twenty
aircraft at Martuba. Back at their base (by now removed from Mersa
Matruh to Kabrit, in the Canal Zone, as Rommel advanced towards
the Nile Delta) Buck had a brief discussion with Carmi on what to do
about Essner. 'He was obviously sick at heart that he had trusted the
two Germans,' Carmi recalled, 'but there was no point in a court

* He recovered from his wounds and went on to serve with the SAS throughout
the North African campaign.

martial.' Instead, he ruled that Essner should be sent back to the PoW camp he had originally come from. Carmi sent for Shai, told him to form a three-man escort party and take Essner away. On a quiet stretch of the road, the vehicle stopped and Shai told Essner to get out and start walking. The German did not argue. When Shai returned, he reported that Essner had been 'shot while attempting to escape'.

There was an intriguing postscript to the episode. On 3 July Ober-leutnant Ernst Klager, a Messerschmitt pilot based at Martuba, was shot down over El Alamein and taken prisoner. He told his interroga-tors what he had heard about the events at Derna on the night of 13–14 June and said that the Germans had received advance warning of the raid. Another member of the same squadron, Leutnant Friedrich Korner, who was shot down two days later, confirmed this, saying they had been aware 'for some time' of a pending raid 'organized by an English colonel' – surely a reference to Stirling. He added that on the morning after the raid, a wounded man had presented himself at the field hospital in Derna, claiming to be a German soldier in need of treatment. 'For some reason the doctor became suspicious and on examination it turned out that he was not a German soldier but a Jew from Palestine.' As for the turncoat corporal who betrayed the Derna party, 'he is said to have been awarded the German Cross in silver'.*

But was it really Bruckner and/or Essner who gave advance warning of the airfield raids? It seems most unlikely that they would have had the opportunity or the knowledge to contact Axis intelligence from the SIG's remote campsite. Was their defection to the British, from the outset, merely a ploy to escape the hardships of a PoW camp? Possibly, and it is conceivable that Bruckner's betrayal of the French commandos at Derna was an act of spur-of-the-moment opportunism, once he found himself among his own again. As for Essner, who paid the price for Bruckner's betrayal, there is no evidence either way, apart from guilt by association, as to his motives and intentions. Some pre-war German members of the French Foreign Legion were indeed

---

* Bruckner survived the war and, with the peace, was readmitted into the French Foreign Legion, serving in Algeria. During this period he told a British fellow legionnaire about his time as an instructor to the SIG and claimed that Rommel decorated him in person for his betrayal of the Derna raiders. He was apparently afraid that the British might hunt him down as a war criminal.

anti-Nazis, as Essner and Bruckner claimed to be. However that may be, Essner must have known he was doomed once the Frenchmen blurted out the news of the Derna detachment's fate.

The best evidence is that the Germans received advance warning of the raids from the hapless Colonel Fellers (whom we have already met). Long after the war, Dr Herbert Schaedel, in charge of the Nazi radio intercept station near Nuremberg, revealed that his staff had picked up and decrypted a message from the US attaché dated 11 June 1942, detailing British plans to infiltrate sabotage groups and attack key Axis airfields simultaneously with sticky bombs on the following night. Fellers' information was incorrect in only one respect: the attacks occurred one night later.

And if the SIG-conducted raids on Derna and Martuba were partly successful, it was not enough. True, Stirling's men managed to destroy a considerable number of Messerschmitt-110s and Junkers-52s at Barce, but they failed to penetrate the airport defences at Benghazi, where they had to content themselves with blowing up fuel storage tanks and a number of trucks and half-track vehicles in a parking lot. The raids, in short, did little to save the two Malta-bound convoys. Under heavy surface and air attack, only two supply ships of the east-bound convoy reached the island, while the entire west-bound convoy was forced to turn back to Egypt.

In the air and on the sea, the Mediterranean war continued unabated; but for over three months, following Rommel's recapture of half of Cyrenaica, there were no major land engagements. During the lull, both sides began to reinforce, each hoping to become strong enough to attack first.

Crossing the Mediterranean was far less hazardous for the Axis, now that Malta had been all but neutralized, and German morale was particularly high. Everywhere the Wehrmacht remained invincible, its only major setback in two and a half years of war having been its failure to capture Tobruk. But Libya would surely be the scene of fresh victories, despite the Führer's reluctance, his mind on Russia, to give Rommel the extra Panzer divisions he demanded.

Rommel's existing divisions were, however, being brought back to something like full strength, and for the young German soldiers going out to join the Afrika Korps a journey to a Mediterranean shore tended to be a great adventure. Most of the arriving officers and not a few of the men knew by heart Goethe's '*Kennst du das Land, wo die Zitronen blühen? Im dunkeln Laub die Gold-Orangen glühen . . .*' ('Do you know the land where the lemon trees grow?/Where amid dark foliage the golden oranges glow?') Although the Afrika Korps had experienced its share of upsets and casualties – and although, except in a handful of Italian settlements, the newcomers would find few lemon trees or golden oranges – there existed among the Germans a romantic enthusiasm for the North African campaign that few British soldiers, more accustomed to exotic overseas postings, would have dared admit for fear of ridicule. The diary of Ralph Ringer, a Panzer Grenadier lieutenant, reflects a kind of 'my generation' camaraderie coupled with a breathtaking *naïveté*: 'We are all twenty-one years old and crazy. Crazy because we have volunteered of our own free will to go to Africa and have talked about nothing else for weeks and haven't been able to think about anything else either . . . tropical nights, palm trees, sea breezes, natives, oases and tropical helmets. Also a little war, but how can we be anything but victorious? . . . Like madmen we jumped around and hugged each other, we really were going to Africa!' Ringer would fly to Libya in a Junkers-52 with a nonchalant crew who knew exactly how to deflate enthusiastic and unblooded foot-sloggers. Life-jackets were useless, the neophytes were told, because they would be flying so low nobody would have time to get out of the plane if they were shot down. And the machine-gun behind the cockpit that was their only protection was, of course, purely cosmetic, being hopelessly jammed with sand.

Africa was much closer for the Germans than it was for the British, most of whom arrived via the tortuous route around the Cape – far longer but far safer than running the gauntlet of dive-bombers and U-boats in the Mediterranean. By the time they had stopped in West Africa and then in Cape Town and Durban, before sailing up the Red Sea and through the Suez Canal, the voyage might take over six weeks. By contrast, an Afrika Korps reinforcement could board a troop-train in Munich on Monday morning, be in southern Italy two days later and in Tripoli by Saturday. The troopship convoys formed up at Naples, where units were split up so that if a ship went down, an entire battalion would not drown with it. Usually it took no more than three days to make the crossing. Belt-fed machine-guns would be removed from their greasy wrappings and set up on stands as a welcome addition to the ship's anti-aircraft firepower. But while the men on watch would be looking out for British aircraft, an almost holiday mood sometimes prevailed, with card games and sing-songs around a piano-accordion. Even kit inspections were reassuring, a reminder of how well the Wehrmacht was preparing them for the adventures that lay ahead.

I could hardly believe what wonderful things German soldiers got for war [wrote Ringer]. I received as my most important bit of furniture a huge rubber sealed tropical chest. The contents were really precious – a tropical helmet, a tent, a mosquito net with carrying case, a face veil, a sleeping bag, a pair of desert boots, a pair of tropical shoes, long trousers, short trousers, breeches, coat, blouse, string vests, a body belt of lambs wool . . . goggles and much, much more . . . to which were added a wonderful rucksack, blankets and the usual officers' accoutrements like binoculars, map case, pistol and ammunition pouch etc. . . .

Lambswool bodices, mosquito nets, face veils – there was, by Wehrmacht standards, always something special, almost pampered, about the Afrika Korps. All over the world, from Reykjavik to Rangoon, British soldiers marched in the same type of boot; by the end of the year, many German soldiers would endure a second Russian winter without adequate cold-weather clothing. But from the beginning, the Afrika Korps were issued with a special lightweight tropical boot, a knee-high canvas version of the jackboot with herringbone laces running from just below the knee to the instep.

Once his well-shod feet were on African soil, though, the German soldier found himself at least partly at the mercy of Italian logistics. His main meat ration, the Axis equivalent of bully beef, was sausage meat issued in cans embossed 'AM' for Aministrazione Militare. The Germans soon insisted that this was really code for '*Alter Mann*' ('Old Man'), while the Italian soldiers said it stood for '*Arabo Muerto*' ('Dead Arab'). The 'AM' was supplemented by standard Wehrmacht rations of a soft cream cheese that could be squeezed out of a tube like toothpaste (quite a novelty in 1942), sardines in olive oil and the clever Italian packets of dehydrated minestrone which had amazed O'Connor's troops, plundering Italian supplies in the winter of 1940–41.

When the Afrika Korps were very lucky they had freshly baked white bread from their field kitchens whose ovens were fitted with a distinctive stove pipe they called 'goulash cannons'. Most of the time they had *Dauerbrot*, a moist and long-lasting black bread made of rye or wheat and wrapped in tin foil to keep it fresh longer. British soldiers, when they came upon it, usually thought *Dauerbrot* quite awful, but it was the kind of health food that by the 1980s would become acceptable fare all over Western Europe.

Inevitably in a desert war, both sides had water problems; near the coast they often drank sea water desalinated by distilling through copper tubing into 40-gallon oil-drums. Attempts to purify supplies from other sources with chlorine and other chemicals invariably made it taste even worse. To a certain extent the British got over this problem by drinking a good part of their water ration as 'char', that extraordinary army brew of tea-leaves, condensed milk and as much sugar as they could get hold of which, later in the war, an astonished American soldier would describe as 'hot ice cream'.

The men of the Afrika Korps preferred coffee to tea, but by 1942, with the United States in the war and trade with South America almost at an end, few Germans could remember what Brazil's biggest export tasted like. They were having to make do with ersatz coffee, a substitute rumoured to be made from powdered acorns which tasted foul even when boiled with domestic tap water. The Eighth Army may have loved its tea, but the *Afrikaners*, as Rommel's troops were beginning to call themselves, loathed their coffee. They called it 'nigger sweat'. Together with the chemicals in the water, the ersatz coffee was blamed for the high rate of dysentery and diarrhoea which, along with hepatitis, seriously depleted Rommel's Panzer Army. The worst cases often had to be flown to Greece or Italy for treatment, followed by convalescent leave in Germany.

Concern for the health of the Afrika Korps was such that Hitler ordered them to be issued with vitamin pills. When the British captured some and figured out what they were, their reaction was one of scorn and contempt. Fleet Street, no doubt with official encouragement, took up the story with a vengeance.* This flagrant flying in the face of nature was obviously all part of the Nazi plan to breed a race of Aryan supermen, said the popular press. There were pledges, which would not survive the war, that such vile potions would never be visited upon imperial troops.

As it happened, the recipients were not all that impressed with their Führer's dietary supplements. The Afrika Korps were inclined to think that the enemy were much better fed than they were. Greatest proof of this, and one which would have astonished the Eighth Army, was their enthusiasm for captured bully beef (canned corned beef). This was not only consumed with relish but was sometimes reverently parcelled up and sent back home so that the whole family could enjoy these spoils of war. Even more wonderful in German eyes were the canned fruits found in captured British supply dumps, one of the choicest items being Californian peaches.

By the spring of 1942 the Americans were beginning to send the British something rather more lethal than peaches. They called it the M3 tank, although the British, in deference to its makers, dubbed it

---

* An entirely mythical Nazi drug culture was a common theme in British propaganda during the first half of the war. The defeat in Crete was partly explained away by fanciful tales of the fanaticism displayed by narcotics-charged German paratroopers whose physical reaction to their chemical rations had purportedly left their faces with a tell-tale greenish tinge.

the Grant,★ after Lincoln's favourite commander, Ulysses S. Grant. Its main armament was a 75-mm cannon and for the first time the Eighth Army had something that outgunned the Mark III Panzers, whose armour it could pierce from almost a mile away. Admittedly, the Grant could still be out-ranged by the 88-mm anti-tank guns that usually accompanied German armour, but not by all that much. And at last the British had a tank with high-explosive shells that could kill and maim 88-mm gun crews with a near miss, instead of needing to score a direct hit with solid shot. At some two and a half inches, the Grant's thickest armour-plate was half an inch thinner than the Matilda's but, despite its huge gun and a five-man crew, it was almost twice as fast as the British tank.

Nevertheless, the Grant was essentially a stop-gap affair while the Americans put the final touches to their M4, the Sherman; and nobody pretended it was perfect. Its principal fault was that its main gun was too heavy for its turret, which instead carried a smaller, 37-mm cannon, not much bigger than the British two-pounder. The main 75-mm gun was mounted in a sponson, a gun port in the right side of the hull, which gave it a limited traverse so that, instead of rotating a turret, it was necessary to point the entire tank to draw a bead on the enemy. Nor could it be fired from the 'hull down' position favoured by tank crews, in which the main body of the tank is behind cover, with only the turret showing. To get a shot off, the entire tank had to be exposed.

Roosevelt saw to it that Auchinleck was sent 167 Grants, even though the United States – far from being the superpower that would emerge from the war† – was desperate to build up its own armed forces. Amazingly enough, given the inadvertent indiscretions of Colonel Fellers' messages to Washington, German intelligence did not learn about the Eighth Army's new tank until a few days before 26 May, when Rommel decided that he was at last strong enough to break the stalemate and attack first.

★

★ There was also a less numerous version known as the Lee, after the Confederate commander, but most of these went to Burma.

† The politics of isolationism saw to it that the US was even less prepared for war than Britain. In September 1939, when Germany invaded Poland, its regular army, at about 200,000, ranked nineteenth in size in the world – slightly larger than Bulgaria's and slightly smaller than Portugal's. Luckily for Western democracy, its industrial potential was in rather better shape.

The balance of forces at this point was still very much in favour of the Eighth Army. Ritchie had 850 tanks, compared to Rommel's 560, of which 228 were Italian. The latter had been improved slightly both by the manufacturers and by the crews who, to increase the thickness of their armour, festooned them with as much extra track and sandbags as they could lay their hands on. In the hands of the better Italian troops, like the Ariete Division, they could sometimes inflict a nasty surprise on the over-confident; but without doubt they remained the least effective tanks in the desert, and the Italians knew it.

Rommel's main *Panzerkampfwagen* was the Mark III – of which he had 223 – with its stubby 50-mm main gun, only marginally better than the two-pounders (40-mm) on all the British-made tanks, though mechanically more reliable. Rommel had another sixty tanks fitted with various main armaments, among them nineteen Mark III Specials with a long-barrelled 50-mm gun similar to the very effective 88. Four experimental Mark IV Specials with an even more powerful 75-mm long-barrelled gun were still awaiting ammunition when the offensive began.* In addition there were his anti-tank guns, not only the 88 which time and again made a mockery of British numerical superiority, but the 50-mm piece and some very good captured Russian guns which the Wehrmacht had refurbished. Nevertheless, the Eighth Army had enough men and equipment to beat the Panzerarmee Afrika. What it lacked was the kind of resolute leadership needed to 'grip it', in the slang of the day, and deal with a ruthless, brilliant and unpredictable opponent like Rommel. Instead, there existed a debilitating and often paralysing crisis of senior command, of which most of the men about to face the Panzers were blissfully unaware.

The root of the trouble was Neil Ritchie. The Eighth Army commander was a large, affable Scot who, in build and temperament, bore a superficial resemblance to his mentor, Auchinleck. He had first impressed Auchinleck with his capacity for hard work when, in 1940, Sir Claude was trying to shore up the defences of southern England against invasion and Ritchie was on his staff. In four years Ritchie had risen from major to major-general, yet his aptitude as a staff officer perhaps owed more to his ability to get on with people than to a particularly sharp mind. And until the 'Crusader' battles of 1941, when

---

* The Panther and Tiger tanks that would easily restore the German edge in armoured warfare had yet to make an appearance in North Africa.

Auchinleck had been standing close behind him, Ritchie had never commanded anything bigger than a company in action, and that over twenty years previously.* He had been snatched from the Cairo desk he occupied as Auchinleck's Deputy Chief of Staff and sent to the desert to take over an army in the middle of what would turn out to the most complex battle of the campaign. Ritchie had jumped at the chance, though he seems to have had some difficulty in adjusting to the rigours of campaign life. The visiting American journalist and playwright Clare Boothe Luce, wife of the founder of *Time* and *Life* magazines, was amazed to discover that Ritchie had his freshly laundered shirts flown up from Cairo. Originally, Auchinleck regarded his appointment as temporary, because he felt there was no time to wait for the arrival from England of a permanent replacement for the sacked Cunningham. 'The Auk' did not want to promote one of the Eighth Army's two corps commanders, because he thought they were doing too good a job where they were. But in the euphoria that followed the relief of Tobruk, Churchill had declared Ritchie to be the new commander of the Eighth Army, and winning British generals were too scarce a breed to be easily discarded.

Still, having won the 'Crusader' battle largely thanks to Auchinleck's guidance, Ritchie had failed miserably when Rommel went back on the offensive. One of the prized corps commanders, Lieutenant-General Godwin-Austen, would later ask to be relieved of his command, claiming that Ritchie was unable to delegate and had countermanded his orders with disastrous results. Auchinleck, feeling he had to support Ritchie, would with regret allow Godwin-Austen to go.

Yet Auchinleck was concerned enough to do something curiously out of character for a man who had a justified reputation for straight dealing. He decided that the Eighth Army's organization and deployment should be looked over by 'Chink' Dorman-Smith. 'We must modernize ourselves . . . he is excellent at this sort of thing . . . he is NOT snooping!' Auchinleck assured Ritchie. But that was exactly what he had briefed Dorman-Smith to do – and specifically, following

---

* As a teenage subaltern, Ritchie was seriously wounded at the battle of Loos in 1915 and later served against the Turks in Mesopotamia, where he participated in the capture of Baghdad and the conquest of Palestine. In 1938 he briefly commanded a battalion on counter-insurgency duties in Jerusalem during the Arab rebellion.

Godwin-Austen's departure, to find out how much confidence other
senior officers had in Ritchie.

Like Wavell, Auchinleck had long been an admirer and a friend
of the acid-tongued master-tactician who had given O'Connor the
blueprint for his victory at Sidi Barrani before returning to the relative
obscurity of headmastering the Haifa Staff College. The friendship of
'Chink' and 'The Auk' was strengthened by shared mutual dislikes, a
list which included a fellow member of the Anglo-Irish ascendancy
named Lieutenant-General Bernard Montgomery, who was currently
commanding a corps in England. Dorman-Smith was eight years
younger than Montgomery and had first clashed with him years before
at Camberley Staff College where Dorman-Smith was a student and
Montgomery a lecturer. Auchinleck's falling-out had been much more
recent when Montgomery had served under him, with ill-disguised
disdain for his ideas and methods, as a corps commander in England
during the invasion scare of 1940–41.

Although Dorman-Smith's uncompromising nature and cruel wit*
had by the age of forty-seven made him many enemies of the kind
who could impede his career, a discerning few admired his brilliance,
among them Britain's leading military philosopher, Basil Liddell-Hart.
In contrast to Ritchie, 'Chink' was bad with people and, though
clever, not clever enough to relax with his intellectual inferiors, to be
clubbable in a profession that understandably demanded camaraderie
more than most other qualities. This was why he had been banished
to the Haifa backwater. Nevertheless, despite opposition from General
Sir Alan Brooke – also of the Anglo-Irish gentry and now at Churchill's
side as Chief of the Imperial General Staff – Auchinleck had got
'Chink' on to his team as Deputy Chief of Staff with the rank of
major-general. A faction at GHQ regarded Dorman-Smith as the
resident Rasputin, full of crackpot ideas and a malign influence over
their chief; and he was indeed the only officer allowed to accompany
'The Auk' on his morning walk or run around the dusty racetrack at
the Gezira Club – 'the dawn patrol', as Chink called it.

Dorman-Smith returned from his two weeks of snooping in the

---

* When a senior staff officer whom he thought an absolute booby received a
knighthood in the 1942 Honours list, 'Chink' penned a verse that went: 'They
knighted him because, forsooth/He cheered us up at GHQ./But that is not the total
truth./He helped to cheer up Rommel, too.'

desert with a new witticism. What was wrong with the Eighth Army, he said, was an '*embarras de Ritchies*'. This was by no means a disinterested opinion. Ritchie represented everything Dorman-Smith despised. 'Chink found him patronizing, limited and assured . . . too repellent to be classified in the fond "Bear of Little Brain" category,' concluded Lavinia Greacen, Dorman-Smith's biographer. These views were echoed by every divisional commander Dorman-Smith interviewed, including Jock Campbell, the hero of Sidi Rezegh.* Other senior Eighth Army officers consulted included 'Strafer' Gott, who after Godwin-Austen's departure had been made commander of XIII Corps, with the rank of lieutenant-general. Gott also seems to have been disparaging, or at least to have expressed reservations, about Ritchie, which is about as far as he ever went in saying a bad word about anyone.

Auchinleck considered Dorman-Smith's mission too important to be discussed on his 'dawn patrol' morning walk around the Gezira racetrack. Instead, he arranged a very private picnic lunch on the banks of brackish Lake Fayum, south-west of Cairo. Here 'Chink' told him that everything he had heard and seen indicated that Ritchie should be replaced. Auchinleck was not pleased. He pointed out that he could not sack another Eighth Army commander, especially one who was deemed to have been successful, so soon after getting rid of Cunningham. And he admitted that there was another reason he did not want to get rid of Ritchie: there was a danger that Brooke would replace him with the difficult and insubordinate Montgomery. To his credit, Dorman-Smith replied that personal prejudices had to be set aside and if Montgomery was the right man for the job he should get it. Although Auchinleck's own doubts about Ritchie's competence had been amply confirmed, he was still adamant that there would be no more sackings.

Churchill, like the men under Ritchie's command, knew none of this. So far 1942 had seen nothing but humiliation for British arms, notably the surrender at Singapore on 15 February of about 80,000 Australian, British and Indian troops to an inferior number of Japanese. The Prime Minister was relying on the reinforced Eighth Army to

---

* Along with his Victoria Cross, Campbell had been rewarded with command of 7th Armoured Division, the famed Desert Rats. Only hours after being interviewed by Dorman-Smith, he was killed in a road accident on a hairpin bend in Halfaya Pass.

wipe away the stain of defeat by surprising Rommel and delivering the kind of land victory last seen against the Italians. He had no inkling that the Eighth Army would go into battle under a man whom none of his senior commanders trusted.

The British desert command did not hold a monopoly on backbiting and intrigue. As well as the perennial friction with their Italian allies, senior German officers were by no means above internecine feuding, especially in the atmosphere of mutual recrimination following the failure of their attacks on Tobruk.

Rommel's file at the Wehrmacht High Command groaned with complaints, several of them from officers Rommel had sent back to Germany – 'put on his camel', as they said in the Afrika Korps. 'Was it so hot down there that you all just got on each other's nerves?' wondered Field Marshal von Brauchitsch, Germany's top soldier, answerable only to Hitler. He was talking to the sacked Streich, who had called to see him with his tales of woe about Rommel.

It was partly to avoid this kind of friction that a compact and highly trained staff had been attached to Rommel, professionals intensively schooled in the conduct of war. They were led by Lieutenant-General Albert Gause, a Prussian who had previously worked as a liaison officer with the Italians. Initially, Gause had been in the anti-Rommel faction but he soon became a firm believer in his genius. By May 1942, however, the strain of working with this genius had often left his nerves in shreds.

Gause's staff consisted of forty-three officers, backed up by 150 signallers, clerks, drivers, medics, cooks and about twenty civilians who were either journalists and cameramen, there to feed Goebbels' propaganda machine, or diplomats of a sort whose role was to smooth ruffled Roman feathers. The staff officers included the Hungarian László Almasy, a renowned pre-war desert explorer who had been seconded by his government, an ally of the Nazis, as desert adviser to Rommel with the rank of captain in the Luftwaffe.★

Rommel's personal clerk was Rolf Munninger, a twenty-year-old fellow-Schwabian. In civilian life Munninger had been a clerk in a

---

★ Long after the war, Almasy would receive posthumous and somewhat spurious international celebrity as the romantic protagonist of the Booker Prize-winning novel and multiple Oscar-winning film, *The English Patient*.

hardware dealership and won prizes for shorthand-typing. Rommel's Chief of Staff Westphal, displaying that rather patronizing humour towards Other Ranks of officers the world over, preferred to tell him that he had been selected mainly because he 'didn't speak German properly' – a reference to Rommel's desire to have some fellow-Schwabians around him. Even the arrogant Prussians had to admit that these south Germans were hard workers.

Munninger and the rest of the staff followed Rommel about in a caravan of forty-six vehicles, often far fewer as Rommel detached himself and got involved at the front. It was a considerably smaller staff than its Eighth Army equivalent, which needed at least 100 drivers. The German concept of operational command was to paint with a broad brush and not to give detailed orders below the level of unit commander, where the man in charge was likely to have a much better understanding of how to carry out a given task. The British tended to do the opposite; few details were beneath the attention of their hard-working planners, an approach that tended to discourage changes of plan and showed a reluctance to adapt to fast-moving events. After almost three years of war the Germans still found most British operations 'sluggish'.

Ritchie had deployed his command in a line that started at the coastal town of Gazala and stopped at Bir Hacheim, the Well of the Wise, some forty miles to the south and on the very edge of the Great Sand Sea. Here, a position extending a couple of square miles around an old Ottoman fort was manned by a Free French brigade under Brigadier-General Marie-Pierre Koenig. The only Britons with him were the crews for six Bofors guns, reinforcing an anti-aircraft unit of French Marines; some signallers to keep him in radio contact with XXX Corps headquarters; his liaison officer, Captain Edward Tomkins; an adventurous young Englishwoman named Susan Travers who was both Koenig's personal driver and his mistress; and a couple of other plucky Englishwomen who had been recruited as nurses for the Free French in Beirut.

The Gazala line was not continuously manned. At Bir Hacheim, and northwards up to the coast, the Eighth Army lay behind broad and densely planted minefields in what were known as 'boxes'. These were strongholds manned by infantry brigade groups. In the unlikely event that they became cut off from the Eighth Army's supply dumps to the east, they had enough rations and ammunition to hold out for several days. The infantry were supported by artillery, anti-aircraft and anti-tank guns. Of the latter, only a few were the new six-pounders whose range and punch gave crews a fair chance of destroying a Panzer.

Within the boxes it was a troglodytic existence. Men spent days digging two-man slit-trenches, and when they had finished these they went to work on the hard, flinty soil again to dig latrines and four-foot-deep bivouac holes, where they might sleep easy when off duty. It was hard work. Positions were constantly being improved, fire lanes worked out, communication trenches dug. Entire battalions went underground in a way reminiscent of Flanders, 1914–18, but without the awful mud. Unless men were working 'on top', it was often very difficult for soldiers to find their positions in this practically featureless terrain, even in daylight.

The way Ritchie had deployed the Eighth Army was predictable enough, thus providing plentiful ammunition for his critics such as Dorman-Smith. The obvious tactical weakness of the boxes was that they were often too far apart to be mutually supporting. In the northern sector, the 2nd South African Division under Major-General Bernard Klopper had taken up positions around Tobruk, where the anti-tank ditch and other relics of the old defence perimeter were dilapidated and filling with sand, and the port's warehouses and underground stores were crammed with supplies and munitions for the offensive which Ritchie planned. Also in the north, Gott's XIII Corps had most of the infantry, the 1st South African Division and the north country Territorial battalions of the British 50th Division.

In the south, below the desert track known as the Trigh Capuzzo, Willoughby Norrie's XXX Corps included the 7th and 1st Armoured Divisions, with most of the British tanks. In this sector, there was defence in depth. The armoured divisions were deployed about twenty miles behind the Free French box at Bir Hacheim. The 201 Independent Guards' Brigade, mechanized infantry with plenty of anti-tank guns,* were on a crossroads on the Trigh Capuzzo in a box appropriately codenamed Knightsbridge. More mechanized infantry, the veteran 3rd Indian Cavalry Brigade who had broken out of Mechili and then fought alongside the Australians at Tobruk, were closer to

---

* Eighteen months before, some of them had made their début in the desert wearing the blue greatcoats and white gloves required for ceremonial duties in London.

the enemy, just to the south-east of the Free French. All was in readiness for the next round – but once again it was Rommel who would throw the first punch.

Rommel's plan of attack called for Crüwell to make a feint in the north with four Italian divisions, stiffened by a couple of Panzer Grenadier regiments. They would be closely followed by trucks fitted with aero-engines on the back whose propellers would whip up enough dust to make the British believe that every tank in the Panzer Army was right behind them. Close air support was to be contributed by the Luftwaffe and the Regia Aeronautica, whose bombers would launch raid after raid on both the minefields and the South African and British infantry dug in behind them.

The real attack would come in the south, where Rommel would personally lead all three German divisions – 21st Panzer, 15th Panzer and 90th Light – plus the Italian Ariete Division in a hook around the British left flank. They would then split up, the Panzers heading north towards the coast and Tobruk, while 90th Light, which had more armoured cars and mechanized infantry than tanks, would head east into the British rear to play havoc with the Eighth Army's lines of communications.

During the initial attack, Rommel gave the Ariete Division the crucial role of capturing the Free French defensive box at Bir Hacheim, the southern anchor of the Gazala line, while his tanks lunged ahead to complete their outflanking move. Bir Hacheim was held by 3,700 troops drawn mainly from France's colonial possessions – Africans from Senegal and a battalion of Pacific islanders, including a contingent from Tahiti, whose junior officers tended to be colonial civil servants or white settlers. There were also two very reduced battalions of Foreign Legionnaires, about 500 in all. These included some German leftists who had fought in the International Brigade against Franco in the Spanish Civil War and then, unable to go home after the republic was defeated, had marched into France and joined the Legion. It seems that some of these German-born legionnaires had reasons other than their politics not to go home: they were Jews. Captain (later Lieutenant-Colonel) Michael Parker of the Royal Artillery gave a lift to a white-kepied legionnaire en route to Bir Hacheim and got quite a surprise:

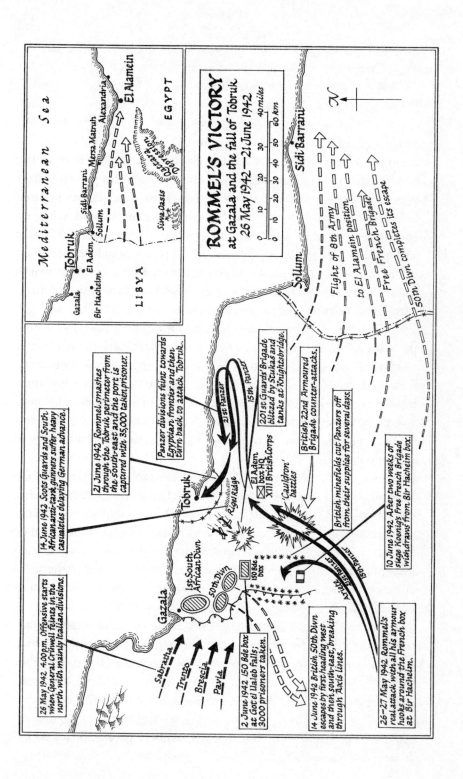

ROMMEL'S VICTORY
at Gazala and the fall of Tobruk
26 May 1942 – 21 June 1942

0 10 20 30 40 miles
0 10 20 30 40 50 60 km

Mediterranean Sea

Tobruk
Gazala
Bir Hacheim
El Adem

LIBYA

Sidi Barrani
Mersa Matruh
Alexandria
El Alamein
Sollum
Siwa Oasis

EGYPT

Flight of 8th Army
to El Alamein position
Free French Brigade
50th Divn completes its escape

Sidi Barrani

Sollum

14 June 1942. Scots Guards and South African anti-tank gunners suffer heavy casualties delaying German advance.

21 June 1942. Rommel smashes through the Tobruk perimeter from the south-east and the port is captured with 35,000 taken prisoner.

Panzer divisions feint towards Egyptian frontier and then turn back to attack Tobruk.

201st Guards Brigade blitzed by Stukas and tanks at Knightsbridge.

British 22nd Armoured Brigade counter-attacks.

British minefields cut Panzers off from their supplies for several days.

10 June 1942. After two weeks of siege Koenig's Free French Brigade withdraws from Bir Hacheim box.

26 May 1942. 4.00 p.m. Offensive starts when General Cruwell feints in the north with mainly Italian divisions.

2 June 1942. 150 Bde box at Got el Ualeb falls; 3000 prisoners taken.

4 June 1942. British 50th Divn escapes by first heading west and then south-east, breaking through Axis lines.

26–27 May 1942. Rommel's real attack with all his armour hooks around the French box at Bir Hacheim.

21st Panzer
15th Panzer

El Adem
box HQ
XIII British Corps

'Cauldron'
battles

Tobruk
Rigel Ridge

Gazala
1st South
African Divn
50th Divn

150 Bde
box

Sabratha
Trento
Brescia
Pavia

Ariete Panzer
Trieste Panzer

'Inevitably, I asked him where he came from. He said, "I'm a Cherman, a Cherman Chew". I hope he escaped capture.'

Individual Germans had always served in considerable numbers in the Foreign Legion. By 1942 there was a company of Panzer Grenadiers in the Afrika Korps largely composed of ex-legionnaires who had either left the Legion before the war or deserted at the outbreak of hostilities. Nevertheless, as Captain Parker discovered, there were still German-born legionaries at Bir Hacheim. These were mostly Communist and Socialist survivors of the Thaelmann★ Battalion, the German contingent to Republican Spain's International Brigade. How many were Jews is not known.

In an order to Rommel dated 13 June 1942, Hitler referred to 'numerous German political refugees with Free French forces' who should be 'immediately wiped out in battle'. Where they escaped being killed in battle they were to be shot out of hand 'unless they have to be temporarily retained for the extraction of information'. Hitler forbade this order being passed on in writing, enabling Rommel to make an ambiguous response. 'We know what to do with this, gentlemen,' he reportedly told his staff, crumpling the message form on which the order arrived. Quite apart from ethical considerations, to shoot prisoners would have gone against Rommel's practice of encouraging the enemy to surrender by cultivating a reputation for magnanimity.

The Italians expected the assault on Bir Hacheim to be something of a walkover. Leutnant Alfred-Ingemar Berndt, one of Goebbels' propaganda experts attached to Gause's staff, had written off the defenders as 'mere Gaullists, swashbucklers, and criminals of twenty different nationalities'. What he failed to understand was the determination of Koenig and his officers to seize the first chance France had been offered since 1940 to avenge the shame of defeat.

Lieutenant-Colonel Romano Prestissimone's 132nd Tank Regiment launched the first assault, advancing with pennants flying and the usual talisman of spare track clattering reassuringly against the inadequate armour of their M13s. Koenig's well-dug-in anti-tank

★ Ernst Thaelmann was the German Communist leader who survived eleven years of imprisonment, only to be murdered by the SS in Buchenwald nine months before the war ended.

gunners waited until the Italians were close enough to be seen through their own dust and then put down a withering barrage. Before long the 132nd had lost thirty-two tanks. Prestissimone had been blown out of three of them himself and, though wounded, was looking for a fourth when he was snatched by some legionnaires in a Bren gun carrier that was hunting down dismounted crews for interrogation. The failure of the Italian assault raised the curtain on the epic siege that would end only after Rommel took personal charge.

Meanwhile, well aware that the enemy did not have the troops and tanks for a fully fledged two-pronged attack, Auchinleck had correctly assumed that Rommel would feint in one direction and strike in the other. But he called it wrong, thinking Rommel would throw the dummy punch at Bir Hacheim and land the real one in the north, with the object of driving straight on to Tobruk.

Crüwell's diversionary attack achieved a certain amount of surprise by starting at mid-afternoon and was fully under way, with the moon well up, when the Axis armour began to move off on the night of 26–27 May. Their progress around Bir Hacheim was monitored by a squadron of South African armoured cars, darting about in the pre-dawn dark, then stopping to listen to the hum of distant tank engines growing into an ominous rumble. Acknowledged experts at the old light cavalry scouting role, the South Africans had learned how to use terrain to get close enough to identify an enemy and, if spotted, the importance of getting off a radio message before they were killed or captured.

As dawn broke, Lieutenant David Parry, the artillery officer who wanted to use anti-aircraft guns against tanks, was standing by his radio near Bir Hacheim when the operator picked up an 'in clear' exchange between a scout car and a rear headquarters. Over the years the ensuing exchange remained etched on Parry's memory and he could make rather a party piece out of it:

SCOUT: There is a cloud of dust to the south. It has the appearance of a military formation.

HQ: There are no, repeat no, troops to your south.

SCOUT: The cloud of dust to the south is growing larger. It is undoubtedly a military formation.

HQ: We repeat, there are no, repeat no, troops to your south.

SCOUT: Through the haze I can now identify tanks . . . possibly German Mark IVs.

HQ: We repeat, there are no, repeat no, troops to your south.

SCOUT: I can now positively identify German Mark IV tanks, together with motorized infantry. It appears to be a large German force.

HQ (sounding irritated): We repeat no, repeat no, forces in your vicinity.

SCOUT: I am counting Mark IVs – one, two, three, four, five, six, seven – there is no, repeat no, doubt that this is a large German force . . . moving at a speed of approximately thirty miles an hour towards El Adem.

HQ (sounding resigned): There are no forces in your area.

SCOUT: I have been spotted by the enemy and am under fire [background noise of exploding shells]. I repeat, it is a large enemy formation . . .

HQ (sounding bored): There are no enemy forces in your area.

SCOUT: It is undoubtedly the Afrika Korps moving at high speed towards El Adem. I am under . . . [silence and end of transmission].

It took the British twenty-four hours to accept that the hook around Bir Hacheim was the real thing and not a feint. By that time the 3rd Indian Cavalry Brigade had been overrun, surprised by artillery and tank fire at about 6.30 a.m. as they were brewing tea for breakfast over sand-and-petrol fires. Eleven officers and more than 200 men were killed and many wounded. Among the 1,000-odd prisoners taken was Sir Walter Cowan, a seventy-one-year-old retired British admiral, captured as he valiantly emptied his revolver at an oncoming German tank. His interrogators discovered that they were dealing with the 3rd Cavalry's 'liaison officer', an ambiguous title Cowan had secured by dint of strenuous string-pulling and an unquenchable desire to smite His Majesty's enemies.*

One of the first to go and check out persistent reports of enemy armour south of the Bir Hacheim box was Major John 'Shan' Hackett,† a regular officer of the 8th King's Royal Irish Hussars, who was commanding a reconnaissance squadron of fast and thinly armoured Honey light tanks. He crested a low ridge when 'there in

---

* Admiral Cowan had won a first DSO fighting with Kitchener (and Churchill) in the 1898 River Nile campaign. In 1943, declared 'too old to be dangerous', he was released by the Italians in a prisoner exchange and promptly joined a commando unit in which he eventually won a second DSO, forty-six years after his first.

† General Sir John Winthrop Hackett, DSO and bar, MC, would be wounded twice in the Western Desert. Later he would command a parachute brigade at Arnhem, where he was wounded for a third time, hidden and nursed by Dutch civilians for over three months and evading capture.

front of me was the whole bloody German army, as far as I could see – coming my way. I put up a black flag to say "Attack!" . . . and like a mug forgot to take it down again. Any tank flying a flag is of course a controlling element and attracts fire, so I attracted all the fire there was. I suppose mine was the first tank in the Eighth Army to be knocked out that day, which was about three minutes after putting up the black flag.' Hackett limped off in search of a new tank. Several of his men were not so lucky. Behind him columns of black oil smoke billowed from their funeral pyres.

But at least the British could now be certain where the *Schwerpunkt*, the main enemy thrust, was coming from. And despite his early gains, it soon began to appear that this time Rommel had underestimated what he was up against. Outflanking the Gazala line was one thing, moving on from there in any meaningful way was quite another. In fact, the Afrika Korps and its allies of the Ariete Division were in a terrible tactical position. They were trapped between the minefields and fortified boxes of the Gazala line on one side and a vastly superior number of British tanks, among them the new Grants, on the other. But, as usual, the British were never quite able to make proper use of their tank superiority and co-ordinate their armour in one devastating simultaneous blow. Instead, Ritchie's four armoured brigades, though their attacks sometimes overlapped, were thrown into battle in a way that meant they were often outnumbered by the Axis armour.

At times the battle took on the fluidity and layered muddle of the encounter at Sidi Rezegh, six months before. As laid down in his original plan, Rommel's 90th Light Division had gone the furthest east, causing havoc among the British rear echelons. They even overran 7th Armoured Division's headquarters, briefly capturing Major-General Francis Messervy, its commander, who slipped his badges of rank off his shirt epaulettes and passed himself off as the officers' mess cook.

'Aren't you a bit old for a private?' a German officer inquired.

'You're right,' Messervy replied with all the mock-indignation he could muster. 'It's a bloody disgrace they've called me up at my age.'

Shortly afterwards, when their captors came under heavy artillery fire, Messervy escaped with some of his staff.

While the 90th Light were harrying hapless headquarters troops and generally panicking the Eighth Army's blunt end into flight, their own supply columns were receiving similar treatment from the British armour, and Rommel called them back. By now Ritchie was beginning to sense victory. 'Rommel on the run,' he signalled Auchinleck, who replied: 'Bravo Eighth Army! Give him the *coup de grâce*.' Here was evidence that his and Dorman-Smith's doubts about Ritchie had been wrong.

Ritchie's optimism was by no means misplaced. Rommel himself appeared to concede that he was on the brink of defeat and might have to surrender. 'I agree that we cannot go on like this,' he told Major Archer-Shee, a British prisoner who had been captured when the Panzers steamrollered over the 3rd Indian Cavalry.* 'If we don't get a convoy through tonight I shall have to ask General Ritchie for terms. You can take a letter to him for me . . .'

Rommel's armoured hook was beginning to weaken through sheer lack of sustenance. If the British armour had been sufficiently organized to attack *en masse* he would have been hard pressed to hold them. A way had to be found to bring water, food, ammunition and petrol through the British minefields and around the two most bothersome Eighth Army boxes from which mobile raiding parties were constantly harassing Rommel's convoys: Bir Hacheim and Got el Ualeb a little to its north, which was held by the British 150 Brigade, mostly Yorkshire Territorials.

In the event, an Axis supply convoy did get through, as Rommel – despite his gloomy prognostication to Archer-Shee – must have guessed it would. Two days before, he had found a route and guided a supply train in himself. German and Italian drivers took their trucks, bumping and lurching, after Rommel's staff car, praying that 'Erwin's' famous intuition had not deserted him. It was the kind of personal attention to detail that defied the Wehrmacht's belief in delegation and drove Rommel's staff officers to near despair as they traipsed after him with frantic radio messages from every part of the battlefield.

With three ways of escape now open, the Germans' Chief of Staff,

---

* Archer-Shee spent two days with several hundred parched Indian soldiers, some obviously close to death, in a makeshift PoW cage not far from the parked vehicles that made up Rommel's tactical HQ. He urged Rommel that, if he could not give his prisoners enough water, he was honour bound to let them go. 'You are getting exactly the same ration of water as the Afrika Korps and myself, half a cup,' Rommel informed him. Shortly afterwards, however, he did exactly what Archer-Shee had urged. Six hundred Indian prisoners were released and told to start walking in a south-westerly direction. They eventually staggered into Bir Hacheim and were evacuated from there.

Gause, urged Rommel to take advantage of them and return the Afrika Korps and the Ariete Division to safe harbour. For even as the west–east supply routes had been established, the Germans were confronted by another setback: the capture of Crüwell. His Storch had been hit by machine-gun fire after straying over the 150 Brigade box. The pilot was killed and Crüwell was extremely lucky to be alive. Seated behind the dead pilot, there was no way he could reach the controls, even had he known what to do with them. But by some aeronautical fluke the little high-wing monoplane made a near-perfect landing unaided and out stepped a shaken but intact Crüwell, to be received by jubilant members of the East Yorkshire Regiment. Later, they served him a gazelle steak for dinner while arrangements were made to evacuate him to Cairo. There he continued to be treated with the courtesies the British and Germans reserved for each other's captured generals. Shown the outside of Shepheard's Hotel, he commented that it would make a wonderful headquarters for Rommel – brave words, considering the dire situation he had left behind.

At that point, only Rommel himself seemed to have faith that he would win the unfolding battle. Dismissing all suggestions of retreat, he delivered a dazzling display of generalship during the next twenty days, running on adrenalin and thirty-minute naps, but seemingly never too tired to make the right decision as he adapted his plans to fit the new realities. First, he concentrated his replenished and rejuvenated armour in a position the Germans called '*Der Hexenkessel*' and the British 'The Cauldron'. To the north and east of this position two ridges provided good anti-tank positions, while to the west a British minefield contributed to his own defence. Ritchie's flailing '*coup de grâce*' increasingly resembled a man pursuing an angry tiger into a shallow pit, and from the Cauldron, Rommel was able to keep the main counter-attack at bay, with enough left over to attack Brigadier Clive Haydon's 150 Brigade at Got el Ualeb with an enormously superior force.

Rommel was impressed by the 'considerable skill and courage' of the British infantry who stopped several Panzers there with their new six-pounder anti-tank guns. But the end was a foregone conclusion. The box was isolated, 150 Brigade was mercilessly shelled and dive-bombed and Ritchie's tanks could not break through the German anti-tank screen to relieve them. After forty-eight hours, Rommel sensed that the will to resist was beginning to wane.

'Wave a white flag and they'll surrender,' he ordered a Panzer Grenadier captain whose men were closing in on what had been some stubbornly held slit-trenches. To the captain's astonishment, the ploy was successful. In a few places the defenders refused to give in, or were never given the chance, but in the end, after the Italian Trieste Division joined the fray from the west, some 3,000 prisoners were taken. Among the dead was Brigadier Haydon.

Unlike Ritchie, Rommel never had any difficulty co-ordinating simultaneous attacks. Indeed, it was almost his speciality. One unhappy witness to the Desert Fox at work at about this time was Edward Tomkins, General Koenig's liaison officer at Bir Hacheim, who had been captured in a sandstorm after losing his way while returning from Ritchie's HQ to the French box.

Taken to Rommel's tactical headquarters, Tomkins found himself in the unique position of being the only man on the battlefield to observe both commanders in action on the same day. The difference could not have been greater. 'At Ritchie's headquarters there were some thirty ADCs dancing about and an awful lot of paperwork,' he would recall. By contrast, Rommel had two signals vehicles, one presumably for outgoing messages and the other for incoming. He was sitting between them in some kind of scout car, barking out orders or writing notes, then handing them to people to deliver to his wireless operators, and dashing off to lead from the front when he judged the situation to be critical. Tomkins who, unknown to his captors, spoke fluent German was 'deeply impressed'.

Rommel's frequent excursions to the sharp end had obvious risks. Soon Westphal and Gause paid the price of sticking too close to him and were in a field hospital with shell wounds that would send them back to Germany for the rest of the summer. Rommel himself had one narrow escape after another but lost nothing more than the heel of his boot to a piece of shrapnel. After his headquarters vehicles were bracketed by a particularly accurate 25-pounder salvo, his clerk Munninger found himself briefly alone with Rommel, all his surviving staff officers having run off into the desert. 'Don't worry, they'll be back,' said Rommel.

Despite the enormous hole in the Gazala line where the 150 Brigade box had once been, the Eighth Army commander continued to believe that he had Rommel on the ropes. But again he failed to concentrate all his available forces into a German-style *Schwerpunkt*, and his Operation

'Aberdeen' was a shambles. It began as a night attack shortly before 3 a.m. with an artillery barrage that would have been impressive had it not, as a result of faulty intelligence, fallen on empty desert. As the dawn came up, British and Indian infantry, supported by Grant, Crusader and Matilda tanks, advanced on an enemy who, warned by the useless barrage, was expecting them. Once again Rommel had been given far too much time (and he never needed much) to deploy his usual screen of 88-mm guns.

Among those on the receiving end was the fire-eating Rea Leakey, the Kenya-born tank officer who had won a bar to his MC fighting with the Australian infantry at Tobruk and now – on leave between safe staff jobs in Syria and Iraq – had run off to rejoin his old regiment. He was manning a 37-mm gun in the turret of one of the new Grants in place of a gunner who had been wounded.

In the first second we must have received at least four direct hits from armour-piercing shells. The engine was knocked out, a track was broken and one shell hit the barrel of the 75-mm gun and broke it. Then quite a heavy high-explosive shell dropped on the mantlet of my 37-mm gun and pushed it back against the recoil springs . . . I suffered nothing more than a 'singing in the ears'. But a splinter hit the subaltern [the tank commander] in the head and he fell to the floor of the turret dead . . . Almost every tank in that battle met with the same treatment and the whole line was halted on the crest of that small ridge.

Rommel was amazed at the incompetence of Ritchie's attack. 'What is the advantage of enjoying overall superiority if you allow your enemy to smash your formations one after the other?' he wrote in the journal he was keeping as the basis for a future book.★

Having won the day, Rommel now headed south-west for his unfinished business at Bir Hacheim. There, Koenig had rejected a surrender note, scribbled on a signals pad, that Rommel had sent by Tomkins' driver:

Any further resistance will only serve to shed more useless blood. You will suffer the same fate as the two [*sic*] British brigades which were exterminated

★ *The Rommel Papers*, edited by the British military historian Basil Liddell-Hart, would be published posthumously after the war.

at Got el Ualeb two days ago . . . We shall cease fire when you raise the white flag and come towards us without arms. Rommel.

While he had been seeing off Operation Aberdeen, Bir Hacheim had been under relentless aerial attack, but the Luftwaffe had paid a heavy price, for the box was well within range of RAF airfields. Stuka dive-bombers had a top speed of less than 250 mph and, though terrifying for those beneath them, were as easy a target as a plump pheasant for any half-decent shot in the cockpit of a Hurricane or even a slower Kittyhawk. '*Bravo! Merci Pour la RAF,*' Koenig signalled after one particularly successful interception left the wrecks of more than a dozen Axis aircraft (some reports say just over twenty) smouldering around his perimeter. '*Merci à vous pour le sport,*' came the RAF's reply.

For them, the good times soon ended. The Germans responded by increasing the number of Me-109Fs flying escort to the dive-bombers, and the RAF had nothing to match them. In one encounter, Hans Joachim Marseille,★ Goering's twenty-three-year-old desert ace, took just eleven minutes to shoot down five lumbering Kittyhawks from a South African squadron, though not before another nine Stukas were littering the desert.

'Smiling Albert' Kesselring, who commanded all the Axis air forces in the Mediterranean, found these losses, and the French resistance generally, enough to wipe the customary grin from his face. Even when the RAF failed to break through the fighter screen he wrapped around his dive-bombers, the Bofors anti-aircraft guns at Bir Hacheim could be almost as effective. Kesselring urged Rommel to stop pussy-footing around and to make good the threat he had made to Koenig to put in the kind of overwhelming assault that had carried the day against 150 Brigade. Free from his commitments in the Cauldron, Rommel took personal charge of the siege, and Kesselring flew to the scene from his headquarters in Rome to make sure no effort was being spared.

Despite his earlier reservations, more close air support was laid on

---

★ Marseille, the descendant of French Huguenots who fled to Germany in the seventeenth century, died in a flying accident four months after the air battles over Bir Hacheim, having shot down no fewer than 158 British aircraft, more than any other flier in both world wars, including the legendary Baron von Richthofen. He is commemorated by a pyramid grave, not far from El Alamein.

and German combat engineers managed to seize a hillock used by the Free French as an observation post for their artillery, and even to go briefly beyond it, before they were pushed back. For the first time there was close-quarter fighting. Panzer Grenadiers under Lieutenant Colonel Ernst-Gunther Baade★ entered a warren of French weapons pits around the old Ottoman fort and, after a hard fight, ended up digging in only 200 yards from its crumbling mud walls. The noose was undoubtedly tightening.

Air attacks became heavier and more frequent. A Stuka could carry a 1,000-pound bomb under its fuselage and four smaller ones under its wings. One bomb hit a field dressing station and killed nineteen wounded men. Another hit an ammunition dump, another a food store. Water was short. Sometimes the doctors and British nurses did not even have enough to clean wounds. Still the Free French hung on. Two years after the summer of France's defeat and occupation, there was talk of 'reborn glory', of a Verdun in the Sands.

'General Koenig,' said de Gaulle in a broadcast from London, 'know and tell your troops that the whole of France is looking at you and you are her pride.'

Koenig replied: 'We are surrounded. Our thoughts are always with you. Long live Free France.'

Much to Rommel's chagrin, though, their encirclement was not complete. After fifteen days and nights, feeling that enough had been done for the Eighth Army and Gallic pride, 7th Armoured Division HQ (Koenig's immediate superiors in the chain of command) ordered a breakout. It took place at night, under constant illumination from German parachute flares which revealed the garrison's agonizingly slow progress along a lane about 150 yards wide that had been cleared through a minefield. Panzer Grenadiers tried to plug the gap and there was savage fighting. In the darkness cohesion broke down, trucks went off in different directions and some of them detonated mines. Koenig's British driver and mistress, Susan Travers, the only woman ever to become an officer of the French Foreign Legion,† has recorded

---

★ Baade claimed Scots descent on his mother's side and had been known to go into action wearing a kilt and carrying a claymore.

† After the war, Miss Travers was awarded the Légion d'Honneur and in 2000, wheelchair-bound at the age of ninety, she published her memoirs of the war, *Tomorrow to Be Brave*.

her recollections of the nightmare drive as she led the way through the minefield and a terrifying gauntlet of enemy fire: 'Shells were falling around us like rain and sudden, violent explosions tore the night, showering our car with burning metal. The German cannon were upon us . . . The wounded who could walk were ordered to get out and continue on foot to lessen the weight of the vehicles picking their way through the mines. From starting off as a reasonably well-planned evacuation it had become a shambolic flight.'

Shambolic or not, 2,400 of Bir Hacheim's 3,700 original defenders – among them Pierre Messmer, a future French prime minister – managed to reach the safety of the British lines. Not all of them, however, seem to have been pleased by the order to abandon their position and break out. Lieutenant Parry would recall that when some of 'these tough, bearded Frenchmen' passed through his mobile repair workshop, 'they were almost in tears when they described their anger and frustration . . . They would have preferred to stay and die as their predecessors had done [in 1916] at Verdun.' In sheer scale, the siege of Bir Hacheim had, of course, been nothing like Verdun ('They shall not pass') where 350,000 Frenchmen lost their lives. But Koenig's defiance had held up and deflated Rommel, inflicting casualties he could ill afford on some of his best troops, and had restored the deeply wounded pride of a defeated and occupied France. As de Gaulle proclaimed in a characteristic flight of rhetoric: 'When a ray of glory touched the bloodstained brows of her soldiers at Bir Hacheim, the world recognized France.' And in the fullness of time he would bestow the name Bir Hacheim on one of Paris's Métro stations.

Despite the loss of the Gazala line's two most southerly defensive boxes, neither Auchinleck nor Ritchie considered the Eighth Army to have been beaten. On the contrary, Auchinleck was convinced that Rommel's troops would soon be exhausted and overstretched. He had seen it happen at Sidi Rezegh the previous November. It was just a matter of outlasting them. After all, thanks largely to improved recovery techniques, the British still had more tanks than Rommel.

And so it might have been, had not the Allied fighting soldiers been so poorly served by their British senior officers, those professionals of brigadier rank and above with their scars and medals from the trenches of 1914–18, spared by a capricious fate to lead the next generation. They were, in the main, good men: brave, courteous, caring (if absent) husbands and fathers, careful of the men's welfare whenever possible, considerate of one another's feelings almost always. Above all, they were *clubbable*, for no army could tolerate too many Dorman-Smiths (or Wingates or Montgomerys, for that matter) and who could deny that any large organization works better if there is among its senior executives a mutual respect based on common values?

But the men around Ritchie lacked one particular virtue that the Germans had in abundance: the habit of instant obedience. 'We made it out a favour if an order was obeyed,' laments a British soldier in Kipling's poem★ about a battalion that cracked in action. There is no better epitaph for Ritchie's immediate subordinates. And the blame for this must lie with Auchinleck for putting Ritchie over the greatly more experienced Gott and Willoughby Norrie – both senior to him in the Army List – in the first place. To get over his understandable embarrassment at finding himself in this position, and because he very much needed not only their advice but their full co-operation, Ritchie consulted them at every opportunity. Thus, the Eighth Army was virtually being run by a triumvirate.

A photograph taken at the time shows Ritchie in conference with Norrie and Gott. Norrie, obviously the older man with his white moustache, is pointing something out on a map to an attentive Ritchie. An uninformed observer would assume that Norrie was in command. Contemporary photographs of Rommel in a similar situation could not be more different, usually depicting him in the act of giving orders to frankly admiring subordinates.

The atmosphere of debate that governed Ritchie's relations with his corps commanders permeated the upper echelon of his entire command. Just as in Kipling's poem, 'every little drummer 'ad 'is rights an' wrongs to mind,' so it seems every Eighth Army divisional or brigade commander had the right to question an order he disagreed with. In a campaign where so much depended on speed it could be disastrous.

By 12 June, the seventeenth day of Rommel's offensive, Ritchie had only seventy tanks left in running order, which for the first time was fewer than the enemy. The Eighth Army, which only a week

---

★ Called 'That Day', the poem, told through the eyes of a soldier shamefully routed with his comrades during a colonial skirmish, starts: 'We was rotten 'fore we started – we was never disciplined.'

before had seemed to have a great victory within its grasp, was now desperately trying to hold its ground at Knightsbridge, a defensive box in the central sector. Nevertheless, after returning to Cairo on 12 June from a brief visit to Eighth Army headquarters, Auchinleck felt able to report to London: '. . . realities of situation are being faced calmly and resolutely. Morale of troops appears excellent.'

By the time he sent that message, Auchinleck's 'realities' were twenty-four hours out of date and the situation was beginning to unravel fast. The British armour and infantry were trying to regroup in the Knightsbridge box and along the nearby Rigel Ridge, where the Guards, supported by some South African anti-tank gunners, were doing their best to hold the German armour and bar their passage to Tobruk. First of all the Panzers hit the Rigel Ridge, where the defenders fought until the enemy tanks were right on top of them. Captain N. B. Hanmer of the Royal Sussex Regiment, who visited the scene some months later, found that 'Almost every gun had the body of a Scots Guardsman drooped across the shoulder piece or slumped over the breech. Several men were still crouching in slit trenches with rifles, as if they had engaged the enemy with .303 when their guns had been put out of action. There was an officer lying on his face, his finger round the trigger of a Bren gun . . . They seem to have served even in death.'

The remnants of the Scots Guards retired into the Knightsbridge box, which was not much of a sanctuary. The air above it seemed to be in the grip of a sandstorm, so thick was the pall of dust rising from the shells and bombs that crashed around its hard-dug slit-trenches. As the German tanks and infantry edged ever closer, it was decided to abandon the box rather than lose more good infantry, and a force of Matilda tanks under Lieutenant-Colonel Henry Bowreman Foote was sent to cover the withdrawal.

Foote, heavily bandaged around the neck as the result of a shrapnel wound, was already something of a legend for his coolness under fire, often leaving the relative safety of his command tank to direct operations on foot. The terrain at Knightsbridge was so flat that his Matildas had no cover from anti-tank fire, so when the enemy started to get his range he moved his tanks either forward or backwards a few hundred yards to confuse him. 'Luckily, with the help of a sandstorm and the use of smoke we were able to hold out until dark,' he would recall, 'but at the end of the engagement we only had seven operational tanks left.'

Foote's own tank could move but not fight. Twenty-nine direct hits had failed to penetrate its thick hide, though one, against all odds, eventually put it out of action. Puzzled because his two-pounder had suddenly stopped working, Foote had stuck his head out of the turret hatch to discover that the barrel was, 'splayed out like the skin of a banana; an enemy shell had exploded on its muzzle. Like Jock Campbell at Sidi Rezegh, Foote would receive a Victoria Cross for sustained courage over several days of intense fighting.

But individual valour could not save the Eighth Army, even though Rommel's men were so exhausted they were beyond fear or hunger. All they wanted was to sleep, which they did whenever they got the chance, no matter how uncomfortable or dangerous it might be. Only the awesome sight of what they had done to the British at Knightsbridge gave them hope that the end might be near.

His eyes smarting with smoke, dust and fatigue, Rolf-Werner Völker passed through Knightsbridge in the back of a truck, shortly after it had been taken. He could hardly believe what he was seeing: 'It was like a naughty child had had a tantrum and thrown his toys all over the room,' he recalled. 'There were upturned guns, trucks and tanks everywhere – a lot of them burning.' Rommel passed through the abandoned British box stony-faced, but Munninger, his young Schwabian clerk, was shocked: 'I had never seen so many dead Englishmen before.'

The withdrawal from Knightsbridge marked the end of the Gazala line and the beginning of what the Eighth Army, angry, self-mocking and uncertain who to blame for their humiliation, called the 'Gazala Gallop' – an eastward stampede* out of Libya and back to the Egyptian border for all but the men who remained in Tobruk.

Meanwhile, what of Fortress Tobruk?

'Things are going very well indeed with us here, as spirits are very

---

* Except for the two surviving brigades of the British 50th Division who, instead of trying to disengage in an easterly direction, attacked in a westerly one, smashing through the enemy lines and heading briefly towards Tripoli before turning south then east, thus bypassing the Axis concentration along the coast.

high, and I do not think morale could be better,' wrote the South African garrison commander, Major-General Bernard Klopper, to a friend at GHQ Cairo on the evening of 16 June. He must have been blissfully unaware of the calamity that had just befallen the Eighth Army at Knightsbridge. 'We are all looking forward to a good stand and we are supported by the very best British troops.'

When war broke out in 1939, Klopper had been a newly promoted lieutenant-colonel, one of white South Africa's tiny cadre of professional soldiers. He was determined to 'go up north' and by the end of 1941 he was a full colonel on the staff of the 2nd South African Division in the Western Desert. Six months later, after a brief spell as a brigadier, Klopper had become the major-general commanding the 2nd South African Division, and it was now the South Africans' turn to deny Tobruk to the enemy until the tide of battle turned. It was the role that had won Morshead and his Australians so much glory, but Auchinleck did not see Klopper or anybody else as another Morshead.

Although possession of Tobruk was bound to ease Rommel's supply problems significantly, should his advance continue into Egypt, Auchinleck tended to regard the port as a Churchillian obsession that got in the way of more important things. He had already made it clear in an instruction to Ritchie that he did not intend to hold on to Tobruk at all costs and, as he would admit in a post-war interview, he personally 'would have been glad if it hadn't been there . . . It dominated the tactics and strategy of the battle. It was a sort of lodestone.'

This was not what he told Churchill at the time. On the contrary, Auchinleck's policy on Tobruk was full of obfuscation, evasion and downright dissembling. When Churchill was about to leave London to see Roosevelt in Washington, he sought guarantees, not for the first time, that Ritchie's withdrawal from the Gazala line would not mean abandoning Tobruk. 'Presume there is no question in any case of giving up Tobruk,' he cabled Auchinleck, to which Auchinleck replied that while 'he did not intend that the Eighth Army should be besieged in Tobruk,' he 'had no intention whatever of giving up Tobruk'. This reply, Churchill noted mildly enough, 'seemed to us equivocal'.

Auchinleck had ordered Ritchie to fall back on a line that would still be west of Tobruk but, to add to the confusion, Ritchie, in the independent way of the Eighth Army, had decided that he would nevertheless prepare Tobruk for a siege. In this he had the support and encouragement of Gott. The pair of them had flown into Tobruk in a captured German Storch and hurriedly inspected Klopper's preparations, which Gott declared to be 'a nice tidy show'.

Rommel would probably have court-martialled a pair of senior officers who disregarded his orders, but Auchinleck saw their defiance as a way to get Churchill off his back. He gave Ritchie his blessing, saying that he realized Tobruk 'may be isolated for a short period until our counter-stroke can be launched'. Then he told Churchill that 'General Ritchie is putting into Tobruk what he considers to be an adequate force to hold it even should it become temporarily isolated . . .' No doubt Auchinleck did not think a siege was likely and had been led by Ritchie to believe that the Eighth Army was still capable of a counter-attack that would push a tired Afrika Korps back to Gazala and beyond. But by compromising and trying to please everybody, Auchinleck paved the way for what would be the biggest British setback of the war in North Africa.

The truth was that, even had Klopper been a better field commander – even as good as Morshead – his command was never really anything but a sop to placate Churchill: Klopper simply did not have the men or the equipment to withstand the blow that was about to fall on him. True, he had a larger garrison than Morshead, but this was only because he had inherited a good part of the Eighth Army's rear echelon to ensure the smooth working of the port and attend to all the tasks required to keep a large mechanized army in the field.

There were about 10,000 of these base troops, stevedores and every kind of mechanical and electrical technician, as well as signallers and hospital staff and the cooks and drivers needed to keep them all going. A couple of thousand of them were South African blacks of various labour companies who, though in uniform, were unarmed and were essentially regarded as non-combatants. As for fighting troops, Klopper had about the same number as the previous garrison but was trying to hold a slightly bigger area, about 170 square miles, within a perimeter that ran about thirty miles inland and for twenty miles along the coast.

He had plenty of artillery, including some 155-mms, the Eighth Army's biggest guns. Two South African infantry brigades held the coastal, western and southern parts of the perimeter. An Indian Army brigade of two battalions – Mahrattas and Gurkhas – and one battalion of Cameron Highlanders held the south-eastern sector, nearest to the port, which was ten miles away. In addition, as a result of the with-drawal from the Gazala line, the Coldstream Guards and the remnants of two more British infantry battalions came into the fortress, bringing the total of anti-tank guns up to about seventy.

Although there were plenty of Bofors anti-aircraft guns, Tobruk had virtually no air cover. The RAF had withdrawn from its airfields around Gambut and the only fighters with the range to come back over the port were a few slow-moving, US-made Kittyhawks, fitted with long-range tanks, that were no match for the German Messer-schmitts.

Brigadier Andrew Willison, who had commanded Tobruk's armour during the previous siege and now had a total of fifty-four tanks at his disposal, thought the perimeter defences left much to be desired. Over the last seven months, several minefields had been pillaged to shore up the Gazala line and the anti-tank ditch had been allowed to silt up in places. During the previous siege all three infantry brigades had been on the perimeter, but Klopper had put one of them into positions along the coast. Transport was not properly camouflaged, Willison felt, and most of the artillery was too far back to be fully effective. He took his complaints to Klopper, but nothing was done.

Brian Lello, a South African war correspondent, observed that Klopper's own lack of experience of battle command was amply reflected by those surrounding him, who compounded inexperience with constant bickering. 'He had not a single professional soldier on the operational side of his staff,' wrote Lello. In addition, 'there was an unresolved conflict of personalities among what should have been his closely knit staff. Since he had been abruptly called on to take command, there had been no time to weld together his own management team. Events had moved too fast for him to take up the reins properly.'

In the garrison's first contact with the enemy, the Transvaal Scottish Regiment killed eighty Italians and took 200 prisoner, and for three days it seemed that Klopper's confidence was justified. Some Axis troops, mostly Italian, came up to the western and southern parts of the perimeter and there was a little patrol activity around its south-eastern corner. But Rommel's two Panzer Divisions, plus the Ariete and the 90th Light, seemed to have passed Tobruk by in pursuit of the Eighth Army. Then, as dusk fell on 19 June, they disengaged from the retreating Eighth Army and headed back towards Tobruk.

In the dark, this was a difficult operation for Rommel's exhausted 'Afrikaners', as he liked to call them, but all the Panzers and their supporting infantry were in place well before zero hour, which was 5.20 a.m. – dawn. Among them, shivering with the cold and anticipation, was Heinz-Werner Schmidt, the young officer who had been on Rommel's staff.

We lay on our bellies . . . to one side we heard the rat-tat of the Vickers gun, followed by a shorter but quicker burst from a German machine-gun . . . then all was quiet again . . . day broke. Our guns opened up. First singly then with growing intensity . . . The first shells burst only a few yards ahead of us. I began to fear we should have to fire a Very light as a warning and that would betray our position. But the barrage crept forward. Then a full-throated roar: our Stukas were approaching. Carefully we laid out the identification strips we had brought with us. We had been given the taste of our own Stuka bombs before . . .

Rommel had crept up on Tobruk like a tiger stalking a tethered goat. His plan of attack was simple: stealth would achieve maximum surprise and the kill would be made with a stunning Blitzkrieg of air and armoured might. Kesselring had arranged for every German and Italian aircraft in North Africa, and even some based in Crete, to attack Tobruk and its perimeter in a series of continuous raids. 'Never have I seen such a mountain of dust and smoke that towered in the sky after those bombers had done their work,' one Coldstream Guards officer recalled. 'They came again and again and I realized that from now on we should get this hourly . . .'

Sergeant Ike Rosmarin of the 6th South African Infantry Brigade, on the south-west sector of the perimeter, found the waves of Stuka attacks 'terrifying'. Worst of all, he would recall, 'was the fact that we didn't know what was happening as there were no orders from our officers. Confusion reigned, with fear and panic. Rumours were rife and facts were few.'

A good many of the Stukas' bombs landed on a single Indian battalion, the 2/5th Mahratta Light Infantry, in the south-eastern sector. Entire platoons of Mahrattas emerged, trembling, from their collapsing trenches to surrender to the first Panzer Grenadiers they saw. Through this breach in the line poured well over 100 German and Italian tanks, and shortly after midday Rommel and his staff were among the lead tanks overlooking the port. The Desert Fox has left his own account: 'On we went. Soon we reached the slope down to the town. A British strongpoint held on here with outstanding tenacity. I sent Second Lieutenant von Schlippenbach to call on the defenders to surrender. The Tommies' response was to pour fire on our staff vehicles. Our outrider, Lance-Corporal Huber, after a time managed to storm the position with six anti-aircraft gunners and succeeded in silencing it with grenades.'

By late afternoon all that stood between the German armour and Tobruk town and harbour were some British and South African gunners firing over open sights. The time they bought enabled army engineers and the Navy's permanent shore-party to start demolitions, but it was too late to destroy anything but a fraction of the stockpiled a million and a half gallons of fuel and 130,000 artillery rounds. Even better news for thirsty Panzer crews was the discovery of a warehouse full of Löwenbräu beer, brewed under a pre-war licence in Egypt.

In the narrow lanes between the mud brick houses around the port, sailors with rifles tried to keep the Panzer Grenadiers at bay while the demolition parties did what they could before trying to get away in small boats. These were wickedly vulnerable to the tanks and guns gathering above the port. 'Shoot, man, shoot! You can almost spit into the harbour!' Rommel yelled at the commander of an 88-mm anti-tank gun who hesitated momentarily. Captain Frank Smith, the senior naval officer in Tobruk and among the last to leave, was mortally wounded when the lighter he had boarded was hit.

At the garrison hospital, German and British wounded lay alongside each other: the hospital had been captured, but the British doctors and nurses were so hard-pressed that they hardly noticed. One of their patients, Lieutenant (later Major) A. O. McGinley of the Royal Tank Regiment, recorded that, although German wounded had been coming through their hands for some time, 'it wasn't until they realized that some of the surgeons working alongside them were Germans too' that the British medical staff realized what had happened.★

★ Eventually, said McGinley, a pattern developed whereby a team of mixed British and German doctors would visit the wards and discuss each patient. And when a male orderly complained that kit was being looted from the hospital and it transpired that Italian soldiers were to blame, 'the German doctors gave sharp orders; the Italians were booted out and a notice went up on the gate saying, "British and German personnel only"'.

According to the war diary of 21st Panzer, the town and port of Tobruk was in German hands by 7 p.m. – some fourteen hours after the attack had started. At what point Klopper realized that the game was up is unclear. Some time during the late afternoon, before he and his staff made a dash for the western side of the perimeter, he reportedly cried out: 'My crust is broken!' The metaphor was apt: Rommel had hammered a triangular wedge, like a slice of pie, through the south-east corner of Klopper's defences, with the apex at the port.

Nevertheless, most of Klopper's command was entirely intact. The South African infantry still held the western and southern sectors or were dug in uselessly, just as Willison had pointed out, along the coast. The majority of them had not fired a shot. They were all volunteers and, in the words of one British liaison officer, 'itching to fight'.

As Klopper and his staff agonized over what to do next, darkness fell over a Tobruk lit by orange flame from blazing buildings and alive with the crackle of thousands of .303 rifle rounds going off in blazing ammunition dumps. The Germans, exhausted and wary of snipers, bedded down where they could. Sometimes within hearing distance, isolated parties of British and South African troops did the same thing, knowing that, at best, the morning would bring capture.

Gunner W. A. Lewis was among the men of 202 coastal defence battery who, having spiked their guns, took shelter in one of the cold concrete-lined tunnels the Italians had built. After midnight, his battery commander, Captain Scott Atkinson, asked for volunteers to crawl with him to the officers' mess, about 100 yards distant, to 'liberate' some bottles of gin. The gunners got as drunk as lords, consuming a dozen bottles and singing patriotic songs such as 'There'll Always Be an England' while, as Lewis recalled, 'all appeared quiet outside, except for occasional snatches of 'Deutschland über Alles'. With daybreak, German troops entered the tunnel and took the gunners prisoner. 'The town resembled a shambles,' Lewis recalled. 'Bodies lay everywhere . . . At what was once the town square we found thousands of other prisoners . . . My God, the humiliation of it all!'

Less than twenty-four hours after the start of Rommel's offensive, Klopper sent a message from the western perimeter saying that his mobile troops would try to break out and the rest would 'resist to the last man'. Four and a half hours later, having received an erroneous report that tanks were massing against one of his South African brigades, Klopper sent out emissaries under a white flag. 'They've surrendered?' asked one bewildered young South African soldier. 'But why? We haven't beaten them yet.'

Last to lay down their arms were the Cameron Highlanders, who held out until the morning of 22 June, when it became obvious that there had been a general capitulation. While some of his men tried to escape on foot, the Camerons' commanding officer, Lieutenant-Colonel Colin Duncan, marched his battalion into captivity with heads high and pipes playing the regimental march 'Pibroch o' Donuil Dhu'. An over-zealous German major, objecting to this display of Scots swagger, tried to order the Camerons off the road, and Duncan felled him with a blow of his fist.* Some 200 of the Camerons tried to escape on foot, but most were rounded up. A truck convoy containing about 400 British soldiers, of whom half were Coldstream Guards, did manage to reach the Eighth Army, having found a way through the Italians in the south-west, before turning east through endless German supply columns. For weeks after its fall, a steady trickle of escapees would contrive to reach British lines, some with the assistance of 'Popski's Private Army', the smallest of all the special forces, run by the White Russian, Vladimir Peniakoff.

Shortly after Klopper went into captivity with the majority of the Tobruk garrison, Rommel allowed him to address his fellow prisoners through a loudspeaker at a temporary PoW cage in Derna. He was heckled and booed and had to withdraw without delivering his message. 'Everyone believed he had sold out to the enemy,' Gunner Lewis explained. After the war, Klopper faced a court of inquiry but was exonerated.

Tobruk was the second-largest British capitulation of the Second World War, after Singapore. In all, 35,000 prisoners were taken, of whom 13,400 were South Africans, 2,500 Indians and 19,000 British, mostly base troops, including sailors. 'Defeat is one thing, disgrace is another,' said Churchill when he heard of its fall. His humiliation was

---

* This incident was widely attested to by South African ex-prisoners on their release from an Italian PoW camp in 1943 (see *Daily Express*, 24/4/43). It is not mentioned in the Camerons' regimental history because, as Colonel Duncan's son Andrew pointed out to the authors, it was written by his formidable father who 'didn't want to seem to be blowing his own trumpet'.

all the greater for having the news broken to him by Roosevelt during a visit to the White House.★

Tobruk fell on Auchinleck's fifty-eighth birthday. Four days later, he fired Ritchie and, accompanied by Dorman-Smith, took personal command of the Eighth Army, which was attempting to stop Rommel at Mersa Matruh, about 220 miles to the east and well inside Egypt.

It was near Matruh that Private Adam Wakenshaw of the Durham Light Infantry found himself part of the crew on one of the older and not very effective two-pounder anti-tank guns. With their first shot they hit a German half-track towing a light gun, but retaliation was swift and accurate. His left arm blown off above the elbow, Wakenshaw used his one good arm to load and fire five more rounds, while another man aimed. The Germans responded, killing the gun-aimer and leaving Wakenshaw, blown aside by the blast, with more grievous wounds. Stubbornly, the twenty-eight-year-old Geordie dragged himself back to his gun, put another round into the breech and was in the act of firing it when he was killed by a direct hit. He was awarded a posthumous VC. Shortly after Wakenshaw's death, his battalion abandoned the position he and his comrades had given their lives for.

Once again, and quite inexplicably to so many of its front-line troops, the Eighth Army was in retreat. Auchinleck had decided to pull the Eighth Army back to the place he had borne in mind for some time as a defensive position of last resort: El Alamein.

★ General Ismay, Churchill's chief of staff, watched as the US President silently passed his guest the pink message-slip he had just been given and for the first time saw Churchill wince.

While Rommel was pushing the Eighth Army back into Egypt, his desert adviser, the Hungarian adventurer László Almasy, was leading a small convoy of four vehicles south from the Axis base at Gialo. It was the start of Operation 'Salaam', a 4,200-kilometre (2,600-mile) trek across the Great Sand Sea to infiltrate two German spies into the Nile Valley and thence to Cairo.

True, the Panzer Army still had its 'little Fellers' as an unrivalled if unwitting source of information on British dispositions and intentions. In addition, Cairo was a notorious hotbed of valuable gossip and rumour. But the Abwehr (German military intelligence), foreseeing that the leak through the US military liaison office must inevitably be plugged sooner or later, had decided to put in an agent of their own. They had just the man for the job, kitted up and ready to go: a German-born Egyptian citizen named Johannes Eppler, otherwise known as Hussein Ghaffar. And in Almasy, Rommel had just the man to put Eppler in place.

In *The English Patient*, the fictional Almasy reluctantly gives the Germans his desert maps in return for the loan of a light aircraft in order to recover the body of his mistress from a cave. In real life, Almasy was unquestionably an enthusiastic supporter of the German war effort and quite possibly an Axis spy well before the conflict began.*

The son of a landed but untitled Austro-Hungarian family, Ladislaus Edouard de Almasy was born in 1895 in Borostyanko, now Bernstein, in eastern Austria. His father, a noted explorer in some of the remoter parts of Asia, sent him to finish his education at a small private school in Eastbourne, on the south coast of England, to perfect his knowledge

---

* How far a novelist is justified in bending the facts about a historical personage – even a little-known one like Almasy – to fit a work of fiction is, of course, a subject for hoary debate. But Michael Ondaatje, the author of *The English Patient*, might easily have avoided any suggestion of misrepresentation by giving his protagonist a fictitious name.

of English and learn the ways of what was then the world's most admired and envied imperial élite. Paternal Anglophilia★ notwith-standing, when the First World War broke out in 1914, the young Almasy became a fighter pilot in the infant Austro-Hungarian air force, going into action against Britain's ally, Russia.

Some uncertainty surrounds László Almasy's claim to the title of Count. A passionate royalist, he claimed to have been elevated to the aristocracy by the last of the Habsburg kings, the exiled Karl IV, in return for his help in two vain post-First World War attempts to restore the Austro-Hungarian monarchy. Although known as Count Almasy in pre-war Egypt, he never used the title in his native country. There is similar uncertainty about his sexuality. Although portrayed in *The English Patient* as the passionate lover of another man's wife, he was known to his inter-war acquaintances as an active homosexual. There exists written evidence, in the form of love letters, of an affair between him and a young German officer who would subsequently be killed in action.

Almasy, a big-boned, hawk-nosed man of undoubted courage and resourcefulness, made his Egyptian début in 1926 when, as representa-tive of the Austrian Steyr motorcar company, he test-drove one of their vehicles from Alexandria to Khartoum. He followed this with a series of gruelling and hazardous geographical and cartographic expeditions into the deep desert. These paralleled, and more than once overlapped with, the pioneering use of the motor vehicle in desert exploration by the LRDG founder, Ralph Bagnold. In this period, Almasy's outstanding coup was the discovery of prehistoric paintings of swimming men in a cave, deep inside the massive and forbidding Gilf Kebir plateau, proving that there must once have been abundant water in one of the most arid regions on earth.

★ In later years, the Almasy family's English friends would include the eccentric, pro-Nazi Lord Redesdale, two of whose daughters, Unity and Diana Mitford, were inter-wars guests at the family Schloss, Burg Bernstein. Unity Mitford, infatuated with Hitler, would achieve notoriety by attempting suicide while visiting Germany on the outbreak of the Second World War; one sister, Nancy, would achieve post-war fame as a satirical novelist, biographer and essayist (the inventor of 'U and non-U'); Diana married Sir Oswald Mosley, the British fascist leader, and was interned with him during the war. By contrast, a fourth Mitford daughter, Jessica, inhabited the extreme left of the political spectrum and, living in California, wrote trenchantly on American social and political foibles.

Intriguingly, that particular discovery was made during a joint expedition in 1932, in which Almasy shared leadership with Wing Commander H. G. Penderel, a British intelligence agent, and which included four future leading lights of the LRDG: Patrick Clayton, Rupert Harding-Newman, Guy Prendergast and William Kennedy Shaw. Bagnold would later affirm that Shaw 'never trusted [Almasy]' to start with, having no doubt that he was a spy for future enemies, Italy and Germany. And it is clear that official British suspicions of Almasy were the reason for his expulsion from Egypt in 1938, despite his personal friendship with Prince Kemal ed Din, desert-loving younger son of Egypt's King Fuad.

It was Rommel who gave Almasy the opportunity to return to the desert he loved, three years later, his attention having been drawn to Almasy's published accounts of his desert expeditions.* By that time Hungary was in alliance with Nazi Germany and, with the approval of the Hungarian dictator, Admiral Horthy, Almasy was seconded from his country's air force to Rommel's staff with the honorary rank of captain in the Luftwaffe. As desert adviser, Almasy undoubtedly had the knowledge and expertise to create a German long-range desert group to rival the one sponsored by Wavell and created by Bagnold.

But Rommel, the master of the big battlefield, had no time and little inclination for such sideshow activities, and Almasy found himself limited to providing the Germans with maps indicating the location of tracks and waterholes and giving advice on desert survival techniques. For him Operation Salaam was an opportunity to demonstrate what a German long-range desert group might have achieved, given the chance.

Johannes Eppler, the spy he was to conduct as far as the Nile valley, was the son of a German Jewish father and an 'Aryan' German mother, a *Mischling* who, under different circumstances, would surely have qualified for admission to one of Hitler's death camps. After his father's death, Eppler's mother married an influential Egyptian who adopted the boy and had him converted to Islam. Under the name of Hussein Ghaffar, Eppler grew up the typical sprig of a wealthy Cairene family: a spoiled playboy addicted to gambling, drink, fast cars and faster women. The Abwehr spotted him early on as a potential asset, a

---

* *Récentes explorations dans le Désert Libyique (1932–36)*, pub. 1936 by the Geographical Society of Egypt; *Unbekannte Sahara*, pub. 1939, Leipzig.

German (notwithstanding his 'tainted' blood) who could pass as an Arab. The Abwehr chief in Turkey recruited Eppler in 1937 and had him sent to Germany for training.

Eppler's partner and wireless operator for the forthcoming operation in Cairo was Peter Sanstede, who had worked on oil rigs in the United States, spoke good American-English and could pass as a Scandinavian-American. They seemed an ideal combination, but Almasy quickly conceived none too high an opinion of either and derisively nicknamed them 'Pit and Pan'. Nor, as his diary* of Operation Salaam reveals, did Almasy have a very high opinion of the three members of the Brandenburgers (the Abwehr's shock troops) who accompanied them on their long and hazardous trek across the high desert.

Almasy's game plan was to take his four-vehicle convoy south from the Axis base at Gialo, along the Palificata – a trail blazed by the Italians and marked with oil drums – to within a few miles of Kufra, by then in Allied hands, then to detour across the sand sea towards his old stamping grounds around the foot of the Gilf Kebir plateau, before heading east towards the Nile Valley. 'Pit and Pan are not overjoyed at driving through Kufra,' Almasy noted. 'They fear an encounter with the enemy . . . I drove through it purposely during noon-time; that's when Tommy is asleep too.' Beyond Kufra, Almasy came across what he called 'the big surprise' – due east of Giof, the main village of the Kufra Oasis complex, there were 104 fresh truck tracks made by Allied vehicles. 'I had no idea that enemy columns were running from the east towards Kufra. They must come directly from the Gilf Kebir then? So we alter course and follow the tracks eastwards. Duny sand, heavy going, Tommy has also ploughed in deeply and often stuck . . .'

By now, Almasy was beginning to lose patience with his signaller, Corporal Woehrmann, who had failed to make contact with either of their two listening stations, codenamed Otter and Tortoise, and was slack about his other duties.

He has no initiative and I have to keep on asking and ordering everything. The men still cannot understand anyway that . . . a long-range expedition through this realm of Death is nothing else than a flight. Flight from the

---

* Almasy handed his diary over to British intelligence officers in Austria after the war. A transcript is now in the Imperial War Museum, London.

desert itself. The terrain is horrible . . . forever having to change course and check bearings for finding ways through. Since Woehrmann is not capable of reckoning bearings and distances for me I am continually forced to stop and to check the courses on the useless Italian map.

Nearing the Egyptian frontier, but still several hundred miles from his destination, Almasy found himself on familiar territory – 'even on my own map. *Allahu akbar!*' – and entering the narrow defile which he named 'the gateway to Egypt'. 'Now everything is familiar to me . . . In May 1932 I discovered this mighty plateau. I was the first to drive along it here, groping and searching; the war has drawn its traces with gigantic claws in this hidden and secret world.'

Now Almasy had to leave one of his trucks behind, intending to push on with three vehicles to conserve petrol and water. He parked the fourth vehicle in a rock cleft, after painting over its identification markings, removing all other evidence of its origins and putting a notice in French on the inside of the windscreen: 'This vehicle is not abandoned. It will be returning to Kufra. Do not remove any part.' Almasy would need the vehicle, and the cache of water and petrol he left with it, on his return journey. 'The Tommies are to think the vehicle belongs to their Gaullist allies. The maps and log-books hitherto used are hidden. If they catch us they can rack their brains as to where we have come from.'

The next morning, Almasy showed his companions the caves where he had discovered the prehistoric rock-paintings of swimming men in 1932. One of his men picked up an eraser dropped there by a member of Almasy's expedition while making copies of the cave pictures. Further on, at a feature Almasy called the Three Castles, he discovered eight cans of water he had left ten years before – a cache which he claimed saved the lives of Bagnold and others in 1935 when they broke an axle near by and had to wait eight days for rescue. 'Some cans are rusted through and empty, but four are full and I open one cautiously in order not to shake up the water. We pour it into a cooking pot. It is clear and odourless. Each of us takes a sample of the 1933 [*sic*] vintage and we find the water excellent!'

In the plain below, Almasy saw a group of enemy vehicles, unattended. He drove down with Corporal Munz to investigate and found six five-ton trucks, not abandoned but parked. On the lead vehicle were chalked the words 'Refuelled for return journey'. Each truck had two full petrol tanks, making a total of 500 litres. Almasy brought down one of his own vehicles, laden with empty petrol drums, and siphoned off the enemy's fuel. Then he removed the oil filler caps, poured sand into each engine-block and replaced the caps 'very carefully and cleanly so that nothing should be noticeable . . . They shan't fight against us any more.'

Two days later, Almasy was feeling less triumphant. He had mistaken his route and had to double back, while 'Pit drives as usual like a wild man and instead of following my tracks drives . . . head over heels down over the steep part of the tail dune. A miracle that the vehicle does not turn over at the bottom. Result: broken track-rod of the shock absorber. Altogether: except for Munz the men cannot drive . . .'

On 21 May, the seventh day of the trek, Almasy had yet more cause for complaint. His eyes 'ache terribly from eternal compass driving' and 'wireless communication has broken down again'.

Woehrmann reports that the transformer is not working. The men mess around with it for an hour, then come in with the thing still out of action . . . Three radio operators and a mechanic are not in a position to find out what is wrong! . . . I always have to do absolutely everything myself. Pit and Pan, who are riding in the radio car, are the most untidy fellows I have ever had under me. The inside of the radio car looks frightful – loads, personal effects, weapons and food all mixed up together.

Radio communication was a constant problem. When Almasy's party did manage to get their equipment working, the receiving stations failed to pick them up and as a result Almasy was not receiving the air drops he had been promised.

I have scarcely enough petrol to get back. Everything was discussed and planned in detail. I was only to radio and they would drop fuel, water and food for me in any grid square I liked. Now the instrument which is tuned in to our point of departure has fallen out and the called station on the other does not answer. Probably there's another 'shift' going on there. I *begged* them to leave '*Schildkröte*' [tortoise] at one fixed point.

But if Rommel's listening posts were not picking up Almasy's messages, the enemy's were. At Bletchley Park, the rambling country estate that was Britain's top-secret code and cipher headquarters, his faint Morse signals were being decrypted. What they revealed was not enough to disclose the precise purpose of Operation Salaam, but the British were able to follow Almasy's progress as he made his way towards the Nile Valley.

To reduce his fuel consumption, Almasy decided to drive through the Kharga Oasis by road instead of bypassing it, unseen, over the dunes. Five kilometres short of Kharga, he halted and told Munz, Woehrmann and 'Pan' in the back car to stay close as he led the way into the town, 'to halt when I halt and to start off when I start off'.

The sub-machine-guns are held at the ready, but arms should not be resorted to unless I myself have started it. We drive past the railway station. There's nothing stirring there yet . . . On the small round square in front of the way up to the Markaz [local government offices] there stand two Egyptian ghaffirs [night watchmen], only one of them carries a pistol. Both of them stand in the road and I stop, unruffled . . .

Almasy exchanged greetings in Arabic and told the ghaffirs that he was the advance guard of a British Sudan Defence Force convoy whose commander was coming along behind in a third car. They waved him on, and Almasy and the following car continued on their way 'in the glow of the rising sun . . . through the most beautiful of all oases. On our right the Temple of Isis, then on the left an early Christian necropolis, the Roman citadel and the small watchtowers and in between the most glorious spots of oasis with its bright green fields, the great shady lebah trees and the countless palms.'

Following the excellent tarred road and encountering no other traffic for several hours, Almasy turned off, twenty-nine kilometres short of the city of Assiut, and left one of his two vehicles, containing Koerper and Woehrmann, concealed behind a limestone hill while he continued on with Pit, Pan and Munz, navigating by compass until they reached the edge of the plateau. Below them lay 'the huge green valley with the silver, glittering river, the large white city, the countless estabahs and country houses. Not many words are said, a few handshakes, one last photograph, a short farewell, and then I am driving back on our own tracks with Munz.'

Operation Salaam had been completed★ and now became Operation 'Condor' as Eppler and Sanstede were deposited at the edge of the desert, a short walk from the railway station at Assiut. Eppler, once again Hussein Ghaffar, and Sanstede, posing as the American Peter Monkaster, aroused no suspicion as, claiming to be travellers whose car had broken down a mile or two up the road, they wandered into town with their suitcases. One case contained their 40-watt transceiver, the other several thousand pounds in expertly forged British and Egyptian banknotes. If Eppler is to be believed,† the road into town ran through a British army camp where he and Sanstede bluffed their way through so successfully that they were treated to whiskies and soda in the officers' mess, followed by lunch, before being sent on their way to the railway station.

At the station they booked themselves two first-class seats on the afternoon Luxor–Cairo express and then hired one of a crowd of Nubians hanging about in the marketplace to be their houseboy in Cairo. Nubian servants had (and still have) a well-deserved reputation for honesty and utter reliability and, to avoid the likelihood of their suitcases being searched on arrival, Eppler handed them over to their new employee, who was travelling third class, confident that the Nubian would not be stopped and searched by the military police, as Eppler and Sanstede might well be. He was equally confident that his new employee would not make off with the cases.

The Nubian's instructions were to meet his new employers with the luggage outside the Midan al Mahata exit of the Cairo main station. At this ruse, 'Sandy gasped and looked frightened enough to faint,' Eppler would recall; but sure enough, as they emerged from the station, 'there sat Mahmoud, waiting patiently on the bottom step, a suitcase on either side'.

The two spies checked into a villa Eppler had previously rented in the smart Gezira district of central Cairo and Eppler lost no time in getting in touch with a belly-dancer named Hekmat Fahmy, an old girlfriend from his days as a free-spending young man-about-town.

★ Almasy returned to Gialo seven days later, after a trek as hazardous as the outward leg. He was rewarded with the Iron Cross, First Class, and promotion to Luftwaffe major.

† In a somewhat incoherent and totally self-serving postwar memoir, entitled *Operation Condor: Rommel's Spy*.

She was obviously a woman of considerable allure, particularly for the British officers – either attached to GHQ or on leave from the battlefront – who frequented the Kit-Kat nightclub where she performed. Eppler considered her an ideal partner for his espionage operation, well equipped to pick up useful titbits of information from besotted Brits, which he could then pass on to Rommel's HQ.

According to Eppler, his own charms were such that the luscious Hekmat agreed quickly to take part in this dangerous game, and after a few days he and Sanstede rented a luxurious houseboat close to hers on the Nile at Zamalek. Sanstede installed his transceiver under the houseboat's mahogany cocktail bar while Eppler set about recruiting other Cairo good-time girls as paid purveyors of interesting pillow-talk. Dressed in khaki drill and passing himself off as a lieutenant in the Rifle Brigade, Eppler did some fishing on his own account, spending his counterfeit bills freely in bars frequented by British officers and keeping his ears open.

After some initial difficulties, Sanstede managed to make radio contact with the Panzer Army's forward interception station, now located on a hill close to El Alamein. As yet, Eppler had no specific information to give them, but it was important to establish the link, prior to preparing intelligence summaries. These were to be coded by reference to page and paragraph numbers in Daphne du Maurier's best-selling novel *Rebecca*. In the event, the first test transmission was their only successful contact. When repeated attempts failed to get through again, Eppler decided to seek help from the Egyptian army's clandestine Free Officers Organization, young nationalists who naïvely believed that an Axis victory would bring them independence.

The Free Officers sent one of their number, a twenty-two-year-old signals lieutenant named Anwar el Sadat, to take a look at the houseboat spies' equipment and get it up and running. The ardently nationalistic Lieutenant Sadat was shocked by what he found – not by the state of the transceiver, which was in perfect working order, but by Eppler's and Sanstede's dissolute life-style. Their houseboat was 'a place straight out of "The Thousand and One Nights",' he would recall, 'where everything invited indolence, voluptuousness and pleasure of the senses . . . the young Nazis had forgotten the delicate mission with which they had been entrusted.' Eppler's version of events was (naturally) somewhat different, depicting himself and Sanstede as dedicated professionals unaccountably let down by their superiors.

From Hekmat's sources, I had received some essential information about the Allies' growing military superiority . . . Hundreds of brand new American tanks were ploughing through the sand on their way to the front . . . Hekmat had wasted her time and risked her life in vain . . . In vain had I been nosing about at the Turf Club, the meeting place of Allied staff officers. In vain had I crept round the perimeter of the Eighth Army supply depot to take down details of what was being loaded and unloaded there . . . Sandy kept on transmitting, although he realized that nothing was being received at headquarters.

There was good reason for this. On 7 July Australian troops had overrun Rommel's 100-strong Wireless Reconnaissance Unit 621, a vital radio interception station deployed as far forward as possible at Tel el Eisa, the Hill of Jesus. This unit's many functions included listening out for Eppler's reports and passing them back to headquarters. However, this was by no means their most important duty. Their main task was to eavesdrop on British radio communications and, thanks to slack Eighth Army wireless procedures and the brilliance of their commander, Captain Harald Seebohm, they had been snatching a steady flow of high-grade tactical intelligence out of the airwaves. Seebohm was killed and the loss of his unit was a serious blow to Rommel.

Among the code books and other paraphernalia the Australians captured at Tel el Eisa were two copies of *Rebecca* in English. They had obviously been purchased in neutral Portugal, for they were priced in escudos and bore stickers with the name of a bookshop in Lisbon. Urgent inquiries quickly elicited the information that the shop had sold five copies of Du Maurier's best-seller to the German military attaché. Clearly, the book was to be used as a code manual by an agent or agents operating somewhere inside Allied territory.

In the event, British counter-intelligence were already on the trail of 'Pit and Pan', thanks to Eppler's extravagantly free-spending habits in various Cairo bars, where he dispensed expertly forged five pound notes supplied to him by the Abwehr.

In the small hours of the morning one day in mid-July 1942 a team from British Field Security, headed by its director, Major A. E. W. Sansom, quietly surrounded the spies' houseboat. Eppler awoke and shouted a warning to Sanstede, who began to flood the boat from below. As the houseboat began to sink, the two spies were arrested at gunpoint, and it was not long before they were making a full confession. One of those they implicated was Sadat. He was relieved of his duties, stripped of his rank and imprisoned. The future President of Egypt escaped the death penalty because Eppler and Sanstede were themselves spared a firing squad. Sadat assumed that this was their reward for making a full confession; Sansom thought it was because Eppler's stepfather was regarded as 'a friend of Britain'.

Five and a half years after the end of the war, the two great desert explorers, Almasy and Bagnold, met again. The occasion was a glittering event in Cairo, to which the Egyptian government invited 500 high-profile guests – including the Vice-Chancellors of Oxford and Cambridge Universities and the Presidents of the Royal Colleges of Physicians and Surgeons – to discuss 'desert problems'. Bagnold does not appear to have been overjoyed at renewing his acquaintance with Almasy, dismissing him briefly in his memoirs as 'a Hungarian desert enthusiast we had known before the war who had lately served on Rommel's staff'.

On that visit to the Egyptian capital, Almasy was nominated to become Director of the Desert Institute of Cairo, but the desert killed him before he could take up the post. A severe attack of dysentery, contracted during a final excursion into the sand sea, laid him low on his return to Austria, where he died aged fifty-five in hospital in Innsbruck.

So what was the truth about the real 'English Patient'? Was he a committed pro-Nazi or simply, as some would have it, an apolitical romantic, in love with the desert but indifferent to the nature of the cause he served? After the Russians occupied Hungary in 1945, they held Almasy briefly as a suspected war criminal but released him without charge. The following year a Hungarian People's Court in Budapest tried him as a Nazi collaborator but acquitted him for lack of evidence. In Britain, an obituarist writing in the *Journal* of the Royal Geographical Society tried to have it both ways, but probably got it about right: Almasy, he wrote, was 'a Nazi but a sportsman'.

After the Gazala Gallop and the Tobruk Stakes came the race for El Alamein, each army trying desperately to be first to get there. To the Panzerarmee this bastion was, as Rommel noted on 29 June, 'the last obstacle to our advance on Alexandria. Once through, our road to the Nile was clear.'

Although individual British and Commonwealth formations fought well, the Eighth Army as a whole seemed by this time to have lost heart. On the other hand, Rommel's men were tired and running desperately short of supplies. Though spurred on by their tireless commander's personal example, the German and Italian tank crews and infantry were virtually sleepwalking and were so exhausted that even the adrenalin high of serial victory was beginning to fade.

This made it possible for the British to win the eastward race, prepare defensive positions and about-turn to face Rommel. They were reinforced by the Australian 9th Division under General ('Ming the Merciless') Morshead, rested after six months of garrison duty in Syria and honed by fresh training.

While seemingly determined to stop the Panzerarmee short at El Alamein, Auchinleck had another, possibly conflicting, priority. 'At all costs, and even if ground has to be given up, [I] intend to keep the Eighth Army in being,' he emphasized in orders to senior commanders issued at 4.15 a.m. on 26 June, after an understandably sleepless night. Consequently, defences were prepared in the Nile Delta and as far back as Palestine's Gaza Strip, in case the Eighth Army should be pushed out of Egypt altogether. Arrangements were even under way to ensure that there were enough Palestine pounds available in the Mandate to meet an Eighth Army pay parade.

Inevitably, such highly visible contingency plans sapped morale and contributed to an Eighth Army desertion rate high enough to induce some senior officers to ask Auchinleck to consider restoring the death penalty, abolished in 1930, for desertion in the face of the enemy.★

★ Auchinleck turned it down flat as 'undemocratic' (Lawrence James, *Warrior Race*, p. 695). During the First World War, very few of the 266 British soldiers executed for desertion or cowardice were officers.

Nor did it help when the Royal Navy decided, with Rommel only sixty-five miles away, to abandon its base at Alexandria and disperse the Mediterranean Fleet to Haifa and Beirut. With the harbour ominously empty, the women of Alexandria's once flourishing Italian community, their menfolk long since rounded up and sent to internment camps in the Canal Zone, began to make plans for a victory ball for Rommel's German and Italian officers. Axis air raids became heavier, and among the targets hit was a brothel much favoured by British officers.

The damage to Alexandria would have been much worse, but for the presence in the Eighth Army of Major Jasper Maskelyne of the Royal Engineers, famous as the music-hall illusionist Maskelyne the Magnificent. In a stunning enlargement of his peacetime skill he 'moved' the harbour. Exactly how he did it is still a secret locked in the bowels of the British Public Record Office and not due for release to the general public until 2030. Mirrors, searchlights and smoke were undoubtedly some of the props. With these, Maskelyne was somehow able to trick some German and Italian pilots into bombing an image of the harbour that was no more than a sea-borne mirage and thereby saved Egypt's second city from considerable destruction.

In Cairo, meanwhile, there was a run on the banks, householders fashioned swastika flags to hang from their windows and street mobs taunted British troops with cries of 'Advance Rommel.' All polite pretence that Egypt was a sovereign and independent country had long since been stripped away and many resentful Egyptians now thought that deliverance was at hand.

Major H. P. Samwell, an officer with the recently arrived 51st Highland Division, found that 'the attitude of the shopkeepers and even the shoeshine boys was rude, offhand and almost gloating. In one small shop I was surprised to see the Italian flag prominently displayed, with a picture of Mussolini and King Victor Emmanuel on either side.' As for the German prisoners of war Samwell encountered when his company stopped alongside a PoW cage, they were openly contemptuous, calling out: 'You're just in time to see Rommel's victory march through Cairo,' and 'More prisoners for the Afrika Korps.'

Lieutenant-General Thomas Corbett, in overall charge in Cairo, ordered all officers to carry revolvers at all times and imposed an 8 p.m.

to 7 a.m. curfew on central Cairo. This ruined the capital's famous wartime night life and many British civilians and officers were glad to find a place on the packed trains that left Cairo's central station daily for Palestine, Lebanon and the Sudan. Others flew to South Africa.

Among the interested spectators of all this was the Oxford classicist and philhellene, Monty Woodhouse, then a young officer in the Special Operations Executive, and about to be parachuted into Greece to help guerrillas blow up a vital railway bridge carrying Rommel's supplies to the port of Piraeus and thence to North Africa. Woodhouse could see that some of the staff officers in the Cairo headquarters of SOE, which ran agents all over the Balkans, were more interested in packing their bags to catch the Palestine Express. 'Compromised' civilians were supposed to go with them, but the most compromised of all – German and Italian Jews working for British intelligence as translators and interrogators – found themselves barred by the Mandate's rigid controls on Jewish immigration, however temporary.

To add to the sense of crisis, somebody (probably Corbett himself) ordered that classified documents choking the filing cabinets of GHQ should be incinerated. It was done with great panache in 40-gallon oil drums at the back of the building and, since it happened on a Wednesday, 1 July, the day soon became known as Ash Wednesday. From a security point of view it was not entirely effective. Much of the paper was only lightly scorched before smoke wafted it above the perimeter wall to flutter down into the street outside. There the peanut- and bean-vendors, who normally fashioned their paper cones out of newsprint, were quick to exploit a new packaging possibility. Ash Wednesday was the low point of the period the British called 'the Flap' and, judging by the gallows humour of the time, they took a certain masochistic delight in it. 'Just wait till Rommel gets to Shepheard's – that'll slow him up,' became a much repeated joke, the service in Cairo's premier hotel being notoriously slow.

Sir Miles Lampson, the British ambassador and, many thought, the real ruler of Egypt, decided that the best way of advertising his intention to stay put was to be seen on the normal social round. He took Lady Lampson to dinner at the Mohammed Ali Club, which had one of the smartest restaurants in town. There, Prince Abbas Halim, Egyptian royalty's best-known Nazi sympathizer, was heard to toast Rommel's health, adding the hope that 'he doesn't fall at the last fence'. Halim's pro-Axis credentials were swiftly confirmed by his arrest and internment. Much more subtle was a British black propaganda campaign, possibly the joint product of the embassy and SOE, which started the rumour that if the Axis occupied Egypt the country was to be presented to Mussolini as an Italian colony. Stories began to circulate that the Italians had already cast a victory medal with Mussolini and the pyramids on one side and the inscription 'Summa Virtus et Audacia' on the back. It was also whispered that the Axis were preparing a 'victory' postage stamp for Egypt bearing the portraits of Hitler and Mussolini.

In some quarters this kind of talk was taken very seriously. The clandestine Egyptian Free Officers Organization, not suspecting that they might merely exchange one occupier for another, more ruthless, was ready and willing to help their enemy's enemy. They decided that a young pilot among the conspirators should fly to Rommel with a message promising an uprising in Cairo in return for a guarantee of Egyptian independence. He never got there. Once over Axis territory in a British-built Blenheim light bomber, he was shot down and killed by the very people he was hoping to contact. Shortly afterwards, some of the Free Officers' leaders were arrested, among them the young Lieutenant Sadat and another future Egyptian president, Gamal Abdel Nasser.

British propaganda concerning Axis intentions in Egypt was probably not all that wide of the mark. Eight days after the fall of Tobruk, Mussolini had arrived in Libya in person, having flown to Derna on 29 June, accompanied by his favourite charger on which he intended to take the salute at the Cairo victory parade. His entourage even brought with them 200 drums of black shoe polish with which the Italian soldiery were to burnish their boots for the occasion.

For Il Duce it looked as if patience had been rewarded. After all Fascist Italy's setbacks and humiliations, his army, thanks to Rommel and his 'Afrikaners', had won back Italy's North African possessions and were now at the gates of Alexandria. But Mussolini soon had reason to suspect that Count Cavallero, chief of the Comando Supremo, had sent for him prematurely. The British, it seemed, were not quite finished yet. The RAF were making it very difficult for Axis shipping to use Tobruk. Rommel's troops were at the end of a long supply line and were exhausted, and Rommel himself was far too busy to spare time for a meeting with Il Duce. Cavallero's generals were not impressed by talk of victory parades. What they wanted to talk to their Duce about was the chronic shortage of fuel, transport and almost everything else that mattered.

Despite these shortages Rommel was in high spirits. He was convinced that one more supreme effort by every officer and man under his command would get them to Cairo. The capture of Mersa Matruh, so soon after Tobruk, with another 6,000 unwounded prisoners, had reduced his respect for the British. 'Trust your Corps will now find itself able to cope with so contemptible an enemy,' he signalled one senior Italian commander. Harsh words, though in the desert, sooner or later, men on both sides tended to give in once they felt they were in a hopeless position.

A typical enough case was that of Sergeant Nell of the Green Howards, a Yorkshire infantry regiment. After some close-quarter fighting, he found himself and the remains of his platoon cut off in some shallow dug-outs on the outskirts of Mersa Matruh, being gradually surrounded by advancing German troops who had no idea they were there. Nell, a regular NCO and veteran of pre-war skirmishes in the Khyber Pass, decided to surrender.

One man, Frank Robinson, wanted to fight, I pointed out to him that we should all be killed without advancing our war effort in the least . . . He cried, actually sobbed, and pleaded with me to fight it out. But fighting was out of the question, so I very carefully crawled out of the trench, stood up and, trying to look much braver than I felt, walked over to the Germans. It was only a short distance but it seemed an awful long way to me. One of them saw me. He shouted, 'Come on, Tommy! Come on, Tommy!' I shouted, 'All right lads, come out!' They came out with their hands up . . . I felt a little ashamed . . .

In the same engagement the New Zealand infantry division gave a rather better account of themselves. Encircled and without armoured support on an escarpment south of Mersa Matruh, they broke out in a wild night attack with fixed bayonets, yelling Haka war-cries of the kind later made familiar around the world by the All Blacks rugby team. There was little of the vaunted spirit of chivalry about the New Zealanders' treatment of the Panzer Grenadiers, whom they literally caught napping as they lay around their lagered transport in bedrolls. As their trucks erupted in flames around them, the Germans fled into the dark, pursued by howling Kiwis. Some wounded Germans were picked up and thrown on to blazing trucks. Others were killed as they tried to surrender. One wounded New Zealander struggled to his feet and ran when he realized that his comrades, coming up behind, were thrusting their bayonets into any human form they saw on the ground, dead or alive, 'and it was hard to distinguish between friend or foe'. The Germans would later accuse the New Zealanders of 'filling themselves full of brandy and fighting like Bolsheviks'.

Rommel, who told a captured New Zealand brigadier that his men had used 'gangster methods', was very nearly caught in the breakout himself. 'My headquarters were soon surrounded by burning vehicles and became the target of persistent British fire,' he recalled. 'One could barely conceive of the confusion which reigned that dreadful night. One could not see one's hand before one's eyes. While the Royal Air Force bombed its own troops, German soldiers shot at each other and the sky was filled with multiple streaks of tracer fire.' Almost 10,000 New Zealanders got away in the breakout, but Rommel was not unduly perturbed, spurring his exhausted troops on to what would become known as the First Battle of Alamein.

In all the North African desert, nowhere fitted Auchinleck's requirements for a defensive battle better than the position which started on the shores of the Mediterranean around the little railway halt of El Alamein and ended some forty miles to the south at the northern cliffs of the Qattara Depression. This 7,000-square-mile basin sinks to almost 450 feet below sea level; a large part of its surface consists of deceptively sand-encrusted saline lakes and marsh, punctuated by small, table-topped hills and weird sand sculptures chiselled by centuries of arid wind. There were tracks through it, but it was difficult for camels, let alone tanks, and wheeled vehicles stood a very good chance of getting bogged down.★

Between El Alamein and Qattara are three low and narrow ridges, running more or less parallel with the coast and called, from north to south, Miteiriya, Ruweisat and Alam el Halfa. Auchinleck established his forward tactical headquarters on the eastern part of Ruweisat, from

---

★ Much to the consternation of Auchinleck's staff, during the retreat a Lieutenant Randall Plunkett of the Guides Cavalry, an Indian Army regiment, had found a way through for his troop of armoured cars.

where his deputy chief of staff and ideas man, 'Chink' Dorman-Smith, wrote to his latest lady friend (another officer's wife) that 'the Boche is flat out for victory and if he doesn't get one he is going to experience a tremendous reaction'. Dorman-Smith seems to have viewed the coming battle entirely without trepidation. 'I'd rather be here than anywhere else in the world,' he wrote, apparently impervious to how his latest love might view his priorities. (She would become the second Mrs Dorman-Smith.)

Most of the line had not been prepared, nor was it held continuously; there were simply not enough troops left to do so. Rather, the line was manned in a series of boxes, rather like the lost Gazala line. Astride the coastal road and railway was the El Alamein box, which had been dug, mined and partly wired; fifteen miles to the south of it, the Qattara box blocked an east–west dirt road known as the Barrel Track and had been dug but not mined; just north of the Qattara escarpment, the Naqb Abu Dweis box was on good, firm sand and very little work had been done on it. Behind the boxes was most of the remaining armour, and some infantry and artillery was deployed on the ridges.

As he steeled himself for the showdown with Rommel, Auchinleck was by no means certain of the mettle of his own Eighth Army, or of British troops in general. An Indian Army officer, he had a profound admiration for the loyal and hardy peasant mercenaries of the sub-continent, but he had never commanded British troops in action until the disastrous Norway expedition in 1940. As his official report of that event shows, he was not impressed: 'By comparison with the French, or the Germans for that matter, our men for the most part seemed distressingly young, not so much in years as in self-reliance and manliness generally. They give an impression of being callow and underdeveloped, which is not reassuring for the future, unless our methods of man-mastership and training for war can be made more realistic and less effeminate.' By the summer of 1942, and despite better training, Auchinleck was not the only senior British officer to feel this way. 'If the British Army cannot fight better than this we shall deserve to lose the Empire,' noted Brooke, the CIGS, after the fall of Singapore.

It is of course not uncommon for middle-aged men (Auchinleck was now fifty-eight) to deplore the 'softness' of the younger generation. What pained him most, as he stood alongside the coastal road

watching the Eighth Army's transport heading back towards El
Alamein, was the sight of all the paraphernalia of a pampered army:
the mobile canteens, the trucks piled high with NAAFI stores, camp
beds and office furniture. Such fripperies had not come the way of his
regiment, the 62nd Punjabis, when they chased the Turks across the
Mesopotamian plain to the very gates of Baghdad during the First
World War and he resolved to set an example by keeping an austere
headquarters and sleeping on the desert floor, like any other front-line
soldier.

Battle was joined on 1 July. At 2.30 in the morning Rommel left his
field headquarters, which was bombed by the RAF shortly afterwards,
and went in the darkness to the headquarters of his armoured divisions.
Before him the night was lit up by flares and flashes from British
artillery fire which soon began to fall on the coast road. For the rest
of the day Rommel and his staff edged further forward and if he
snatched any sleep he does not mention it. By late afternoon they
were with a small formation of tanks and mechanized infantry known
as Battle Group Kiel, which was supporting the 90th Light Division.
The advance had slowed and Rommel had received reports of 'murderous British artillery fire'. Shortly afterwards, he learned exactly
what his men were talking about. 'British shells whistled in from
north, east and south . . . Under such an overwhelming weight of
firepower our attack ground to a halt. We hastily spread out our
vehicles and took cover as shell after shell hurtled into our position.
Bayerlein [his chief of staff in place of the wounded Westphal] and I
had to lie in the open for two hours.' Field marshals are not supposed
to be cut off for two hours from the headquarters of the armies
they command, and by the time Rommel returned his attack had
everywhere come to a halt and could not be restarted. After a certain
amount of reorganization the next day, and heartened by Luftwaffe
reports that the British fleet had left Alexandria, Rommel tried again.
But Auchinleck and Dorman-Smith proved a formidable team.
Dorman-Smith was particularly adept at interpreting the often frac-
tured Ultra intercepts of German radio messages.

When the Afrika Korps resumed with a push to the north-east, the
Eighth Army ducked and weaved, feinted a retreat, then hit the
Panzers on their unprotected south flank. Soon both Panzer Divisions,
the 15th and the 21st, found themselves on the defensive, outnumbered

by British tanks, among them some of Auchinleck's few remaining Grants with their superior 75-mm gun.

Then, during a sandstorm which might have worked to their advantage, the 90th Light stumbled on to a strong British position long before they expected contact; they panicked and, for the first time in their illustrious history, bolted. The Ariete, whose performance at Gazala and Knightsbridge had so pleased the Germans, crumbled under attack by the New Zealanders. Four hundred Italians were taken prisoner and almost thirty field-guns captured. Time and again Axis units felt the awfulness of the British artillery and the omnipotence of the RAF. The Germans in particular were unused to being at a material disadvantage and Rommel himself was concerned that the advent of the Grant and the six-pounder anti-tank gun meant that German tanks had lost their qualitative superiority.

But he knew that the main difference was the Eighth Army's change of command and he felt constrained to praise Auchinleck for 'deploying his forces with considerable skill'. On the third day of his offensive, Rommel was writing to his wife, 'The battles for the last positions before Alexandria are hard.' The next day, 4 July, was even harder: 'Dearest Lu! Unfortunately things are not going to plan here. The resistance is too great and our own strength exhausted. Hopefully some way will be found to reach our objective. Am always tired and over stressed.'

On the fifth day, Rommel realized that his troops were exhausted. He ordered a pause to rest and absorb German infantry reinforcements being flown in from Crete before he returned to the attack. Auchinleck beat him to it. At 5 a.m. on 10 July, Rommel, sleeping in his transport after being evicted from a captured bunker by 'the fleas the British had left behind',★ woke to the persistent thudding of a heavy artillery barrage. It was in support of Morshead's Australians, astride the coastal road in the north. They were about to rout the Italian Sabratha Division, taking 1,556 prisoners, as well as overrunning the wireless reconnaissance unit at Tel el Eisa.

The barrage that shook Rommel from his slumbers was, yet again, the direct result of Dorman-Smith's insistence that artillery should

---

★ Accusations of bad front-line housekeeping are made by all the combatants and not just against their enemies. Everybody seems to have believed that they kept a cleaner trench than everybody else.

be concentrated. Veterans of 1914–18 compared it to the rolling 'drum-fire' of France's Western Front.

Rommel, who was in part of the Qattara box that the British had abandoned, called for the start of his new offensive and rushed up north with elements of 15th Panzer to plug the gap. But the Australians had their tails up and were hard to stop. Corporal James Hinson, an English immigrant from Manchester, won a Distinguished Conduct Medal by getting close enough to an enemy tank to disable it by attaching a sticky bomb. For several days the Australians continued to beat off German counter-attacks, often with devastating effect. Corporal Victor Knight, a London-born former British merchant seamen, won another DCM for the leading role he played in repulsing an attack on Tel el Eisa with his four Vickers machine-guns.

Jimmy Nimmo – who'd been over the hill to pick up ammunition – said, 'Hey, Vic, they're coming in from the other side.' So I scrambled up the hill and saw tanks and infantry coming in at the rear. I grabbed the blokes and took the guns over the other side – there was no cover – and began firing at the advancing Germans for about three hours. We had to urinate on the barrels to keep them cool enough to keep firing. We had oil available and we simply poured it from a four-gallon drum into the working parts, keeping the guns firing all the time.

The Germans were from 104 Infantry Regiment, newly arrived from Crete, and despite some artillery and Stuka support they never got within 300 yards of Knight and his mates. Several accounts put their casualties, including those killed from shellfire, at 600 – just over 50 per cent. Rommel accused his infantry of being 'too late to take advantage of the preliminary bombing'. It was the early days of Tobruk all over again and exactly the kind of action he wanted to avoid.

The initiative had now swung to Auchinleck. There was particularly vicious fighting around the Ruweisat Ridge, where a New Zealand officer, Captain Charles Upham, a sheep farmer who had already won a Victoria Cross in Crete the year before, became the third man in the history of the award to win it twice – and the only one to survive. Upham won his second VC in a surprise night attack against mechanized infantry. Already twice wounded, he managed to get close enough to a truck crammed with Panzer Grenadiers to ruin most of its occupants with grenades. He was wounded again and could have

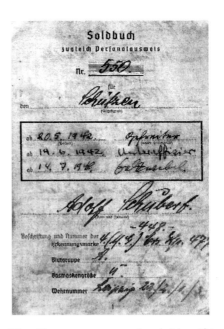

18. Ariye Shai, one of the German-speaking Jews serving in the Special Interrogation Group, on leave in Cairo in the British uniform (the headgear is from a Highland regiment) he rarely fought in.

19. The German army pay book identifying Shai as Corporal Adolf Schubert. Capture in enemy uniform would have meant a court martial and a firing squad – the fate, later in the war, of German special forces caught in American uniforms in Europe.

20. Two members of the Long Range Desert Group monitor Axis traffic along the coast road. Although the LRDG did mount raids and ferry SAS raiding parties to their targets, one of its main tasks was reconnaissance.

21. A German half-track outside an Italian fort in Cyrenaica. The British never did develop one of these useful hybrids.

DANGEROUS DESCENT
DRIVE IN BOTTOM GEAR

22. The real 'English Patient'. László Almasy, the Hungarian explorer who became Rommel's desert adviser, poses by a British signpost during his epic trek to infiltrate German spies into Cairo.

23. 'The Unwitting Spy'. Colonel Bonner Fellers, US military attaché in Cairo, whose intercepted briefings to Washington gave Rommel priceless intelligence.

24. Italians laying captured British Mark IV anti-tank mines.

25. Germans putting up barbed-wire entanglements around one of their 'devil's gardens'.

26. The cerebral 'Chink', Major-General Eric Dorman-Smith (*left*), talking with General Sir Alan Brooke. Dorman-Smith, Auchinleck's military guru, thought the Eighth Army's main problem was an '*embarras de* Ritchie'.

27. And Lieutenant-General Neil Ritchie himself.

28. Brigadier Jock Campbell VC driving the popular Lieutenant-General 'Strafer' Gott into Benghazi after Rommel's withdrawal from Cyrenaica. Both would be dead before another year was out.

29. 26 November 1941. After almost eight months of siege, the Tobruk garrison's Matilda tanks under Brigadier A. Willison (*centre, in beret*) break out and meet the advancing New Zealanders on the El Duda ridge. But the link-up lasted only a few hours and the British army's longest siege would run for another eleven days.

30. As the Tobruk siege comes to an end, men of the British 70th Division emerge from a gap in their own barbed-wire entanglements and move into the El Duda salient.

31. Free French Foreign Legionnaires doubled
up under fire as they rush an Axis position during a
counter-attack at Bir Hacheim.

32. The passing British crew of a newly delivered American Grant stare curiously
at smouldering Axis armour during the Gaza fighting in June 1942.
The arrival of the Grant meant that for the first time the British possessed a tank
gun that equalled anything the Germans had.

33. 21 June 1942. Tobruk falls. German medics pose for pictures in front of the clearly marked Sweeney Todd's barber shop, now under new management.

34. Some of the 35,000 prisoners, taken when the South African commander, Major-General Klopper, surrendered, receive water from their German captors. This was Britain's most humiliating defeat in the desert war.

35. Afrika Korps soldiers take a shower – a luxury for
all the combatants in the desert war.

honourably retired to the nearest casualty clearing-station, but Upham would have none of it. A short, wiry man, with the build of a scrum-half, he rejoined his battalion in time to take part in a dawn attack. Held up by four machine-gun posts supported by tanks, Upham immediately charged. 'His voice could be heard above the din of battle cheering on his men,' reads the official citation. Wounded yet again, Upham was captured; he was not an easy prisoner, made several escape attempts and ended the war in Colditz, the Oflag for persistent escapers.

For the next two weeks, Auchinleck followed Dorman-Smith's advice and concentrated on the Italians. After the rout of the Sabratha by the Australians came the turn of the Brescia, Trieste and Pavia infantry divisions. All in turn were badly mauled by the Eighth Army, often in night attacks. Sometimes the lines of Italian prisoners, glad to be out of it, were almost long enough to remind old hands of the good times under O'Connor. They would have been even more cheered had they been privy to Rommel's almost daily notes to his beloved 'Lu' as he ran his German troops ragged, rushing them hither and thither to mend holes made in the Italian positions.

14. Jul.42
Dearest Lu!
My expectations for yesterday's battle were bitterly disappointed. It achieved nothing at all. The blow must be borne, further operations undertaken with renewed spirit. Today I am wearing shorts for the first time this year. [Rommel, with his stocky physique, did not look well in them.]

17. Jul.42
Dearest Lu!
It is going pretty badly for me. The enemy's superior infantry is taking out one Italian unit after another. German units much too weak to halt them alone. It makes one cry!

18. Jul.42
Dearest Lu!
The past, crucial, day was particularly bad for us. Once again we got away. It cannot go on much longer or the front is lost. Militarily these are the worst days I have lived through.

On 20 July a dispirited and exhausted Mussolini returned to Italy and in Rome there were rumours that he was dying of amoebic dysentery. One of his ministers said that it was more likely that Il Duce was suffering from a terminal dose of humiliation. As it happened, for the time being at least, the worst was over for the Panzerarmee Afrika. Now it was the Germans' turn to show how resolute they could be in defence.

To keep up the pressure, Auchinleck was obliged to use an armoured brigade so recently arrived from England that they had done hardly any desert training. Even worse, most of their tanks were Valentines, well armoured but mostly armed with the old inadequate two-pounder gun. The product of two years of intensive training in England, 23rd Armoured Brigade charged the enemy with all the eagerness of troops who have never been in action before. Their opposition were the veterans of 21st Panzer. In the space of an hour, eighty-six of their ninety-seven Valentines were lost, most of them on a screen of anti-tank guns. 'Two years of training, a sea journey half-way around the world – and in just half an hour it's all over for us!' one of its captured officers told his German interrogators.

Rommel knew that, despite his superior numbers, there was no way Auchinleck could afford losses like these. Once again his German soldiers and their equipment had proved more than a match for the British, and in a signal congratulating his troops Rommel added: 'I am sure further enemy attacks will be met with the same resistance.' Yet despite the losses suffered by 23rd Armoured Brigade, Auchinleck was pleased by the way things were going and in a Special Order of the Day on 25 July he urged his troops to make one more effort: 'You have done well. You have turned a retreat into a firm stand and stopped the enemy on the threshold of Egypt. You have done more. You have wrenched the initiative from him by sheer guts and hard fighting and put HIM on the defensive in the last weeks. He has lost heavily and is short of men, ammunition, petrol and other things . . . You have done much but I ask you for more. We must not slacken. If we can stick to it we will break him. STICK TO IT.'

But some felt that they had done rather more than their fair share of 'sticking to it' and Auchinleck was suddenly faced with a high-level mutiny. Morshead, in common with the New Zealand commander Freyberg, had long been dissatisfied with the performance of the British armour. More often than not, the tanks had difficulty co-ordinating with the infantry and they turned up at the wrong place at the wrong time – if, indeed, they turned up at all. Even when they were doing some good, they were apt to disappear, like Cinderella, long before midnight, insisting that they could not see in the dark. And when the spirit did move them to attack, it was often in the unscientific manner adopted by 23rd Armoured Brigade. The survivors swiftly left the field and once more the infantry were without tank cover.

So now Morshead, whose division had already performed miracles, was declining to attack again on the grounds that he had 'no confidence' in the armour. If Auchinleck insisted, he would have to consult his government. Auchinleck's initial reaction was to blow his top. As if he did not have enough on his plate, there were fears that some of the British troops in the Middle East might have to be switched to the defence of the Persian oil-fields because of German successes in the Soviet Caucasus. Churchill wanted him to beat Rommel before this happened. But once his anger had subsided, Auchinleck decided it would be more politic to conciliate the commander of one of his best divisions. For the most dangerous part of the attack, he offered Morshead British troops – one of 50th Division's tired north country brigades which had been in action continuously for over three months.

Morshead agreed to do it, but the attempt came to nothing. The British brigade put in a muddled night attack and lost 600 men captured or killed. An entire battalion from Western Australia was cut off and surrendered after its tank support was repulsed with heavy losses and the Panzers got there first. Some years later, one of the almost 500 Australian prisoners taken described the final act: 'As the [German] tanks closed in on Battalion Headquarters a Bren gunner ran to an exposed position to open fire. His .303 bullets were useless against thick steel and he was shot down by one of the other tanks. The loss of this life convinced Lieutenant-Colonel McCarter of the futility of further resistance. He stood up in his weapon-pit, and with an upward wave of his hands signalled to his battalion to end the hopeless struggle.'

The next day, 28 July, Auchinleck called off his offensive, saying he lacked enough 'fresh, well trained troops'. As both sides reinforced, the Eighth Army getting much more than its opposition, the First Battle of El Alamein ended in exhausted stalemate. Nevertheless, even Rommel thought that Auchinleck had reason to be pleased with himself: he had done what mattered most. The advance of the Panzer

Army had been halted, and it would be some weeks before it was ready to try again.

Others, notably Winston Churchill himself, were less impressed and were bent on change.

PART FOUR
Enter Monty

They are rolling up the guns for tomorrow's battle.
I must not be late to hear Death rattle
In my enemy's throat.

> – Denis Saunders ('Almendro'),
> South African Air Force

Although Auchinleck had stopped Rommel cold at Alamein, Churchill's impatience with what he called 'the inexplicable inertia of Middle East Command' had by now become acute. His excruciating embarrassment at receiving news of the Tobruk débâcle while in conference with Roosevelt had been somewhat mitigated when the US President immediately ordered 300 brand-new Sherman tanks* to be withdrawn from a US armoured division and handed over to the Eighth Army. But on his return to England Churchill found this striking affirmation of Anglo-US solidarity offset by an equally striking, though considerably less agreeable, affirmation of the strength of British democracy in adversity: a no-confidence motion in the House of Commons.

Following the loss of Singapore and Burma, the fall of Tobruk had been Britain's third significant land defeat of 1942. At sea, Japanese aircraft had sunk two capital ships, the *Prince of Wales* and the *Repulse*, while in the Atlantic German U-boats were threatening to starve Britain into submission. And at home 3,000 civilians had been killed or injured between April and June by the Luftwaffe's 'Baedeker raids'† on cities of historical importance such as Canterbury and Bath. For a vocal minority in Parliament, the Tobruk fiasco was the last straw, inspiring a censure motion against Churchill's conduct of the war. And although Churchill weathered the challenge by a massive majority of 475 votes to 25, the public squabble inevitably eroded the image of a nation united in total war.

For Churchill, it was the deciding factor that would crystallize his resolve to go to the Middle East, find out what was wrong and put it

---

* The Sherman, successor to the Grant, had its 75-mm gun mounted in the turret rather than the hull, making it a match for any of Rommel's Panzers as far as armament went.

† The raids, in response to the British carpet-bombing of Rostock and Lubeck, were so called when the Germans announced they would hit sites marked with three stars in the Baedeker *Guide*.

right, even if this should mean replacing Auchinleck. After Cairo, Churchill intended to go to Persia and then on to Moscow for a meeting with Stalin. This was not something he was looking forward to, for he would have to break the news to Russia's dictator that there would be no Anglo-American Second Front in Europe that year. Instead, they were to concentrate on the total defeat of the Axis forces in North Africa by launching Operation 'Torch', the invasion of Vichy French Morocco and Algeria. This would be a big enough undertaking, to be sure, but a sideshow compared to the titanic struggle being waged in the Soviet Union.

Churchill and his entourage set off on their perilous 3,500-mile flight to Cairo in one of two American-piloted B-24 Liberator bombers which left an airfield in Wiltshire on 2 August and arrived the following day, after one stopover in Gibraltar. For only part of the journey was it possible to protect the Prime Minister with a fighter escort. And though the Liberators' route lay well to the south of the desert battle zone, they had to cross the North African territories of Spain and Vichy France where, as Churchill wryly observed, 'it would have been very tiresome to make a forced landing'.

Quite apart from these hazards, it was a far from de-luxe flight for a sixty-eight-year-old who had first visited Egypt as a Victorian cavalry officer. Earplugs notwithstanding, the bomber's four engines made a noise that a later generation of air travellers would have found intolerable. Worse, the aircraft was unheated. 'Razor-edged draughts cut in through many chinks,' noted Churchill, who was travelling with his doctor, Sir Charles Wilson (later Lord Moran). They slept side by side on one of two shelves in the after-cabin. Wilson had reason to worry about his patient's pulse rate for, despite the discomfort, the Premier's growing excitement was obvious. 'Instead of sitting at home waiting for the news from the front I could send it myself,' wrote the former war correspondent. 'This was exhilarating.'

At the same time, the CIGS, General Sir Alan Brooke, was flying to Cairo via Malta in another Liberator and in a similar degree of discomfort 'with a wooden box between my legs'. He arrived in Egypt a couple of hours before the Prime Minister. Churchill and Brooke were joined in Cairo by Field Marshal Jan Christian Smuts, the South African Prime Minister, who had flown up from Pretoria. Churchill admired the septuagenarian Afrikaner as 'a fount of wisdom' who, having fought the British as a Boer commando, had embraced the

British Empire with such fervour that in both world wars he became a supernumerary member of the London War Cabinet.

Brooke, who met with Churchill on an almost daily basis in London and regarded himself as a necessary brake on the Prime Minister's wilder schemes, had been hoping to visit Cairo alone. He knew that Churchill wanted 'Strafer' Gott to take over command of the Eighth Army and was not at all sure this was a good idea. Gott came highly recommended by Churchill's Foreign Secretary, Anthony Eden, for reasons that were more sentimental than practical. In the 1914–18 war Eden, like Gott, had won an MC while serving in the Rifle Brigade (otherwise the Green Jackets) and, although never a professional soldier, he remained fiercely loyal to his wartime regiment.* Gott was one of the few senior Eighth Army officers who was well known and well liked by the rank and file. A tall, silver-haired man with piercing blue eyes and a high forehead, he was the son of a vicar and nephew of a bishop and was given to quoting a line from *The Pilgrim's Progress*: 'God will not count your medals but your scars.' With a DSO and bar as well as the MC, Gott had earned plenty of both, starting in 1917. In the desert war, a quarter of a century later, his climb from lieutenant-colonel to lieutenant-general in under two years had earned him several more wounds, one of them while daringly evading capture in an open car.†

Gott was the veterans' veteran of the desert war. 'All, high and low, turned [to him] for advice, sympathy, help and encouragement in difficulty,' recalled Michael Carver, a twenty-seven-year-old major in 7th Armoured Division who would survive the war and eventually become a field marshal. Even so, Carver thought that Gott's goodness sometimes got in the way: 'Perhaps he was too great a man to be a really great soldier.' Carver probably got it right. Gott may have met most of the criteria for Chaucer's 'verray parfit gentil knyght', but a cold appraisal of his soldiering in North Africa reveals no stunning display of tactics or the kind of Rommel-esque grip that bends scared

---

* In the spring of 1941, when they were desperately short of officers, Eden had seen to it that seventeen Americans, most of them just out of Ivy League colleges, were commissioned into the regiment – this at a time when the US was still neutral.
† Cut off from his headquarters as German vehicles closed in, Gott scorned the soft option of surrender and ordered his driver to charge through them. One enemy bullet came close enough to give the general a flesh wound, but he escaped and made sure his driver was decorated for gallantry.

and exhausted men to the will of the born leader. In common with several other officers, he had enjoyed a good beginning to the campaign, particularly during the initial Italian invasion, but he had never demonstrated any of O'Connor's panache. At Sidi Rezegh, where he had commanded 7th Armoured Division, the real glory belonged to his subordinate, Brigadier Jock Campbell, who time and again persuaded tank crews to follow him across that lethal plain.

Years after the war Auchinleck would tell an interviewer that he did not think Gott was 'all that bright', and it is true that as a corps commander Gott had failed to distinguish himself when Auchinleck took command of the Eighth Army. On the contrary, it had been Gott whose orders had left the New Zealanders in the lurch at Minqar Quaim. Brooke shared some of Auchinleck's doubts about Gott, considering him 'no longer as fresh as he might be'. These suspicions were reinforced by Gott himself when they went on a tour of front-line positions and returned to Gott's headquarters for a chat. 'It was not until we were sitting at tea together that he began to open out his heart to me. He said, "I think what is required out here is some new blood. I have tried most of my ideas on the Boche. We want somebody with new ideas and plenty of confidence in them."'

Brooke had the very man in mind: Lieutenant-General Bernard Montgomery, Auchinleck's difficult subordinate in Southern Command during 1940, and the man Auchinleck had feared Brooke would send out if he sacked Ritchie. There was no doubt in Brooke's mind that Montgomery, who had served under him in France in 1940, was the best tactical commander in the army. 'I never interfere with Monty in tactical matters,' he once averred. 'He's generally right.' But he had to convince the Prime Minister, who seemed set on promoting Gott.

Churchill had his first and last meeting with Gott on 5 August, after a visit to Auchinleck's tactical headquarters on Ruweisat Ridge. From there his next stop was lunch with Air Vice-Marshal Arthur Tedder at RAF headquarters in Borg el-Arab, and he had Gott drive him there 'in order that I might form an impression of him'. According to Churchill's post-war account, Gott told him that he would be 'better off for three months' leave in England' although he remained 'quite capable of taking any responsibilities confided to him'. If this distinctly tepid response gave Churchill second thoughts about Gott, they did not last very long.

Churchill's earlier meeting that day with Auchinleck at Ruweisat

Ridge was not a happy occasion for either host or visitor. The Auk's attempt to provide a fly-free eating area failed to impress. 'We were given breakfast in a wire-netted cube,' Churchill recalled tartly, 'full of flies and important military personages.' This lapse might have been forgiven if Auchinleck and Dorman-Smith had even pretended to share Churchill's enthusiasm for a renewed offensive. But both were adamant that there could be no full-scale attack until mid-September at the earliest. 'I remember noticing that the prime minister did not like this attitude,' recalled Francis ('Freddie') de Guingand, Auchinleck's staff brigadier.

What Churchill failed to understand was that both men, with some justification, were feeling rather pleased with themselves for stopping the Panzerarmee at El Alamein and taking some 7,000 prisoners, most of them Italian. What Auchinleck and Dorman-Smith failed to comprehend was that Churchill thought it disgraceful that, with its superior numbers, the Eighth Army should find itself forced to fight a battle so close to Cairo in the first place. The meeting undoubtedly signalled the end of Auchinleck's career as a field commander.

On the beach at Borg el-Arab, the RAF commander made sure that his hospitality outshone Auchinleck's. As Churchill would recall, there was a splendid luncheon, the food flown in from Shepheard's in Cairo, complete with gleaming silver and snow-white napery – 'a gay occasion in the midst of care, a real oasis in a very large desert,' the Premier noted. Senior air force officers' criticisms of the army's performance served only to convince him how necessary it was to initiate a thoroughgoing shake-up.

On his return to Cairo, and before Brooke could properly make his case for Montgomery, Churchill astonished the CIGS with a proposal of his own. Brooke had long argued that Middle East Command was too big and that Iraq and Persia should be a separate entity. The Prime Minister agreed that the division should be made, but he wished Brooke to assume Auchinleck's role in what would now be known as Near East Command. Auchinleck would retain the title of Middle East commander, but his fief would be reduced to Iraq and Persia. As an added inducement, Brooke could have Montgomery as Eighth Army commander.

Brooke was sorely tempted. 'This made my heart race very fast!' he recorded. Nevertheless, he felt he must remain in charge of the War Office to act as a curb on Churchill's 'impetuous nature'. The Prime

Minister dispatched the artful Smuts, whom Brooke greatly admired, to tempt the CIGS with predictions of the glory that surely awaited him if he would relent. 'For a few moments I hesitated and then, thank Heaven, I remained firm.'

Given Brooke's determination to remain at his post as CIGS, Churchill named Lieutenant-General Sir Harold Alexander – previously earmarked to command the British element of the Anglo-American invasion of French North Africa – to take over the new Near East Command in place of Auchinleck. Montgomery would go instead of Alexander to 'Operation Torch', and Brooke, keeping his 'serious misgivings' to himself, acquiesced in Churchill's decision that the Eighth Army command should go to the tired and dispirited 'Strafer' Gott. The scene was surely now set for another disastrous failure of British leadership in the Western Desert. But, as Brooke confided to his diary, 'Fate took the matter in its hands within twenty-four hours of our decision.'

A few days after his meeting with Churchill, Gott left Borg el-Arab as a passenger in a high-wing Bristol Bombay, a twin-engined transport with fixed undercarriage and a top speed of less than 200 mph. He was going for more talks in Cairo and was sharing the aircraft with fourteen stretcher cases, a sergeant medic to look after them, two aircraftmen to handle the loading and a cockpit crew of three. Gott sat in a jump seat next to the rear door. The Bombay was virtually unarmed, with only one fixed forward-firing .303 machine-gun. At the controls was nineteen-year-old Sergeant-Pilot 'Jimmy' James. After take-off he went down to an operational height of fifty feet, where desert camouflage made the lame-duck Bombay less visible to marauding enemy fighters.

They had been airborne for about fifteen minutes when a series of clatters and bangs erupted. At first James thought these heralded engine failure, then he began to smell smoke and through the windscreen he saw the broken orange lines of tracer-fire darting ahead of them. This was followed by his first glimpse of a Messerschmitt-109, which overtook the Bombay slightly to the right. As it peeled off, James noted a blur of yellow markings on the Luftwaffe fighter's belly and nose. It also had the dancing bear of Berlin painted on the cowling over its Daimler–Benz engine, the emblem of Jagdgeschwader 27, a fighter group which normally provided escorts for Stukas. On this day, six aircraft of 11 Staffel, under Unteroffizier Hugo Schneider, were after their own prey.

Schneider's Messerschmitts, attacking in pairs, almost immediately knocked out both of the Bombay's engines. Its teenage pilot was under fire for the first time and, as he would recall, was 'absolutely scared to death. I was yellow, there was no other word for it . . . It started about my hands and it went straight up my spine, hit my brain and literally bounced all the way back down . . . all I wanted to do was go and hide. Then suddenly it all changed. It was like rugby, I went into wild Welshman mode. I thought, I'm not going to let the bastards get me. I'm going to land this damn thing.'

James ordered his crew to prepare for an emergency landing. The navigator went back into the fuselage to help the sergeant medic and the two aircraftmen prepare the stretcher cases for fast evacuation. This required lifting the rear door off its hinges to prevent it jamming on landing. The Bombay was on fire. Fuel dripping down from the punctured tank in the high wing was feeding a thickening curtain of flame between the fuselage and the cockpit. Looking for a place to land, James realized that his joystick had become so hot that it was blistering his ungloved hands. The windscreen began to melt and James ordered the opening of the cockpit's emergency exit – a trapdoor in the floor behind his seat. The wireless operator was slumped in his seat, ashen-faced and clutching his arm; he had been hit by a cannon shell. James himself was quite unaware that he had a splinter wound in his back and a bullet through one calf.

He brought the Bombay to earth along a gentle, downwards slope but couldn't get the tail down to apply the brakes. The Bombay now bore a greater resemblance to a runaway train than to an aircraft as James wrestled with its red-hot controls to stop it ground-looping on to its back. Then the Messerschmitts were back: 'I got a flash of them, six specks on the horizon . . . I thought, Oh God, they're going to have another go at us.'

Eventually, James got the tail down. The brakes had been shot away, but the Bombay hit a patch of soft sand and slowed down to about 20 mph. There was no time to wait until it came to a complete stop: better to risk throwing the wounded off the moving aircraft before the Germans attacked again. James yelled at the crew to start getting the wounded out and he left the controls to help. This probably saved his life, for a burst of fire shattered his instrument panel. The cockpit was now full of flame and smoke, and the floor was buckling with the heat. Dazed and with the *thump, thump, thump* of the Messerschmitts' cannon fire in his ears, James dropped through the escape hatch.

As he crawled clear, the Bombay settled on to its belly, flames dancing along the fuselage. Convinced that he had 'beaten the bastards', the young pilot expected to see twenty-one people around the wreck of his aircraft. Instead there were just four: his navigator, his wireless operator, the sergeant medical orderly and one of the wounded who had somehow dropped through the cockpit escape hatch. James asked where the others were. Somebody pointed to the rear of the aircraft. To his horror, James saw that the door was tightly shut and its camouflage paint was beginning to bubble and blacken. For some reason the door had not been taken off its hinges and had jammed shut, trapping those inside. These included 'Strafer' Gott. Despite his injuries, James set off to get help. He was picked up by a Bedouin, who placed him on his camel until he could flag down an army truck. Although lapsing in and out of consciousness, James insisted on guiding a search party back to the wreck.*

Much later in the war, Brooke and Churchill would marvel at 'the part that the hand of God had taken in removing Gott at the critical moment' – although Unteroffizier Schneider and his Dancing Bears would surely have been amused to be seen as the instruments of Divine intervention. But with Gott gone, the Prime Minister had to give way to Brooke and settle for Montgomery as head of the Eighth Army. All that remained was to tell Auchinleck he was fired, an act that Churchill compared to 'killing a magnificent stag'. The Prime Minister delegated this disagreeable task to his military secretary, Colonel (later General Sir) Ian Jacob, who felt it would be 'as if I was just going to murder an unsuspecting friend'. He handed Auchinleck a letter from the Prime Minister, informing him that Alexander was taking his job and offering him the Iraq–Persia command. 'It may in a few months become the scene of decisive operations,' wrote Churchill.

But Auchinleck was not to be mollified and turned the offer down

---

* James was awarded a Distinguished Flying Medal for this and, later in the war, the Air Force Cross and bar for other acts of gallantry in the air. After the war he remained in the RAF and retired with the rank of Squadron Leader, having commanded the Queen's Flight.

flat. 'I considered myself a fighting soldier, and it was a backwater really,' he explained in an interview, over thirty years later. For almost a year, Auchinleck was idle, and then in June 1943 he returned to the post of Commander-in-Chief Indian Army – the job he had held before taking over from Wavell in the Middle East. Although other professionals, including Rommel, thought he was a brilliant tactician, he was never again given a field command.

As for the brilliant and acerbic Dorman-Smith, he was ousted along with Auchinleck, the clever but conventional CIGS thinking him a malign influence and knowing that Montgomery would not want him. Dorman-Smith's career never recovered. Although he briefly commanded a brigade at the Anzio beachhead in Italy in 1944, he was ultimately reduced to Colonel and retired six months before the war ended.★

Reporting back to Churchill after delivering the fatal blow to Auchinleck, Jacob found the Prime Minister striding up and down in his quarters and crying: 'Rommel, Rommel, Rommel, Rommel! What else matters but beating him?'

★ Embittered, Dorman-Smith returned to his ancestral home in Ireland, assumed his hereditary name O'Gowan (he was head of that Irish clan) and in the 1950s even had a brief flirtation as military adviser to the 'official' IRA, then raiding police and army barracks in Ulster.

Bernard Montgomery arrived in the Middle East full of 'binge' (his term for fighting spirit), an abiding professional contempt for Auchinleck and an utter conviction that he would succeed where his predecessors had failed.

An abrasive, opinionated little cock-sparrow of a man, Montgomery was quite as much the professional as Rommel, but a different kind of professional. Here was a cold, methodical technician of war who rarely risked the intuitive gambles and daring bluffs so beloved of his quicksilver opponent-to-be. Unlike Rommel, he rarely led from the front for he held firmly that no army commander could be in total control of his forces from this position. And, though he was good at delegation, being in control was what Montgomery was essentially all about.

On arrival in the desert he lacked Rommel's personal magnetism and had not yet revealed his startling talent for self-promotion. But what he always had in common with Rommel was the ability to convey an absolute certainty of victory to the men under his command. At fifty-five, Montgomery was almost totally unread and uncultivated in the broader sense, and his military talent was of the careful kind. Results were obtained through relentless training, organization, a firm grasp of tactics, and an ability to motivate subordinates through a clear, concise and direct exposition of his ideas. The wonder was that, since leading an exemplary fighting withdrawal to the evacuation beaches at Dunkirk, he had been kept in Britain and deprived of 'another crack at the Boche' for over two years.

Like Auchinleck, Brooke and Alexander, Montgomery was a product of the Anglo-Irish Ascendancy, most of whom had settled in Ulster in the seventeenth century. His family traced its lineage back to a certain Roger de Montgomerie, one of William the Conqueror's Norman knights. In Ulster, the Montgomerys became merchants, administrators and clergymen, and the younger sons drifted away from the family seat overlooking Lough Foyle, rarely following their fathers into the same occupation.

The family's most successful soldier since Sir Roger was born in Kennington, south London, in November 1887, the fourth child of the Vicar of St Mark's, Kennington – shortly to become Anglican bishop of Tasmania – and an unloving mother, a child-bride turned domestic tyrant. Married at sixteen to a man over twice her age and the mother of five by the age of twenty-four, Maud Montgomery seems to have had a scarcely concealed aversion to her third son, whose childish pleas for love she spurned so brutally that in later life he would reciprocate to the extent of cutting off all contact with her.★

While his father kept in the background, his termagant mother controlled all household affairs, including the family's modest finances. When they lived in London she made her husband an allowance of ten shillings a week and this had to include lunches at his Pall Mall club. On the children she imposed a savage discipline, enforced by vigorous use of the cane. In Tasmania, Bernard was regularly chastised for his lapses into Australian English. 'Disobedience brought swift punishment,' he would recall. 'She made me afraid of her. [I] withdrew into my shell. Certainly, I can say that my childhood was unhappy.'

Maud was utterly philistine, although she came from a cultured background. Her father was the liberal theologian, teacher and writer Frederic Farrar, author of the best-selling Victorian school novel *Eric, or Little by Little*, in which literary critics have since discovered strong homoerotic undertones. Farrar's late marriage is said to have stunned his male friends. Perhaps they were less surprised when one of its progeny, Bernard Montgomery's uncle and a chaplain to Queen Victoria, fled the country after a scandal involving a choirboy.

When the family returned from Tasmania, young Bernard was sent to St Paul's, a celebrated London day school, where he excelled at rugby and cricket if not in class. Team photographs show a small boy with a rather fierce expression and unusually large hands. In 1906 he gained entrance to Sandhurst but was almost thrown out in his last term for his part in the bullying of a cadet who was badly burned.

Montgomery wanted to get into the Indian Army, where a subaltern could live on his pay. He knew he could not expect an allowance from his parents, impoverished by the expenses of multiple parenthood and a huge mortgage on the recently inherited family estate in Ireland.

★ He would not allow his son David to have anything to do with his grandmother and, unforgiving to the end, refused to attend her funeral in 1949.

But there was fierce competition for Indian Army places and Bernard just failed to get in. Instead, he got the next best thing: a commission into a British regiment serving in India, where the food and drink charged to a subaltern's mess-bill was much cheaper than at home. In 1908 he was commissioned into the Royal Warwickshire Regiment and joined its 1st Battalion in Peshawar, on the North-west Frontier of India. The Warwicks, which mainly recruited around Birmingham, were a solid county infantry regiment with none of the expensive social cachet of the Guards or the cavalry.

In August 1914 his battalion found themselves in France, members of what the Kaiser memorably called 'that contemptible little army', the British Expeditionary Force. By October, Montgomery, now a captain, was involved in hand-to-hand fighting during the first Battle of Ypres and led a spirited counter-attack. Like all junior officers of the time, he was carrying a freshly sharpened sword. 'I was confronted by a large German who was about to shoot me [he recalled] . . . no one had taught me how to kill a German with a sword . . . I hurled myself through the air at the German and kicked him as hard as I could . . . the blow was well aimed at a tender spot. I had read much about the value of surprise in war. There is no doubt that the German was surprised . . . he fell to the ground in great pain and I took my first prisoner.'

Shortly afterwards, while standing with his back to the enemy to assess his platoon's position from the enemy point of view, he was shot through the right lung by a sniper. As he lay bleeding in a muddy field, his platoon sergeant dashed out to apply first aid and was shot in the head. This saved Montgomery's life, for the sergeant collapsed on top of him. All afternoon, until the light failed, the snipers kept firing. Montgomery was hit once more, this time in the knee, but the dead man caught most of the bullets. Montgomery's ordeal lasted for over three hours and by the time he was taken to an advanced dressing station he seemed so far gone that a grave was dug for him. But Montgomery survived the night to return to England on a stretcher, where he spent two months in hospital and was awarded the Distinguished Service Order, Britain's second-highest decoration for gallantry.*

---

* Montgomery always made it plain that he felt the DSO was more than he deserved. The Military Cross – the next gallantry medal down – was not introduced until a few months later.

Like Rommel, Montgomery acquired a reputation for absolute fearlessness that inspired his battalion. A story went the rounds that he had received his wounds while arguing with a German officer over the possession of a *pickelhaube* helmet he wanted as a souvenir. Hospital gave him time for reflection on this and he 'came to the conclusion that the old adage was probably correct: the pen is mightier than the sword. I joined the staff.'

In fact, his staff posting was a result of his doctors' verdict that he was unfit for active overseas service and likely to remain so for several months. This enabled Montgomery to shine in a training role, and when he did return to France in January 1916 it was as a brigade major. In the trenches he had several more lucky escapes, including being bowled over, but was otherwise unscathed, by a shell which detonated four feet away from him. He went on to survive the carnage of the Somme, Arras and Passchendaele and ended the war as a divisional chief staff officer with the temporary rank of lieutenant-colonel.

Between the wars, Montgomery's formidable talents as a trainer and administrator were increasingly recognized. 'Clever, energetic, ambitious, and a very gifted instructor' who however 'must cultivate tact, tolerance and discretion,' wrote a perceptive general in his personal report for 1931, when Montgomery was commanding the small British garrison in Palestine.

Peacetime promotion was painfully slow and he was not made up to full colonel until 1934, when he was instructing at the Indian Army staff college at Quetta in what is now Pakistan. He had also done a stint as lecturer at the Camberley Staff College, where he clashed with one of the star students, Dorman-Smith, who had publicly criticized his teaching of tactics. Montgomery confronted him in the students' anteroom. 'He strode in his little-man walk up to me,' 'Chink' would recall. '"What's this I hear, Dorman-Smith? You think my idea of tactics is to take a sledgehammer to crack a nut. Is that true?"

'"Perfectly true, Colonel."

'"Preposterous, preposterous."'

They also differed over Ireland, where both men had served during the Troubles of the 1920s. Dorman-Smith's views were ambivalent, veering from the usual British officer's contempt for the rebels to an admiration of Michael Collins, the doomed republican military leader. Montgomery found the campaign against the IRA to be in many ways 'far worse than the Great War'. It tended to lower British 'standards of decency and chivalry,' he said. Even so, he preached a hard line, writing to a friend that 'Cromwell or the Germans would have settled it in a very short time.'

Shortly before the outbreak of the Second World War, Montgomery was again involved in counter-insurgency operations, having returned to Palestine to fight Arab rebels who were up in arms against British rule and Jewish settlement. The surest way to victory, he said in a letter to the War Office, 'is to direct all our energies now on killing the armed rebels'. And when he came to report in April 1939 that the rebels had been 'smashed', Montgomery confessed: 'I shall be sorry to leave Palestine in many ways, as I have enjoyed the war out here.' No weasel wording here. No attempt to disguise that 'real soldiering' is ultimately about killing the enemy.

In his private life, Montgomery did something that astonished many who knew him. 'Women had never interested me and I knew very few,' he would write. 'My life was devoted almost entirely to my profession and I worked at it from morning to night, sometimes taking exercise in the afternoon.' Then, at the age of thirty-nine, rather in the footsteps of Grandfather Farrar, he took a wife.

Over the years there has been considerable conjecture that marrying late was not the only way in which Montgomery took after his maternal grandfather. Nigel Hamilton, whose award-winning three-volume biography of Montgomery is by far the most exhaustive and who knew his subject personally, was quite categorical about it: 'There can be no doubt that, by temperament and inclination, Bernard Montgomery was disposed towards the male sex rather than the female.' If Montgomery was a repressed homosexual who never, according to all known evidence, allowed himself to give way to his desires, it would certainly explain the lack of sustained interest in the opposite sex so blandly revealed in his 1958 *Memoirs*. What is surprising is that somebody who for over twenty years had largely ignored women★ should make such a good marriage to somebody with such different interests.

Betty Carver (née Hobart), a war widow with two sons, aged eleven and thirteen, was a slim, petite woman 'far from beautiful but popular',

---

★ He did have a brief fling with a seventeen-year-old girl, half his age. He wooed her by explaining his views on infantry tactics and armoured warfare. Not surprisingly, she rejected his offer of marriage.

in Hamilton's estimation. She came from the same caste of Anglo-Irish gentry as Montgomery, but was untypically artistic and liberal in her political views. Some of her acquaintances were, by military standards at least, disturbingly Bohemian (though Montgomery admired the war novel *The Secret Battle* by her celebrated author friend, A. P. Herbert) and Betty was a moderately talented painter and sculptress.

In many ways, then, she seemed rather exotic for the clipped little major she first met through mutual friends while on a skiing holiday with her sons in Switzerland. He proposed to her a year or so later on the fives court at Charterhouse, where her boys were at school, and they married on 27 July 1927.

Betty Montgomery was 'terribly disorganized, really,' her son Dick would recall and Monty ran their household 'on military lines'. But the Carver boys became fond of their stepfather and he of them. They both followed him into the army and Dick Carver, for one, seemed to have no doubt that his mother and her second husband were very much in love.

In August 1928, aged forty, she bore Montgomery a son, David. She travelled with her husband to postings in Palestine and India and was altogether, as Montgomery wrote, 'a very good Colonel's lady'. Then, safely returned to England from all the health hazards of the sub-continent, the colonel lost his lady in a most bizarre and distressing way.

In the summer of 1937, while on the beach at Burnham-on-Sea, Betty was bitten on the foot by some kind of insect. Blood-poisoning set in and she was admitted to a local hospital. At first Montgomery, busy with manoeuvres on Salisbury Plain, failed to realize how sick she was. But as her condition worsened he was soon making regular 200-mile round trips to visit her.

The septicaemia spread. Only the coming war would bring into general use the antibiotics which might have cured it. As a last resort the leg that had received the bite was amputated. Even this failed to save her. After almost two months of suffering, Betty Montgomery died in her husband's arms on 19 October 1937. He had just read the 23rd Psalm to her. Montgomery was heartbroken. 'I was utterly defeated. I began to search my mind for anything I had done wrong, that I should have been dealt such a shattering blow ... my soul cried out in anguish against this apparent injustice. I seemed to be surrounded by utter darkness; all the spirit was knocked out of me, I had no one to love except David and he was away at school.' Montgomery threw himself with renewed intensity into his vocation, and his eccentricities became more marked. Having been comprehensively rejected by his mother, he had transferred his need for affection to Betty. Now she was gone and Montgomery completed the process of alienation by cutting off all further contact with the now-widowed Maud Montgomery.

Then, for the first time in his life, he became seriously ill himself. It happened in the summer of 1939 when, the Arab revolt in Palestine over, Major-General Montgomery was due to return to England to command an infantry division. Instead, he was taken on board the liner *Ranchi* at Haifa on a stretcher, with four nurses in attendance and suffering from suspected tuberculosis. Montgomery insisted that it was merely his old war wound playing up. 'He thinks he's going to serve in the war that's coming,' the ship's doctor told Montgomery's sister, Winsome, whose husband was a serving officer and who by coincidence was also travelling on the *Ranchi*. 'Well, he's not – he'll never see action.'

Confounding that verdict, Montgomery walked, unaided, off the ship at Southampton, and the military hospital at Millbank gave him a clean bill of health. Rest, sea air, good food, attentive nursing, and gentle promenades around the deck had done the trick. 'It was just sheer guts, will power,' said his sister. 'He wasn't going to give in.'

In France, following the outbreak of war, the British Expeditionary Force was under the overall command of General Lord Gort, a man of undisputed personal bravery who in 1914–18 had won the VC, the DSO and nine Mentions in Dispatches. Unfortunately, though, he had little aptitude for high command. During the so-called phoney war, from September 1939 until spring 1940, Montgomery chafed under Gort's command, conscious that if and when serious fighting broke out, the BEF would suffer the consequences of poor leadership. Gort's abiding fault was that he let himself get bogged down in detail. He found it difficult to delegate and there was little that he did not consider worthy of his attention.

Despite his own lack of interest in the opposite sex, Montgomery had always shown indulgence towards his men's need for what he liked to call 'horizontal refreshment'. When his battalion was serving in Egypt, he had made sure that the Alexandrian brothels were managed in a way that would leave the Warwicks in good health. But when he tried the same thing in France in November 1939, he nearly got the sack. Alarmed at the incidence of venereal disease in his division, he issued written orders that condoms should go on sale at NAAFI canteens and that the men should be urged to use the cleaner brothels in Lille. Gort was outraged by such candour and vowed to make Montgomery withdraw the order. Even granted the prevailing British hypocrisy on sexual matters in the 1930s, it was ludicrous for an army commander to become involved in such trivia, even more so when he was hopelessly wrong. Montgomery dug his heels in and refused to withdraw the offending order. In the end, Brooke, then Montgomery's corps commander, intervened, persuading him that Gort meant business and would send him back to England if he didn't back down. The so-called VD Affair was sadly typical of Gort's priorities.

In the débâcle that followed the Germans' Blitzkrieg attack of May 1940, Montgomery's division was one of the few Allied formations to maintain its cohesion. It made an exemplary withdrawal under fire to the evacuation beaches at Dunkirk. There, Montgomery found Gort 'a pathetic sight', a judgement which was unfair as well as unkind: given the collapse of the French army, there was probably little Gort could do. And by retreating to Dunkirk he at least saved enough of the pre-war regular British army to lay the foundations for the massive force of civilians in uniform that was about to be raised.

Back in Britain, Montgomery's cool competence under fire in France earned him promotion to lieutenant-general and command of V Corps, while his fanatical ruthlessness in dealing with subordinates whom he considered 'useless' (his favourite expression of contempt), his niggling perfectionism and his overbearing self-confidence earned him the title 'the mad general'. This 'madness' included an apparently irrational hatred for his immediate superior, Auchinleck, who was in overall charge of defending the south of England against an expected enemy invasion.

Physically and in terms of personality, Auchinleck was everything Montgomery was not: tall, handsome, urbane and charming. But the small, beaky-faced, squeaky-voiced Montgomery had something 'the Auk' lacked: '100 per cent binge' and the terrifying single-mindedness of an intellectually and emotionally limited man with no outside interests. He had no time at all for Auchinleck's tactical ideas, openly disparaging him for spreading his defences along the beaches instead of defending key locations and keeping the bulk of his forces in an emergency reserve, ready to move at short notice to wherever the danger was greatest.

As soon as he became convinced that no invasion was imminent, or even likely, Montgomery more or less dispensed with the idea of defence altogether and began thinking in terms of the offensive operation he hoped to lead against enemy forces somewhere overseas. His whole objective was to kill Germans – not an expression of hatred but once again of a cold professionalism and an abiding belief that killing the enemy was what soldiering was all about. He realized that the bumbling amateurishness displayed so far against the brilliant cohesion and ruthless effectiveness of the Wehrmacht could only end in defeat for Britain.

In April 1941, Montgomery was sent to command XII Corps where, in his own words, he 'burst like a 15-inch shell' on the comfortable and complacent corps HQ at Tunbridge Wells, Kent. He sent officers' wives and families home by the trainload and dismissed 'useless' subordinates by the sackful. His objective was to build what an admiring *Times* military correspondent called 'the new British Army'. And even though he entitled his directive '12 Corps Plans to Defeat Invasion', his real purpose was to train himself and his men not so much for the defence of England as for the invasion of France.*

But an overseas posting continued to elude Montgomery. The despised Auchinleck had been sent to overall command in the Middle East, but Montgomery remained at home. In November 1941 he was appointed General Officer Commanding Southeast Command, which he promptly re-named Southeast Army, declaring that 'our worst enemy is defensive mentality. The troops will be indoctrinated with that state of infectious optimism which comes from physical well-being [he declared in an Order of the Day]; they must have in their make-up that spirit that will make them want to kill Germans. The powers of endurance of all ranks will be brought to the highest pitch.

---

* He was, in fact, to be one of the planners of the Dieppe raid of 19 August 1942, a masterpiece of misdirected 'binge' in which of the almost 5,000 Canadians who took part only 1,500 got back. The majority, roughly 2,500, were captured and about 900 were killed or died of wounds in what came to be seen as a quite unnecessary dress-rehearsal for the invasion of Hitler's 'Fortress Europe'. Montgomery withdrew his support for the operation shortly before he went to Africa and in recent years most of the blame for the fiasco has been attached to Mountbatten, Head of Combined Operations at the time.

Every officer and other rank must be able and mentally wishful to take part in a real rough-house, lasting for weeks. They must be 100 per cent enthusiastic for battle and must possess 100 per cent binge.'

As GOC, Southeast, Montgomery continued driving, prodding, provoking, tirelessly and compulsively. He made few friends but many admirers; he became eccentric and egotistical almost to a pathological extent. By now his personal asceticism had hardened into teetotalism, something almost unheard of in the British military. Then came the call to take over command of the Eighth Army.

In the previous year three British generals had tried to take on Rommel in the desert: Cunningham, Ritchie and then Auchinleck himself. Montgomery, the fourth, had never commanded anything bigger than a division in battle, apart from a few days when Brooke handed over his corps to him during the Dunkirk evacuation. Montgomery had never fought in the desert, indeed he had not fought anywhere for over two years. He was about to face the most brilliant exponent of armoured warfare the world had ever seen. He was inheriting a command that, in Churchill's words, was 'vast but baffled and somewhat unhinged'. In the circumstances, could Bernard Montgomery really expect the Eighth Army to share the enormous confidence he had in himself?

He arrived at Eighth Army headquarters on Ruweisat Ridge at about 11 a.m. on 13 August and did not like what he saw: it was 'enough to lower anyone's morale . . . no mess tents, work done mostly in trucks or in the open air in the hot sun, flies everywhere. I asked where Auchinleck used to sleep; I was told that he slept on the ground outside his caravan. Tents were forbidden in the Eighth Army; everyone was to be as uncomfortable as possible, so that they wouldn't be more comfortable than the men. All officers' messes were in the open air where, of course, they attracted the flies . . . The whole atmosphere . . . was dismal and dreary.'

Shortly before sunset, de Guingand, the staff brigadier who had been one of Montgomery's regular squash and tennis partners in England, had all the staff officers assembled; their new commander wished to address them. It began badly. Montgomery, whose obsession with punctuality was manic, arrived half an hour late after his escorting officer led him into a minefield while on a tour of forward positions. To extricate themselves they had been obliged to reverse cautiously along their own tracks. By then the RAF fighters that had been circling the Ruweisat HQ in a protective umbrella had disappeared into the gathering easterly gloom and the fifty waiting officers were impatient for their dinner. They sat on the sand while Montgomery spoke to them from the steps of Auchinleck's old trailer.

The first thing they noticed was how much he lacked the Auk's natural authority. Instead of a handsome, towering presence, there was this small, wiry man, with a beaky nose and the pale skin of the newcomer. But for his peaked hat and badges of rank, he could almost have been one of the ops room clerks. Then, in his somewhat high-pitched voice, Montgomery started speaking. 'I want first of all to introduce myself to you. You do not know me. I do not know you. But we have got to work together . . .' It was hardly the Gettysburg Address. And many of his audience thought they had listened to rather too many pep-talks from new commanders of the Eighth Army. But by the time Montgomery had finished, which was less than ten minutes later, they were under his spell. 'Brilliant, absolutely brilliant,' was de Guingand's verdict.

Montgomery's message was a simple one. It had about it the battle cry of his Ulster loyalist stock: No Surrender.

Here we will stand and fight; there will be no further withdrawal. I have ordered that all plans and instructions dealing with further withdrawal are to be burnt, and at once. We will stand and fight here. If we can't stay here alive, then let us stay here dead . . . Now I understand that Rommel is expected to attack at any moment. Excellent. Let him attack. I would sooner it didn't come for a week, just give me time to sort things out. If we have two weeks to prepare we will be sitting pretty; Rommel can attack as soon as he likes after that and I hope he does . . . Meanwhile, we ourselves will start to plan a great offensive; it will be the beginning of a campaign which will hit Rommel for six right out of Africa . . . He is definitely a nuisance. Therefore we will hit him a crack and finish with him.

Churchill and Brooke returned to Egypt on their way home from Moscow, where Stalin had been predictably rude about the British war effort. On 19 August the Prime Minister and his new commander-in-chief drove from Cairo, past the pyramids and out into the desert, to visit Montgomery in his new headquarters alongside the RAF at Borg el-Arab 'amid the sand dunes by the sparkling waves. After our long drive [Churchill recalled] we all had a delicious bathe. Three hundred yards away about a thousand of our men were disporting themselves on the beach. Although I knew the answer, I asked "Why do the War Office go to the expense of sending out white bathing drawers for the troops? Surely this economy should be made." They were in fact tanned and burnt to the darkest brown everywhere except where they wore their short pants.'*

The next day the tireless Churchill toured the area south-east of the Ruweisat Ridge, where the mass of the British armour and hundreds of artillery pieces were concealed under camouflage. The Prime Minister had decided that his famous dark-blue, zip-up boiler suit was suitable desert wear. Although he topped off his ensemble with a pith helmet and pale blue umbrella, the boiler suit was a mistake. 'He was perspiring profusely and dropped into a chair which had been prepared for him and mopped his brow furiously,' recalled Major A. R. Flatow, a Royal Tank Regiment squadron commander.

For Churchill the exertion was obviously worth it. Generals may have resented his nagging calls for action, but for the ordinary soldier the idea that 'Winnie' was among them, making his famous V-sign and even handing out the occasional cigar, was a tremendous morale-booster. Near a field cemetery in which a number of their comrades had newly been buried, he inspected his old regiment, the 4th Hussars.

---

* Churchill was intrigued by the way perceptions had changed since his days as a subaltern in the Sudan, forty-four years previously, when 'the African sun must at all costs be kept away from the skin'. Now the received wisdom seemed to be that going hatless and almost naked in the desert sun did no harm.

'Gentlemen, you will strike an unforgettable blow against the enemy,' he told them. 'The corn will be ripe for the sickle and you will be the reapers.'

Visiting Freyberg at the HQ of the 'splendid' New Zealand division, Churchill sat down in the noonday heat to 'a scalding broth of tinned New Zealand oysters, to which I could do no more than was civil'. Montgomery declined to join them at table, explaining that he made it a rule never to accept hospitality from subordinate commanders. 'So he sat outside in his car eating an austere sandwich and drinking his lemonade with all formalities,' noted Churchill, reflecting that his ancestor Marlborough 'would have entered and quaffed the good wine with his officers – Cromwell, I think, too.'

Despite Montgomery's dismal lack of conviviality, Churchill detected 'the reviving ardour of the army' and a growing enthusiasm for his teetotal general. 'Refreshing' was how Morshead, the Australian commander, described his first meeting with Montgomery. 'Everybody said what a change there was since Montgomery had taken command,' Churchill wrote. 'I could feel the truth of this with joy and comfort.'

Churchill left for home on 23 August, well satisfied that the situation in the desert had been put to rights. A week later Rommel attacked, seeking to outflank the British with an armoured hook from the south, just as he had done at Gazala. As Montgomery predicted, the Eighth Army was by then 'sitting pretty' and his doctrine of maximum co-operation with the RAF paid dividends. What started as a moonlit night attack was slowed by the RAF, who lit up the desert with dozens of the parachute flares the Germans called 'Christmas trees' and started to hit vehicles that should have been invisible with unnerving accuracy. When dawn broke on 31 August the Panzer regiments were still stuck in unexpectedly deep British minefields and being subjected to increasingly painful air strikes and artillery bombardment.

Nehring, the commander of the Afrika Korps (that is, the 21st and 15th Panzer Divisions and the 90th Light), was wounded in an air attack. The talented von Bismarck, commander of 21st Panzer, who had sent his men into battle to the strains of a regimental band playing Prussian marches, was killed by a mortar bomb while well forward. Rommel's own *Kampfstaffel* (his tactical HQ) had several killed in a bombing raid, and the Desert Fox himself had yet another of his miraculous escapes when an eight-inch bomb splinter that would have almost cut him in half landed inches from him.

Then, when the Panzer regiments finally arrived at the Alam el Halfa Ridge, they met a wall of dug-in steel and their troubles really began. It was too much to ask of any army. On the morning of the third day, 2 September, Rommel gave the order to withdraw. It was the furthest easterly point the Afrika Korps ever reached.

Ten years after the war, Colonel Friedrich von Mellenthin, one of Rommel's intelligence officers, wrote that the battle of Alam el Halfa marked not only the high-water mark of Rommel's progress across North Africa but was also 'the first of a long series of defeats on every front which foreshadowed the defeat of Germany'. This was a large claim for a relatively small battle. Total Axis losses amounted to just under 3,000 killed, wounded, captured or missing, and total British casualties were 1,750. The Panzerarmee lost forty-nine tanks and the Eighth Army sixty-seven, some of them in raids not directly connected with the Alam el Halfa fighting.

Auchinleck had correctly predicted from which direction Rommel's next attack on the Alamein line would come – a penetration just above the Qattara Depression, wheeling north to the Alam el Halfa Ridge, which runs west–east and is the last obvious defensive position before the coast. This led to post-war claims that 'the Auk' had laid the foundations of Montgomery's Alam el Halfa victory; but most trained military minds confronted by the same situation would probably have made the same prediction.

It was Montgomery's preparations and mind-set that were so crucial – his determination that there should be no more withdrawals, not even contingency plans for them; no talk of the paramount importance of preserving the Eighth Army no matter how much territory had to be sacrificed. This was a bold decision for a man who had no experience of desert fighting and who had just been entrusted with the largest army Britain had in the field. Certainly it lends weight to the argument that Montgomery's reputation for undue caution was often undeserved. By putting most of his chips on the El Alamein line and leaving the Delta virtually uncovered, he was concentrating his forces in a win-or-lose situation: 'If we can't stay here alive then let us stay here dead.'

What Montgomery had reason to be grateful for was that the

disasters of the early summer had obliged the Eighth Army to fall back on the El Alamein line which thus reduced the scope for mobile warfare and suited his talents. Once he had decided, which he did very quickly, how he was going to fight his first battle with Rommel, preparing for it was not difficult.

Some defence works had been started on Alam el Halfa but they were thin. Montgomery decided to reinforce the line with the newly arrived 44th Infantry Division, whose anti-tank guns and artillery were languishing in the Delta. Most of his tanks were also dug in around the ridge, hull down so that only their turrets were exposed. These included the 170 or so surviving Grants with their 75-mm guns (the first of the Shermans were only just being unloaded at Port Said) and armoured brigade commanders were under strict orders, which ran contrary to all their instincts, to stay put.

Montgomery was not going to attempt a battle of manoeuvre with Rommel; he knew who would win. Even so, slugging it out toe-to-toe with the Panzerarmee took some nerve. If you were not prepared to move, there was always the chance that Rommel might find a hole in your defences and crash through. At one point, Major-General Alec Gatehouse, commander of the 10th Armoured Division, was alarmed to see that the advancing enemy, avoiding the dug-in tanks, seemed about to steamroller over his headquarters. 'I don't want you to think we're peeing in our bags here,' Gatehouse radioed to 'Pip' Roberts, commander of the 22nd Armoured Brigade, 'but you may have to come out of your position and attack him from the rear.' In the event, it was unnecessary. Shortly afterwards the Panzers obligingly turned their attention to the Grants of Roberts's City of London Yeomanry, who held their fire until the enemy were little more than half a mile away.

Despite Montgomery's orders to stay put, some regiments were not disciplined enough and paid for it. The Sherwood Rangers Yeomanry, mobilized in September 1939 but in action for the first time, found the temptation presented by some 'black dots' on the skyline irresistible and advanced to within 150 yards of them. The German anti-tank gunners held their fire until the Rangers were almost on top of them. When they opened up, two C Squadron tanks were hit immediately and went up in flames. Now the whole regiment advanced and came under intense enemy fire. Six C Squadron tanks and one from B were hit and blazed. Four more were disabled. But in most cases the

Panzerarmee's tried and tested show-and-kill tactics that had so often lured the British armour to its destruction failed. 'The swine isn't attacking,' Rommel complained to Kesselring, who was visiting the front.

Rommel's defeat at Alam el Halfa proved that British forces had already been strengthened to the point where they were too strong to be attacked successfully. For although the Axis still deployed ten divisions – six of them Italian – to Montgomery's six, the British had 700 tanks to the Panzerarmee's 450, of which 240 were Italian. Nothing could match the German 88 as an anti-tank gun, and at least 100 of the German tanks were better gunned than the Grants, carrying new long-barrelled 50-mm and 75-mm cannon. But there were not enough of them. The heady days of the summer, when Alexandria and Cairo and that first enticing glimpse of a felucca on the Nile seemed just around the corner, were gone. Only if Hitler could be persuaded to take his mind off Russia long enough to spare the Panzerarmee at least another couple of armoured divisions, with air cover to match, could the Axis hope again for a victory parade with the pyramids as the backcloth.

An army addicted to victory found the cold turkey of defeat hard to take. Some, Kesselring among them, blamed Rommel for the setback at Alam el Halfa, saying he was tired and sick, that the Panzerarmee had got through the minefields, outflanking the British, and that the old Rommel would have pressed on. There were accusations that Hitler's newest field marshal had allowed himself to become demoralized by his fears of fuel shortages following the sinking of several Italian tankers in the Mediterranean. But Rommel was ever the realist. A year before, some of the same critics had probably been telling him he was wrong to give up the siege of Tobruk and abandon Cyrenaica. The fact remained that Rommel was still only sixty miles from Alexandria, with all of Italy's North African possessions recovered. If he had pressed on at Alam el Halfa, he might have ended up sacrificing all his precious German armour in a series of useless frontal assaults.

Nevertheless, Rommel was a sick man. It may have been that he was simply 'run down', for his ailments appear to have been a cocktail of stomach and liver complaints, complicated by high blood-pressure and the misery of sinusitis and a sore throat. Every day Junkers transports with huge red crosses painted on the fuselage, or the hospital ships that sailed to and from Tripoli, took dozens of his young soldiers to hospitals in Greece and Italy with ailments such as dysentery and jaundice. On 23 September 1942, Rommel went too. He handed over to General Georg Stumme, a Russian Front veteran, before returning, via Rome and an audience with Mussolini, to Lucie and the teenage Manfred. Ahead of him lay at least six weeks' leave and the adulation due a national hero. In Berlin on 3 October, he told a press conference for journalists from neutral countries that the Germans would soon be in Alexandria.

Paradoxically, Montgomery must have found this reassuring. If any further proof were needed that the enemy was at present incapable of launching another offensive, Rommel's presence in Berlin seemed to confirm it. 'Egypt has been saved,' the Eighth Army commander told the American industrialist and Republican presidential candidate Wendell Wilkie, whom Roosevelt had made a presidential envoy after narrowly defeating him in the 1940 election. Visiting the Eighth Army on a fact-finding mission, Wilkie was impressed by Montgomery, who gave him a guided tour of the Alam el Halfa battlefield, delving into derelict Panzers to produce charred British rations that had been captured at Tobruk. 'You see, Wilkie, the devils have been living on us,' he told his guest. 'But they are not going to do it again.'

It was at about this time that Montgomery started to become 'Monty' to a wider public. For both sides until now, the most famous general in the desert had been Rommel. British soldiers, officers included, were so bemused by his reputation as a master tactician, and at the same time a stickler for the Geneva Conventions, that they came to believe the most unlikely stories. One that had wide circulation was that he had personally shot an Italian he caught abusing wounded British prisoners.

Auchinleck had become so concerned about the 'Rommel cult' that he sent out a written order forbidding senior officers to use the R-word when 'the enemy' or 'Axis forces' would do. 'There exists a real danger that our friend Rommel is becoming a kind of magician or bogey-man to our troops,' said Auchinleck. But his order served only to amuse the Germans and make matters worse: surely there never was an army so besotted with an enemy commander.

Montgomery decided to tackle the charisma problem head on. What his soldiers needed, he decided, was 'not only a master but a mascot. The Eighth Army consisted in the main of civilians in uniform, not of professional soldiers [he would recall]. And they were, of course, to a man, civilians who read newspapers. It seemed to me that to command such men demanded not only a guiding mind but a point of focus . . . And I deliberately set out fulfilling this second requirement. It helped, I felt sure, for them to recognize as a person . . . the man who was putting them into battle.' It was one of Montgomery's many conceits that everything that occurred around him was in accordance with some master plan. 'This analysis may sound rather cold blooded,' he says in his *Memoirs*. Well, yes. It is not all that credible that within days of taking command and fighting an important battle he should have found time to set about building this mascot figure in such a deliberate way. More likely it was a role he drifted into at first, then he began to realize it was no bad thing, and ultimately relished it.

It was not difficult for him. Unlike Auchinleck, there was not a diffident fibre in Montgomery's body. And he was, as Churchill had spotted over the business of the sandwiches in the car, a genuine eccentric. One of the milder symptoms of this was his taste for incongruous hats. As an instructor at the Quetta staff college he had amused his students by wearing a topi so antique that it might have belonged to Lord Curzon. In the desert he almost immediately acquired one of the Australians' trademark slouch hats that can be clipped up on one side, and it was soon studded with the cap-badges of regiments he had visited. Before long, Montgomery equipped himself with the kind of mobile tactical headquarters that Rommel used – and with it a new type of headgear, which he was to use throughout the war.

The mobile HQ included a modified Grant tank with its top 37-mm gun removed and replaced by a wooden dummy to make more room inside for an extra map-table. The driver was Lance-Corporal (later Warrant Officer) James Fraser, a decorated veteran from the 6th Royal Tank Regiment, the other three crew members being staff officers. The Grant flew a general's flag and, in order to see and be seen, Montgomery liked to stand in the open turret. Unless he remembered to pull the chin strap down when he did so, his Digger hat tended to blow away. Time and again the tank had to halt while somebody went off to retrieve it and driver Fraser was 'getting a bit cheesed off. So I took off my beret – it was sand- and oil-stained – and handed it on, saying, "Tell him to try this on and if he wears it we'll get there a lot quicker." To everybody's surprise, he tried it on and after that he kept on wearing that beret for some time.'

Generals did not often wear berets in those days and Montgomery tended to sport his in the kind of sloppy fashion that does awful things to a sergeant-major's blood-pressure. But after Alam el Halfa the baggy beret, bearing the badge of the 6th RTR as well as a general's insignia, became a familiar sight. 'What started as a private joke . . . became in the end the means by which I came to be recognized,' Montgomery would recall.* Another means he adopted of being recognized was the risky recourse of having the name 'Monty' painted in 18-inch Gothic letters on the side of his tank.

Montgomery quickly realized that although the Eighth Army was 'composed of magnificent material, it was untrained' and he resolved not to launch an all-out offensive without intensive training. As the old hands went through their paces, green reinforcements poured in. The latest to arrive were the reconstituted 51st Highland Division, which had replaced the formation captured by Rommel in France. They were prepared for the coming showdown by being broken up into small groups in order to spend time with the battle-hardened Australians in the northern part of the line where the occasional artillery duel and 'stand-to' at dawn and dusk gave them their first taste of action.

Newcomers and desert veterans alike expected the battle to begin any day. But, to Churchill's mounting frustration, Montgomery refused to be hurried, sticking to the promise he had made to his staff when he first addressed them not to attack until he considered the Eighth Army was ready. The Prime Minister's impatience was understandable. If the Eighth Army did not take the offensive before the Allied landings in Morocco and Algeria, the Axis might be able to deal first with the landings and then with an attack from the El Alamein line. And above all Churchill yearned to demonstrate to his American and Russian allies that, after three years of reverses, Britain could inflict a major land defeat on the Germans. On 17 September Churchill

---

* After a while one of Montgomery's ADCs acquired a new beret for his boss, who returned Fraser's stained and battered hat to him. Montgomery might not have become so attached to this kind of headgear had he realized that the deeply disliked Dorman-Smith had been the one to introduce it into the British army, having recommended it as suitable for tank crews after seeing the Basque beret while carousing in Spain with his friend, Ernest Hemingway.

sent Alexander a signal – 'I am anxiously awaiting some account of your intentions' – which in effect urged him to make Montgomery get a move on. Alexander, ever the diplomat and conscious of the fact that the Eighth Army commander, four years his senior, had been his instructor at staff college, knew better than to hassle Montgomery.

As Brooke had realized when recommending him for supreme command in the Middle East, Alexander might have 'no ideas of his own' but he had other qualities that made up for that lack. In Eighth Army parlance, Alex did not flap, and it was probably this more than anything else that explains how during the First World War he had become, at the age of twenty-four, one of the youngest battalion commanders in the history of the British army. However bad the situation became, Alexander retained his rock-like composure and charm, qualities so abundant that jealous colleagues sometimes said it was the composure of a man untroubled by imagination.

Apart from his nerve, Brooke spotted that Alexander had the leadership knack of getting all kinds of people to work as a team, not only to delegate but to co-ordinate talent and deploy it where it was most needed. Alexander, recognizing that Montgomery was a much more talented tactician than he would ever be, knew that part of his job was to shield him from Churchill's demands. Consequently, on receiving Churchill's message of 17 September he flew immediately to Eighth Army headquarters at Borg el-Arab to discuss how to reply.

As Montgomery would recall: 'I said that our preparations could not be completed in time for a September offensive, and an attack would fail: if we waited until October, I guaranteed complete success . . . Alexander backed me up wholeheartedly as he always did, and the reply was sent on the lines I wanted.'

In fact, it seems clear that Alexander did more than back Montgomery up, actually allowing him to frame the reply to Churchill. 'Freddie' de Guingand, Montgomery's chief of staff and the only other person at the meeting, was taking notes and later recorded: 'Montgomery said: "Now Alex, I won't do it in September. But if I do it in October it'll be a victory." And Alex said: "Well, what shall I say to him?" Monty said: "Freddie, give me the pad" – I always carried a note pad – and he wrote the message himself for Alex to send.'

Privately and out of de Guingand's earshot, Montgomery told Alexander that if Churchill insisted on an attack in September he would have to find somebody else to do it. 'My stock was rather high after Alam Halfa! We heard no more about a September attack.' Churchill accepted the inevitable and cabled Alexander: 'We are in your hands and of course a victorious battle makes amends for much delay. Whatever happens we shall back you up and see you through.'

So Montgomery got his extra time, and a date was set for the start of Operation 'Lightfoot' – 23 October, the night before a full moon. Alexander arranged to send Churchill a one-word telegram to notify him when the offensive had begun. That one word would be 'Zip!', a joking reference to the fastening on the boiler suit Churchill had unwisely worn on his visit to the desert in August.

Gradually, according to rank, the nearly 170,000 men of the Eighth Army were let into the secret. By the end of September all the divisional commanders and their brigadiers knew; by 10 October battalion commanders had been told; by 17 October company and battery commanders; by 21 October all other officers, many of them the young subalterns who would lead the infantry platoons in the first assault. The Other Ranks, in which the British army bracketed everybody who did not hold the King's Commission, from regimental sergeant-major down to the humblest private, were the last to know. On 21 October, all leave to Alexandria and Cairo was stopped, the explanation being that information had been received that Rommel himself might go on the offensive.

In the interim, Montgomery had issued a memorandum calling on officers to promote a kind of bloodlust among their men. In the war to date 'far too many' unwounded British soldiers had surrendered to the enemy, said Montgomery, and 'they must be worked up to that state which will make them want to go into battle and kill Germans'. On the same theme, Montgomery 'brought the house down' at one officers' meeting by declaring that 'even the padres' were included in the injunction to kill Germans: 'One on weekdays and two on Sundays.'

It is doubtful whether Montgomery hated the Germans at all. As a professional soldier he had a great admiration for their officer corps. What he wanted was infantry of the same mind-set as the regulars he had led, sword in hand, across a Belgian field, over a quarter-century before. Instead, he commanded an army of mainly citizen-soldiers whom he still considered insufficiently trained, men who, however bravely they had fought, had known almost nothing but defeat.

While the build-up to Operation Lightfoot continued, GHQ Cairo finalized plans for a major sideshow. Undeterred by the failure of previous commando raids, they ordered a combined-operations attack on Tobruk to cripple the vital port facilities which the Eighth Army had virtually handed to Rommel on a plate three months previously. Simultaneously, a long-range group was to go overland to attack the more westerly Axis port of Benghazi.

However, as in the raid on Rommel's supposed headquarters the previous November, and in the airfield sabotage raids seven months later, a combination of poor planning, loose security and bad weather would once again lead to disaster. This time the security leakages could not be laid at Fellers' door; he had already been sent back to Washington. Nevertheless, far too many people with no 'need to know' were aware of the pending raids, scheduled for the night of 13–14 September and codenamed Operation 'Agreement' for Tobruk and Operation 'Bigamy' for Benghazi. (There were also to be three smaller operations, including an attack on the Italian airfield at Barce.)

In its original conception, 'Agreement', which was by far the most important operation, might have worked. It was born in the fertile mind of Jock Haselden, the peacetime Cairo cotton-broker and fluent Arabic-speaker who was by now a lieutenant-colonel attached to the SAS at Kufra. Using Buck's Special Interrogation Group German-Jewish volunteers once again to act as 'guards' over a group of 'prisoners', he planned to introduce a compact commando force into Tobruk to destroy harbour installations and shipping carrying vital supplies for Rommel's army. According to intelligence estimates, only 'low grade elements' of the Italian Bologna Division and German technicians or specialists, 'and therefore poor fighting material', were likely to be encountered there.

Middle East Headquarters liked the idea – so much so, they decided that a small-scale raid by Haselden's unit was not sufficient. It should be enlarged into a major combined-services operation, involving the Royal Navy, the Royal Marines, the RAF and conventional army units and carried out in co-ordination with the parallel raid on Benghazi, 200 miles to the west.

Neither Haselden nor the SAS commander, David Stirling, who was to lead 'Bigamy', was comfortable with the expanded plan. It seemed to them altogether too complex and unwieldy, presenting too many opportunities for things to go badly wrong. But by now the GHQ planning machine had developed an unstoppable thrust of its own. The two raids were originally intended as a curtain-raiser to the Eighth Army offensive at El Alamein; but when Montgomery and Alexander postponed the showdown for a month, GHQ nevertheless ruled that 'Agreement' and 'Bigamy' should go ahead as planned.

Very early on, rumours that something big was in the offing began to leak out in the bars and clubs of a Cairo teeming with enemy informants and sympathizers. 'Lovely dark Syrian heads on crumpled pillows listened carefully to their blond bedfellows; military plans mingled with the raw pleadings of inexperienced passion,'* recalled Vladimir Peniakoff, commander of the raiding and reconnaissance unit known as 'Popski's Private Army'.

A more mundane insight into the kind of leakage that so seriously compromised Operation 'Agreement' is to be found in an official report headed 'Serious Breach of Security' which tells of a loud-mouthed Royal Marine corporal, sent from Haifa to Kabrit with his unit to train for the raid. He had been heard sounding off in the NAAFI canteen about the movement of two cruisers, four destroyers and hundreds of marines, signifying that 'some big operation must be on'. Said the report: 'This man has been spilling his mouth at every step on his way down from Haifa and much damage may have been done.' Exactly how much would eventually become clear to the Marines' commanding officer, Lieutenant-Colonel E. H. M. Unwin, when his German captors tauntingly asked him 'why my force had arrived late!' Rumours of a large-scale raid in the offing were even circulating as far away as Beirut, where a barman at the St Georges Hotel who was generally thought to be an enemy agent 'seemed much too well informed'.

---

* In his post-war memoirs, Peniakoff would claim to have been convinced from the start that the 'Agreement'/'Bigamy' project was unworkable. The intelligence was faulty, the planning was reckless and light-hearted and Haselden, an old friend, 'should have known better,' he wrote (*Popski's Private Army*, p. 212).

The SIG's warrant officer, Israel Carmi, who was plugged into Cairo's unofficial Jewish intelligence network through his Haganah connections, was well aware of the security seepage and warned his junior comrades not to volunteer for 'Agreement'. He also warned Captain Buck that there was far too much loose talk about a pending raid. But by that time Buck had committed himself and his second in command, Russell, to go with five of their German-speaking Palestinians on the operation. They were to lead the way into Tobruk aboard a convoy of three-ton trucks, carrying Haselden and a company of his raiders posing as PoWs.

Although the small SIG contingent was a vital component of the raiding force, the top brass were belatedly having second thoughts about the propriety of sending men behind the lines in enemy disguise. Two weeks before the launch, Haselden was expressly and categorically forbidden to use the Palestinian Jews of the SIG in this role. 'You are to clearly understand,' said a 'Most Secret and Personal' message to him (and Stirling) from GHQ Middle East, 'that under no circumstances will either you or the troops under your command be permitted to wear any article of German or Italian uniform while on operations.' Haselden, for one, chose to ignore this instruction.

Operation 'Agreement' was divided among three forces: Force A, the Royal Navy destroyers *Sikh* and *Zulu*, the heavy cruiser *Coventry* and a cluster of smaller vessels, which were to bombard Tobruk from the sea; Force C, a mixed force of Royal Marines and Royal Northumberland Fusiliers, who were to be landed from a flotilla of lighters and motor torpedo boats; and Force B, Haselden's 80 commandos, who were to travel overland from Kufra in eight three-ton Chevrolet trucks, escorted by an LRDG patrol that would hive off when they were within striking distance of Tobruk. Haselden's objective – 'the most hazardous phase of the operation' – was to occupy Mersa Sciausc, a cove just east of the harbour mouth, put the coastal defence and anti-aircraft batteries there out of action, and guide the MTBs of Force C in to shore by signal light.

After a 1,800-mile, seven-day drive through the desert, three vehicles of Force B duly penetrated the Tobruk perimeter without raising the alarm. The Chevrolet trucks, now adorned with Afrika Korps markings on the sides and roofs, would arouse no suspicion; so much British transport had been captured that 'enemy' vehicles were in commonplace use by the Panzerarmee. At the perimeter they were waved through by an Italian guard and Haselden's men reached the target area just as RAF and newly arrived US Army Air Force planes started bombing Tobruk to distract the defenders.

Force B went rapidly into action. Buck, Russell and five SIG rankers – named Berg, Steiner, Weizmann, Wilenski and Hillman – stormed a villa haphazardly guarded by an Italian section and set up Haselden's headquarters there. Meanwhile, other members of Haselden's force attacked Axis coastal defence batteries and got into position to guide the sea-borne assault forces in by signal lamp. These initial successes were quickly reversed. Far from low-grade Italian troops, the raiders found themselves up against first-class German infantry, who mounted an unexpectedly spirited series of counter-attacks and re-took the coastal batteries before their guns could be spiked. As HMS *Sikh*, *Zulu* and *Coventry* and their accompanying MTBs approached, they came under heavy fire.

Rough seas hindered the progress of wooden lighters towing a battalion of Marine commandos in to shore. To make matters worse, the engines of some of the towing lighters failed and the craft began to founder as enemy searchlights picked them out, 800 yards offshore. For the Germans, it was like shooting fish in a barrel. All but seventy men of the Marine battalion drowned and, of those who did get ashore, only twenty-one survived the ensuing battle.

The Fusiliers aboard the MTBs fared little better. A mix-up in the signalling arrangements made it almost impossible for them to find their way into the cove. Six MTBs were sunk by enemy fire and only two got to the cove, where they ran aground. The destroyer *Sikh* was so badly damaged that it had to be scuttled. And later, as the warships withdrew towards Alexandria, both *Zulu* and *Coventry*, which had taken the badly damaged *Zulu* in tow, were sunk by Stuka dive-bombers, with heavy loss of life. Allied losses included eight British and American bombers, and when the final tally was made it would be found that 'Agreement' had cost the lives of 750 men.

Stirling's Operation 'Bigamy' ran into similar difficulties. His 220-man column, designated Force X and totalling forty vehicles, including two light tanks, did reach the Benghazi perimeter, intending to 'take the garrison by surprise and once inside to destroy everything we could lay hands on'. But there was no surprise: the Benghazi garrison were waiting for them. The bazaar had been full of rumours about a raid for days and, as Fitzroy Maclean, who took part in it, would discover, 'a strong German machine-gun detachment had arrived, as well as Italian infantry reinforcements. Minefields had been laid at different points around the city perimeter, including the place where we hoped to force our way in. Finally, the actual date of our attack – 14 September – was being freely mentioned.'

As the raiders approached the perimeter with headlights full on – a typical Stirling ploy to fool the defenders into believing it was a friendly force – they ran into a well-laid ambush: 'A dozen machine-guns opened up at us at point-blank range,' Maclean recalled, 'then a couple of 20-mm Bredas joined in, and then some heavy mortars, while snipers' bullets pinged viciously through the trees on either side of the road.' Heavily outgunned and taking severe losses, Stirling ordered the retreat and headed for a line of distant hills and wadis, where they were pounded by Axis close-support planes.

Before Stirling could limp back to Gialo, his jump-off point, he had lost a quarter of his men, killed, wounded or missing, and three-quarters of his vehicles. Lieutenant James Sherwood of the Special Boat Section, who took part in 'Bigamy', grumbled afterwards that 'we headed out of it, having achieved nothing at all; a complete fiasco, the whole operation'. The Germans were cock-a-hoop. 'The British have gone through another Dieppe,' said their official radio the next day – a reference to the large-scale commando raid on the French seaport that had come to spectacular grief only four weeks before. The Tobruk and Benghazi raids had been carried out 'in the same amateurish manner,' sneered the Germans. They did not mention the Long Range Desert Group's raid on the airfield at Barce, where about twenty-five aircraft were destroyed and most of the raiders made good their escape. This was the only British success of the night.

The lethal fiasco at Tobruk left Force B in dire straits. Haselden, Buck, Russell and the rest of the SIG group were virtually isolated around Haselden's headquarters, with the enemy closing in. Before making an attempt to break out, Buck told one of his SIG men, Austrian-born Ernst Hillman, to go down to one of the trucks, change out of the German uniform he was still wearing and get into British khakis. 'After I had gone about 100 yards,' Hillman recalled, 'Colonel Haselden came running from the direction of the trucks. He was alone and he shouted that there was an ambush 50 yards ahead. Colonel Haselden stayed there alone and opened fire with his TSMG [Thompson sub-machine-gun] while I went back to warn the others.'

Hillman rounded up Buck, Russell, a Lieutenant Sillito and Privates Watler and Roer, and together they went to help Haselden, who gave the order to charge in an attempt to break out of the encirclement and reach an MTB which was beached in the cove. It was too dark to see the enemy, but Hillman estimated there were about ten of them. Little by little, the British drove them back, allowing a truck carrying a number of their wounded to break through. Then Roer was wounded and Buck carried him into the shelter of a wadi, calling for Hillman to follow. Hillman reckoned he was needed more urgently by Haselden, and that was the last he saw of Buck.* 'We continued to hold back the enemy for another ten minutes until we ran out of ammunition,' Hillman recalled. Then Haselden was hit and fell into a wadi. 'I saw the colonel lying, face down, and not moving. I shouted his name two or three times but he did not move.'

With the Force B commander dead, and Buck nowhere to be found, Hillman, Watler, Russell and Sillito made their way to the beach, where they linked up with a small party headed by Lieutenant Tom Langton,† another of Haselden's officers, and including a few of the Northumberland Fusiliers who had come in on the MTBs. Those vessels were out of action and the only escape route lay overland, through the perimeter defences of Tobruk.

The group split into two to make detection more difficult. Russell went off with one group; Hillman joined up with Langton and five others, including a pair of identical-twin Fusiliers, surnamed Leslie. Three hundred miles of virtually waterless desert lay between them and the British lines at El Alamein. Hillman had lost one of his boots in the breakout and badly lacerated one heel on barbed wire. 'He also had the added burden of knowing he would be shot if caught,' Langton recalled. 'We changed his name there and then to Kennedy and he was known thus until we were safe.' Before setting out on the trek to safety behind British lines, 'Kennedy' recovered a good pair of boots from the corpse of a German soldier.

Langton's party laid up by day in caves or wadis and moved only

---

* Buck, luckily in British uniform, was taken prisoner. He survived the war in a PoW camp only to die in a post-war air crash while on his way to a posting with the occupation forces in Germany.

† Langton, a pre-war Cambridge rowing blue, was instrumental in designing the SAS regimental emblem – a pair of parachute wings on an Oxford-and-Cambridge dark-blue and light-blue background.

after dark to avoid detection by patrolling enemy aircraft. They started out with only a bar of chocolate, a small can of cheese, four biscuits and half a gallon of water between them, but many evenings they would find a Bedouin encampment where, thanks to 'Kennedy's' fluent Arabic, they were able to negotiate for food and water. The fact that 'Kennedy's' Arabic was Palestinian-accented helped allay the suspicions of the local tribesmen, who knew well the punishment that had been meted out to those of their fellows who had given aid to Italians posing as British soldiers on the run. Accordingly, whenever Langton's party approached an Arab village 'Kennedy' would go in ahead to get on good terms and establish their credentials. The first time they did this, the Arab villagers gave them biscuits and marmalade and all the water they could drink. 'I don't think I shall ever forget that meal,' Langton would recall. 'We set upon it like animals, quite unashamedly . . . Later, we were to learn through "Kennedy" how to conduct ourselves as visitors.'

By the time Langton's party reached British lines on 13 November, it had been reduced to four – two British Other Ranks, Hillman and Langton himself; the others had one by one succumbed to dysentery, dropped out and given themselves up. At about the same time, another small party, which included the SIG's Lieutenant Russell, also reached safety. This was effectively the end of the brief and controversial existence of the SIG. In the absence of its progenitor, Captain Buck, the unit was disbanded and its members dispersed among less adventurous formations.

Montgomery had nothing to do with the planning of the 13–14 September raids, though it was within his power to stop them, and in his memoirs he makes no mention of them. As the survivors struggled back towards British lines on 14 September he issued an order concerning the state of his army's morale for the coming battle: 'Morale is the big thing in war. We must raise the morale of our soldiers to the highest pitch. They must be made enthusiastic and they must enter this battle with their tails high in the air and the will to win.'

There had been nothing wrong with the morale of the men whose lives were squandered at Tobruk and Benghazi. On the contrary, they were among the best the British army had. They just deserved better leadership and planning.

PART FIVE
Alamein

It will become a staid historic name,
That crazy sea of sand!
Like Troy or Agincourt its single fame
Will be the garland for our brow, our claim,
On us a fleck of glory to the end;
And there our dead will keep their holy ground.

John Jarmain, 51st Highland Division

22

For all Montgomery's insistence on maintaining the morale of his foot-soldiers, the men required to storm the Axis positions were obliged to spend the last long day of waiting in the most potentially demoralizing of circumstances. To achieve maximum surprise, enormous care was taken to conceal preparations for the attack and most of the British and Commonwealth infantry had been moved up the night before to deep slit trenches just behind their 'start lines'. By the time the dawn came up behind them on 23 October, bringing with it the first of the enemy's daily reconnaissance flights, they were invisible from above and were under strict orders to remain concealed in the trenches – generally small two-man affairs – from dawn to dusk, about thirteen hours.

Calls of nature had to be answered in the trench and too bad if your mate had 'gippy tum'; a shovel was provided for disposal, while for sustenance each man had a can of bully beef, hard biscuits and water. Almost everybody smoked heavily, both to calm the nerves and to keep the flies away. They groused, of course, but the men knew the discomforts were in their own interests, to ensure that the enemy got as little warning as possible. Even so, senior officers fretted that keeping a man in a trench all day with little to do but swelter and brood on what fate might have in store was hardly ideal.

When 'Ming the Merciless' Morshead discovered that there was a possibility zero hour might be brought forward by an hour so that his Australians would step out of their cramped trenches and go straight into battle, he protested. 'I cannot conceive anything psychologically worse than such solitary confinement in a tight-fitting, grave-like pit awaiting the hard and bloody battle,' he told his XXX Corps commander, General Oliver Leese. 'There must be some relaxation before the fight . . . these troops will not be able to emerge until close on 19.00 hours. Then they will have dinner – in the semi-darkness – and they will not want to be rushed off as soon as they have eaten.'

Morshead got his way. The infantry would not leave their start lines until 10 p.m.

★

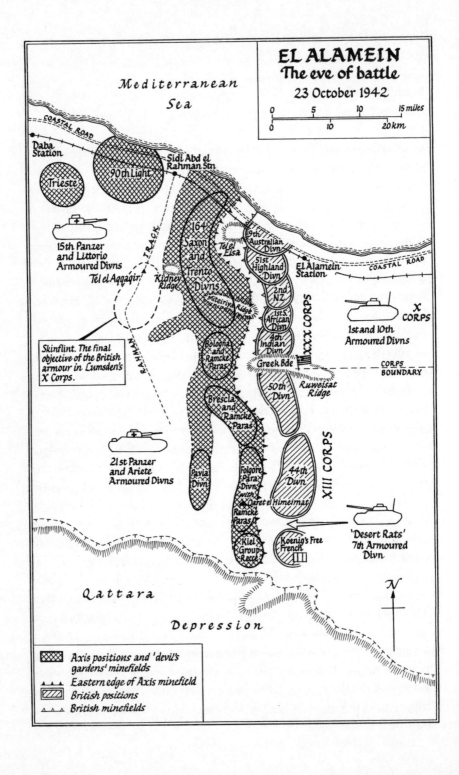

EL ALAMEIN
The eve of battle
23 October 1942

Mediterranean Sea

COASTAL ROAD

Daba Station

Trieste

90th Light

Sidi Abd el Rahman Stn

15th Panzer and Littorio Armoured Divns

Tel el Aqqaqir

TRACK

164 Saxon and Trento Divns

Kidney Ridge

Tel el Eisa

9th Australian Divn

51st Highland Divn

El Alamein Station

COASTAL ROAD

2nd NZ

Miteiriya Ridge

1st S. African Divn

XXX CORPS

X CORPS

1st and 10th Armoured Divns

4th Indian Divn

Skinflint. The final objective of the British armour in Lumsden's X Corps.

RAHMAN

Bologna and Ramcke Paras

Greek Bde

CORPS BOUNDARY

50th Divn

Ruweisat Ridge

Brescia and Ramcke Paras

21st Panzer and Ariete Armoured Divns

Pavia Divn

Folgore Para Divn with Ramcke Paras

44th Divn

XIII CORPS

Qaret el Himeimat

'Desert Rats' 7th Armoured Divn

Kiel Group Recce

Koenig's Free French

Qattara

Depression

N

Axis positions and 'devil's gardens' minefields

Eastern edge of Axis minefield

British positions

British minefields

Since the beginning of the desert war, just over two years before, there had never been anything, in size or conception, quite like the battle the Eighth Army was about to fight. Montgomery's plan was brutally simple, its main features being a feint in the south and a broad infantry frontal assault in the north, where they would punch holes in the enemy's defences for the armour to pour through. It was a rehash of exactly the kind of 1914–18 horror that the desert generals had endured as subalterns and tried so hard to spare another generation. Montgomery had decided there was no other option.

As Auchinleck had spotted, the El Alamein–Qattara Depression line, with its unturnable flanks, favoured the defender, in this case the Axis. At Alam el Halfa in August, Rommel had attempted to get around the line with one of his outflanking armoured hooks that normally worked so well but which for once had failed dismally. Now it was the turn of the British to attempt an attack, and Rommel had laid the foundation for some truly formidable defence-works before proceeding on home leave on 23 September, suffering from a variety of minor ailments and general exhaustion, and handing over temporary command to the large and affable General Georg Stumme.

Axis troops were protected by what were probably the world's biggest minefields. Known to their Italian and German defenders as 'the devil's gardens', these consisted of some half a million mines, sown in two enormous fields at least a mile apart. Most were round Teller anti-tank mines fitted with a pressure fuse. They weighed about nineteen pounds, more than half of which was explosives. A man's weight would rarely detonate a Teller, though vehicles much lighter than tanks could. The Italians had a trick of tying a long rope to an axle and tyres, then dragging it over a freshly laid minefield to lure enemy vehicles along what appeared to be a well-used route.

To discourage the clearance of the Tellers, they were sometimes surrounded by S-mines, a wickedly ingenious anti-personnel weapon. The S stood for '*Springen*' and later in the war American troops would call them 'Bouncing Bettys'. Once touched off, an initial charge sprang a canister crammed with 360 ball-bearings to about waist height, where it exploded. S-mines were hard enough to spot in daylight, let alone at night. Often, they and other booby traps were triggered by a trip wire. Luckily for the British, S-mines were not as plentiful as Rommel might have wished.

Between the main fields, more mines were laid in a ladder pattern, so that any enemy troops who got through the first field would, finding mines on either side of them, be channelled on to the next field by a route covered by artillery and machine-gun fire.

The forward minefields were lightly garrisoned with machine- and anti-tank gunners in place on their perimeters or in outposts within the minefields themselves. Manned defence started in depth at the rear edge of the second minefield, where there would be plenty of 50-mm anti-tank guns. Behind them, in reserve and poised to respond wherever they were most needed, lurked the Panzer Divisions and the 88s that so often kept them from harm. These anti-tank guns could still outrange any Eighth Army tank, including the newly arrived Shermans. Fortunately for the British, General Stumme seems to have inherited no more than about forty, though, as it turned out, these were almost enough.

Axis troops at El Alamein totalled about 104,000 men, of whom 50,000 were German and the rest Italian. They had approximately 500 tanks, of which nearly 280 were the inferior Italian models. There were some 1,200 artillery pieces, just over half of them German, and about 350 serviceable aircraft, of which 150 belonged to the Luftwaffe. This did not include those available in Crete, Greece and Sicily.

By now, Montgomery had received enough reinforcements to enjoy a considerable advantage in men and equipment, although nowhere did he have the three-to-one ascendancy staff colleges usually insist on as the proper ratio for an attacking force. Eighth Army had just over 1,000 tanks, of which about 300 were the heavily gunned Shermans and Grants able to match all the Panzers with the exception of thirty or so Mark IV Specials with their long 75-mm guns. At Alam el Halfa the Specials had demonstrated that, in the right circumstances, they could pick off Grants with impunity; it was hoped that the untested Shermans would fare better.

The British had almost twice as much artillery as the Axis – 2,311 pieces – and their Desert Air Force had 530 serviceable aircraft, almost 200 more than their opponents. The United States Army Air Force presence was now up to about eighty aircraft, with the arrival of more twin-engined Mitchell bombers and Warhawk fighter-bombers. In all, the Desert Air Force now consisted of nineteen RAF, nine South African, seven American and two Australian squadrons. More important than numerical superiority was that some squadrons at last had the latest Spitfires. The days were over when the Luftwaffe's

Messerschmitt-109s and the Regia Aeronautica's excellent, if rare, Macchi-202s could fly rings around anything the British put in the air. Also, by the beginning of October the Luftwaffe had lost three of its top desert aces, including Marseille, who baled out, collided with his tail-unit, and was unable to open his parachute.

To get the best out of his Italian formations, Rommel mixed them with German units, which almost invariably meant that the Italians came under German command. In the north, near the coast, the 15th Panzer Division was grouped with the Italian Littorio Division and in the south 21st Panzer was combined with the Ariete, probably the best of the Italian armoured formations.

The veterans of the Afrika Korps' 90th Light Division were also grouped with an Italian formation, the Trieste Motorized Division, about three miles from the front and the nearest to the coast. This was in case Montgomery, notwithstanding the recent disaster at Tobruk, tried to cut the road with an amphibious landing.

Italian tank crews, despite all the taunts about a superabundance of reverse gears, often fought very bravely, just as their artillery did. Mixing them with the Panzers was a reflection rather on the inferiority of their tanks than on their morale. The same could not be said of Mussolini's infantry which, since the campaign began, had generally fought poorly and sometimes not at all. One of the main reasons for this seems to have been indifferent junior leadership. There was an almost eighteenth-century chasm between officers and men in the Italian regiments of foot, somewhat at variance with the egalitarian notions of the Fascist creed. Wounded German officers on an Italian hospital ship were outraged to discover that their enlisted men were put on inferior rations and insisted that they got the same. By contrast to the Italians, the high percentage of British infantry officers who became casualties – far greater than the Other Ranks – was ample proof of a worthy *noblesse oblige*.

The majority of Stumme's infantry was Italian and, faced with the certainty of a major British attack, their morale was more uncertain than ever. In order to give them the kind of backbone that might prevent a repetition of July's rout of the Sabratha Division by Morshead's Australians, they were far more densely mixed with German units than were the Italian armour.

The majority of these 'corset staves', as the Germans called them, were from Major-General Karl Lungerhausen's 164th (Saxon) Light

Division, which had been on garrison duty in Greece and Crete. Its 10,000 men included a number of ethnic Germans from the Czech Sudetenland and Polish-speaking *Volkdeutscher* from the coalfields of Silesia. Prisoners taken by the Australians in a raid on the Saxons revealed that their division had not yet received its full complement of anti-tank weapons. Overall, Eighth Army intelligence were unimpressed by these newcomers. Said a 'Top Secret' memo: '[T]he troops of this division cannot be considered equal to the German infantry we have so far met in Africa although, when properly armed, they should be at least good defensive troops.' The memo added that 'a considerable proportion of the new personnel seem to be affected by the usual maladies from which most new arrivals in Egypt suffer'.

Far more daunting than the Saxons, if only a quarter of their number, was the Germans' Ramcke Parachute Brigade. These had arrived at the beginning of August and participated in the closing stages of the Alam el Halfa battle, where one of their battalions had made a spirited counter-attack against Freyberg's New Zealanders on the Ruweisat Ridge. Their morale owed a lot to their leader, Colonel Hermann Ramcke, ex-merchant seaman, ex-ranker in the Kaiser's war and ex-Freikorps stalwart during the chaos of post-war Germany. Like all senior officers in General Kurt Student's parachute division, Ramcke had last fought in Crete, where British and Commonwealth troops under Freyberg had exacted a terrible price for German victory, a price that was the main reason why Ramcke's 2,800 paratroopers now found themselves foot-slogging in Egypt's western desert.

For almost a year they had helped to train Italy's newly raised Folgore Parachute Division for Operation 'Herkules', an airborne invasion of Malta. This was cancelled at the last moment by Hitler, fearing that the casualties might be even heavier than in Crete – and conscious, perhaps, that no military fiasco is so unambiguously public as an airborne fiasco. Instead, the Folgore and Ramcke paratroopers were sent to the desert. Initially they believed they were to be dropped over the Suez Canal, ahead of a glorious overland advance. Then their parachutes were taken away and it became plain that there was to be no Valkyrian arrival: they were going to fight (and die) in an entirely conventional infantry role.

The airborne 'corset staves' were spread along the front in the hope that they would bring firmness to those places where the Italians might sag. In the north, two of the Ramcke Brigade's four battalions, with some Bersagliere attached, were between the coast and the railroad. Next came Lungerhausen's 164th, which was mixed in with the Trento and Bologna Divisions. Then a third battalion of paratroopers was deployed in packets of no more than 100 among the Brescia Division, which held the middle section of the front between the ridges of Miteiriya and Ruweisat.

In the south, almost on the rim of the Qattara Depression, was Major Otto Burckhardt's 'Experimental' battalion, which was field-testing some of the Wehrmacht's latest weapons. These included the kind of small arms most European armies would not see for another twenty years: a fully automatic rifle, a flare pistol modified to fire a small high-explosive charge, a mortar bomb which bounced before exploding to spread its shrapnel over a large area at chest height. They also had a couple of what a later generation would come to know as the 'recoilless rifle', a light, 75-mm field-gun with a flat trajectory, which could be dropped in pieces by parachute and then easily assembled. But undoubtedly their most effective weapon, and one all the Ramcke Brigade had in abundance, was the brand new MG-42 belt-fed machine-gun made out of a light alloy that was virtually sand-proof. It rarely jammed and had the phenomenal rate of fire of 1,200 rounds a minute; a Bren gun fired 500. They also had a magnetic anti-tank bomb, fitted with a four-second delay fuse, started by a sharp tug on a cord once the device had been attached to its target.

Burckhardt's battalion was attached to the Italian Folgore ('Lightning') Division, who were the linchpin of the southern section of the Axis front line, just north of the impassable Qattara Depression. About 5,000-strong, the Folgore were everything the Italian infantry generally were not. Like the German and British parachute troops, they were all volunteers. They had that self-esteem which comes to men who have conquered fear in earning their parachute wings while weaker spirits balked at the jump and were 'returned to unit'. With this came the kind of *esprit de corps* normally found only in formations that have fought a successful battle. It made the bond between officers and men considerably closer than in most of the Italian infantry. In addition, Ramcke's training teams had given the Folgore a very thorough grounding in fieldcraft and tactics and inculcated some of their own shocktrooper spirit.

At first the Italians took great pains to disguise the presence of their new airborne division in the desert, probably because they wished the

British to believe that an invasion of Malta was still on the cards. The Folgore were told to remove their hard-earned '*paracadutino*' shoulder-flashes. In August, when a twelve-man Folgore foot-patrol was captured close to the British lines, their interrogators noted that these Italians were 'physically well above average'. Attempting to disguise their provenance, the captives confessed to membership of a unit they called the Cacciatori d'Africa ('Hunters of Africa'), a rather sporting title that could have meant almost anything. When the lieutenant in command was discovered to have carelessly kept on him a letter-headed paper for '1st Battalion, Parachute Division', he insisted gamely that it had nothing to do with him and his men.

The British did not have to wait long to confirm their suspicions that part of the southern sector was held by Italian troops of a quality they had not met before. At the end of September a brigade of infantry from 44th (Home Counties) Division, as newly arrived in Africa as the Folgore, mounted a local attack intended to lop off part of a salient. Partly because of poor co-ordination between the artillery, armour and infantry, they walked into a trap and most of one battalion was lost.

The Folgore's lightning struck two companies, about 200 men, of the 1st/5th Queen's, a tightly knit Territorial unit, many of whose original volunteers had known each other in civilian life. One company surrendered more or less intact. The other was raked by Breda machine-gun fire, leaving the stunned survivors huddled among the dead and the dying. Corporal Ernest Norris thought things were going splendidly until the covering British artillery barrage stopped prematurely, leaving him and his mates feeling 'so naked you can't describe it'.

In a matter of seconds they were firing tracer bullets at us. It was still dark and they seemed too slow to be bullets . . . Captain Clarke was mortally wounded and I heard him call out 'Carry on, Mr Cole-Biroth. I've been hit.' Then my Bren gunner screamed and went down . . . We got down behind what cover we could find. I looked round: Captain Clarke was dead, Mr Cole-Biroth was pretty badly wounded and Mr Whittaker had most of his face shot away. We had no officers left . . . they began mortaring us . . . We were being fired at from behind as well as in front . . . we tried to reply to their fire as best we could. Eventually we heard voices . . . Then we saw them standing above us and making signs to throw our rifles down and come out. And that's what we did.

The Germans were delighted to see what a little Wehrmacht training could do for their allies and presented the Italian paratroopers with eleven Iron Crosses (Second Class). This humiliating little defeat by the despised Italians was bound to rekindle Montgomery's worst fears. Winning a defensive fight such as Alam el Halfa was one thing. But was the Eighth Army capable of going on the offensive and beating a well-prepared, resolute and skilful opponent buoyed by the know-ledge that, in three years of war, he had never lost an important battle?

It was not so much that the men of newly arrived divisions such as the 44th Home Counties or the 51st Highland lacked determination or such infantry skills as can be honed by constant and sometimes alarmingly realistic practice. But if 131st Brigade's performance was typical, it was worrying. When the test came, all their unblooded enthusiasm had been squandered by poor intelligence and sloppy staff-work. They had been informed they were attacking a much weaker position and then, when they most needed it, their artillery support had ceased. Nor, it seemed, had Montgomery's strictures about 'too many unwounded prisoners' had much effect. When they found themselves in a hopeless position, those who still could had put their hands up.

Montgomery realized that his was still very much 'an untrained army', lacking the kind of officer corps that enabled Panzerarmee Afrika to think on its tracks, react quickly and weld armour, anti-tank guns, infantry and artillery into one controlled and seamless killing-machine. Bearing this in mind, he had rewritten his plan of attack until it was about as simple as he could make it.

For the coming battle, he was working with an Eighth Army divided into three corps, designated XXX, XIII and X. The first two were mainly made up of infantry. X Corps, optimistically styled a Corps de Chasse, consisted of the tanks, armoured cars and the truck-borne infantry of two armoured divisions. It was under Lieutenant-General Herbert Lumsden, who had led 1st Armoured Division during the Gazala débâcle and, some thought, might have saved the day, given a free hand.

Lumsden was a long-legged cavalier, fond of tailored sartorial frills and coloured neckerchiefs. Despite his height, he had been an amateur jockey, brave and skilled enough to win a Grand National. Too arrogant to be as well liked as Gott had been, he nevertheless had a following among the old desert hands. All in all, he was just the type Montgomery was bent on culling from his new model Eighth Army.★ But against his better judgement, Montgomery had let Alexander persuade him to keep Lumsden: 'I had already imported two new Corps commanders from England,' he rationalized, 'and did not want the Eighth Army to think that none of its senior officers was fit for promotion.'

The new corps commanders, Lieutenant-Generals Brian Horrocks and Oliver Leese, were not exactly Monty's friends (he did not have many) but were men almost a decade younger than himself whom he thought worthwhile and whose careers he had been in a position to nurture. In return, they gave Montgomery their unquestioning obedience and loyalty.

At the Ruweisat Ridge the front was divided into northern and southern sectors. In the northern part was Leese's XXX Corps, with Morshead's Australians nearest the coast, then Major-General Douglas Wimberley's 51st Highland Division, followed by Freyberg's New Zealanders, Pienaar's South Africans, and the 4th Indian Division under Major-General Francis Tuker.

South of the ridge was Horrocks's XIII Corps, in which Major-General Nicholls's north country Territorials of the 50th Division had been reinforced by a brigade of Free Greeks to make up their losses at Gazala. Then, facing the Folgore, came Hughes's 44th Division, in which the battered 131st Brigade had been brought back up to strength with reinforcements from the Canal Zone.

Slightly south-east of 44th Division was 7th Armoured Division, the original 'Desert Rats'. Their latest commander was Major-General John Harding who, like Leese and Wimberley, had been a pupil of Montgomery's at Camberley Staff College. When Montgomery arrived in the desert, Harding had been a brigadier on Auchinleck's staff and working on contingency plans to withdraw to the Nile Delta and even beyond, if necessary. The new commander had no intention of falling back under any circumstances and, anyway, he considered Harding's job to be a peculiar waste of time and talent. He gave his

---

★ 'I agreed he was delightful,' Montgomery recalled of one victim famous for his knowledge of the bunkers on the course at the Gezira club. 'Unfortunately the game we were about to play was not golf ' (Montgomery, *Memoirs*, p. 99).

old pupil promotion and the Eighth Army's best-known division, where Harding soon acquired a reputation as a dangerous man to go on reconnaissance with.

In the extreme south and guarding the Eighth Army's left flank were Koenig's Free French Brigade, the heroes of Bir Hacheim. From their forward positions they could see the flat-topped mountain of Qaret el Himeimat, at 1,300 feet the highest ground for miles around and a wonderful observation post for the Folgore. Himeimat and its surrounding British minefields were about the only gains from the Alam el Halfa battle that Rommel had retained.

When Horrocks, uneasy that his corps was overlooked like this, wanted to try to get the high ground back, Montgomery had refused him permission. He told Horrocks it suited his purposes 'that Rommel should be able to have a good look'. This was because all the preparations taking place on the southern flank were a feint.

Up until then it had normally been the other way around: both sides, however fierce the fighting on the coast became, tried to finish the bout with an armoured swing northwards from the desert side, aimed at cutting the enemy's lines of communications at the coast. Given their two-to-one superiority in tanks, there seemed no reason why the Eighth Army should break with this pattern, but Montgomery thought otherwise. 'The fact that a certain tactic had always been employed by all commanders in the desert seemed to me a good reason for doing something else. I planned to attack neither on my left flank nor on my right flank, but somewhere right of centre; having broken in, I could then direct my forces to the right or the left as it seemed most profitable.'

The main fight, then, was to be in Leese's northern XXX Corps sector, where the tough and experienced Commonwealth infantry from Australia, New Zealand and South Africa had been joined by the 51st Highland Division. In the first twenty-four hours they were required to hack out two corridors through which the 1st and 10th Armoured Divisions of Lumsden's X Corps, entirely British formations, would pour.

At first Montgomery had envisaged his armour going through and taking on the German armour in a pitched tank-battle, dealing with the Axis infantry later. But by the beginning of October, after the Folgore had shown the Queen's Brigade what happened when co-ordination between the artillery and the infantry was bad, he concluded that the Eighth Army was probably not up to it. 'If I was not careful, divisions and units would be given tasks which might end in failure because of the inadequate standard of training.'

So Montgomery decided to reverse the plan so that the Eighth Army would first concentrate on destroying the enemy's infantry, their first line of defence, by what he called a 'crumbling process'. This 'crumbling' – perhaps one of the oddest euphemisms for military mayhem ever coined – would be brought about by concentrating on attacking the Axis infantry not only from the front but, whenever possible, from the flanks and rear so that they were cut off from their supply lines.

Meanwhile the British armour and accompanying anti-tank guns, having come through their corridors in the minefields, would pause to block any attempt by the Panzerarmee to rescue their beleaguered infantry. Far from being dreaded, a Panzer counter-attack was to be welcomed: the Germans would not be allowed their customary tactic of impaling a British advance on their dug-in anti-tank screen.

'Having thus beaten the guts out of the enemy . . . the eventual fate of the Panzerarmee is certain,' Montgomery predicted. 'It will not be able to avoid destruction.' In his emphatic way the new commander of the Eighth Army briefed his senior officers that the battle would be 'a dog fight lasting about twelve days'. And he warned: 'Our troops must not think that, because we have a good tank and very powerful artillery support, the enemy will all surrender. The enemy will not surrender and there will be bitter fighting.'

For the enemy in question 23 October 1942 began as just another day in Egypt's Western Desert. Some of them had been occupying the same dug-outs and trenches and waiting for the British to attack them ever since the battle of Alam el Halfa, almost two months before. As the days wore on, a faint hope began to take root that it might never happen, at least not in 1942. After all, the first winter rain would soon turn sand into a mud that, churned by track and wheel, could glue tanks to the landscape and ruin dreams of armoured manoeuvre. Already the nights were growing colder. Dawn stand-to saw Rommel's men emerge, shivering, from their dug-outs, still in the greatcoats they had slept in, and glad of the Afrika Korps' watery ersatz coffee so long as it was hot. But the day quickly warmed up. Long before noon the greatcoats and sweaters would be off and working parties out improving the defences by laying more barbed wire or re-covering mines exposed by mischievous night breezes.

Italian anti-tank gunners could be seen stepping warily out into their own minefield, whitewashed posts in hand. These were usually hammered into the ground about 300 metres from their guns as range-finding markers. If posts were not available as markers, loose stones would be piled into cairns and finished with some scrub on top.

Three months after their arrival, the Folgore had still not received their full quota of anti-tank guns. By way of protest Captain Gino Bianchini of the 186th Regiment had taken to wearing a huge spanner on a string around his neck 'to take the enemy's tanks apart'. The Italians had plenty of the same suicidal anti-tank limpet mines the German experimental battalion carried. But their anti-tank guns, like their transport, were either awaiting shipment in Italy or Greece or were at the bottom of the Mediterranean.

Transport was limited and truck convoys preferred to make the journey by night rather than risk being shot up by the Desert Air Force, who by now had established an almost total supremacy. Lack of equipment was not the Folgore's only problem. Some forty-five miles from the Axis main supply route on the coast, they were chronically hungry. 'We received less than the minimum of food and water and were all but starving,' recalled Lieutenant Raul di Gennaro, commanding a company of sappers. The only fresh meat was provided by the occasional camel that strayed into one of the 'devil's gardens' and either set off a mine or came close enough to be shot.

In an attempt to solve their supply problems, units with enough mechanically minded soldiers would cannibalize the numerous wrecks at hand until they had restored some to running order and could go and collect their rations. But this brought its own problems. Oberjager (Parachute Corporal) Fritz Neumaier was serving in Burckhardt's battalion alongside an Italian unit. After the sinking of the ship carrying their transport, his company found themselves with one motorbike and twenty-five litres of petrol between them. Neumaier and others set to work on the graveyard of Fords, Mercedes and Fiats that littered their rear areas and the minefields. But when they did get some of them going and drove them in triumph to Mersa Matruh, there was another problem. The Feldpolizei had orders to confiscate all unauthorized vehicles and placed them in a central pound for redistribution to deserving causes.

Despite such trials, and the disappointment of not being used for the airborne assault they had trained for, the *esprit de corps* of the German and Italian paratroopers remained high. The unblooded Folgore were probably the only formation in the Italian army which had never experienced defeat. They might be short of anti-tank guns but, like Ramcke's men, they had plenty of automatics: Breda and Fiat-Revelli heavy machine-guns. Officers and NCO's often carried the new Beretta 38 sub-machine-guns which weighed half as much as the American Thompsons carried by some of the British. Those involved in the action against the battalion from the Queen's had acquitted themselves well and had the satisfaction of seeing a crestfallen column of British soldiers being marched into captivity.

Perhaps a few had themselves known the terror of ambush, even temporary capture, while serving with other regiments in the desert, but the majority had volunteered for the Folgore fresh from recruit training. They were cocky, the way jump-qualified airborne troops usually are, with the knowledge of fear conquered.★ Among their officers were men who had first fought for Fascism as volunteers in the Spanish Civil War. But the paratroopers do not seem to have been as overtly 'political' as the Young Fascist battalions. If they had anything in common with them, it was that they were predominantly from northern Italy. Typically, eighteen-year-old Aroldo Conticello was from a village near the town of Orvieto in Umbria, where his father was the local cobbler. His eldest brother was already in the army, serving in the occupation forces on Rhodes, when Aroldo, a baker's assistant, volunteered for the Folgore 'because I wanted to do something for my country' and because rising at dawn to mix dough was 'boring'.

Conticello was by no means the only teenager in his unit. Private Umberto Galati was another, and his long dark hair was always getting him into trouble with his company commander, Second Lieutenant Giovanni Piccinni, an 'old man' of twenty-seven. No matter how many times Piccinni told him to get it cut, Galati invariably found some excuse to avoid a Prussian crop from 176th Company's barber. Piccinni found this challenge to his authority irritating. Second lieu-

---

★ In 1942 military parachuting was still in its infancy and by no means as safe as it has since become. It was not, for instance, general practice to carry a reserve chute in case the main canopy did not open.

tenants did not usually command a company, and he was trying to fill the boots of a wounded veteran of Spain and Ethiopia. Command was quite difficult enough without the provocation of Private Galati's musical locks. In most military units of whatever country, haircuts would have been beneath an officer's notice and a matter for an NCO. But the Folgore's junior officers had learned from their trainers in the Ramcke Brigade to take a greater interest than usual in their men.

The same could probably be said of the Ariete Division and some of the other Italian armoured formations that had won the respect of the Panzer regiments by the dogged determination they sometimes displayed in their toytown tanks. But in general, after twenty months of campaigning together, the Axis allies increasingly viewed each other through the distorted prism of the national stereotype. Italians were operatic, unreliable, cowardly and comically equipped. Germans were arrogant, brutal and robotic, only as good as their admittedly superior equipment, and they could not match the Italians' ability to endure hardship. On the contrary, the *tedesci* were spoiled hypochondriacs, addicted to vitamin pills and the like who were sent back to the Fatherland on a hospital ship as soon as they had a runny tummy.

Finding themselves at war with the United States only increased the Italians' anti-German tendencies, so many of them, especially southern Italians, had relatives in America. Was cousin expected to kill migrant cousin? Nor were the Germans and Italians traditional allies. Only twenty-five years before, Rommel had won his best medal fighting the Italians.

Now the Germans, believing this was good for morale, liked to give awards for valour to the Italians. The combat sappers' commander, Colonel Caccia-Dominioni (who would write what was probably the best account of the Italian side of the desert war) was one of those comparatively elderly Italian officers who had fought the Germans as a young man. At Alamein he was in his early forties and, his unit attached to the Folgore, he witnessed an incident in which two Italian soldiers objected to taking part in a medal parade in which each was due to be awarded an Iron Cross by General Stumme himself. One of the two had lost a father in the Kaiser's war and the other a brother, and it was only with great difficulty and 'in the interests of harmony' that they were persuaded to accept their medals. Dominioni noted that the presentation was made by a red-faced Stumme (the German suffered from high blood-pressure) who was 'almost bursting out of a uniform a size too small for him, with his monocle positively screwed into his eye socket'.★

How Stumme must have envied his (mainly) homogeneous enemy. In the Eighth Army there was rivalry among national groups, but far less ethnic tension. The official Australian war historian, Barton Maughan,† may have overlooked the participation of relatively small French and Greek contingents in describing the Eighth Army as 'a roll call of the Empire'. And he may have failed to take account of the hundreds of professional Indian soldiers and those South African troops who were Afrikaans-speaking and, unlike Churchill's friend Smuts, not particularly of a British mind-set. Yet for the most part it remained true that in trenches and dug-outs along the forty-five miles of front line, men born thousands of miles apart but speaking the same language, practising the same religion and the same brand of democracy, measuring in feet and inches, weighing in pounds and ounces and professing allegiance to the same King-Emperor, were about to hurl themselves at Europe's New Order. It was essentially, as Maughan would write, 'that grand, old fashioned "British Commonwealth of Nations" fighting its last righteous war'.

As the long day wore on, those on the British side with something to do before zero hour were the lucky ones, although sometimes what they had to do contained elements of farce. Captain Basil Miles, a Royal Army Medical Corps doctor serving with the armoured cars of the King's Dragoon Guards in the southern sector, was filling in forms. While his orderlies were preparing shell dressings, splints and checking their supplies of morphine, Miles was doing his best to account for the loss of a thermometer that had exploded under the heat of the midday sun.

Being technically a 'Scientific Instrument', we had to fill in a complicated form in quadruplicate. The listed price was, I think, eleven pence, but for

---

★ This description, however it might play to the Italians' innate dislike of the Germans, does not do Stumme justice. He was a brave and experienced soldier who had proved his worth as a tank commander in Russia. Ever since his arrival in North Africa he had gone out of his way to smooth Latin feathers often still ruffled by their last encounter with Rommel.

† Maughan was a lieutenant with the Australian infantry at El Alamein. Later he fought in New Guinea, where he won the Military Cross and finished the war as a lieutenant-colonel on the staff of Mountbatten.

some inscrutable reason we had to add ten per cent and later subtract ten per cent, which rounded up to eleven pence again. A nearby MO, falling into the spirit of this farce, after a similar catastrophe answered the written question, 'How was the Scientific Instrument lost?' with 'Chewed in half by a maniacal patient.'

Major Flatow, the recently arrived Yorkshire Territorial who in August had watched Churchill pouring with sweat as he visited the troops, snatched time to write Christmas cards home. By surface mail they would just about get there in time and he found himself 'wondering rather wistfully if I would be alive when they were delivered'. His squadron of 45 Royal Tank Regiment (originally the Leeds Rifles) had now refitted from Valentines to Shermans – a Ford to a Rolls-Royce in tank terms. After three years of war and intensive training in England 45 RTR had yet to fire a shot in anger. Its crews were encouraged to give their tanks names. In the interests of confusing the enemy, Flatow had chosen 'Attila'.

Another recent arrival in the desert was Private Arthur Kennett, a driver with the Royal Army Service Corps' 509 Ammunition Company, attached to 44th Division in the southern sector. Their three-ton Bedfords were loaded with boxes of 25-pounder artillery shells. Not long before, Kennett had been working in Sussex as a driver for the Meat Transport Pool, taking livestock from markets to abattoirs. It was a 'reserved occupation', considered essential to the war effort and it exempted him from military call-up. But all his friends were going into the services and Kennett began to feel left out, so he volunteered. As an experienced driver there was no question of his going into the infantry. One in the family had been enough: his older brother Ernest, who had been with the Royal Sussex at Dunkirk, had come back a broken man and had eventually been given a medical discharge.

That night the Ammunition Company's three-ton Bedford trucks were loaded with boxes of 25-pounder shells, but nobody told them anything 'special' was on. In any case, for Kennett 23 October had always been special. It was his birthday. This one was his twentieth.

Major Robert Snowdon of the 4th South African Armoured Car Regiment had money on his mind. Few personified a 'roll call of Empire' better than he: born in Tasmania, educated in England (Harrow and Reading Agricultural College) and a farmer in South Africa when war broke out, he immediately volunteered for the 4th, a fashionable, polo-playing regiment. Among Snowdon's brother officers was the diamond magnate Harry Oppenheimer who, a few days before, had given him a hot tip to invest in gold shares. Snowdon, who was twenty-seven and about to get married, decided to put every penny he had on them (in the circumstances, financial risks seemed the least of his concerns). But getting word to his London broker was difficult. All leave was stopped and the regiment was virtually incommunicado. Eventually, Snowdon managed to persuade some-body who was going back to Alexandria to take an overseas telegram for him. But Alexandria had recently suffered heavy air raids and there was no guarantee that the Marconi Radio Telegraph Company was still operating. Even if it were, it might not be allowed to handle non-military traffic. It was all very frustrating.

Snowdon might have been reassured by a chat with Corporal Jed Cope, who was with the anti-tank company of the Green Jackets' 2nd Battalion, which had been pulled out of 7th Armoured Division in the south and sent north with the rest of 7th Motor Brigade to join 1st Armoured Division. A few weeks before, Cope had written to his girlfriend Doreen Roots, a solicitor's clerk in Morden, Surrey, asking if she would marry him. Carefully folded in its envelope between the covers of his AB 64 (a passport-sized document that was both paybook and ID card) was the Marconi telegram he had just received in reply: YES DARLING ALL MY LOVE.

Although the Eighth Army dress code was notoriously relaxed, by tacit agreement Other Ranks rarely donned anything more eccentric than an extra sweater, a balaclava or perhaps a sleeveless leather jerkin. But as the weather cooled, most of Cope's battalion officers (like their men, almost all desert veterans) donned their winter garb of corduroy trousers and smelly Hebron coats of uncured sheepskin from Palestine. Cope's company commander was Tom Bird, the architectural student whose brother had been killed at Calais. He was now Major Bird, with a bar to his MC, won for a raid he led during the Gazala fighting in July which had netted fourteen prisoners without taking casualties.

Two days before, Bird had written to his father, a wounded veteran of the 1915 fighting against the Turks at Gallipoli, being careful not to upset the censor or alarm his parents. He customarily kept his letters as light-hearted as possible and often included sketches. This letter included a drawing of himself in winter costume, plus news of friends he had introduced to his parents in previous letters. 'Hugo Salmon still my second in command, and Jack Toms another great standby. I should hate to be without either of them now.' The only hint that anything momentous might be about to occur comes right at the end: 'I may not write again for a little bit. Best of love, Tommy.'

In the lines of the Argyll and Sutherland Highlanders, Major H. P. Samwell spent the first part of the day memorizing objectives and their code names from the over-printed map he had been given, purporting to show all the enemy positions in his company's sector. When he had studied it long enough, he tried to settle down with a book he had received from his wife together with a recent picture of her and their two small children. So far he was pleased to find he was without fear, detached, 'a spectator for a great event'. Even so, he would have chosen rather more escapist reading matter: his book was about the Guards in France in 1940 and was called *They Died with Their Boots Clean.*

All around Samwell, the infantrymen who would be in the first wave of the attack were sewing thin strips of white cloth in diagonal St Andrew's crosses on to the back flaps of their small packs for identification in the dark. None of the other divisions seem to have done anything like this but, after training losses by 'friendly fire' among the Black Watch, there was concern to show artillery observation officers where they were. That it was a St Andrew's Cross, potent symbol of Scottish national pride, was most likely the idea of the Highland Division's commander, Major-General Douglas Wimberley, a gangling figure who could not sit in a jeep without his folded knees coming perilously close to his chin. Although his paternal grandfather had been English, Wimberley was so stridently Caledonian that his men had nicknamed him 'Tartan Tam'. Wimberley tried to keep not only the English but also even the Lowland Scots out of his Highland Division. It was a losing battle. The division's heavy machine-gun battalion were the Cockneys of the Middlesex Regiment. And most of the Highland infantry battalions sheltered a minority of Glaswegians and deracinated English conscripts. Then, just before the 51st sailed for Egypt, the War Office delivered the final blow, bringing the division up to strength with drafts from various English county regiments, among them the South Staffordshires, the Warwickshire Yeomanry and the Leicestershires.

Among those who would not have passed the Wimberley admission test was Private John Bain of the Gordon Highlanders, Scottish Command's 1941 middleweight boxing champion. Although Bain's paternal grandfather was a Highlander and his father was wounded serving with a Scots regiment in the First World War, his mother was English and so was his upbringing. For most of his twenty-one years he had lived in Aylesbury in Buckinghamshire, where his father was a commercial photographer. Bain* had left school at fourteen to work as a clerk in an insurance office. Four years later, shortly after war was declared, he volunteered for the army 'as a lark'. The boxing had started at school and he had been good enough to become all-England Schoolboy Champion of 1935. But Bain was also a bookish boy, indiscriminately devouring Thomas Hardy's poetry and the thrillers of Edgar Wallace. By the time he joined the Gordons, his acquaintance with literary heavyweights would have astonished and puzzled his platoon mates. To them, he was simply a bruiser and, well muscled, the obvious choice to carry his section's Bren gun.

At dusk that evening, before battle, the cooks brought up a hot stew, which the men washed down with tea that was milkless because some purifying chemical added to the water had made even tinned milk curdle. Afterwards, Bain sat in his slit-trench chain-smoking. Like most of the division, he had not been in action before and was not in the least infected by what Montgomery called 'binge'. Nor was he particularly frightened. Mainly he was curious. What would battle be like and how would he respond to it?

Bain had yet to start writing his verse. But a few miles to the east, at the headquarters of 10th Armoured Division, a slightly older poet-in-the-making had been asking himself the same question ever since his arrival in the Middle East, almost a year before. Lieutenant Keith Castellain Douglas was of mixed Scots-French descent, the great-grandson of a French aristocrat who had come to England to escape the guillotine. Douglas and Bain had birthdays one day apart, 24 and 23 January respectively – but that is about all they had common, apart from an appetite for poetry and the more bruising sports. Douglas, who was two years older than Bain, had gone from boarding at Christ's Hospital (a meritocratic public school, founded as a charity

---

* After the war, under the pen-name of Vernon Scannell, Bain would become widely known as an award-winning poet, critic, broadcaster, novelist and memoirist. He also, when times were hard, earned a living as a fairground pugilist and sparring partner to big-time professionals at 'a pound a round'.

for deserving scholars) to Oxford, where his tutor in English literature had been the First World War poet Edmund Blunden.

At Merton College, Douglas was something of an enigma, impossible to label as either a 'hearty' or an 'aesthete', being a bit of both. There was no doubting his academic brilliance and Blunden immediately saw that his verses showed promise. But Douglas displayed just as much enthusiasm for rugby and strutting about in riding-boots and Sam Browne belt as a member of the Officer Cadet Training Unit. By the time he joined the army as a volunteer in 1941, no less an authority than T. S. Eliot had praised his unpublished verse, and he had already appeared in print in an anthology of new Oxford poets.

However, his military career had not run so smoothly. Even by yeomanry standards, the regiment he joined, the Sherwood Rangers (more formally known as the Nottinghamshire Yeomanry) were unusually clannish and feudal. The new subaltern found it hard to fit in. He rode, but did not hunt, shoot or fish. And he could no more drop the names of the county families of Nottinghamshire than recite its telephone directory.

Douglas's arrival to join the Sherwood Rangers in Palestine in 1941 coincided with the regiment's conversion from horses to tanks. Unlike most of his superior officers, Douglas had done a lot of armoured training, which should have made him a welcome addition. But he was not always as tactful as he might have been and some of his seniors began to resent the frequency of his advice. In Palestine he had completed a course in camouflage; he sketched and painted almost as well as he wrote. And when divisional headquarters, who had been told that its tanks must be made as invisible as possible, demanded his services as a camouflage expert, Douglas's CO made no great effort to get him back.

Far from being pleased with this 'cushy number' at HQ, well out of harm's way, Douglas was in an agony of guilt, boredom and frustration. After Alam el Halfa, where the Sherwood Rangers lost nine tanks and had seven killed in an impetuous charge, he begged his regiment to lobby for his return before the big attack. His old squadron commander insisted that he was doing his best, but by the evening of 23 October Douglas's prospects were unchanged. He was still at Divisional HQ, where he had been put in charge of a two-ton truck in preparation for the division's roll westwards. This was not what he had in mind at all.

Lieutenant Neville Gillman of the County of London Yeomanry was exactly where Douglas wanted to be. The twenty-four-year-old had joined the regiment as a Territorial four months before the outbreak of war, when he was studying accountancy, and had worked his way up through the ranks. Now his unit was going to be in the vanguard of the thrust against the Axis southern flank. But first – and on the very eve of battle – the army was about to demonstrate to his squadron its reassuring concern for their long-term welfare. As the minutes to zero hour ticked slowly by, and after they had already taken on ammunition and fuel, his men were ordered to line up at a mobile dental unit to have their teeth checked.

After dusk fell and the Australian infantry had left the foul holes where they had been made to spend the day, to eat and smoke and, if they were lucky, drink a little navy rum served from stone jars, their commander, Leslie Morshead, sat down and wrote a letter to his wife.

[I]n exactly two hours' time by far the greatest battle ever fought in the Middle East will be launched. I have settled down in my hole in the ground at my battle headquarters which are little more than 2,000 yards from our start-line . . . At the present time I can see and hear all the forward movement to battle positions – it is bright moonlight, tomorrow being full moon . . . a hard fight is expected and it will no doubt last a long time . . . But we shall win out and I trust put an end to this running forward and backward to and from Benghazi . . . In the preliminary and opening stage of a battle a commander can do little or nothing. He merely waits and hopes . . .

Shortly before zero hour there was a faint but insistent hum, hardly audible at first, until, according to one witness, it grew slowly in volume to become a 'rhythmic, surging, sound'. These were the night bomber squadrons of the Desert Air Force, the Wellingtons and Halifaxes whose bombs would be mixed with the artillery barrage. Then, several miles to the east of Morshead's command dug-out, a few dozen pinpricks of light appeared. They were the muzzle flashes of 5.5-inch howitzers firing, seconds before zero hour, so that their heavier shells would land simultaneously with the shorter-range 25-pounders that were the mainstay of the British artillery. Great care had been taken to give a minimum of warning so that the first salvo might find the Italians and Germans out of cover.

In the north, in the sector of Wimberley's Highland Division, a single searchlight was switched on, its beam almost vertical, quickly followed by a second one. Gradually the beams were lowered so that they formed a St Andrew's cross.

Almost forty miles to the south, near the Qattara Depression, an officer with the 'Tin Tummies' (as the First Household Cavalry was known because of the breastplates it wore when on ceremonial duty guarding Whitehall) looked east from his armoured car and saw the night sky lit up with flashes.

At that moment, at Middle East HQ in Cairo, General Alexander sent his prearranged, one-word code message to Churchill at the Cabinet War Room in London: 'Zip.' The Prime Minister immediately signalled President Roosevelt in Washington: 'The battle in Egypt began tonight at 8 p.m. London time.'

For the CIGS, Sir Alan Brooke, it was a moment of 'great possibilities and great dangers'. Writing in the confidential diary that he kept as a kind of emotional blotting paper to soak up the strains of the day (especially his often vitriolic rows with Churchill) he observed: 'It may be the turning point of the war or it may mean nothing. If it fails I don't quite know how I shall bear it.'

Operation 'Lightfoot' began with the biggest artillery barrage the British army had laid on since the First World War. Almost 1,000 guns participated and, had they been evenly distributed, this would have worked out to about twenty-five guns per mile, or one every seventy yards. As it was, they were concentrated in batches. Oliver Leese's XXX Corps in the north, which had a slightly shorter front than Horrocks's XIII Corps in the south, had 474 guns of various calibres behind his Highlanders, Australians, New Zealanders, South Africans and Indians.*

The first fifteen minutes of the barrage was aimed exclusively at Axis artillery batteries, either spotted from the air or located by foot patrols behind enemy lines. Targets were concentrated on one at a time, so the rate of fire was intense: a terrible forty-eight shells a minute from some of the heavier British guns. After the counter-battery fire there was a pause of five minutes then at exactly 10 p.m. the guns opened up again with rolling barrages on all the Axis forward positions. This went on until 3 a.m. and resumed four hours later, shortly after daybreak.

Italian and German accounts of the barrage cannot seem to find the words to do it justice without lapsing into hyperbole and cliché. It was 'as though a giant had banged his fist down on a table,' said General Lungerhausen, commander of the 164th Division, whose headquarters were near the coast. 'The peaceful stars were shaken in their heavens,' wrote Heinz-Werner Schmidt, who was in reserve with his anti-tank unit. It was 'one sheet of incandescence from end to end,' said Dominioni.

---

* The purely British contribution to the overseas Commonwealth divisions was much larger than their titles suggest. All had a certain amount of British armour attached to them – the New Zealanders an entire brigade – while the Indian Division included three battalions of British infantry, and its artillery and support arms were almost entirely British. Leese also had in reserve the 23rd Armoured Brigade, comprising not only tanks but a battalion of motorized infantry from the Rifle Brigade.

Some of the British, including the gunners who were delivering it, appear to have found the barrage almost as terrifying as the recipients. In 1942 there was no such thing as ear-defenders for British artillery-men. Some attempt had been made to provide cotton-wool earplugs, but many of the gunners had rejected them as being rather effete.

Lance-Sergeant George Waddington was commanding a 25-pounder supporting 44th Division's Queen's Brigade in the south. He had been firing for about an hour when the bombardier in charge of one of the other guns came running across to him. 'His sergeant (always thought to be a real tough guy) had gone raving mad and was shouting all sorts of things and seemed to be going off his head. He was taken away.'

Another veteran in action that night was Sergeant-Major Harold Harper of the 'Acorn Gunners',* the South Notts Hussars Yeomanry, who had fought at Tobruk and Gazala, where he had been wounded and captured before making a daring escape through a minefield. Now the Acorn Gunners, originally firing 25-pounders, had been re-formed as a medium artillery regiment with the new 5.5-inch heavy gun and Harper, old soldier though he was, was dumbfounded by the din. 'Nothing had been seen like it before or after,' he would recall.

The entire lot started firing at the precise second and the whole sky seemed to burst. After firing ten or twelve rounds I suddenly thought, 'Blimey, this is beginning to get hard work!' Then I noticed that one bloke was missing, hiding in a slit trench behind the gun. So I dragged him out by the scruff of the neck . . . I threatened to shoot him if he didn't get back on the job. I had to do something drastic because if you do that sort of thing in action and do nothing it becomes contagious. I would have shot him if I had to . . . He went back to the gun but was never quite the same again.

The vast majority of the 6,000 or so men manning the guns did not, of course, crack up. Training and team spirit, the satisfaction of maintaining this extraordinary rate of fire, gradually made them impervious to the din, though some of the men who had refused earplugs were beginning to regret it.

One man who had no need of earplugs was Bernard Montgomery.

---

* So called because of the acorn in their cap badge, fruit of the oak trees that grow in their native Nottingham forest, stamping-ground of the legendary Robin Hood.

Having watched the start of the barrage – 'a wonderful sight' – he put himself to bed at his Tactical HQ in the caravan that O'Connor had captured from 'Electric Whiskers' Bergonzoli at Beda Fomm: 'There was nothing I could do . . . There is always a crisis in every battle when the issue hangs in the balance and I reckoned I would get what rest I could, while I could.'

While Montgomery slept, his infantry left their holes in the ground and advanced towards the enemy. At first it was an oddly unhurried affair, a moonlit stroll with a rifle, as the shells from the British barrage made a whirring sound like geese in flight overhead.

'Scotland for ever and second to none,' was Wimberley's entirely predictable battle message to his troops. Six battalions of the Highland Division, the best part of 5,000 men, advanced on a front almost one and a half miles wide to the sound of their bagpipers. They moved at a stately fifty yards a minute and tried to make it difficult for the enemy machine-gunners by keeping five yards apart, just as their fathers had done on the Somme. The enemy strongpoints that were their objectives had all been code-named after Highland towns. Behind them, two of the division's four remaining battalions were poised to leapfrog through on the flanks, once Inverness, Dundee, Montrose, Arbroath and the rest had been seized.

Nineteen-year-old Duncan McIntyre, splendid in a mainly scarlet Royal Stuart kilt, played the 5th Black Watch into battle to 'Highland Laddie'. Sid Lunn, one of the battalion's Cockney conscripts, found himself as stirred by the tune as any heather-born Jock, though he could only hear the pipes in snatches between the sound of the guns. 'It really got us going,' he would recall.

'Tartan Tam' had insisted that every company should go into action with a piper who, in theory at least, would double as a stretcher-bearer and medical orderly. The pipes had been supplied, free of charge, by the Highland Society in Edinburgh. Pipers and a few senior officers were the only men on the field in kilts, everybody else wearing long baggy 'shorts'.

Private Bain, the Gordons' champion boxer and secret poetry-lover, was struck by the oddly familiar preparations that had been made for the business at hand. The five-yard-wide lanes through the British minefield and the start line itself had all been marked out with white tape. It reminded him of school sports days.

Megaphones were also much in evidence. In the Argylls' sector, Major Samwell could hear the commander of another forward company bellowing: 'Keep up there on the left – straighten up.' Samwell could not remember leaving the start line. One moment he and his company, almost 100 men, were lying prone behind the line, looking at their watches. Then he became aware that he had for some time been on his feet and heading deliberately towards the enemy, ash walking-stick in one hand and a .38 service revolver in the other.

Samwell soon realized that the walking-stick was a mistake and determined to trade it for a rifle; this would make him a less obvious target for a sniper intent on picking off an officer. Sooner or later he would be able to take a rifle from a casualty; if he was hit first, he wouldn't need one.

Tank men, waiting their turn and watching this steady advance of the Highland Division as the pipes skirled, found it an exhilarating sight. Even men like Captain Bill Close of 3 RTR were impressed. A regular soldier, commissioned in the field after Sidi Rezegh, blown out of three tanks at Gazala and recently recovered from a burn wound, he thought the Highlanders looked 'almost as if on exercise'.

For some time there were no incoming shells and when the German and Italian gunners did respond, it was obvious at first that they were seeking out the British batteries in the rear. Then suddenly the artillery supporting the 51st did stop – not because the counter-battery fire had been all that effective but for fear of hitting the Highlanders, who were now almost on their first objectives. In the silence that followed, the bagpipes grew more audible and with their skirl came the first sound of Axis machine-guns. The Highlanders continued to go forward with the kind of measured tread Wellington's regiments might have recognized. 'We'd been told "if a man falls, walk on,"' Sid Lunn would recall, 'and men started falling within minutes.' Corporal Geordie Reay, whom Close thought the coolest tank gunner in his unit, watched in horrified admiration as the survivors advanced over terrain 'as flat as a table. I thought, "They're the only real soldiers in the British Army." Men were dropping right, left and centre – their mates were dropping right beside them, but they just carried on. I turned to Major Crisp [his squadron commander] and said, "Isn't this a bloody disgrace, sir? It's against human nature." It was a terrible sight.'

Among the dead was the kilted young piper, Duncan McIntyre,

his body recovered later with his fingers still on the chanter of his pipes. Some of the Black Watch who passed by him maintain that he continued to play long after he had fallen.

Mortar bombs as well as machine-guns began to take their toll of the Scots infantry. So did booby traps, some of which were connected to small aerial bombs. Samwell, the Argylls officer, spotted a single strand of wire. He cleared it with a running jump despite the encumbrance of boots, walking-stick, and small pack crammed with bully beef, hard biscuits and extra water in a whisky bottle. Behind him, a sergeant laden with rifle, ammunition bandoleers, grenades and an entrenching tool pulled the wire down to step over it. Samwell felt the heat from the blast and never saw the sergeant again. Afterwards, he wondered what instinct made him jump the wire, because he had not been thinking of booby traps.

He and the men around him broke into a run, and Samwell noticed a corporal firing a Bren gun from the hip. Then he almost ran past what seemed to be a head and shoulders growing out of the earth, swivelled round, snapped off three shots with his .38 and ran on. The next thing he knew, he was confronted by a square trench full of Italian soldiers with their hands in the air, 'screaming something that sounded like "Mardray"' (mother).

At this moment one of the Italians threw a grenade. It bounced off Samwell's boot and exploded a few feet away, crippling a sergeant but leaving Samwell unscathed. Enraged, he emptied his revolver into the Italians now cowering at the bottom of the trench. Then he picked up the wounded sergeant's rifle and bayoneted four more Italians before his anger subsided.

I was quite cool now, and I started looking for my pistol . . . At the same time I wondered when I had got rid of my stick, as I couldn't remember dropping it. I felt rather sad; it had been my constant companion for two years at home. I had walked down to the pictures with my wife and had put it under the seat, and on leaving I had forgotten it, and had to disturb a whole row of people to retrieve it. I started then to wonder what my wife was doing at that moment.

Mercurial mood swings, horror piled on horror. Despite the kilted pipers, the neat white marking tape and cosy Scots place-names, nobody had expected the Highland Games. But few of the 51st had been in combat before and they were seeing and hearing things that would stay with them for the rest of their lives.

About a mile from Samwell and the Argylls, on the division's northern flank alongside the Australians, Private Bain of the Gordons was advancing slowly at the high-port with his platoon, himself unscathed but soon to absorb a pitiless lesson. 'There was a sergeant who was quite close to me who always seemed to me almost a kind of father figure – rather a tough, leathery kind of man. And he was badly wounded and hearing his voice sort of sobbing and in fact calling for his mother, his mum, you know, seemed to be so, I don't know, demeaning and humiliating and dreadful.'

Sheltering later in a shallow depression under artillery fire, Bain would notice another reaction common to the infantryman.

All of that shrieking, whining venom is directed at you and at no one else. You hunch in your hole in the ground, reduce yourself to as small a thing as you can become, and you harden your muscles in a pitiful attempt at defying the jagged, burning teeth of the shrapnel. Involuntarily, you curl up into the foetal position except that your hands go down to protect your genitalia. Montgomery doesn't protect his privates, but by Christ, I protect mine.

When Montgomery awoke in his caravan shortly after dawn on Saturday 24 October he discovered that in the north, where the main thrust was, Australian, British, New Zealand and South African infantry battalions had managed to achieve some of their final objectives along what was codenamed the 'Oxalic Line'.* Only about half of them were where Montgomery hoped they would be by 8 a.m. but the rest were not far behind them, and at least Leese and his XXX Corps had hammered a considerable wedge into the broad Axis defences. All this had been won with relatively few casualties. For the twenty-six-hour period until midnight on the 24th they totalled 2,324 wounded and 159 killed. The high proportion of wounded was mainly because of the mines and booby traps. By comparison, the armoured divisions in Lumsden's X Corps had put up a dismal performance, having entirely failed to exploit the infantry's success. Nowhere had

---

* Codenames were, of course, quite deliberately as nonsensical as possible. Oxalic acid is a colourless, crystalline substance, sometimes used as a bleach or metal-cleansing agent.

they broken out beyond the Axis defences in order to establish the
tank screen Montgomery wanted in place to protect X Corps from
the Panzer divisions poised to counter-attack.

Only the 8th Armoured Brigade, with the Shermans of Bill Close's
3rd Royal Tank Regiment and the Staffordshire Yeomanry in the
lead, had even reached the vanguard of the New Zealanders on top
of the Miteiriya Ridge. And they had taken their tanks to the top of
the hill, only to take them down again and into hull-down position
as soon as they started taking casualties from the Axis anti-tank guns
which were dug in on the reverse slope. The rest of the armour did
not even get out of the minefields.

This was not entirely their fault. Clearing lanes through the minefields, even on a moonlit night, was just as hazardous as it sounds.
Sappers, taking casualties from shell and machine-gun fire, could not
always keep up with their demanding timetable. The favourite method
of both detection and lifting was to probe with a bayonet. Electronic
mine-detectors were in their infancy and unreliable. So were the
'Scorpions', old Matilda tanks fitted with a revolving drum and chains
to detonate mines by thrashing the ground ahead. Once a lane had
been cleared, there was also the problem of congestion. An overlooked
mine which blew a track off could block a lane for hours and make a
mockery of numerical superiority.

Vehicles that tried to drive around such blockages could easily
detonate other mines or get stuck in soft sand. The Bank Holiday-style
tailbacks that built up behind the infantry – not only tanks but hundreds
of soft-skinned vehicles of every type – were also prey to the Luftwaffe.
Parachute flares illuminated these sitting targets and enough vehicles
were set alight to make handy beacons for the Axis artillery. In places
the difficult business of threading the British tanks through the infantry
had been turned into a shambles.

All this was a valid excuse for delay, but Montgomery was not a man
to accept excuses; 'bellyaching' was not allowed. Eighth Armoured
Brigade had almost got through, only to seek cover as soon as they
came under fire. North of them Brigadier Arthur Fisher's 2nd
Armoured Brigade was refusing to budge on the grounds that the 51st
Highland had not cleared the way for them as planned. This was
despite Montgomery's orders that, if the infantry became stuck, the
armour must be prepared to fight their own way through. Morshead
and Wimberley, the two divisional commanders on the northern flank,

were both adamant that Brigadier Raymond Briggs's 1st Armoured Division had missed opportunities to break out. Montgomery decided that the armoured divisions lacked offensive spirit and were in need of 'determined leadership'.

I saw Herbert Lumsden . . . So far he has not impressed me by his showing in battle; perhaps he has been out here too long; he has been wounded twice. I can see that he will have to be bolstered up and firmly handled . . . There was not that eagerness to break into the open on the part of Commanders; there was a fear of casualties; every gun was reported to be an 88-mm . . . I therefore spoke to Lumsden in no uncertain voice, and told him that he must 'drive' his Divisional Commanders, and that if Briggs and Fisher hung back any more I would remove them from command and replace them with better men.

It was a convincing display of how much the style of leadership of the Eighth Army had changed since Auchinleck's departure. Lumsden was a product of the old school of British desert tactics that had died with Gott: the school where mobility was everything, where infantry and artillery were employed in penny-packet battle groups, where the cavalry spirit reigned, only the right orders were obeyed, and newcomers knew how to take advice. What did this strutting little man Montgomery know about desert warfare? Alam el Halfa had been a defensive battle and, in any case, it had been laid on for him. Had he ever seen what a battery of 88s could do with impunity to a brigade of British tanks when they breasted a skyline? Had he seen what they did at Knightsbridge? How dare he devise a plan where tanks were required to emerge from gaps in the minefields, where they could be picked off one at a time. But Montgomery did dare and he expected his orders to be obeyed. And, far from being intimidated by Lumsden's experience, he wondered if the man had been 'out here too long'.

Major Bill Williams, a bright young academic at Montgomery's HQ who had been entrusted with assessing the top-secret Ultra intercepts of relevant Axis radio traffic, thought that Montgomery saw right through Lumsden. His effect on Lumsden was 'like a stoat on a rabbit . . . Herbert was scared stiff of Monty . . . He wasn't as good as he was made out to be, but he had tremendous polish, always had the answer to everything, always had such charming manners.'

Brian Horrocks, the acolyte Montgomery had selected to come out from England and command XIII Corps in the south, had enjoyed no

more success than Lumsden. Koenig's Free French had taken the twin
peaks of the Himeimat, only to be pushed off them again by the Kiel
Gruppe, an *ad hoc* formation equipped with fast American Honeys
captured at Gazala and elsewhere. Koenig's men, mostly legionnaires,
had not taken heavy casualties but had been demoralized by the death
of Colonel Dimitris Amilakvari, a Russian prince who was one of
their most flamboyant officers. Montgomery, perhaps unfairly, would
later tell Alanbrooke in a letter that he thought the French had let him
down badly.

Recapturing Himeimat enabled Axis troops to resume their artillery
spotting and give the advancing British merry hell. Horrocks's 7th
Armoured Division, commanded by Montgomery's other pupil, John
Harding, had got through one minefield but then became trapped in
the second. 'My recollection,' Harding recalled of the first night, 'is
of a snake-like procession of a mass of tanks and guns and other
vehicles in an atmosphere of smoke and dust and noise, all vividly
illuminated at one point by a blazing [Bren gun] carrier.'

As the dawn came up, the infantry ahead of them dug in as best
they could and waited for the tanks to catch up. While they waited,
the Folgore and some of Ramcke Brigade's men closed in. Second
Lieutenant Derrick Watson, who had arrived among the reinforcements which brought the 1st/5th Queen's back up to strength after
the September débâcle against the Folgore, was one of its youngest
platoon commanders.

[O]nce daylight came it was dangerous to lift your head, and suicide to stand
up. We had biscuits and bully and water in our bottles. The battalion suffered
heavy casualties . . . I remember young O'Connell had both legs severed by
a mortar bomb and was screaming for help, and then for his mother before
he mercifully died. Major Cooper, who had disappeared from sight when
hit, called out at intervals during the day before he, too, fell quiet.

On the next night the British tanks made another attempt to get
through the last minefield to the infantry. Among them were the
County of London Yeomanry, including Lieutenant Gillman and his
squadron of the recently inspected teeth.

We followed what was left of the Queen's, and there was no element of
surprise now. When we got through the gap everything opened up on us

from the flank and front; my searchlight and periscope were shot off inches from my head as we went through . . . There were lots of mines and a ring of anti-tank guns awaiting us and one by one my squadron went off the air.

Unlike Lumsden, Horrocks had received 'emphatic orders' to husband his armour, and he suspected that after making their feint Montgomery intended to use them elsewhere. The surviving Yeomanry were ordered to return. Gillman, who had hidden his Crusader between two knocked-out tanks, discovered that this was easier said than done. As soon as they reversed out of their cover they were hit.

The shell, an 88-mm I think, came in one side and blew the other side of the turret wide open, killing all the crew except the driver and myself. [Crusader IIs had a crew of four.] Being small, I was not sitting in the commander's seat but squatting on it, and that is what saved me. I felt a blow on my leg and fell into the bottom of the fighting compartment, and all the ammo was on fire, so I hauled myself out over the gun, out of the turret – I don't know how – and rolled off into the sand.

Gillman's leg was broken in two places. He was dragged into a slit-trench by his driver, who went to get help while the lieutenant lay there in the dark, 'feeling a bit isolated'. It is not difficult to imagine the nightmare it must have been for stretcher-bearers to locate a wounded man at night in a contested area under shellfire. By the time Gillman had been brought back to a field hospital, gas-gangrene had started and eventually his leg had to be amputated.

Getting the wounded back quickly was not helped by the Royal Army Medical Corps' conventional ambulances frequently getting stuck in soft sand. Luckier units were served by a band of American Red Cross volunteers who drove four-wheel-drive Dodges. Some of the volunteer drivers were Quaker pacifists. Captain Miles, the doctor with the thermometer replacement problem, was particularly impressed by them. His field aid post was along one of the lanes in the first minefield through which ammunition and fuel trucks were passing. Shells were landing within fifty yards of it. The wounded awaited their turn for evacuation in shallow slit-trenches as the Dodges went back and forth. Miles was left with fond memories of a gallant and eccentric breed.

That splendid American academic from Yale who used to sit . . . reading Chaucer through his thick myopic glasses, was superb, coming back time and again in his unprotected ambulance to pick up more wounded . . . I shall always remember our first, a geologist from Harvard, who joined us in an area where there were silicified remains of a bygone forest. His very first words, before introducing himself, being 'Gee, the cellular structure is well preserved.'

Miles would shortly find himself in an ambulance with shell splinters in his lung and liver and one near his heart which would remain there for the rest of his life.

Derrick Watson and his platoon from the Queen's were subjected to cruelly accurate daylight mortaring and sniping from dawn until the early afternoon of the 24th, when inexplicably it stopped. Shortly afterwards, about twenty Folgore surrendered 'rather sheepishly' to another platoon which had come up in support when Watson's had been pinned down. Around dusk the Queen's received permission to withdraw, and Watson was told he was in command of the rearguard. 'Before I could make any plan there was a sudden rush of feet and disengagement began. I was the last to disengage and have no recollection of clearing two barbed-wire fences and a thousand yards of minefield. However, I found myself in the midst of our tanks carrying two rifles and "escorted" by some fifteen unarmed Italians anxious to be prisoners.'

Watson was one of the lucky ones. Rather closer to the Axis lines was part of another Queen's battalion, the 1st/6th under their commanding officer, Lieutenant-Colonel David Gibbs, a very determined regular soldier who believed in leading from the front. Gibbs was unaware that Harding had been told to conserve his tanks and had pressed ahead, confident that the armour was bound to catch them up, no matter how great the risk. With about 100 men, Gibbs had grenaded his way through the well-dug-in Italian fire centres where two machine-gun nests supported a light anti-tank gun that could have stopped one of the new Shermans only at very close range. Eventually they got to a point where they could hear German artillery officers and NCO's shouting orders to their gun crews and realized they had seized all their objectives.

By then Gibbs and his men, who included his adjutant, two other officers and most of his HQ company, were probably the most westerly soldiers in the entire Eighth Army. They were feeling quite pleased with themselves and had certainly got into a better position than their sister battalion, the 1st/7th. The CO of the latter had also taken them well forward, only to be captured with about ten others, then killed during an escape attempt, probably by 'friendly fire'.

Gibbs, coming under heavy mortar and artillery fire, ordered his men to dig in, convinced that Harding's 7th Armoured would soon catch up with them. They stuck it out for eighteen hours, then the survivors, Gibbs among them, surrendered.★ The Queen's Brigade had lost two of its battalion commanders in a single action, dismal proof that brave and determined leadership was not always enough. That night, as Gibbs lay, shivering, in shirt and shorts under a single blanket provided by his captors, gazing at the star-filled desert sky from within a hastily erected barbed-wire enclosure, his German guards were jubilant. The battle was as good as won, they told him: Rommel was back.

★ Despite his capture, Gibbs was awarded a DSO for the leadership and courage he displayed. After the Italian surrender he escaped, like so many others in Italy, from his PoW camp, reached Allied lines and was back on active service by 1944.

Rommel had made it plain to Stumme when he went on sick leave that in the event of a British offensive he would return to Africa and resume command. Possibly ego had a lot to do with this, but loyalty to the men whose sacrifices had earned him his field marshal's baton undoubtedly played a part: Rommel could hardly reap the rewards and then leave his troops to face the biggest test without him.

The morning of 24 October found him with Lucie enjoying the crystalline atmosphere of the Austrian Alps at the end of a third blissful week at Semmering, near Wiener-Neustadt. When news that the battle had started reached Berlin, Field Marshal Keitel, the German Chief of Staff, agreed that Rommel should get ready to return. At first, though, Hitler preferred him not to cut short his convalescence. He wanted his newest field marshal rested and back on form. Accordingly, he advised Rommel not to go back unless the situation became 'really serious'. Nevertheless, Rommel put himself on standby at Wiener-Neustadt airport and when, around midnight on the 24th, Hitler called again to ask if he felt well enough to go, Rommel kissed Lucie goodbye without further delay.

He was on his way back to a command that was in a state of some confusion. Surprise had been about as complete as it could have been, given that the Axis had been expecting an attack any day. A radio intercept on 15 October, regarding the numbers of stretcher-bearers available, had alerted Panzerarmee intelligence, who, recalling a similar message eight days before a previous British offensive, did their sums and with breathtaking accuracy predicted that the attack would come on 23 October. Luckily for the British, their reasoning was thought to be a bit thin and the prediction was ignored in preference to a High Command estimate that the blow would fall in early November.

Even after several hours of fighting, it remained unclear where the main British thrust was aimed. In the southern sector, Maskelyne the Magnificent and other wizards of deception had woven wonders of illusion. Painstaking labour had produced hundreds of canvas tanks and trucks and a convincing-looking water pipeline heading boldly south. The wireless telegraphists manning a communications centre for an entirely fictitious armoured division had industriously tapped out round-the-clock signals for attentive Axis eavesdroppers. These elaborate deception measures had worked so well that the Panzer-armee's daily order of battle assessment continued to show both of Lumsden's divisions with Harding's 7th Armoured in the south.

Immediately after the opening barrage it proved impossible for the Panzerarmee to obtain a proper overall picture. Shellfire had cut field telephone lines in dozens of places and radio signals had been disrupted by a new form of jamming: circling Wellington bombers packed with electronic devices that transformed radio transmissions into agonized shrieks of storm-lashed static.

Operation 'Slender', in which the Royal Navy provided the back-cloth for Major Maskelyne to stage another grand illusion, diverted part of the 90th Light Division and aircraft that were much needed elsewhere to the coast to repel a phoney landing. On a poetically moonlit sea, three destroyers, eight fast motor torpedo boats, and twelve landing craft had sailed west from Alexandria until they were off Fuka, where the Axis had a large airfield. A thick smokescreen was then laid behind which Maskelyne and his assistants serenaded the enemy with enormously amplified wind-up gramophones on which they played a medley of specially recorded sound-effects. These included an avalanche of rattling anchor-chains, squeaking davits, shouted orders and the sound of naval gunfire. Meanwhile, real shells from the real destroyers were mixed with some very expensive fire-works; dozens of Aldis lamps flashed meaningless Morse; signal flares coloured the night sky and – perhaps cleverest of all – the air was filled with the unmistakable stench of diesel engines close inshore. This was achieved by burning a cocktail of fuels, including diesel, in oil pots aboard one of three small vessels that Maskelyne was using.

Axis coastal batteries responded by blindly shelling the smokescreen while Junkers and Macchis went in search of this 'invasion fleet', managing only to inflict slight damage on a motor torpedo boat. Many British sailors returned to port as mystified as the enemy about what they had been doing. There were no casualties and it was not until daylight that the Axis realized they had been hoaxed.

Then came the kind of bonus that planners can only dream about: Stumme went missing and the Panzerarmee became a headless beast, able to snarl and lash out locally but without the guiding intelligence to co-ordinate its responses to the British. At first light on the 24th, Stumme, having received precious few situation reports from his army, set out to find out what was happening. He was accompanied by his driver, Corporal Wolf, and Colonel Büchting, a signals officer who wanted to see how quickly he could restore the field-telephone system. Stumme decided against taking an escort and a wireless vehicle to keep in touch, saying that he intended to go only as far as the HQ of the 90th Light, just behind the front line on the coast. Finding divisional HQ no better informed than army headquarters, Stumme decided to get closer to the front. How could a man who had stepped into Rommel's boots do otherwise?

There are two versions of what happened next. One has it that Stumme's car was hit by a strafing fighter, the other that, on a deserted stretch of road, he strayed too close to Morshead's Australians and came under anti-tank and machine-gun fire. Whatever it was that hit them, Oberst Büchting received a mortal head wound and Wolf turned his vehicle so violently that he failed to notice that the valiant if corpulent Stumme had fallen out. It was some time before Wolf discovered that he had mislaid the boss. By then he was several kilometres from the scene of the attack. Initially, it was feared that the Australians might have sent out a patrol and captured Stumme, but his body, with no visible wounds, was eventually recovered the following day and the cause of his death established as a heart attack. Whether he suffered it before or after his car was hit was never established.

Lieutenant-General Wilhelm Ritter von Thoma, who commanded the Afrika Korps (the two Panzer Divisions plus the 90th Light), took temporary charge of the Panzerarmee Afrika, comprising all the German units plus the Italian armoured and infantry formations.

It took Rommel about 15 hours to get back to his men, flying via Rome and Crete where he transferred from his Heinkel to a faster Dornier. Once back in Africa he sat behind the pilot in a Storch flying eastwards along the foam-fringed coast with the sun setting behind them. There was not much light left when they put down at a forward landing-strip, from where a car took Rommel on the last leg of the journey to his *Kampfstaffel*. Sentries challenged and saluted. Heavy guns rumbled and cracked. Some of their own batteries were quite close. There was a constant ripple of flashes along the eastern horizon and the massive generators for the signals trucks hummed in their important, reassuring way. Lucie, Trudel, Semmering and the pine-scented Alpine forests were a world away.

'I have taken command of the army again – Rommel.' The signal went out to all units shortly before midnight on the 25th, more than forty-eight hours after the battle began, and officers were not slow in passing the news on to their men. The reaction of the guards around the luckless Lieutenant-Colonel Gibbs and the other captives from the Queen's Brigade on the southern front was probably typical of the effect this had on German morale.

Rommel's own morale seems to have been less certain. 'I knew there were no more laurels to be earned in Africa,' declares a diary entry dated 24 October. And responding to reports he heard during his Rome stopover that yet another tanker had been sunk on its way to North Africa, reducing his fuel stocks to three days' supply, Rommel predicted gloomily that this 'would completely prevent our taking the correct tactical decision and would impose tremendous limitations upon our planning.' And yet the notion that Rommel returned to Africa knowing it was a lost cause needs to be treated with caution. The idea was carefully fostered by him in the diaries, letters and autobiographical notes he kept for a book he planned to write after the war.* Most of it was written well after the events, and diaries are not always kept as punctiliously as their entries suggest. Magnanimous in victory, almost invariably generous to defeated opponents, Rommel was a bad loser. Much better modestly to proclaim that you are but human and that, against insuperable odds, no mere mortal could triumph. 'Sometimes it is a disadvantage to have a military reputation,' he wrote. 'One is aware of one's limits, but others go on expecting miracles and put defeat down to deliberate obstinacy.'

Yet the situation Rommel inherited at El Alamein was far from hopeless. The British had failed fully to exploit their surprise, the death of Stumme or the disruption in Axis communications. It was true they had severely dented the northern part of the Axis defence line, but nowhere had they succeeded in driving a hole through it. Most of the British armour was still stuck behind the infantry. Those regiments

---

* These first appeared in Britain in 1952, as *The Rommel Papers* after they had been annotated and edited by the military historian, Basil Liddell-Hart. A German-language version, *Krieg ohne Hass* ('War without Hate'), was published two years later.

which did manage to get a few tanks through often found they were being picked off as soon as they emerged, one at a time, from the gaps in the minefields. Once again it seemed that the British had devised a way to squander numerical superiority in armour by serving it up in easily digestible pieces.

Initially, the opening barrage had been just as terrifying for the enemy as the British had hoped. Three Axis infantry battalions, one Italian and two German, had been particularly hard hit and there were reports of broken men running to the rear. Since then the British artillery had rarely entirely stopped, going up and down the scales from diminuendo to crescendo and back again when and where required. Even so, it did not take the majority of the Panzerarmee long to learn the old lesson that, providing you dig in well, it takes more to kill you than horrendous noise, a series of small earthquakes and air permanently fogged with dust.

Kannoneer Martin Ranft, quite recently a machinist in a textile factory at Chemnitz in Saxony, was a gun-layer with the 220th Artillery Regiment, not far behind the front line and one of the initial counter-battery targets. Ranft had arrived in North Africa, a very excited twenty-year-old, about three months before, when he was flown in from Crete as part of Lungerhausen's 164th Division. Like most of this division, he had seen very little action, yet he would recall that during the enemy barrage he 'actually fell asleep. When it got light the fire had stopped. We looked out of our holes and it looked like a ploughed field. I could not understand how I still was alive. But nobody had been hurt and all four guns were still intact.'

In the south of the line, the Folgore lieutenant Giovanni Piccinni, temporary company commander and monitor of Private Galati's hair, had a similar experience. Every square metre of ground in front of his position had been blasted into a fine powder, but he and his men seemed to bear a charmed life. 'I actually saw a shell in flight heading in my direction,' he would recall. 'I fell flat on my face and it landed a few metres in front of my slit trench.' Not long afterwards, Piccinni was again under heavy artillery fire and 'skidding from one position to another', when he noticed a lock of dark hair protruding from the sand: 'I ran over and scraped the sand away to reveal Galati's head. His mouth was full of sand and he was choking. He gasped for water and I gave him some from my canteen. He spat the sand out and recovered. If he had obeyed me and cut his hair he would certainly have died.'

Despite his display of private pessimism, Rommel conceded that his army did have 'a certain tactical advantage . . . while the attacker had to contend with being fired at from these dug-in positions'. Certainly, many of his troops, Italians and Germans alike, continued to put up a stubborn resistance. Isolated parties in the first belt of Axis minefields were fighting with the stubbornness of men who had turned the tables on the British before. On the night of his return, some of the Eighth Army infantry in Oliver Leese's northern sector were still trying to capture objectives they were supposed to have taken on the first night.

At about the time Rommel was being driven on the last leg of his exhausting return trip, Major Samwell of the Argyll and Sutherland Highlanders was trying to supervise the distribution of a rum ration. The regulation tot of 90 per cent proof navy rum (since Nelson's day issued daily on His Majesty's ships but only occasionally to the army) was not supposed to exceed a serving spoonful. This was estimated to be enough to maintain morale without losing coherence. In this case there was not enough to go round, and Samwell and most of his sergeants and corporals had to go without.

The Argylls were preparing an attack to secure their left flank, which remained exposed when the neighbouring battalion failed to reach its objectives. This had left the Axis with a useful salient into territory the British had just captured. To ensure surprise, the Argylls attacked without artillery support, but as they advanced under bright moonlight they soon came under machine-gun fire. Samwell got close enough to make out the shapes of a three-man Spandau crew behind their weapon, when he was felled by a bullet which passed through the fleshy part of his thigh. Thinking he was taking cover, some of the Argylls dropped down beside him. Cursing ('for the first time I remember I swore at my men'), Samwell urged them on, dragging himself after them. Then, to his astonishment, the Germans began to surrender, except for the machine-gun crew who had shot him; they sprang out of their pit and tried to make a dash for it. From the ground Samwell fired four shots after them with his .38 revolver. He saw one pitch forward.

Before long, the Argylls discovered that they were cut off and began to prepare the captured position for all-round defence. Samwell was carried well inside the perimeter, where a deep trench was dug for him. When a wounded man in a German uniform was carried into the position, Samwell, who spoke some German, asked for him to be put alongside him and soon discovered that he was sharing a trench with one of the machine-gun crew he himself had shot 'right between the shoulder blades'. His bullet had found an Austrian in his late thirties, a married man with three children who had worked in a cotton mill in Linz before being called up the year before for 'home defence work'.

The wounded Austrian told Samwell he had arrived at the front with other reinforcements the previous day and had been at the machine-gun post for only two hours before the Argylls attacked. While mortar bombs dropped around them, one falling in a nearby trench containing other wounded, the enemies who had just shot each other began to bond. Samwell's shorts were drenched with blood from his unplugged exit-wound; the Austrian was obviously worse off and was finding it difficult to breathe. Samwell gave him his own haversack to use as a pillow, 'and he was pathetically grateful'.

The Austrian machine-gunner showed Samwell a photograph of his wife and three children: two girls and a little boy in lederhosen. As the night wore on, they slept fitfully, awoke to hold a further desultory conversation, then returned to their tortured dreams. Several times Samwell assured his companion that a doctor was coming and that they would soon be in hospital. But dawn of the 26th, the third day of the battle, broke to find them still in their trench. As the light improved, so did the accuracy of the Axis mortaring. When the noise of the barrage became intense, the Austrian awoke and, for some reason, began to lever himself above the trench by placing his hands on its edges.

There was an ear-splitting explosion. At first I thought our trench had been blown in . . . Then I looked at the Austrian; he was lying half propped up against the trench looking curiously at the remains of his left hand; it had been partially blown away. I was nearly sick, but hastily tore my shirt and bound it tightly round the stump. He thanked me weakly and closed his eyes. His breathing was heavy and laboured . . . I thought of his wife and children, of our talks about Austria, how damned stupid the whole thing was.

★

Battles rarely go according to anybody's plan, and El Alamein was no exception. In an attempt to impose some order, the British had laid down a Manhattan-style grid system in the northern sector. Laterally, running parallel to the coast, were six 'streets', named Star, Sun, Moon, Bottle, Boat and Hat. They were crossed by three broader 'avenues', running north-to-south, of which Bombay was the most easterly, followed by Springbok and then Qattara.

Well beyond this 'street plan', the maps in Montgomery's caravan showed the three lines, each a little further west, that his troops were due to reach at various stages of the battle: 'Oxalic' (which included all the Miteiriya Ridge), by 03.10 hours on 24 October; 'Pierson' (including the slight rise known as Kidney Ridge), where Lumsden's tanks were supposed to be by dawn of the 24th; then 'Skinflint', Lumsden's final objective, shown on the maps as a huge goose-egg straddling the north-south Rahman track and embracing Tel el Aqqaqir, a bump in the desert that was not quite a hill. There was no time set for reaching this; once Lumsden got there, the battle, which Montgomery had predicted would last about twelve days, should be over.

By the beginning of 26 October, the third day, the plan and the reality remained very different. Lumsden's tanks were nowhere near the Pierson line. His most forward elements were with the infantry on the Miteiriya Ridge. Most of his Corps appeared to be stuck in a vast, dust-billowing traffic-jam of trucks and armour that was prey to Axis artillery and air strikes, the latter increasingly at night as British air supremacy remained unassailable.

There was another problem. For three days most men had slept very little, and now fatigue was beginning to take its toll. Major Flatow, the stocky Yorkshire Territorial who had named his tank 'Attila', had been told with the rest of his regiment to take the benzedrine pep-pills they had been issued. These amphetamines, whose pre-war use had been pioneered by long-haul pilots, were freely issued to the British army and navy though, acting on the advice of their medical officers, some units refused to take them. After the initial high, which could take effect about half an hour after ingestion, benzedrine users were often beset by hallucinations of the kind later generations would know as 'bad trips'. Flatow's was mild, if perplexing: why should a man on a bicycle be riding across the desert towards his Sherman?

Other hallucinations were less benign. A lieutenant shot down several German soldiers with a tommy-gun when they tried to rush his tank leaguer after dark, only to learn that they were the crew of a knocked-out Sherman seeking the sanctuary of their own lines. Luckily, his aim was not as sharp as his heightened imagination. The same officer also spent several minutes trying to rouse a man lying in the path of his tank, before he realized he was talking to the dead. In the middle of heavy shell-fire a sergeant turned up alongside a tank in a jeep and calmly informed its crew that it was 'only a scheme' (an exercise) and they could go back. Meanwhile, their colonel saw a map in the sky, complete with grid lines, and began to muddle the names of his officers.

Flatow's suspicions that the battle might go either way were heightened when some engineers went out and blew up one of his squadron's new Shermans that had lost a track in the minefields. It might have been recovered and repaired but, rather than risk its falling into enemy hands, the sappers were ordered to destroy it. And Attila's first shots fired in anger, high-explosive shells to cover yet another attempt by the British armour to break through the Axis defensive line, proved to be a baptism of misfire: 'Bell loaded with great eagerness . . . Corporal Hudson took aim at my well-directed fire order and with great ceremony pressed the switch with his foot. Nothing happened! Bell re-cocked and Hudson pressed; again still nothing happened!' The dud was carefully extracted and carried away from the tank and the next round in the breech showed more respect for three long years of training. Soon afterwards, Flatow's squadron, along with the rest of 24 Brigade, were transferred from the 10th Armoured Division to Major-General Raymond Briggs's 1st Armoured and were sent further north.

It did not take Rommel long to conclude that the British were feinting in the south and that the *Schwerpunkt* was to come nearer the coast. One of his first acts was to order his 21st Panzer to pull out from behind the Folgore and head north towards Kidney Ridge, known as Hill 28 on German maps. He knew that he was taking a considerable risk. The only armour he had left in the south were the Ariete and, if Montgomery decided to move all his armour to the south, Rommel would not have the fuel to send his Panzers back to face them. He need not have worried. Montgomery, too, was gradually denuding his southern front, allowing his reserves to be sucked into the vortex that was developing around Kidney Ridge. In the extreme south, 44th (Home Counties) Division had been reduced to one infantry brigade. The three battalions of the Sussex Regiment that composed 133 Brigade had been transferred to 10th Armoured Division, where they were learning a new role as mechanized infantry. The Queen's Brigade, which had been isolated beyond the minefields and mauled by the Folgore, had now become part of Harding's 7th Armoured Division. The Queen's were painting the division's famous stencil of a jerboa, the desert rat, on to their trucks and preparing to head north with the rest of the division.

Despite the 'rocket' he had received from Montgomery on the second night of the battle, Lumsden's tanks had still not broken through. As far as Lumsden and his commanders were concerned, they were being asked to do the impossible. As the fighting around Kidney Ridge developed, the experienced and courageous Gatehouse, commander of 10th Armoured, had flatly refused to take his tanks 'over the Miteiriya Ridge, at night, through an unlifted minefield and be 800 yards down the forward slope of the ridge by dawn the next morning'.

There were more colossal rows and allegations that the armour were not pulling their weight, even lightly veiled accusations of cowardice. Montgomery became particularly incensed when he dis-covered that Gatehouse's HQ was some nine miles behind the front. This was grossly unfair: Gatehouse himself was rarely in it. He had a reputation for putting his own tank at the head of his division – another Prince Rupert – when the moment had come to charge. The trouble was, neither he nor any of his senior officers was yet convinced that this was the right moment.

The evening of 26 October saw another attempt to get Lumsden's armour out in front of the infantry. The plan involved expanding a salient into Kidney Ridge by capturing two localities north and south of it, beyond a line now held by the 51st Highlanders at a location codenamed 'Aberdeen' on the left and the Australian 9th Division, who were almost astride the coastal railway line, on the right.

The intention was to disrupt the Axis anti-tank screen and hold these two new strongpoints as 'pivots of manoeuvre' for two armoured brigades. At XXX Corps headquarters some field-sports aficionado named the objectives 'Woodcock' and 'Snipe' and taking them was to be a task for the infantry. It was an operation that, although relatively small-scale, would prove to be crucial to the ultimate success of Montgomery's grand plan. The attack was to be made by the 7th Motor Brigade, which had been given plenty of the new six-pounder anti-tank guns. Two veteran battalions were involved: the 2nd Battalion of the King's Royal Rifle Corps, also known as 60th Rifles, and the 2nd Battalion of the Rifle Brigade★ where Tom Bird, in his Hebron coat, was commanding the anti-tank company.

The assault was launched at night with artillery support by at least thirty guns, firing a half-hour barrage. Normally, mechanized infantry would dismount at least 500 yards from their objective and close in on foot. The 60th Rifles made a navigational error and found themselves among the Germans at 'Woodcock' long before they thought they were close. Since it would have been suicidal to pause and dismount from their trucks and Bren gun carriers, Major Peter Blundeel in the leading vehicle told his driver to put his foot down and charge, hoping that the rest would follow. They did, and about 100 stunned German soldiers, together with six anti-tank guns, were captured, though not entirely without a fight. 'It shows what can be done by surprise tactics

---

★ The Rifle Brigade was not a brigade but a regiment. For the uninitiated, the nomenclature of the British army, until post-war contraction imposed a certain logic, was about as easy to decipher as pounds, shillings and pence or the rules of cricket.

– especially if the surprise is equally divided between friend and foe,' noted a knowing regimental history. Blundeel got a DSO.

At 'Snipe', a few miles to the south, it was a very different story. The Rifle Brigade battalion under Lieutenant-Colonel Victor Buller Turner was having its own navigational problem: the references on the 1st Armoured Division map they were using were found to differ by about a mile from the 51st Highland Division map the artillery was firing on. Turner decided that the only solution was to follow the barrage, to 'march on the backs of the falling shells', as he put it. Turner was a short, stocky man with an avuncular moustache, a professional soldier from a family of professional soldiers, whose older brother had been awarded a posthumous VC at the Battle of Loos in 1915. A deceptively mild-mannered bachelor, he was well liked by his young officers, who tended to treat him like a respected if somewhat unworldly housemaster from one of the public schools they had so recently left.★

Most of Turner's soldiers were Londoners and conscripts, who had inevitably replaced casualties. But its character as a regular battalion was preserved by the number of pre-war professionals still serving as NCOs. These corporals and sergeants, old sweats in their late twenties, speaking their own Cockney-Urdu-Arabic argot, were the battalion's backbone. 'We were like a family. We knew each other intimately,' recalled Joseph Swann, the son of a West London baker who had enlisted in 1934 and who by 1942 was a sergeant in charge of a troop of anti-tank guns. The battalion had been in the Middle East since before hostilities began and were battle-wise. As their adjutant, Captain (later Colonel) Tim Marten would put it, 'they had long experience of being under fire and getting away with it'.

The battalion had spent the first three days of the battle escorting sappers into the minefields and trying to keep the lanes open, and thus were as tired as everybody else. Most had long since learned the old

---

★ In 1942 it was more or less *de rigueur* that Rifle Brigade officers should be old boys of one of the better public schools. Turner had been to Wellington, but in his own mess he was outnumbered by Old Etonians and Wykehamists. As officer casualties mounted, more 'emergency commissions' were granted, but even then some of the more snobbish regiments tried to discriminate. Major Flatow, the north country tank commander, was appalled to discover one Yeomanry adjutant plotting to establish a separate officers' mess dining table for his regiment's 'temporary gentlemen'.

soldier's trick of catnapping whenever possible. Otherwise, they kept awake on sugary tea and adrenalin. Benzedrine was not issued to this battalion after its medical officer had conducted an experiment and decided that it affected their marksmanship.

By 2 a.m., following the opening barrage, Turner had led his battalion about 2,000 yards from the start line to what he assumed was 'Snipe'. He found a shallow, oval-shaped depression, measuring about 1,000 yards by 400. It was, in fact, about half a mile from where the battalion was supposed to be and, as they were soon to discover, was located between two Axis tank leaguers. But Turner refused to budge. 'Here we are and here we damned well stay,' he told Marten.

Most of the edges of the depression were no more than three or four feet high but, fringed with scruffy tamarisk bushes and camel thorn, they provided ideal concealment for the nineteen anti-tank guns and their crews that were deployed in all-round defence around the perimeter. In most cases there was no need to dig in. Approaching the position, the battalion had captured a score or so German sappers who had put up little resistance. They too had obviously appreciated the merits of this dent in the desert, for Marten discovered a dug-out near its northern perimeter in which he established battalion HQ. It was about ten feet square, with what looked like old railway sleepers for a roof and not quite deep enough to stand upright. Once his two signallers with their radios were inside, the best place Marten could find to seat himself was on the steps. They had to watch where they put their feet. Previous tenants had used its darker corners as a latrine and even at night there were plenty of flies.

Meanwhile, some of the Bren gun carriers announced the battalion's presence by attacking a mixed leaguer of German and Italian armour. Acting more like the leader of an armoured car squadron, their commander, Lieutenant Dick Flower, ventured about a mile west through a gap in a minefield, collecting fourteen prisoners on the way, then surprised the tanks in the act of refuelling. The cavalry spirit displayed by Flower and his crews had a lot to do with their firepower, which was considerably greater than the regulation Bren gun to be found in newly arrived divisions such as the 44th or 51st Highland. Over their two years of campaigning, the riflemen had acquired an arsenal of entirely unauthorized Axis machine-guns and, best of all, the same Vickers K that the SAS used, which they had looted off RAF wrecks before the salvage teams could get to them. Opening fire from about 200 yards, they set light to one of the fuel bowsers and two other trucks. In the ensuing firefight one of the carriers was wrecked, but Flower led the remainder back to the battalion, radioing a situation report to Marten at HQ as he did so.

Shortly afterwards, Turner heard the sound of approaching Panzers and, against the rising moon, saw the silhouettes of about twenty tanks encircling their position. Heading the attack was one of Rommel's Mark IV Specials with its long 75-mm gun – the latest thing in the Wehrmacht's tank armoury. It was followed by an Italian Semovente self-propelled gun, a 75-mm howitzer mounted on an M13 tank-chassis, and then more tanks. Whether they had blundered on to the British position or were in pursuit of Flower's insolent band is unclear. Soon both sides were firing at what little they could see of each other.

One of the six-pounder gun commanders facing the Mark IV was Corporal Savill, a fishmonger in later life. Droning and roaring through its gears, the Mark IV, a monster spitting fire and apparently lacking all connection with humankind, waddled towards them. When a machine-gun bullet removed most of one of Savill's ears, leaving him too stunned to function, Rifleman Chard took over the gun.

Bird always considered Chard, who was slightly buck-toothed, to be one of the quieter members of his anti-tank company. He was surprised to learn later that he had a reputation for being something of a hell-raiser when on leave in Cairo. Now, crouched behind the shield of his gun, it looked likely that Rifleman Chard would never get the opportunity to misbehave again. For a long time nothing happened, it was as if he was frozen in fear. When at last he fired, the Panzer was no more than thirty yards away. The monster ground to a halt. As he reloaded, Chard became aware of some movement about the turret, and at least one of its five-man crew dropped to the ground. Chard fired again. Then the Mark IV did something the diesel-fuelled German tanks (unlike the petrol-driven British) rarely did: it burst into flames, lighting up the Semovente, about 200 yards away. That was also swiftly destroyed. At this point the rest of the Axis armour backed off. Turner sent the few prisoners they had taken back with most of his transport.

At first light the battalion discovered that by an enormous fluke they had inserted themselves right into the belly of the 15th Panzer and Littorio Divisions. Sergeant Swann rubbed his eyes in disbelief. 'It was like a massive car park,' he would recall. 'There were vehicles all over the place. Hundreds of them. I remember a lot of them were ambulances, scooting off in all directions. We were right in his rear echelons.'

Turner hardly had time to take stock of his position before his gunners started shooting. Only a small part of Bird's Company had been involved in the night fight. For most of them, this was their first chance of finding out if their new six-pounders were as good as they were cracked up to be. Within a short time they had hit and disabled fourteen tanks and also destroyed two self-propelled guns, several trucks, an 88-mm gun and a staff car. The six-pounder was proving to be the British infantry's best equalizer since the longbow.

Retaliation came soon in the form of heavy shelling. Men were caught in the open, trying to reposition guns which in daylight were seen not to have a good field of fire or whose recoil had dug them into soft sand. Among the casualties was Hugo Salmon, Tom Bird's friend and second in command, who lost half of his handsome face and took several hours to die. The battalion's medical officer remained at the start line, held up by heavy artillery fire, and it was left to Rifleman Sidney Burnhope, a medical orderly, to take care of the wounded.

Turner's 300 riflemen were virtually cut off from the main British forces, a mile to the east, and were in danger of being surrounded. At first, though, there seemed no great cause for alarm. They were in a natural fortress and had already inflicted considerable punishment, while relief, in the form of 24th Armoured Brigade, was expected at any moment. But when the 24th's Shermans crested Kidney Ridge, Turner's battalion became victims of their own success. The armour had no more idea of the exact position of the British infantry than the riflemen had themselves. Nor were they close enough to comprehend that the largest concentration of Axis machines clustered below them were the wrecks created by Turner's six-pounders. What they saw was a tempting target and immediately began to bombard it and the well-camouflaged position of the riflemen beyond.

Unable to warn off the tanks because they were on different radio frequencies, Turner decided to send his intelligence officer, Lieutenant Jack Wintour, in a Bren gun carrier with an urgent message to stop this 'friendly fire'. Wintour reached the tanks intact and one squadron did cease fire. The other continued to shell the riflemen with some enthusiasm. Only because they were well dug in, and the Shermans' ordinance was nowhere near as lethal as some of the Axis air bursts, did the battalion escape serious casualties. Eventually the firing stopped and the British tanks began to advance on to their 'pivot of manoeuvre'.

At first this worked out quite well. Turner's anti-tank guns picked off some of the Panzers that had turned to face this new threat. The machine-gunners in the Shermans – new to the desert and unburdened by notions of chivalry between opposing tank crews – shot the survivors. But when 24th Brigade got on to Snipe itself, the high-turreted Shermans came under devastating anti-tank fire from the German 88s. Soon, seven British tanks were ablaze and, as Turner's riflemen risked their lives trying to rescue their crews, it became apparent that Snipe was no place for any target that could not be concealed below its low natural parapet. The Shermans accordingly withdrew east of Kidney Ridge, pursued by the taunts of the Germans who got on to their radio frequency and proceeded to demonstrate that they knew an alarming amount about their opponents. The 15th Panzers must have had an energetic propaganda team at divisional headquarters, for Flatow's radio began picking up a very Germanic rendering of English north country voices, spreading alarm and despondency. 'Aye,' said one voice, 'it's the 45th, 41st and 47th regiments, they come from Lancashire and Yorkshire. We'd be much better off at home in our gardens with our wives . . . We can't do anything against the German artillery . . . These 88-mms are so accurate . . . I don't know what we're fighting for.'

'It was all in that strain,' Flatow would recall, 'two soldiers talking to each other . . . Believe me, it was incredibly demoralizing. I switched off my set so my crew couldn't hear it – as it was, they were rather windy.'

Now Turner's men were on their own: the 'cavalry' were not coming to their rescue after all. Few isolated infantry battalions have ever been able to survive in such a position. Almost certainly the riflemen could not have done so had the Luftwaffe still been able to provide close support. But for the rest of the day, inspired by the grit of their NCOs and the unflagging leadership of Turner and Bird, the battalion took on all comers. Guns were knocked out, and a couple just stopped working. Ammunition began to run low, not only the precious anti-tank shells but also .303 bullets for the rifles and Brens.

Rifleman Eddie 'Muscles' Blacker, an athletic six-footer from West Ham who had lied about his age to enlist and was still two months short of his eighteenth birthday, was lying under the remains of the Mark IV that Chard had destroyed. He and his mate, another South Londoner, had crawled out to pick off enemy snipers and were getting through a lot of ammunition. Their opponents were also in among the wrecks, but because they had to shoot downwards to hit a target inside Snipe they were tempted to expose themselves by clambering on to tank turrets. It was a gunfight in a junk yard, and Blacker, a good shot, killed with impunity. 'They didn't know where we were,' he would recall. 'It was ducks in a water barrel.'

But by now the Axis artillery was taking a heavy toll. By midday there were only thirteen of the battalion's six-pounders left in action and the continuous churning up of soft sand by shells made it almost impossible to move them around. Officers and NCOs ran and often crawled between them, distributing ammunition. Flies swarmed in black clouds over the dead and tormented the wounded. On the western flank, six of Flower's parked Bren gun carriers were set alight, sending up columns of black smoke.

At about one o'clock, nine Italian M14/41 tanks, a refinement of the M13 with its machine-gun mounted in the hull, approached this flank, supported by some Semovente self-propelled guns. The M14s were commanded by a Captain Preve and had been detached from the Littorio Division to become part of a mixed German-Italian group under a Panzer colonel called Teege. Preve had chosen a good spot for his assault. Only one gun could be brought to bear on his tanks.

The commander of that gun was Sergeant Charles Vivian Calistan, an Anglo-Indian whose father had served as an NCO in India between the wars. Calistan was one of the battalion's most popular regular NCOs. Small and nimble and an accomplished featherweight boxer, he had recently recovered from wounds received when he won a Military Medal near Bir Hacheim. Now he had been left alone on the six-pounder while two of his men tried to crawl back to him with some ammunition from a damaged gun. A third man's nerve had gone and he was still near the gun, unwilling to leave cover or do anything else.

Turner had been touring his perimeter, helping a short-handed gun crew or tending the wounded when he could, exhorting when he could not. Bird sometimes wished he could find a happier choice of words. 'Come on, you're not dead yet,' he growled at the shaken occupants of a slit-trench who had been almost buried alive by a near-miss. Seeing that Calistan was in trouble, Turner ran over to him, joined by Calistan's platoon commander, Second Lieutenant Jack Toms, a dreamy young man who loved fly-fishing and had won an MC at Gazala. Battalion commanders and their subalterns did not normally man anti-tank guns, but they pitched in alongside Calistan. Turner ordered him to hold fire until the oncoming Italian tanks were 600 yards away. Calm and cool as if on a training exercise, the sergeant knocked out six tanks, one by one. When he was down to his last three shells, Toms left cover and ran under machine-gun fire to a jeep, 100 yards away, that had on board four boxes of six-pounder ammunition. He brought the jeep to within ten yards of the gun when the vehicle was hit by incoming incendiary rounds and burst into flames. 'We managed to pull off the ammunition and bring it up to the gun,' Turner recalled.

An Italian account of the action makes it plain that the British were 'extremely well dug in and camouflaged'. Eyes level with the rim of the bowl, Calistan had the advantage of seeing without being seen. All the enemy could do was shell and machine-gun where he thought the gun was. Italian tanks caught fire easily but had a disturbing habit of continuing to advance long after all aboard were dead or dying. Dominioni witnessed this phenomenon more than once: 'huge, self-propelled funeral pyres shaken by explosions and emitting coloured flashes as the shells inside went off'.

Although six of Captain Preve's M14s had already stopped and some were in flames, the crews of the surviving three demonstrated a courage their poor equipment did not merit. They closed in, machine-guns blazing, while behind them the Semovente self-propelled guns tried to find the anti-tank crews with their 75-mm shells. A splinter sliced through Turner's helmet and penetrated his skull. He fell to his knees, blood pouring over his eyes and down his face. He wanted to carry on, but Toms and Corporal Albert Francis persuaded him to lie down behind a camel thorn bush before they rushed back to Calistan.

They found him crouched by his gun, his forehead pressed against the concertina rubber eyepiece of the six-pounder's telescopic sight while he turned the wheels which controlled elevation and traverse. A burst of machine-gun fire kicked up dust behind him, but Calistan seemed unaware of it. His hand moved towards the firing lever and Toms knelt with a fresh round in his hands, ready to slam it in the breech. Calistan started firing when the first M14 was 300 yards away.

He fired twice more and all three were flamers. 'Hat trick!' yelled the colonel from behind his bush. In the lull that followed, Calistan put a dixie of water on the bonnet of Toms's still-smouldering jeep and brewed some tea. Turner was taken a mug. 'As good a cup of tea as I've ever had,' he always said when he re-told the story.

Officer casualties began to mount. Bird, almost inevitably, was among the next to be hit. Although the surest way to survive at Snipe was to remain in a hole in the ground as long as possible, he spent most of the morning touring the perimeter, supervising the guns. It had become a fashion among young officers (and not only in the Rifle Brigade) to disdain the uncomfortable steel helmet. In the summer they tended to wear peaked service caps and in winter cloth side-caps, preferably as far to the side of the head as possible. Bird was hit as he was lying on the ground talking to Lieutenants Toms and Flower. Toms's right hand was mangled and he would eventually lose two fingers; Flower was hit in the legs, Bird in his unprotected head. It was not as serious a wound as Turner's but it was bad enough. For a while Bird tried to carry on but concussion and heat began to take their toll. Eventually, a space was found for him alongside Turner on the floor of the HQ dug-out along with the signallers, their radios, Marten and the flies. By now Turner had become delirious and was under the impression he was defending a harbour against naval attack. Every now and then he would yell out, 'Sink that destroyer!'

In the late afternoon they again came under friendly fire. This time it was from 2nd Armoured Brigade's 105-mm Priests, brand-new American self-propelled guns which, like the Shermans, were in combat for the first time. Two of Sergeant Swann's men were killed by one of their air bursts and it is unclear how many more casualties were inflicted. 'During an unpleasant day this was the most unpleasant thing that happened,' the battalion's report of the action recalled.

By now, as the shadows lengthened, the NCOs were beginning to take over from the wounded officers. Among their own casualties was the recently betrothed Corporal Cope, happy recipient of Doreen Roots's 'I love you' telegram. His loader had been killed alongside him, but Cope carried on working the gun until he was himself hit by shrapnel. He crawled away to find a replacement crew before waiting his turn for the attention of medical orderly Burnhope. By that time his gun was credited with two Mark IIIs, a Semovente, and an 88.

Every minute closer to dusk increased the riflemen's chances of survival. In 1942 tanks had no kind of night-vision aids and the enemy armour were normally reluctant to press conclusions in the dark. A determined infantry assault might have carried the position, but that was rarely the Axis way. At about 5 p.m., when no more than two hours of good light remained, it was observed with some apprehension that about seventy enemy tanks, divided into two groups, were assembling to attack the British armour beyond Snipe. This was one of the counter-attacks for which 21st Panzer Division had been brought from the south. As in most tank operations inspired by Rommel, it was executed in the way that had so often caught the slothful British on the wrong foot. But this time dash became slapdash.

At least one of the 21st's newly arrived Panzer regiments had not been warned that between them and their objective lay this venomous nest of British anti-tank guns. They might have drawn their own conclusions from the large number of disabled Axis tanks about the place; instead, some of them chose a route which placed their more vulnerable side armour within 200 yards of the hidden six-pounders. Those with the best field of fire were four surviving guns of an attached Royal Artillery battery under Lieutenant Alan Baer, a recent Oxford graduate and keen jazz musician. Until now his crews, dedicated gunners better trained on the six-pounder than the riflemen, had been manning the quietest sector. Now the tempo changed and within minutes they had stopped nine Panzers, some of which were on fire.

As the enemy tanks turned head-on to face their tormentors, they exposed their flanks to the armoured brigade's Shermans and Priests. Despite this enfilade fire, one of the long-gunned Mark IV Specials got to within 100 yards of Baer's battery, machine-gunning all the way, until it was hit by the guns of Sergeants Binks and Cullen. Then Binks's six-pounder was hit by a high-explosive shell. By some fluke the sergeant was unscathed, but one of his crew was decapitated and the other two mortally wounded. This was battle as the men exchanging broadsides on Nelson's ships-of-the-line must have known it, and it seemed there could only be one outcome.

At this point the Panzers pulled back and, once out of range of the six-pounders, settled into hull-down positions in folds in the ground. Clearly they did not intend to let the British get away with their continued defiance. No doubt an experienced eye had noted the growing feebleness of the defenders' fire and drawn the appropriate conclusions. Fifteen Panzer Mark IIIs approached the north-west corner of Snipe, advancing hesitantly. They were not to know that at first only two working six-pounders could be brought to bear on them. One of these was commanded by Sergeant James Hine, who had taken over Cope's gun when his own was destroyed. The other was not far from the battalion HQ dug-out and was neutralized before it had fired a shot. Its crew fled for a nearby slit-trench after three hull-down tanks, about 500 yards away, started to find them with their machine-guns. With the odds now at fifteen to one, adjutant Marten began to burn the radio codes lest they fall into enemy hands.

In the south-east corner of the position, Rifleman Chard's gun was pointing the wrong way and he struggled to turn it around to face the latest threat. His platoon commander, Lieutenant Holt-Wilson, and a sergeant rushed over to help him, and together they managed it. Hine held his fire until the first tank was 200 yards away. Then Chard and the others began to support him. Between them they quickly disabled four Panzers. But two others had bypassed Hine's gun and were safely out of Chard's line of fire. All that stood between them and battalion HQ was the abandoned six-pounder.

Inside the dug-out, Marten and Jack Wintour the intelligence officer were soaking the last of the wireless telegraphy codebooks with petrol before putting a match to them. Watching the tanks closing in on the dug-out was Sergeant Swann, increasingly a supernumerary since his crew had been hit and the number of working six-pounders reduced to about eight. Standing on a slight rise, about 100 yards from the abandoned gun, Swann yelled a warning to its sergeant commander to get back to it. A voice he did not recognize replied that the sergeant was hurt. Later Swann was furious to discover that this was untrue.

He ran down towards the abandoned six-pounder, hit the ground, crawled for a few yards when a machine-gun seemed to be on him, then sprinted for the gun. There was a round in its breech and Swann took aim at the first tank, which was now about 100 yards away, a long-barrelled Special with another directly behind it. Swann fired and the Panzer stopped. Swann was vaguely aware of the turret hatch opening and two men leaping out to the rattle of rifle fire. At this point the six-pounder crew, shamed into it, began to leave their trench and run back towards their weapon.

Swann took his time with the second shot and aimed it, as he had been taught, at the weakly armoured spot just below where its gun barrel met the turret. An incredulous and delighted Marten watched as the tank's main member drooped towards the ground. Beside him, Wintour was jumping up and down like a schoolboy, shouting, 'He's got him! He's got him!' From inside the tank came the sound of a man screaming. It went on and on.

These were almost the last shots fired at Snipe. Three Panzer Mark IIIs remained close enough to machine-gun the battalion from a depression which shielded all but the tops of their turrets. At dusk the rest of the Panzers withdrew and for a few minutes were 'nicely silhouetted against the pale patch in the sky'. The riflemen fired most of their remaining ammunition at them, more as a *feu de joie* than with any serious intent, but their luck held and one of the enemy was hit. They watched it being towed away.

For a while, even in the darkness, the heavy if blind machine-gunning of the Panzers' rearguard in their hull-down position continued. Then the shooting died down and gave way to an unspoken truce, during which both sides were allowed to collect their wounded, the Germans extracting some of theirs from the wreckage of tanks little more than 100 yards from the British positions. This would eventually include the man trapped in the tank Swann had hit.

Meanwhile, German salvage teams moved in and began to tow away those machines that looked repairable. Marten, the most senior British officer left on his feet, did nothing to stop them. His priority was getting as many of the battalion's wounded loaded into the remaining transport as possible. Their casualties totalled about seventy killed or wounded, including ten officers – about 25 per cent of Turner's force. Bird's anti-tank company, so much more exposed than the others, were the worst hit. Most of the dead were buried on the spot, often in the slit-trenches they had occupied.

Later that night the Rifle Brigade was given permission to withdraw and began to do so by companies at around 10.30 p.m. Lack of towing vehicles, most of which had returned to the start line, meant that all but one of the guns were rendered useless by having their breech-blocks removed and abandoned. Only the attached Royal Artillery troop had a vehicle available to save a gun. Most of the riflemen walked away from Snipe. The companies put their wounded in the middle, Tommy gunners fore and aft, and then headed north-east. Before he left the scene with the wounded, Calistan 'did something you may think rather stupid – I went back and kissed my gun'. At the pace of their walking wounded they left the sandy places, wind-rippled into the patterns of low tide. Once they were on harder ground, with ankle-deep camel thorn and colonies of white-shelled snails, they knew the ordeal was almost over. 'Attila's' commander, Major Flatow, saw them come in. He had just pulled back into leaguer when 'some weird swaying figures approached us; they were dressed in British uniforms but I was frightened of a trick and I asked the first wretched man for his AB 64 [paybook]. He nearly cried. "Lord, sir, we've been out there for twenty-four hours and we've been shot at by both sides and we're all in. Here, take my rifle!"'

It was a while before the defenders of Snipe, let alone the rest of the army, realized just how well they had done. Tom Bird certainly did not feel as if he had been involved in a great victory. 'I had lost all my officers [one killed and the rest wounded] and all my guns.' But Eighth Army HQ was in no doubt what the battalion had achieved, and Montgomery was delighted. By their stubborn defence of Snipe, they had frustrated Rommel's efforts to destroy Briggs's 1st Armoured Division and in doing so had inflicted losses Rommel could ill afford on the 15th and 21st Panzer and the Littorio Divisions.

When, some days later, officers from the battalion and others had the chance to revisit Snipe, it was concluded that, by a conservative estimate, they alone had destroyed or disabled thirty-three Axis tanks, five self-propelled guns, a couple of artillery pieces, several trucks and a staff car. They had possibly damaged another twenty tanks which were recovered for repairs that might never have been completed. All this quite apart from the losses inflicted on the enemy by the British armour.

Honours were heaped upon the battalion. Turner was awarded a Victoria Cross for 'an example of leadership and bravery which inspired his whole battalion'. Following his older brother's post-humous award, this made his family* one of the very few to produce two holders of the Victoria Cross. The Anglo-Indian Sergeant Calistan was put up for the VC but, to the disgust of some of his comrades, he received the lesser Distinguished Conduct Medal. (He eventually received a battlefield commission and held the rank of lieutenant when

---

* A very unusual family it was, too. On retirement, Turner went to live with his sister Jane and two surviving brothers on a country estate in Norfolk. None of them ever married. Turner died in 1972. Jane Turner lived to be 101.

he was killed in Italy in 1944.) Tom Bird got a DSO and a 'cushy number' as one of Wavell's ADCs in the Viceroy's house in Delhi. Towards the end of the war he was seriously hurt by a shell in Belgium, his fourth wound, which ended his active soldiering. Like Calistan, Sergeant Swann got a DCM. So did Rifleman Chard. Both men survived the war. Corporal Cope soon recovered from his wounds and was able to tell his Doreen that he had been promoted to sergeant with a Military Medal for gallantry – one of seven MMs awarded, mainly to NCOs. Toms won a bar to his Military Cross and, having lost his trigger finger, spent the rest of the war as an instructor.*

Snipe was one of the turning points of this second Battle of El Alamein. Rommel became convinced that Montgomery was trying to break out from the salient around Kidney Ridge and squandered his precious armour trying to prevent it. It was a wrong move. By now Montgomery was too disillusioned with Lumsden's X Corps to seriously entertain hopes of an armoured breakthrough. He had his eye on other developments.

---

* A less experienced battalion from the Royal Sussex, which was supposed to relieve the Rifle Brigade, went to the wrong spot, failed to get their guns dug in properly, was overrun by Panzers, and most of them were captured.

To date, all of Eighth Army's successes were due to the infantry. A glance at the butcher's bill showed the 51st Highland Division heading the list with around 2,000 dead or wounded, more than four times as many as Lumsden's entire X Corps. The Highlanders' commander, 'Tartan Tam' Wimberley, was himself heavily bandaged but soldiering on after a Teller mine had blown him out of his jeep, killing his driver. The Argylls' company commander, Major Samwell, was among scores of Highland officers and men who woke up between clean sheets in Delta base hospitals.* (So, it seems, was the Austrian machine-gunner he had shot. Samwell had last seen him in a casualty clearing station receiving a blood transfusion.)

Australia's 9th Division came next on the list, with well over 1,000 casualties. It was to them that Montgomery now turned to try and break through. Their division had not only attacked frontally, but had also executed a wide left hook from their original positions. One Axis outpost after another had fallen to them. They were rapidly establishing what Eighth Army HQ was beginning to call 'a thumb' across the coastal railway line and towards the coast. If they succeeded in reaching the sea, they would trap a large part of Rommel's 90th Light and 164th Divisions inside a horseshoe-shaped pocket created by their original front line, their left hook, and the Mediterranean.

In short, Morshead's men were once again showing their fearsome offensive qualities. The grenade, the gangster's Tommy gun, and the fixed bayonet remained their weapons of choice. Time and again when things went wrong some Ned Kelly type would materialize to inspire others to follow him in a rush that saved the day. All were volunteers, but often from very different backgrounds. Two of the 2nd/48th battalion won posthumous VCs during the battle yet all they would appear to share was their age; they were both comparatively old men – positively ancient for front-line infantry. Private Percival Gratwick turned forty just before the battle started and Sergeant Bill

* Samwell was killed in action in northern France in November 1944.

Kibby was thirty-nine. Gratwick was an Aussie of popular myth. Born and bred in Western Australia, he had earned a hard and precarious living prospecting for gold and other precious metals. He was cut down, leading a night attack on 26 October, after his platoon commander, a lieutenant, and sergeant had been killed, leaving seven unwounded men pinned down. Gratwick immediately took charge. He threw two grenades into a sandbagged enemy strongpoint, then climbed into the wreckage and killed the survivors. He was killed by machine-gun fire charging a nearby second outpost. Sensing that Gratwick had unnerved the enemy, his company commander led another assault which captured the position.

Sergeant Kibby, an English immigrant born in Durham and a plasterer in civilian life, won his VC for a series of similar actions, beginning on the first night of the battle when he made a single-handed attack on a German position, killing three with his Tommy gun and capturing twelve. On 31 October he took over command of his company after all the officers had become casualties. He died hurling grenades as he led a bayonet charge.

Posthumous VCs are obviously exceptional. But the general calibre of Australian junior officers and NCOs had been good since the beginning of the campaign and it showed in their high casualty rate. A dour sense of humour – some might call it gallows humour – was characteristic. Rifleman (later Lieutenant) Donald Main of the Rifle Brigade would recall a night engagement in which British six-pounders disabled fourteen enemy tanks. The Australians on their right were not pleased. ' "You rotten Pommy bastards," they cried, objecting to our knocking out the tanks with our six-pounders before they came within range of their two-pounders.'

Some of the Panzerarmee, particularly the Italians, were convinced that the Australians gave themselves Dutch courage with hard liquor. 'The Australians, roaring drunk on whisky, are like madmen,' Captain Luigi Bohner, an artillery officer, noted in his diary. Second Lieutenant Eithel Torelli, whose unit was overrun by Australians with fixed bayonets, recorded that as he grappled with two of them 'they were splitting their sides with laughter; drunk as lords'.

Martin Ranft, the Saxon Kannoneer, would recall how, well behind the front line on the fourth day of the battle, he awoke just before dawn to feel a gentle breeze on his face. 'With the breeze came this distinct smell of liquor. You could almost taste it. We were beginning to ask ourselves what this could mean when we started to come under small-arms fire from the ridge in front of us.' An Australian patrol, Ranft estimated there were no more than twenty-five of them, had broken through. Some made a dash for the battery of German heavy artillery, perhaps with the intention of snatching a prisoner, while others fired at them from the ridge. Ranft heard their youngest lieutenant shout, 'Shoot, lads, we're not finished yet.' He turned in time to see the officer, who was standing in a foxhole with the upper part of his body exposed, suddenly put his hand to his mouth and slump forward. Then he grabbed his rifle and started firing back.

An Australian sergeant got to within a yard of one of the guns before he was dropped by a bullet in the head and they started to fall back. The Germans raced for their guns, depressed their barrels about as far as they would go and started firing their huge shells directly at the ridge. Ranft watched in amazement as the body of the Australian who had got closest to the guns was lifted into the air by the muzzle blast. Soon there was no more rifle fire and two unarmed Australians walked in to surrender, their hands in the air.★ The others had either bolted or been killed by their shells. The only German fatality was the lieutenant Ranft had seen shot. Even so, Kannoneer Ranft and his comrades did not derive much comfort from their small victory. Where, they asked themselves, were the infantry who were supposed to be protecting them? The battle was obviously not going well.

As the fighting intensified in the Australians' sector, Rommel committed more and more of his resources, reinforcing the 164th Infantry and 90th Light Divisions by moving his Panzers north from the Kidney Ridge area. In his own account of the battle he explains: 'We were, therefore, going to make one more attempt, by the tenacity and stubbornness of our defence, to persuade the enemy to call off his attack.'

Oliver Leese, XXX Corps commander, responded by reinforcing Morshead with Royal Artillery six-pounder anti-tank gunners. However, despite the large number of tanks Lumsden had in the rear, no attempt was made to reinforce the two Royal Tank Regiments that

---

★ Ranft was given the job of escorting the prisoners back to a PoW cage. They passed a field kitchen and the cook called the prisoners over and gave them each a heated can of *Leipzigerwallerbei*, a stew of pork, potatoes, beans and gravy that was very popular in the Wehrmacht. After his exciting morning Ranft was hungry too but to his disgust the cook did not offer him anything and the twenty-year-old was too shy to ask.

were attached to the Australians. They were equipped with Valentines, infantry tanks armed mostly with the old, inadequate two-pounder gun. Those that survived to get close enough did knock out some of the Mark IIIs, but their numbers were soon reduced from about thirty to eight.

The Australian infantry were not much given to speaking well of British armoured units. They thought they had let them down too many times, but they praised 40th RTR. 'The courage of these men made their action one of the most magnificent in war,' the historian of 2nd/48th Battalion noted. But, one might ask, why were they sacrificed in the first place? Where were the Shermans and Grants?

Keith Douglas, the poet and tank officer who so badly wanted to be at the sharp end, was looking for them himself. By the fourth day of the battle he had felt too ashamed to remain at his safe job at divisional HQ and had set off in his little Ford truck with a batman and a fitter to find his regiment. 'I like you, sir,' said his batman, a former hunt servant and one of the original Yeomanry volunteers. 'You're shit or bust, you are.' Douglas had decided to present himself to his commanding officer as if the Division had agreed to let him go. In case he was rejected, he had typed a movement order giving himself permission to go to Palestine, where he intended to enjoy himself until he was caught and court-martialled. However, Lieutenant-Colonel Everard Kellett, a Tory MP when he was not commanding a tank regiment, did not reject him; he was too short of officers. The Sherwood Rangers had lost twelve killed and fifty-six wounded in the opening forty-eight hours of the battle. Sixteen of their tanks had been disabled as they tried to get across the Miteiriya Ridge.

On his first day in action, Douglas was involved in some mopping-up operations in the Kidney Ridge area and did well. When an infantry subaltern asked him to help clear some snipers, he leapt from his Crusader with his gunner and assisted in rounding them up. He took forty German prisoners. He came under heavy artillery fire for the first time and discovered he could control his fear. Towards dusk, he participated in a fierce tank battle, during which one of his squadron's fuel trucks was hit and

blazed like a beacon. I crammed shells into the six-pounder as fast as Evan could lay and fire it. Presently the deflector bag was full of shell cases, and Evan, who had now adjusted the Besa [machine-gun], blazed off a whole belt without a stoppage, while I tossed out the empty cases, too hot to touch with a bare hand. The turret was full of fumes and smoke. I coughed and sweated; fear had given place to exhilaration.

Then, to Douglas's surprise, the Sherwood Rangers were pulled out of the battle, along with the rest of Lumsden's Corps de Chasse. A couple of days later, Kellett explained that they had been withdrawn until such time as they were needed to deliver the *coup de grâce*. 'When we've destroyed the enemy's armour and routed his forces we, we shall go back to Cairo, and . . . er . . . have a bath, and leave the other buggers to do the chasing for us,' he said.

When Churchill learned that Montgomery had withdrawn the bulk of his armour and, after six days, the battle seemed to be at stalemate, he was furious, summoning Brooke to his presence and subjecting him to the kind of hectoring he had, during his days in opposition, reserved for the appeasers. The Chief of the Imperial General Staff felt ill-used and, despite his heavy workload, described the incident in his private diary:

What, he asked, was my Monty doing now, allowing the battle to peter out? (Monty was always 'my Monty' when he was out of favour.) He had done nothing new for the last three days, and now he was withdrawing troops from the front. Why had he said he would be through in seven days if all he intended to do was fight a half-hearted battle? etc., etc.

Brooke discovered that Churchill had been egged on by Anthony Eden, his Foreign Secretary. Eden had been at loggerheads with Brooke ever since the CIGS had made it plain that he wanted Montgomery to command the Eighth Army and not Eden's candidate, Gott. Now, over a late-night drink with Churchill, the Foreign Secretary had 'shaken his confidence in Montgomery and Alexander, and had given him the impression the Middle East offensive was petering out!'

At a Chiefs of Staff meeting later in the day, Brooke was able to pour scorn on Eden's grasp of military affairs. He pointed out that, far from doing nothing for the last three days, the Eighth Army had exhausted Rommel by rebuffing one counter-attack after another. As for Monty withdrawing his armour, was it not one of the first principles of offence that reserves must be created for the next attack? It was a bravura performance and won Brooke the support of the South African leader, Field Marshal Smuts, always one of Churchill's favourites. Yet Brooke was nowhere near as confident as he sounded:

I had my own doubts and my own anxieties as to the course of events, but these had to be kept entirely to myself. On returning to my office I paced up and down, suffering from a desperate feeling of loneliness. I had during that morning's discussion tried to maintain an exterior of complete confidence. It had worked – confidence had been restored. I had told them what I thought Monty must be doing and I knew him well, but there was just the possibility that I was wrong and Monty was beat.

Montgomery was not beat, far from it, but he was in the process of heavily rewriting the script. Operation 'Lightfoot' was over; Operation 'Supercharge' was about to begin. It was to be a smaller version of Lightfoot and its main player would be New Zealand's Major-General Bernard Freyberg VC, whom Montgomery considered to be his best divisional commander, followed by the Australian, Morshead. But it was to be Freyberg without most of his men. The New Zealand Division was exhausted; they had been fighting almost continuously since July, when Auchinleck had first established the Alamein line; so for this new chapter of the battle Freyberg was given UK troops. Apart from one battalion of Maoris, his active infantry were to be the 'Durham Brigade' from 50th Infantry Division, composed entirely of three battalions of the Durham Light Infantry, and the Seaforths and Camerons of the Highland Division's 152nd Brigade. Freyberg's tanks were to be the 9th Armoured Brigade, comprising the 3rd Hussars and two Yeomanry regiments, the Wiltshires and the Warwicks, under Brigadier John Currie, a red-head with a temper to match.

Currie's men had been fighting under Freyberg as an integral part of the New Zealand Division since the start of the battle, and they got along well. Once the infantry had seized their objectives, it was intended that Currie's armour should smash a hole through the Axis anti-tank screen running along the track that went south from the coastal hamlet of Sidi Abd el Rahman. The focus of the attack would be a little north of Tel el Aqqaqir, a small hill, and Lumsden's Corps de Chasse would be right behind them, ready to dash through the hole once it was made. That, at least, was the theory.

The Hussars were desert veterans, but Currie's Yeomanry had not served as tank crews before Alamein. As poorly equipped motorized infantry they had fought the Vichy French in Syria, where they had come off rather badly. They had also helped put down an Arab rebellion in Iraq and had been in Persia, where their most potent enemy had been malaria. Only the Wiltshires had been in the desert before, and that had been to man searchlights in Tobruk. But since the battle started they had seen enough fighting to become confident in their own abilities without suffering the kind of casualties which can breed a paralysing caution. The prospect of going back into action alongside the Hussars and the equally battle-hardened Maoris, who were at peak form, appears to have given Currie's brigade confidence and a 'can do' spirit that was sometimes lacking in Lumsden's regiments.

A good dose of that spirit was certainly needed. When the 3rd Hussars' CO, Lieutenant-Colonel Sir Peter Farquhar (known to his men as 'Colonel Push On') heard what Supercharge entailed, he sought out Montgomery and informed him that his plan was 'suicide'. Montgomery did not disagree. 'It's got to be done,' he told Farquhar. 'If necessary, I'm prepared to accept one hundred per cent casualties in both personnel and tanks.' The Hussar was impressed by Montgomery's candour. 'There was, of course, no more to be said,' he would recall.

The sixth Baronet Farquhar was a lapsed professional soldier who had resigned his commission to become a full-time Master of Fox Hounds, but returned to the army as soon as hostilities began. Now he set about organizing his regiment for what he strongly suspected might be the extinction of all of them.

In later life it was Montgomery's greatest conceit to maintain that almost every battle he planned worked out the way he had planned it. Yet at El Alamein he proved that he could think on his feet, adapting and changing as circumstances dictated as readily as his famously flexible adversary. True, he would rarely be the risk-taker Rommel had been in his heyday, lacking the German's vivid tactical imagination, but this was not always necessarily a bad thing. Brooke had been almost right in asserting that Montgomery had withdrawn Lumsden's armour from the fray because he was planning a new attack. But, initially at least, he had not done so to create reserves for the next stage of his offensive but because he had utterly lost faith in them. His instinct was to finish the battle with his infantry, exploiting the Australians' success on the extreme northern flank without using Lumsden's armour until the battle was practically won.

Even when Rommel pushed so many reinforcements into the northern sector that the Australians' momentum began to slow, Montgomery was tempted to match the Axis reinforcements, raise the stakes and slog it out. Then it became noticeable that Rommel was running short of men as the whole notion of 'corseting' the Italians to the south with German units began to unravel.

Churchill's harangue with Brooke left Montgomery in no doubt as to the necessity of finishing the battle before Operation Torch, the Anglo-American landings in Vichy-controlled North Africa, on 8 November. It was also vital to recapture the Martuba airfields, west of Tobruk in the Cyrenaica Bulge, giving the RAF the range to cover a convoy which was due to leave Alexandria for Malta around 16 November with desperately needed fuel and food. If this convoy did not get through, the island might yet fall.

These priorities had been confirmed when Alexander visited Montgomery's HQ, accompanied by the Australian Richard Casey, who was the Cairo-based Resident British Minister in the Middle East. This was not an entirely happy event. Freddie de Guingand, Montgomery's loyal chief of staff, was particularly on edge and when, at one point, Casey suggested, out of Montgomery's earshot, that he ought to warn Churchill that all was not well, de Guingand flew at him. 'If you do, I'll see that you're drummed out of public life,' he warned – an empty threat, since Casey was at that point a senior civil servant and in any case was not a part of UK public life.

Despite the tensions, it was in the end a productive visit. Out of it came the final plan for Supercharge. Afterwards, several people tried to take the credit for persuading Montgomery to move the axis of his attack away from the Australian sector. But as far as Montgomery could be influenced by others, the kudos for pointing out that the thrust should go further south through the increasingly uncorseted Italians seems to belong to de Guingand.

Rommel was already looking over his shoulder and had ordered a reconnaissance of Fuka, the port and airfield off which Maskelyne had conjured his phoney landing, to see whether it might be a good place to withdraw to and buy time until reinforcements arrived. 'I haven't much hope left,' he wrote to Lucie on 29 October in his daily letter home. 'At night I lie with my eyes open, unable to sleep for the load that lies on my shoulders.'

By now both Montgomery and Churchill knew from Ultra intercepts that Rommel was growing desperate. The demands being made on the Italian navy to deliver the supplies and reinforcements he needed to hold the line were becoming increasingly intemperate. Cavallero, the Italian Supreme Commander in Rome, was losing a lot of good men and vessels trying to do just that. The fish had grown fat on seamen who had drowned while trying to run the British sea- and air-blockade. On 26 October the ammunition ship *Tergestea* and the tanker *Proserpina* had been sunk; two days later it was the turn of the tanker *Louisiana*, then the freighter *Tripolino*. And although three Italian destroyers got into Tobruk harbour, under almost constant air attack, carrying 190 tons of supplies, it was little more than a brave gesture.

Montgomery decided that his *Schwerpunkt* for Supercharge would be just north of Kidney Ridge, on the junction where the Italian and German formations met, 'but overlapping well on to the Italian front'. On Friday, 30 October, exactly a week after the start of the battle, he sat down in his caravan and wrote out his plan for Supercharge. 'I always wrote such orders myself and never let the staff do it,' he explained in his memoirs. 'This was the master plan and only the master could write it.'

Once again the master discovered that he could not entirely control events. Zero hour for Supercharge, another night attack with artillery support, was set for 1 a.m. on 1 November. But Freyberg was not ready and begged for a twenty-four-hour postponement. Montgomery reluctantly agreed while in London Brooke sweated and Churchill fumed.

Realizing that delay would only help the enemy, Montgomery ordered that the depth of penetration be extended from 4,000 to 6,000 yards – 'the whole under a very strong barrage'. 'I should add,' he would later write, 'that there were doubts in high places about Supercharge . . . These doubts I did not share and I made that clear to everyone.' Except to Brooke. On 1 November Montgomery sent a message containing a paragraph that, from Monty of all people, could have done nothing to ease his superior's private anguish:

If everything goes really well there is quite a good chance we may put 90 Light and 21 Panzer both in the bag. *But battles do not go as one plans* [authors' italics], and it may be that we shall not do this. We have got all the Germans up in the north in the Sidi Rahman area, and I am attacking well south of that place. There will be hard and bitter fighting as the enemy is resisting desperately and has no intention of retiring.

Zero hour was 1 a.m. on 2 November. All along the start line came a clicking sound as infantrymen fixed bayonets. Bofors anti-aircraft guns lowered their barrels and fired tracer to help battalions keep direction. Walking behind a creeping barrage, the Highlanders again went into the attack to the sound of their pipers.

Among the Germans and Italians who heard them was Rolf-Werner Völker, the Panzer Grenadier who had accidentally shot up the wing of the Junkers-52 bringing him to North Africa. Fewer than twenty of the 400 men of his battalion who had crossed the Mediterranean with him, some seventeen months before, were left. Most of one company had been captured in the fighting before Alamein in July

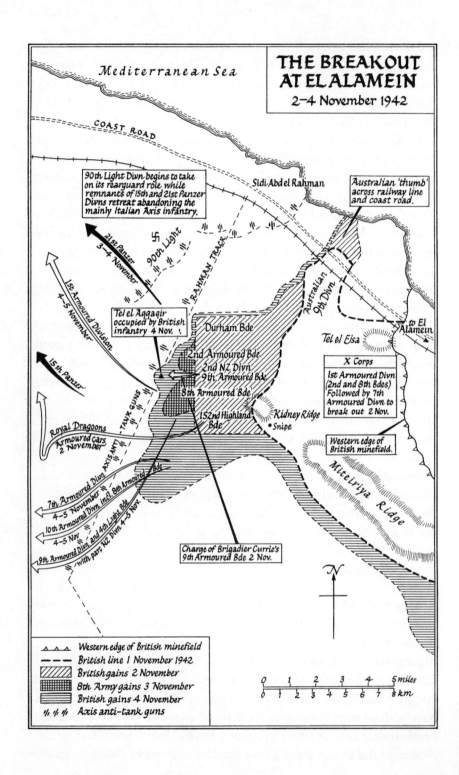

THE BREAKOUT AT EL ALAMEIN
2–4 November 1942

Mediterranean Sea

COAST ROAD

Sidi Abd el Rahman

90th Light Divn begins to take on its rearguard role while remnants of 15th and 21st Panzer Divns retreat abandoning the mainly Italian Axis infantry.

Australian 'thumb' across railway line and coast road.

21st Panzer 3–4 November

90th Light

RAHMAN TRACK

1st Armoured Division 4–5 November

15th Panzer

Tel el Aqqaqir occupied by British infantry 4 Nov.

Durham Bde

Australian 9th Divn

to El Alamein

Tel el Eisa

2nd Armoured Bde
2nd NZ Divn
9th Armoured Bde

8th Armoured Bde

X Corps
1st Armoured Divn (2nd and 8th Bdes) Followed by 7th Armoured Divn to break out 2 Nov.

Royal Dragoons Armoured cars 2 November

TANK GUNS

152nd Highland Bde

Kidney Ridge
• Snipe

Western edge of British minefield.

7th Armoured Divn 4–5 November incl 8th Armoured Bde

AXIS ANTI

Bde

Miteiriya Ridge

10th Armoured Divn 4–5 Nov

9th Armoured Divn and 44th Light Bde with part NZ Divn 4–5 Nov.

Charge of Brigadier Currie's 9th Armoured Bde 2 Nov.

N

▲▲▲ Western edge of British minefield
– – – British line 1 November 1942
//// British gains 2 November
▦▦▦ 8th Army gains 3 November
||| British gains 4 November
⫻ ⫻ ⫻ Axis anti-tank guns

0   1   2   3   4   5 miles
0 1 2 3 4 5 6 7 8 km

and the rest had been killed or invalided home, wounded or sick. Like many desert veterans, Völker found the Afrika Korps had changed. Quite a lot of the more recent arrivals had fought in Russia. 'They thought Africa would be easier,' Völker would recall. 'They changed their minds at El Alamein.'

Völker, now a corporal, was in command of a long-barrelled Pak 38 anti-tank gun along the Rahman track. This was the area the British had codenamed 'Skinflint' and where Montgomery hoped his armour would eventually congregate and break through. In the nine days since the battle started Skinflint had been shelled so much that its sand had been reduced to a fine dust. Every time a shell landed, it kicked up a cloud that was as dense as a smokescreen. At times visibility was down to fifty yards. Nor could the Germans dig their guns in properly; they had to lay sandbags on the traces of their Pak to try and stop the recoil from shifting it after each shot.

Earlier in the year, like so many of his comrades, Völker had been evacuated to a Wehrmacht hospital in Greece suffering from dysentery. Now he seemed to be going down with it again, with persistent bouts of diarrhoea and what felt like the beginnings of a fever. He was shivering under a blanket in a slit-trench close to the gun when he first heard the unearthly wail and drone of the pipes, rising and falling as they came towards him.

At first I thought I was dreaming. It was a strange feeling. It wasn't frightening. It's hard to explain but it reinforced this feeling we sometimes had that we were all front-line fighters together – that we had more in common with our British enemies than we did with the generals and their staffs and the rear echelon troops behind us. It was almost as if we were all taking part in some kind of pageant.

Major Wilfred Watson of the 6th Durham Light Infantry, to the right of the Highlanders, could see them moving, ghost-like, through the smoke and sand thrown up by the barrage. After a while he saw 'figures with their arms up looming out of the mist – Germans and Italians surrendering. After we'd done about 880 yards we received enemy fire from our right which slowed us down a bit. Also we must have walked over some Italians who lay doggo as we advanced and undoubtedly one of them killed my RSM, the doctor tending the wounded and a sergeant who played cricket down in Dorset.' Shortly before dawn, most of the British infantry had seized their objectives, as had the Maori battalion which captured over 300 Germans and Italians for thirty-three of their own killed, among them their colonel.

Now it was the turn of Currie's brigade. For the last forty-eight hours they had been struggling to make ready. The lack of standardization in most British armoured brigades complicated logistics enormously. Four different types of tank – Shermans, Grants, Honeys and Crusaders – required three different kinds of fuel. Between them they carried nine different calibres of cannon and machine-guns. Nor did their problems end there. Many of their tanks were replacements for vehicles the brigade had lost during their encounters on the Miteiriya Ridge the previous week. Most of these were 'recovered vehicles' – abandoned machines towed or transported off the battlefield after losing a track or worse. In the workshops just behind the front line, fitters and mechanics sweated around the clock to get them ready in time, but in some tanks the guns were still not functioning properly; in others the radios were faulty.

Currie, like Farquhar a fox-hunting man, had decided to call the operation 'The Meet of the Grafton Hounds'. It is not difficult to imagine what his overworked signallers, struggling to encrypt and tap out messages in Morse, thought of this. Grafton, as it became known, was due to start at 5.45 a.m., about an hour before first light. It was intended to get the tanks through and behind the Axis anti-tank screen on the Rahman track, where Völker and the other Panzer Grenadiers were waiting, while it was still dark. But Currie had to postpone the attack by half an hour because the Warwickshire Yeomanry were delayed getting to the start line by unsuspected minefields and pockets of determined enemy infantry with a few anti-tank guns.

To achieve maximum surprise, the plan called for the tank crews to shed their usual inhibitions about moving in the dark. Ultimately it was hoped that they would be among or even beyond the anti-tank gunners on the Rahman track before dawn. But inevitably people got lost. One squadron strayed into a field kitchen of the Highland Division, much to the alarm of its early porridge shift. Closer to the front, they were required to feel their way along narrow channels cleared through minefields. As on the opening night of Lightfoot, these channels came under artillery fire.

The Sherwood Foresters, the brigade's motorized infantry and anti-tank gunners, took some casualties. All soft-skinned transport was vulnerable; truck loads of fuel and ammunition were soon offering unwelcome illumination. And despite the frantic last-minute servicing, the brigade was considerably reduced by mechanical break-downs. Thirteen of the Wiltshires' forty-four tanks and ten of the Hussars' thirty-five failed to reach Grafton.

At 6.15 a.m. the creeping barrage started and about ninety tanks began to move away from the Grafton start line. The Hussars were on the right flank, the Wiltshires in the centre and the Warwicks on the left. Since they did not have any infantry support, the tanks had been issued with extra grenades so that their commanders could throw them into trenches and foxholes as they went by.

At first all went well for Currie. As a night tank attack was unusual for either side, it came as a considerable shock to enemy troops who had just endured another dose of what Rommel called 'the terrible British artillery'. The Wiltshires saw German infantry 'running in all directions. They could not avoid the tanks and many were killed by machine-gun fire or run over. Those who surrendered were directed back to the British lines, but when light came many were able to take up fresh positions and continue fighting.'

Then the 9th were betrayed by the dawn. It came up behind them long before they were through the anti-tank guns, silhouetting their tanks as plainly as in a recognition manual.

On the right flank the Hussars were subjected to fire from their front and both flanks. It was every bit as bad as Farquhar had predicted and his response was precisely what Montgomery had expected of him. 'Soon the battlefield was thick with black smoke from burning tanks,' notes the regimental history. The smoke may well have been the saving of the survivors, who were able to get among the guns and wreak a terrible revenge, in some cases crushing man and machine alike.

The Hussars claimed the destruction of fifteen anti-tank and four field-guns. By this time their 'runners' were down to seven, including Farquhar's headquarters tanks. All radio communication between them had broken down. Farquhar himself seems to have borne a charmed life, despite having to dismount and give orders by running from tank to tank under fire.

The Yeomanry reacted in exactly the same way. On the left flank the Warwicks, having mistaken another small hill for Aqqaqir, advanced on a more southerly bearing than was intended. This immediately brought them up against a battery of four Italian field-guns whose crews fired over open sights and quickly accounted for one of the Warwicks' leading Crusaders, killing the second-in-command of the reconnaissance squadron. Then the British got their machine-guns on to the Italian emplacements and they were overrun.

A frenzy seems to have gripped some of those involved. Sergeant Jack Ballard was commanding a Crusader III, the latest model, when both its six-pounder and its Besa machine-gun malfunctioned. At this point he could have retired honourably from the fray. Instead, he ordered his driver to press on while he fired from the turret with a Thompson sub-machine-gun.

In the centre the Wiltshires were confronted by a battery of 88s. These began to pick off the British tanks with their usual ease. Before long, the Wiltshires' lieutenant-colonel and all three squadron commanders were wounded. It was clear to the Wiltshires that they were much too close for retreat to save them, so valour became the better part of discretion. They closed with the guns, machine-gunning madly, ignoring their casualties.

Then the surviving Shermans and the Grants were all over the 88s, an armour-plated lynch mob which trampled over gun pits and gunners alike, competing with each other to do their worst. The 9th's own casualties were considerable. In all they lost 270 killed or wounded and out of their ninety tanks only nineteen were still capable of movement.

When Captain Clive Stoddart of the Warwicks tried to radio his commanding officer, a German-accented voice came in on his wavelength to inquire, 'Isn't it nice, seeing all your beautiful new toys going up in smoke?' Stoddart had just baled out of his blazing Grant and was trying to use the radio in another abandoned tank that had failed to catch fire. It was as if he was being watched.

Later, British war correspondents with the Eighth Army made much of the 9th's charge, inevitably comparing it with that of the Light Brigade at Balaclava. But though the courage and sacrifice may well have matched Lord Cardigan's 'gallant six hundred', there was a crucial difference. The 9th's charge was much more than tragic error and futile gallantry: almost the last act of the battle of El Alamein, it redeemed the performance of the armour. 'If the British armour owed any debt to the infantry of the 8th Army,' said Montgomery some time later, 'the debt was paid on 2 November by the Ninth Armoured Brigade in heroism and blood.'

Between them, Currie's three regiments were estimated to have destroyed about thirty-five of Rommel's anti-tank guns along the Rahman track, and if they did not punch a hole in the Axis line they certainly left a crack that was ripe for exploitation.

Some British armoured cars, Humbers and Daimlers of the Royal Dragoons, had already got well behind enemy lines, shooting up transport, fuel dumps and any other soft and unsuspecting targets they chanced upon. A few hours after Supercharge started, they had moved in the dark through Freyberg's infantry to bluff their way through the enemy formations lined up either side of 'A' track, miles behind the front line. As the dawn came up behind them, the Dragoons held their breath and could hardly believe their luck.

Sleepy Axis guards sat rubbing their eyes with the backs of their hands, or ran over to consult with one another about the strangers passing through their position. They surely could not be the enemy, so far from the battle and arriving in column of march in their Humbers and Daimlers. If they looked British, then they must belong to the 90th Light, which had a squadron equipped with captured British vehicles.

Despite Freyberg's pleas for them to get a move on, Brigadier Fisher's 2nd Armoured Brigade, which followed Currie's men on to the field, could not match the dash of the Dragoons. After their losses, the Wiltshires felt particularly bitter about the 2nd's failure 'to take advantage of the hole punched through the enemy gun line'. One problem appears to have been lack of liaison: nobody was there to tell Fisher what had been achieved and what could be done next. All his men could see were wrecked British tanks. It certainly did not look like a good place to go rushing into. In any case, the moment soon passed. Once Rommel understood what was happening, he reacted with his customary swiftness and moved what was left of the 21st and 15th Panzer Divisions from the northern sector to block Montgomery's latest move. The biggest tank action of the battle now began to build up on the Rahman track around Aqqaqir.

Fisher's 2nd Armoured Brigade, supported by the remnants of Currie's command, bore the brunt of it, but the action was soon sucking in more and more of the British armour. At Rommel's behest, the Afrika Korps commander, von Thoma, had moved his headquarters to Aqqaqir to take personal charge of it. But this was intended to be a rearguard action. By the end of the day, Rommel would have fewer than fifty German tanks in running order; Montgomery still had at least ten times that number. Partly thanks to the destruction wrought by Currie's brigade, Rommel was also short of anti-tank guns. He had only twenty-four 88-mm guns left to face the British tanks in the salient that Freyberg had created. It was obvious now that Montgomery's nerve would hold and that he would not call off his offensive as Auchinleck had done in the summer. Nor could the Panzerarmee possibly expect to win a battle of attrition.

That evening Rommel sent a message to the Comando Supremo in Rome saying that the only hope he had left was to 'extricate the remnants' of his army. He warned that those Italian formations without transport would have to be abandoned.

Thanks to Ultra, Brooke learned of the message's contents the following day, 3 November, and 'felt as if I was treading on air'. The next day a delighted Churchill greeted Brooke with another Ultra intercept: Hitler had ordered Rommel to 'stand firm' and offer his men 'no path but to victory or death'.

A great victory was obviously within Montgomery's grasp and the Prime Minister knew just the way to celebrate it. Britain's church bells had been silent since the 1940 invasion scare, when it was decided that they would be pealed only to sound the alarm if enemy paratroopers were dropped. Once the Alamein victory was beyond doubt, Churchill would order the bells to ring out all the way from Land's End to John O'Groats.

Like the jubilant Churchill, Rommel recognized Hitler's message as a death sentence for his army. But he could not bring himself to disobey his Führer's order to stand and die. Von Thoma tried to persuade him that 'minor withdrawals' were acceptable, but Rommel knew that the situation called for more than this: what was needed was a general retreat before Montgomery at last got his armour through and outflanked him. There was not a minute to be wasted yet this *Führerbefehl* paralysed him. Several times he started to draft replies but sent none of them. In the end he was moved to utter the ultimate blasphemy. Six hours after receiving Hitler's order, he told Elmar Warning, a junior staff officer while pacing up and down outside his command vehicle: 'The Führer must be crazy.'

Despite the pressure he was under that night, 4 November, Rommel found the time to scribble one of his notes to his illegitimate daughter

Trudel. They are very much the words of a soldier who is by no means certain whether he will live through the next twenty-four hours. 'The battle is coming to an end and I'm sorry to say it is not to our own profit,' he wrote. 'The enemy's strength is too strong and they are overwhelming us. It is in the hands of God whether my soldiers will survive. To you I send my heartfelt greetings and wish you and your family all the best for the future. Your Uncle Erwin.'

Eventually Kesselring, the senior Wehrmacht commander in the Mediterranean and Rommel's superior, flew in from Rome and persuaded him that Hitler's order did not have to be interpreted so literally. He made a personal telephone call to Hitler and on the evening of 4 November got the order rescinded. By that time there had been another important development: Montgomery had dined with General von Thoma. The commander of the Panzerarmee had surrendered at about midday to Captain Allen Grant Singer★ of the 10th Hussars after his command vehicle was hit and most of his *Kampfstaffel* destroyed in fighting around Tel el Mampsra, another small hill not far from Aqqaqir. Montgomery arranged to be photographed receiving von Thoma. Brendan Bracken, the Irish journalist who had become Minister of Information, thought this very unwise and said so in a memo to Churchill. 'The incident, trifling in itself, roused an altogether disproportionate amount of disapproval,' said Bracken. 'Montgomery remains the hero of the hour, but that he should entertain a German general to dinner and allow himself to be photographed receiving him appears to have struck the home public as symptomatic of an attitude they fear and resent.' Later in the war, Eisenhower made it a point of honour not to meet any captured German generals.

Certainly, Montgomery did not come well out of the photo-opportunity he had arranged. Von Thoma, tall and looking rather younger than his fifty-one years, appears every inch the dashing Teutonic knight with his leather-gloved right hand touching his cap in salute, while Montgomery – wearing a long-sleeved pullover that looks a size too small for him and with his thumbs hooked in his

---

★ Singer was killed the next day, and in a letter to his widow von Thoma wrote: 'I shall always keep an honourable memory of this knightly foe on the battlefield, who also took me to General Montgomery and beg to express my sincere sympathy with you, most honourable, gracious lady.'

trouser pockets – looks as though he might have been disturbed while gardening.

At the dinner party that followed, Montgomery told von Thoma through an interpreter that he had 'enjoyed the battle very much' and asked after Rommel's health. He was in boastful mood and told von Thoma: 'I met Rommel once in August and I beat him; and I have met him again now, and I shall do the same thing.' He claimed that the Eighth Army had captured Fuka, a position von Thoma knew Rommel might try to hold, though Montgomery was nowhere near Fuka: Gatehouse's 10th Armoured Division would not be there for another thirty-six hours.

Among the wounded at 21st Panzer's field hospital was Corporal Völker. He had received a painful though not serious leg-wound when infantrymen from one of the Highland regiments had got close enough to hurl grenades at his anti-tank gun before they were beaten off. Casualties were being evacuated by air to Mersa Matruh two at a time in Fiesler Storch spotters. But the doctor would not allow Völker to go because the fever brought on by his dysentery was too high. A few hours later, when news came that the British had broken through, the walking wounded were ordered to save themselves by heading east and hitching lifts. 'Typical of the army of course,' Völker thought. 'One moment I'm too sick to fly, the next I'm told to walk.' There were fifteen of them and they walked for an hour and a half, cursing the stream of Luftwaffe trucks which made them eat their dust as they sped past. Eventually an old flat-bed laden with empty oil-drums drew to a halt and its Italian driver took them on board.

They spent the next three days in his company, picking up food and water from supply dumps that were about to be demolished or booby-trapped. Sometimes they crawled along at night in nose-to-tail convoys, praying that the RAF's 'Christmas tree' flares would not make them a bomber's target. Fortunately for them, the RAF Wellingtons and Hampdens were not really suitable for the job, while the fighter-bomber squadrons that could have cut them to pieces had been unable to move their airfields forward fast enough because of the traffic-jams on the British side of the lines.

On the southern front, quiet after Horrocks's initial feint had been so easily rebuffed, there were no traffic-jams. Those who wanted to get away had to walk. Ramcke, the man of iron, got out. He and about

600 of his paratroopers reached Mersa Matruh by hijacking a convoy of fifty or so British ration trucks carrying supplies for one of the armoured brigades that were trying to cut off the Axis retreat. Most of the rest of Ramcke Brigade, about 2,000 strong, were captured by British armoured units and in some cases were glad to be so, as food and water had begun to run out and every step westwards became more painful.

Burckhardt's Experimental Battalion were among them, captured by the Household Cavalry's armoured cars. While the rest of his battalion were being rounded up, Burckhardt hid for a couple of hours but eventually surrendered. The 'Tin Tummies' were unimpressed by the boastful Major Burckhardt, whom they thought 'a phenomenal snob' after he tried to ingratiate himself by telling them: 'I have never seen armoured cars work like that before. You have learned all we can teach, and now we must learn from you.' His vanity remained enormous. As he was led off for interrogation, he shouted to his men, 'I am Burckhardt. They want me. Farewell, lads, look after yourselves and remember, you have known Burckhardt.'

Fritz Neumaier, a corporal in Burckhardt's battalion, was also taken prisoner. 'I was captured by British tank troops and treated by them the best way you could imagine,' he would recall. 'At the front the British were good to us because they had to live like us. But as we went back towards Alexandria our treatment became progressively worse. At one point we had rotten tomatoes thrown at us and were hit by rifle-butts when we had to get into trucks.'

Few of the Folgore escaped. Most of those who did had been wounded in the early stages of the battle and had been sent to hospitals well behind the lines. Among these was Aroldo Conticello, the teenage baker's apprentice. On the third day of the battle, the British had raided the Italian trenches at about dusk, getting close enough to throw grenades. Conticello remembered putting his hands in front of his face, then waking up in a field hospital at Mersa Matruh, where doctors amputated what was left of his hands and wrists. They saved the sight of one eye and began to extract over fifty pieces of metal from his body. Many of his unwounded comrades died of thirst, trying to walk to freedom when the front collapsed. Private Carmel Calio, aged twenty-three, his battalion commander's personal dispatch rider, recalled that by 3rd or 4th November they received the order to withdraw.

We started walking during the night. We dug ourselves in to rest and were fired on by the British. They approached under a white flag and called on us to surrender but some of us replied with shots and they withdrew. We kept withdrawing through the 6th. It rained all day, which brought some relief from heat and thirst, but as the sun went down our commander, General Frattini, said: 'Boys, it's all over, there's nothing more to be done. Those who can make it on their own are free to go.'

   Lieutenant Piccinni, rescuer of the long-haired Private Galati, surrendered when the British suddenly appeared on the brim of a bowl-like depression he and his unit were sheltering in. His commanding officer, fearing a massacre, yelled at his men to drop their weapons.

The British separated us according to rank. One British soldier took my dagger then felt my tunic, looking for any more hidden weapons. He found the parachute badge that we had been told to remove from our sleeves. 'Folgore!' he said and, obviously impressed, he picked up my dagger and handed it back to me – an honour of the kind we'd never had from our own lousy government. I shall never forget that moment. That British soldier's gesture was worth more than a medal to me.

According to Dominioni, some elements of the Folgore initially refused to surrender, even after three British armoured cars with loudspeakers turned up to praise their courage and offer them honourable terms, threatening 'complete annihilation' if they refused. 'The paratroopers shouted "Folgore!" and opened fire,' says Dominioni and 'the armoured cars made off.'

   In the end, thirst and hunger proved unbeatable. British accounts suggest that all those who failed to get away from the southern sector eventually surrendered, with the possible exception of small groups who starved to death or who were picked off by the Senussi. The number of prisoners on the southern front soon became an embarrassment to the British. They held up the advance as the captured Folgore were joined by ordinary infantrymen from the Pavia and Brescia Divisions. Picking up these thirsty and hungry men began to resemble a relief operation of the kind generally mounted in the face of earthquake or famine. RASC Driver Arthur Kennett, of the auspicious 23 October birthday, was one of those ferrying them back to temporary PoW cages. 'We used to pick up twenty Italians at a time. I had my rifle in the cab, but there were no guards. They used to clamber into the back and if we hit some soft sand in our Bedfords, which were no good for the desert really, they'd all get out again and start pushing.'

Inevitably, there were some among the British who could not resist taking advantage of the Italians' plight. George Greenfield, an intelligence officer in a battalion of the Buffs, was examining a map in his jeep when a member of his section asked for some advice.

'Do you know the Italian for water, sir?' he asked.

'Aqua, I think.'

'And for watch?'

'God knows. The French for clock is *horloge*. Try "orlogio".'

I went on with my map calculations and then the penny dropped. I jumped out of the jeep . . . There was my man standing by the track side as the prisoners shambled by, holding up a chagul [canvas water bag] . . . He was shouting 'Aqua?' and then, pointing to his wrist with the other hand, 'Orlogio.' . . . Four or five handsome wrist-watches were strapped above his left wrist. A watch for a mouthful of cold water . . . I ordered him to hand them back to their owners, an impossible task, but at least he would not score from the deal. And then I told our new intelligence sergeant to put him on extra duties for the next week.

In the northern sector, the Panzerarmee was now in full flight, but in the main was mostly avoiding attempts to trap and annihilate them. However, the remnants of the Ariete, Rommel's favourite Italian tank division, were cut off by 'Pip' Roberts's 22nd Armoured Brigade, which destroyed twenty-nine Italian tanks and countless soft-skinned vehicles and took 450 prisoners. One of his Honey light tanks was damaged; none of his men were killed.

Then Brigadier Custance managed to get to the coast with his 8th Armoured Brigade in time to destroy a mixed force of about forty Italian tanks and half a dozen Panzers. They also captured an Italian artillery battery and around 1,000 Axis prisoners. The Sherwood Rangers played a key role. In his Crusader, Keith Douglas found himself driving at speed alongside a column of Chevrolet trucks which at first he assumed to be British. Then he realized that these were captured vehicles, probably Tobruk booty, and that he was looking at a German driver.

The German glanced casually sideways at us, and away again. Then a terrible thought struck him. All this was comically visible on his face. He looked sideways again, seemed to confirm his worst fears and swerved violently into the railway embankment, jumping out before the truck stopped moving. Men came piling out of the back in colossal confusion ... I suppose we could have killed a good many of them as they ran, with my revolver and our Tommy gun. But this seemed a futile thing to do.

From von Thoma's capture on 4 November it took Montgomery nine days to reach Tobruk, by which time he had received a knighthood and been made a full general. 'We have a new experience,' said Churchill. 'We have victory – a remarkable and definite victory.' On Sunday, 15 November, the church bells rang out all over Britain for the first time in three years, their peals relayed by the BBC Overseas Service in a special outside broadcast from Coventry Cathedral, where only the spire and bell tower had survived German bombs. 'Did you hear them in Occupied Europe?' a gleeful radio commentator asked. 'Did you hear them in Germany?'

After more than three years of war, Alamein was the first indisputable victory over a German-led army, some three months before the even more momentous German surrender at Stalingrad. It was also (though Churchill did not yet realize it) just about the last hurrah of Empire, as the United States gradually exerted its role as dominant partner among the Western Allies. Even so, only in the last ten months of the war against Germany, from July 1944, did the Americans have more troops in the field than the British.

Montgomery's 'crumbling' tactics had not proved as expensive as some of his staff had feared. The Eighth Army's total casualties in killed, wounded or missing were 13,500, or about 8 per cent. Most were in Leese's XXX Corps in the northern sector. The Australian Division, who on the eve of Supercharge were tying down the bulk of the Panzerarmee, incurred 2,827 casualties of all kinds; the 51st Highland Division were next with 2,495, followed by 2nd New Zealand with 2,388 and 1st South African with 922. Slightly over half the casualties were UK British.

Reliable Axis casualty figures are harder to come by. The most accurate is probably the number of prisoners taken: 30,000 out of an army of just over 100,000. Ten thousand of these prisoners were Germans. Major-General (later Field Marshal Lord) Carver estimated that another 20,000 were killed or wounded, though the Axis official count was much lower. This was not at all slaughter on the scale of the Somme or Verdun in the First World War. Nor, in the second global conflict, did it compare to Stalingrad or the intensity of the Normandy campaign. But the battle was no less significant. As Churchill would say, it was not the end or even the beginning of the end, but it was the end of the beginning of Nazi Germany's downfall.

PART SIX

Endgame

For these will live,
They are quit of killing and sudden mutilation;
They no longer cower at the sound of a shell in the air,
They are safe.

John Jarmain, Captain, 51st Highland Division

Churchill's order for church bells to be rung throughout Britain was not as widely welcomed as he had expected. The outcome of the battle was, of course, 'a fine stimulant', said a War Cabinet Report on Home Opinion, signed by Churchill's protégé and propaganda chief, Information Minister Brendan Bracken. But the ringing of the bells 'was received with an awed disquiet' and 'approval and disapproval were fairly even'.

In Malta there were no such equivocations. Victory at Alamein and the subsequent capture of the Axis air bases at Martuba meant that the long aerial siege of the island was effectively over, and the inhabitants of the most heavily bombed territory on earth gave thanks in their cathedrals with heartfelt 'Te Deums'. By this time Malta had acquired a new governor, one who was less reliant on the whims of the Almighty than Dobbie. The CIGS, Brooke, had instigated Dobbie's removal, ostensibly because 'the strain on him was intense and he could not be expected to carry it indefinitely'. But undoubtedly Brooke had been incensed by Dobbie's refusal to allow troops to train or work on the Sabbath and, even more to the point, by his indirect responsibility for the loss of thousands of tons of vital supplies from two merchantmen that limped into harbour during March 1942.

Even battle-hardened British servicemen had found the task of unloading cargoes while under intense aerial bombardment distinctly unnerving. Chief Petty Officer Ernest Dillingham, who was in charge of one such work party, recalled that 'quite frankly, some of them were scared shitless'. The men in his party had seen plenty of action at sea, yet 'at one point I thought I had a mutiny on my hands'. Hardly surprising, then, that Maltese civilian dock workers, weakened by sleepless nights and a starvation diet, were even more scared than disciplined British soldiers and sailors.

Consequently, when the cargo vessels *Pampas* and *Talbot* – all that survived of a convoy from Alexandria which had run the deadly gauntlet of Stuka dive-bombers – limped into harbour on 25 March with 16,500 tons of desperately needed food, fuel-oil, ammunition and spare parts, local stevedores refused point blank to unload them. Far too late, Dobbie called on the army to carry out the unloading, and troops of the Cheshire Regiment were sent in to do the job. As wave after wave of Stukas dive-bombed the two merchantmen, the Cheshires managed to salvage a few hundred tons of supplies. But the rest went, with the two ships themselves, to the bottom of the harbour – a devastating loss which foresight and planning could surely have prevented.

Dobbie's critics, for instance, felt that he should have sent the troops in straight away, instead of leaving the unloading to frightened civilians, and that he should also have taken the elementary precaution of shrouding the harbour area in smoke to conceal the two target vessels from Kesselring's Stukas. But Dobbie had failed to acquire any smoke-pots, even though these were readily available in Alexandria. Nor had he made any coherent plan to remove the off-loaded cargoes quickly by road to storage depots around the island. 'The governor was dead to blame', is how Sergeant (later Major) B. A. Pond of the Royal West Kent Regiment remembered the incident. 'Everyone said what a wonderful man he was. An inspiration, they called him. Well, I say he was a bloody fool. He kept saying "Don't worry. God will take care of everything." Well, God didn't unload those bloody ships, did he?'

When, towards the end of April, Brooke went to 10 Downing Street to urge Dobbie's replacement, Churchill at first resisted. By his own account, he 'did not at first accept what I was told'. But Brooke pressed the point and eventually Churchill conceded that 'this Cromwellian figure' would have to go. To succeed Dobbie, the PM and the CIGS agreed on Lord Gort VC, commander-in-chief of the ill-fated British Expeditionary Force in France in 1940, who had latterly been Governor of Gibraltar. At fifty-six, he was seven years younger than Dobbie and, although he had failed to distinguish himself during the French débâcle, he was correctly thought to have the right qualities to handle the situation in Malta.

Gort arrived by Sunderland flying-boat on the night of 7 May 1942, landing in Marsaxlokk Bay while an air raid was in progress, and bringing with him the George Cross (Britain's highest civilian award for gallantry) that King George VI had bestowed on the people of Malta in a grand propaganda gesture the month before. Gort met Dobbie for the handover in a bomb-damaged hut ashore. There, according to Mabel Strickland, an irate Lady Dobbie demanded of Gort: 'What do you mean by taking William's job?' After Gort had been sworn in by the island's Attorney-General, the Dobbies and their spinster daughter Sybil left by the same aircraft that had brought Gort from Gibraltar. Dobbie returned to well-earned obscurity (and retirement) after Malta, living on until 1964, when he died aged eighty-five.

The January-to-May blitz was the high-water mark of Malta's ordeal by bombing. Following Kesselring's boast that the island had been neutralized, several squadrons of his bombers and their fighter escorts were redeployed to the Russian front, where it was felt they were more needed. In Malta the air raids continued, to be sure, but at considerably lower intensity. After all, there was not very much left to bomb.

In July, elements of the Italian navy, all too conscious of the Regia Aeronautica's poor performance and seeking to redeem national honour, made a gallant if foolhardy attempt to bring Malta to its knees by launching a human-torpedo attack on Grand Harbour. In the dark just before dawn, fourteen one-man craft – small motor-launches with torpedo-head bows, whose drivers were supposed to leap off just before hitting their targets – were launched from a mother ship lying nine miles offshore. An alert Maltese coastal defence gunner heard their engines as they approached and sounded the alarm. Displaying superb marksmanship the Maltese gunners destroyed all but one of the approaching enemy craft. The one survivor was beached in St George's Bay. The gleeful populace, roused by the sound of gunfire, rushed out to watch the slaughter from the bastions overlooking the harbour. It was another tremendous morale-booster.

As the German air raids slackened off and air-dropped mines were cleared from the Grand Harbour and its approaches, the submarines of the Royal Navy's 10th Flotilla slipped back to resume their harassment of Axis supply convoys to Rommel's troops. In all, more than 650,000 tons of Axis shipping would be sent to the bottom by the Flotilla; three of its skippers, Lieutenant-Commander Malcolm Wanklyn of HMS *Upholder*, Commander John Linton of HMS *Turbulent* and Commander Anthony Miers of HMS *Torbay*, would win the Victoria Cross.

Malta won a further respite, this one unearned, when in late June Hitler vetoed Operation 'Herkules', the well-advanced joint

German-Italian plan to launch an airborne invasion of the island. The Führer had no wish to repeat the experience of Crete, in which, although the operation was successful, German losses had been enormous. Also, he had learned by bitter experience that the Italians were not to be relied on. 'They do not possess the necessary fighting spirit,' he told General Kurt Student, the hero of Crete, who had been nominated to lead the Maltese invasion force. Nevertheless, the Germans remained determined to reduce Malta: if they couldn't occupy it or bomb it into submission, they would starve it out.

They came close to doing so. Stocks of flour, fuel-oil, kerosene and ammunition became so reduced that a committee consisting of the Deputy Governor, Sir Edward Jackson, and the three service chiefs calculated a secret 'Target Date', around the end of August 1942, beyond which the island could not hold out unless it were substantially resupplied. Churchill was determined that it should be sustained, no matter what the cost, thus setting the scene for the titanic 'battle of the convoys' that was waged in the summer of 1942.

Since the turn of the year, thirty-one merchant ships had tried to get through, of which ten had been sunk and eleven so badly damaged that they had been forced to turn back. Of the ten that had reached Malta, three had been sunk in harbour. Now, a massive two-pronged effort was launched to relieve the island which, as Churchill put it, was being 'pressed to the last gasp'. On 12 June, eleven merchant ships carrying 72,000 tons of cargo set out from Alexandria, escorted by no fewer than forty-six warships. This convoy was codenamed Operation 'Vigorous'. Simultaneously another convoy, consisting of six merchantmen carrying 43,000 tons of cargo, escorted by twenty-nine warships and codenamed Operation 'Harpoon', left Gibraltar travelling east.

As the 'Vigorous' convoy entered 'bomb alley', the narrows between Crete and Cyrenaica, it came under furious attack by Axis aircraft, submarines and E-boats. One merchantman was sunk and three others so badly damaged that they had to drop out of the convoy. A cruiser was crippled and a destroyer sunk. And when it was learned next day, after a second British cruiser and two destroyers were crippled, that a powerful Italian surface fleet, including two battleships and four cruisers, was closing in, naval headquarters ordered the convoy to return to Alexandria.

Meanwhile, Harpoon had encountered a similar reception while passing through the straits between Sicily and Tunisia. It had already lost one merchant ship and had one cruiser disabled. Now it came under furious air attack, and three more of its six cargo vessels were sunk or so badly damaged that they had to be scuttled. Only two, carrying 15,000 tons of supplies between them, made it into port.

This time, the island was properly prepared to receive them. Determined not to duplicate Dobbie's failure, Gort had mobilized a force of 2,500 troops and civilians, including a group of boys from the island's reform school, to be on hand at an hour's notice to unload the ships. Five hundred trucks were standing by to remove the cargoes rapidly to inland storage sites along one-way routes marked with individual coloured signs, while smoke-pots were in place to provide a screen to foil the Stukas. The two cargoes were successfully unloaded. This was the clincher, although barely enough to keep the island going on a starvation diet which, already at 1,200–1,500 calories a day, would now have to be reduced even further. As of 1 July adult males were to receive a twice-monthly ration of two ounces of rice, twelve ounces of preserved meat, eleven ounces of preserved fish and ten ounces of cheese. (Women and children received proportionately less, on the grounds that they were smaller and had to work less hard.) In addition there was a daily ration of thirteen ounces of heavily adulterated bread. A certain amount of local produce, such as eggs, chicken, fruit and vegetables, was available at government-controlled prices and, inevitably, there was a flourishing black market in which, for example, eggs were available at thirty shillings (£1.50) a dozen, six times the controlled price. Queenie Lee met a woman who said she had traded a suite of furniture for a few pounds of potatoes. Black-market cigarettes were as much as four shillings (20p) each, as compared with an 'official' price of one shilling for a pack of twenty, and 'some people smoked bamboo,' recalled Mabel Strickland, whose *Times of Malta* never missed an issue.★

To get around the shortage of fuel for cooking and to stretch food supplies further, the government set up a series of 'Victory Kitchens' which provided civilians with one cooked meal a day. These were to be collected, at the cost of sixpence and half a day's ration coupons, at either noon or 5 p.m. and were decidedly skimpy. Queenie Lee

★ After the war she was awarded the OBE in recognition of her steadfastness during the siege. Characteristically, Miss Strickland called it 'the Order of the Bad Egg'.

recalled collecting 'three thin sausages and fifteen peas for the three of us'. To make matters worse, the island's spring potato crop failed and, since by this time all the island's goats had been slaughtered and eaten, there was no fresh milk, 'only two tablespoonfuls of powdered milk to last two weeks and a few tins of milk reserved for babies'.

As Churchill would say, 'the strain was at many points more than could be borne' and if the island was to be saved a stupendous new effort must be made. The curiously named Operation 'Pedestal' was the result – an armada of four aircraft carriers, two battleships, seven cruisers, twenty-eight destroyers and numerous smaller naval craft as escort to fourteen cargo vessels. This huge fleet, starting out from Scotland, passed through the Straits of Gibraltar into the Mediterranean on 10 August, observed as a matter of course by enemy agents who proliferated in Franco's Spain. A formidable force of twenty-one Axis submarines, twenty-three E-boats and 540 aircraft was deployed to ambush the convoy. On 11 August, 550 miles west of Malta, the enemy inflicted their first casualty: the aircraft carrier *Eagle*, sunk with the loss of 260 lives by a salvo of four torpedoes from a German U-boat. At dusk on the same day, the Luftwaffe came in with Junkers dive-bombers and Heinkel torpedo-bombers but were driven off by anti-aircraft fire and fighters flown from HMS *Indomitable*. When the enemy bombers returned the next morning, diving through a deadly curtain of flak, *Indomitable* was crippled by three direct hits and several near-misses.

Now the battered convoy was approaching the most dangerous stretch, where the battleships *Rodney* and *Nelson* and the surviving aircraft carriers *Victorious* and *Furious*, unable to manoeuvre in the narrows between Sicily and Tunisia's Cape Bon, would have to turn back, leaving escort duties to the smaller, nimbler cruisers and destroyers. In the narrows, more E-boats and U-boats lay in wait and on Sicily, a few minutes' flying time away, Kesselring's bombers revved up their engines.

As 'Pedestal' entered the narrows, the cruisers *Nigeria* and *Cairo* were hit by torpedoes and sunk. Also hit and set on fire was the fast American-built tanker *Ohio*. This vessel, skippered by Captain Dudley Mason of the British merchant marine, was the most important target: it carried 11,500 tons of kerosene and diesel oil, without which the Maltese could not continue to cook their food and the Navy would not be able to fulfil its strategic role as a base for attacks on Rommel's supply ships. After a long struggle Mason and his crew managed to put out the fires, but the convoy was now scattered over a twenty-mile area and the enemy pressed home his attack with bomb and torpedo. Soon only eleven of the original fourteen merchantmen remained afloat, their protective screen reduced to two cruisers and ten destroyers, while sighting reports said that a powerful force of Italian surface vessels was heading their way.

That night, four more merchant vessels fell victim to sustained E-boat and U-boat attacks. Daylight on 12 August would surely bring more air attacks and shells from the big guns of the approaching Italian fleet. But when almost within striking distance of the British convoy the Italian task force, consisting of six cruisers and eleven destroyers, turned back. Denied air cover by the Luftwaffe and fearing attack by Malta-based British bombers, their commander had lost his nerve.

By this time, five of Pedestal's surviving merchantmen were sailing in convoy, with two more, the *Brisbane Star* and the *Ohio*, limping behind. The *Ohio*, with no working compass and manoeuvring only by means of primitive emergency steering gear, was being led by the destroyer *Ledbury*. Malta was still 170 miles away. And wave after wave of Stukas attacked. One of them, hit by anti-aircraft fire from the *Ohio* itself, crashed into the tanker's starboard side. Still the tanker ploughed on, bombs bursting on either side of it, until one bomb knocked out its engines. Now the *Ohio* could no longer make way and lay, immobile and low in the water, far behind the convoy and a sitting duck for fresh waves of enemy bombers. They were not long in coming. Fierce defensive fire from the *Ohio*'s Bofors and Oerlikon 'pom-pom' anti-aircraft guns, augmented by barrages from the accompanying destroyer, HMS *Penn*, drove off a number of attacks. But eventually a bomb hit the *Ohio* amidships and all but broke its back. The escorting destroyer nosed alongside and Mason and his crew abandoned ship. Seventy miles short of Malta, it seemed that the *Ohio* and its so-valuable cargo were lost.

But miraculously the *Ohio* remained afloat and that afternoon its captain and crew, refreshed after four hours' sleep aboard HMS *Penn*, went back aboard. *Penn* attached a tow-line to the stricken tanker and began dragging it, swinging wildly and making about four knots, towards Malta. A second destroyer, HMS *Rye*, arrived to assist in the towing operation. She attached herself by a second line to check the *Ohio*'s swings.

Soon the enemy bombers were back. Another bomb hit the *Ohio*, and several more fell around it. Still the tanker remained afloat. As darkness fell and the air raids ceased, *Penn* and *Rye* tried to resume towing. Malta now lay sixty miles to the east. At dawn the next morning, 14 August, the destroyer *Ledbury* arrived to join the rescue operation. By mid-morning, when they were making about six knots, the enemy bombers came again. The *Ohio* and its escorts put up a tremendous barrage which forced the Germans to drop their bombs short of target. Then, as another wave of Junkers came in, sixteen RAF Spitfires from Malta appeared on the scene and the sky above the *Ohio* became a mêlée of dogfighting planes.

By this time the surviving five merchantmen of Pedestal had staggered into Malta in convoy. The *Ohio*, with forty-five miles still to go, was being kept barely afloat by emergency pumps. At this point, and as darkness fell, the *Ohio*'s destroyer escort decided to change tactics. Instead of tugging and pushing, they would sandwich the tanker between two warships, lashed tightly alongside, and take it into port in a dual embrace, like a drunk being held up by two fellow revellers. *Penn* was already coupled to the starboard side. HMS *Bramham* took up position on the port. Soon they were moving forward at five knots; any faster, and the creaking and groaning *Ohio* might literally fall apart.

Just past midday *Bramham*'s tow-wire parted. Painfully, the exhausted crew attached a new line. A few hours more and Malta was in sight. Destroyers circled the tanker and its escort, dropping depth-charges to scare off enemy submarines; when the shock waves threatened to finish off the *Ohio* they were forced to desist. Now night had fallen and, as the *Ohio* and its escort approached Malta, the enemy made a last desperate attempt, this time with E-boats. Malta's coastal batteries drove them off.

Dawn brought the danger of renewed air attack but, as thousands of Maltese manned the ramparts and a band played 'Rule Britannia', the *Ohio* made it safely into Grand Harbour, still sandwiched between its two destroyer escorts. Its deck was awash and it seemed that the tanker might sink to the bottom of the harbour at any moment. There was no time to waste and, within minutes of tying up, the *Ohio*'s cargo of oil was being pumped ashore. Pedestal had succeeded, if only just, and Admiral Burrough signalled Captain Mason: 'I'm proud to have met you.'

Altogether, the *Ohio* and the five other Pedestal merchantmen who made it into Grand Harbour delivered 55,000 tons of stores and fuel, enough to keep the island going for another three months, if not to alleviate its population's hardships. Malta remained on starvation rations, resupplied but not yet relieved. But it was victory enough until the breakthrough at El Alamein, three months later.

Knighted, promoted and rarely off the front page, in a matter of a few weeks the commander of the Eighth Army had become the most popular British general since Wellington. Yet, despite these plaudits, Sir Bernard failed to crown his victory at El Alamein by cutting off the remnants of the Panzerarmee and destroying it. 'The German people will not worry if we go back to El Agheila again,' von Thoma had warned him at their famous dinner.

For a while it seemed as if Montgomery was not all that concerned either. Time and again, the 90th Light Division and some attached Italian units who comprised most of the rearguard thwarted British left-hooks designed to cut them off. For a while they would hold up their pursuers on the coast road with anti-tank guns. While they were doing this, their engineers, Italian as well as German, laid mines and ingeniously booby-trapped objects, including even palm trees, that might attract human contact. Then, as soon as the ponderous, much-telegraphed hook was spotted coming across the rain-soaked desert goo, they would slip away down the Via Balbia, leaving the British pincers to clang uselessly together enclosing nothing but empty road.

After twelve days of battle at Alamein, some of the Eighth Army were simply burned out and in need of a rest. Many could not remember the last time they had enjoyed six consecutive hours' sleep. Nor was the exhaustion confined to troops at the sharp end. At Montgomery's tactical HQ, de Guingand, who had borne the brunt of the army's administrative problems and been awarded a DSO, became so exhausted he had a kind of breakdown and had to be sent back to Cairo to recover.

With an end to the campaign in sight, some were beginning to think that they should not be pushing their luck. Michael Carver (later Field Marshal Lord Carver), who as a member of Harding's staff in 7th Armoured Division was in the vanguard of the chase, refers to 'the feeling that, having miraculously survived the ever-present dangers of the battle among the minefields, it would be folly to fling away one's life too recklessly when victory was at hand.'

For a few days Montgomery allowed Lumsden to have his head. But, for one reason or another, the armoured brigades proved no better at pursuit and pillage than most of them had been at breaking through. Some of this was due to sheer bad luck. Tanks poised to cut off large Axis formations ran out of fuel at the crucial moment because the supply columns coming along behind them ran into soft sand. On another occasion a large, uncharted minefield that caused hours of delay turned out to be a British dummy field put down during Auchinleck's retreat. It consisted of no more than a single strand of wire bedecked with the kind of symbols that are hard to ignore.

Even so, much of the armour's failure could be attributed to its usual mixture of incompetence, indolence and sometimes a maddening insouciance towards the task at hand. Brigades ordered to push on through the night stopped doing so after half an hour because they had not been trained to manoeuvre in the dark and were getting in a muddle. Yet it was not two years since O'Connor's troops had successfully completed a peerless night's drive to cut the Italians off at Beda Fomm. Gatehouse's 10th Armoured Division dawdled at the gates of Mersa Matruh, which was eventually taken by one of the left hooks which had then entered the town from the west, only to find it empty. Earlier, the port had been the scene of some personal tragedy for Montgomery. Somebody had wrongly reported that the enemy had cleared out and as a result Montgomery's stepson, Major Richard Carver, who was on his staff, had gone forward with another officer and a few men to establish an advanced headquarters there and was captured.

Perhaps this incident was the final straw so far as Lumsden was concerned. A couple of weeks later, Montgomery sacked him.* This was not entirely fair; Freyberg, who had directed Supercharge, had been just as dilatory in pursuit. But Montgomery liked Freyberg.

The rains continued to turn large stretches of desert into something resembling a badly ploughed field. The Eighth Army's sluggishness,

---

* Churchill, however, seems to have rather taken to Lumsden, who certainly looked much more like his idea of a soldier than Montgomery did. He was knighted, made the Prime Minister's personal liaison officer to General MacArthur and sent to the Pacific. On 6 January 1945 he was killed when a Japanese kamikaze pilot hit the bridge of the USS *New Mexico*. MacArthur described him as 'England at its best'.

when that was the case, was mainly to do with too many troops trying to get down too little road. It took a while to streamline the army for the pursuit. But before long there was a new Corps de Chasse comprising 7th Armoured Division, 51st Highland, and the New Zealanders with some extra armour. Everybody else was held back. The newly knighted Morshead and his Australians, with Montgomery's thanks and praises ringing in their ears, were going home anyway, first for epic punch-ups with the recently arrived Americans (which reached riot proportions in Brisbane), then for encounters of a more lethal nature, fighting alongside their new allies in the jungle war against the Japanese in New Guinea.* The South Africans were just going home, though later in the war some of them would re-emerge as an armoured division to fight in Italy. Pienaar, their general, was killed in an air crash on the way. For the moment Freyberg's New Zealanders and the Indians would be the only 'imperial troops' remaining in the Eighth Army.

Even before Lumsden's departure, the Eighth Army started to roll. Mersa Matruh fell on 8 November, and three days later the New Zealanders had seized Halfaya Pass with a couple of thousand prisoners and crossed the Egyptian frontier into Libya. Then came all the familiar, blood-soaked milestones of the Cyrenaica Bulge. Rommel declared Tobruk to be only of 'symbolic value' and the little port which had earned him his field marshal's baton was vacated on 13 November; Derna on 16 November; Benghazi on 20 November.

For the first time the Germans were tasting real defeat. It was not yet defeat on the scale the British had suffered in the three years of blunders and misplaced effort that sooner or later had marked its every confrontation with the Wehrmacht. But defeat it was, with all its humiliations, cruelties and the desperate heroism of men refusing to accept that they were beaten.

A few hours before the British reached Tobruk, the pilot of a huge four-engined Focke-Wulf flying-boat based in southern Italy put down among the half-submerged wrecks in the harbour to airlift the

---

* Friction was inevitable between these veterans and unblooded American troops, who seemed to have stepped straight out of Hollywood so far as many Australian young women were concerned. Even before the Australian troops had returned, Goebbels had fanned the flames with propaganda leaflets dropped over their desert positions. Beneath the divisional insignia of platypus and boomerang they asked: 'Aussies! The Yankees are having a jolly good time in your country. And you?'

36. *Above:* Montgomery in the Australian slouch hat he acquired soon after his arrival in the desert and which he later decorated with regimental cap badges. Montgomery is talking to the 22nd Armoured Brigade. On his right is General Sir Brian Horrocks.

37. *Right:* Rommel's terrifying aerial artillery: Stuka dive-bombers.

38. *Left to right:* Alexander, Churchill – playing with the zip of his siren suit – and Montgomery on a visit to the front, shortly before the battle of El Alamein.

39. 'When are they coming?' German machine-gunner near the coast road awaits the British attack along the El Alamein line.

40. The British start their massive night bombardment at El Alamein.

41. Sherman tanks, first seen at El Alamein, go in to the attack. Montgomery accused the British armour of being too cautious until Currie's 9th Armoured Brigade charged regardless of cost.

42. Some of the survivors from the Rifle Brigade Battalion which repulsed the Panzers at Snipe. Major Tom Bird, who commanded the anti-tank company, stands in the centre with his head bandaged. Sergeant Calistan is second from the extreme right. 'They had long experience of being under fire and getting away with it.'

43. Direct hit. A Panzer knocks out a British tank in a rare night action.

44. The ubiquitous 25-pounder. Axis troops learned to dread British artillery fire.

45. A piper plays to both German and British wounded at a forward dressing-station near El Alamein.

46. A long line of German and Italian prisoners are marched to the rear during the first day of El Alamein.

47. The scourge of the British armour. An 88-mm anti-tank gun.

48. Outnumbered and eventually outgunned, the German armour lost its ascendancy. A naked and eviscerated member of a Panzer crew alongside his wrecked machine.

49. The Fox in flight. Rommel begins his 1,700-mile retreat across the desert to Tunis.

50. Monty in victory. The Eighth Army commander accepts the surrender of General Ritter von Thoma – and invites him to dinner. Standing between them is Captain Singer of the 10th Hussars, who captured von Thoma and who was killed the next day. Some weeks later from prison camp, von Thoma wrote a letter of condolence to his widow.

51. The British and Americans at last link up in Tunisia and the days of the Axis in North Africa are numbered.

52. The End. On a Tunisian beach an Italian soldier lies dead beside the boat he hoped to use to get home. Fewer than 1,000 Axis soldiers escaped from North Africa. Well over 100,000 gave themselves up.

wounded out. His passengers were squeezed into every available space; Corporal Völker, healing nicely from his grenade wounds, flew beneath the fuselage in the belly gunner's bubble.

Then the Luftwaffe tried to repeat this feat with an air evacuation of Benghazi, and it ended in tragedy. Montgomery, who possessed an enthusiasm for close air support hitherto unknown in the British army, had insisted that the Desert Air Force be allowed the road space to transport all the paraphernalia necessary to keep its airfields as far forward as possible. As a result, Benghazi was in range of its Hurricanes and newly arrived Spitfires, who massacred the virtually unarmed Junkers and Heinkel transports.

By this time Rommel was being threatened from the west by Eisenhower's Anglo-American army, which had landed in Morocco and Algeria on 8 November – four days after the breakout at El Alamein. Allied troops commanded by Britain's Lieutenant-General Kenneth Anderson were heading for Tunisia, the north-eastern colony close to the Axis airfields in Sicily. It was the only part of Vichy French North Africa where the Anglo-Americans had not established a presence.* British and American paratroopers made unopposed drops on the airfields at the Algerian port of Bône, just west of the Tunisian border, and on Tebessa inside the colony. From there the American paratroopers moved eighty miles south-eastwards to capture the airfield at the oasis town of Gafsa in the southern part of Tunisia. Meanwhile, Allied tanks and infantry were assembling on the colony's western border with Algeria where Anderson had ordered them to pause and 'concentrate' before proceeding.

It was a costly error. The Anglo-Americans did not reach their objective in time to stop Hitler rapidly deploying an expeditionary force of his own, determined to delay as long as possible what would obviously be the next stage: an Allied invasion across the Sicilian channel which would give them a first toehold in continental Europe

---

* Vichy troops had started off opposing the Allies. Over 1,000 American soldiers were killed, and two small British warships sunk, by the Armée d'Afrique. But Admiral Jean Darlan, who commanded all the Vichy military, happened to be visiting Algeria. Even before the Royal Navy's July 1940 attack on the French fleet at Oran to prevent it falling into German hands, Darlan was an Anglophobe: his great-grandfather had been killed at Trafalgar. However, he agreed to talk to the Americans who, since Vichy was officially neutral, maintained a US Consulate in Algiers. On 10 November, two days after the Allies landed, a ceasefire was signed.

and, he feared, knock Mussolini out of the war. It is not quite 100 miles from Tunisia's Cape Bon to Sicily's Marsala.

The race for Tunisia was one of the Wehrmacht's finest performances. It showed them at their fast-moving, improvising, bluffing and brave best. Hitler heard of the North African landings at a railway station in Thuringia, on his way from the Wolf's Lair (his head quarters in East Prussia) to Munich where he was due to make the annual speech to the Nazi party faithful at its famous Bürgerbräukeller. He immediately called Field Marshal Kesselring in Rome and demanded that he send all the troops he could spare to Tunisia.

This turned out to be two battalions of paratroopers who had been going to join Rommel in Libya and the company of infantry who normally protected Kesselring's headquarters. To these were added in piecemeal fashion a paratroop company that had been formed in Athens from the remnants of some of Ramcke Brigade, many of them convalescents; a recently formed parachute brigade training in France; an engineering battalion from Crete, and some Luftwaffe squadrons, including Stukas, with supporting anti-aircraft guns to protect their landing-strips. A couple of battalions of Italian infantry were sent up from Libya and some marines from Sicily.

Numbering the resident French garrison with the Allied troops who had already entered Tunisia from the west, this meant that about 3,000 Axis soldiers were about to take on at least five times that number, probably more. They were commanded by General Walther Nehring, who was still being treated for wounds received at Alam el Halfa almost three months earlier.

Nehring's orders were to try and secure a line along the Tunisian-Algerian border and to disarm or push back the poorly equipped French before they could co-operate with the Anglo-Americans. Inevitably, this was not always possible. French troops holding an important bridge across the Medjerda river at Medjez el Bab, some thirty-five miles west of Tunis, had already been reached by a British parachute battalion and a regiment of American field artillery. This should have been ample to hold Medjez el Bab, but Tunisia was the first time British paratroopers had taken part in anything bigger than commando raids. Most of them were as green and unblooded as the American gunners fighting alongside them. Furthermore, the defenders, far ahead of the Allied airfields in Algeria, were without adequate air cover. Nor did they have much in the way of anti-aircraft guns. Americans, British and French were all unnerved by a squadron of Kesselring's Stukas dive-bombing with an impunity they had not enjoyed for some time.

The bombing was quickly followed up by ground attacks by an under-strength German parachute battalion of some 300 men under a Captain Knoche* which was made with such vigour that the Allies thought they were facing something much stronger. As soon as it got dark, Knoche got some of his men across the river, using logs and anything else that would float. Once across, they created enough mayhem to give the impression that a sizeable bridgehead had been created in the Allied rear. Small parties infiltrated the town and created considerable panic among the French colonial troops there, demolishing rooftop machine-gun positions with ear-splitting satchel charges of high explosive. By midnight the British officer in charge had decided to pull back from the bridge.

Knoche's clever and relentless action at Medjez el Bab was typical of the kind of aggression that secured the Axis bridgehead in Tunisia. But Nehring had some bad moments. The worst occurred when seventeen American-manned light tanks, Stuarts under Major Rudolph Barlow, blundered on to and then charged the airfield at Djedeida, where the Luftwaffe had been flying in reinforcements. The airstrip had already been softened by recent rain and rendered almost useless for the day, and the assembled Junkers-52 transports and Messerschmitt Bf 109's were almost literally sitting ducks. A brave attempt to stop the tanks by the crews of some light 20-mm flak guns was brushed bloodily aside. At least twenty aircraft were destroyed. Some pilots did try to take off, but their wheels became glued in the mud, propellers whirring uselessly.

Djedeida is less than thirty miles from Tunis. Nehring was so alarmed by what had happened at its airfield that, much to Kesselring's annoyance, he abandoned Medjez el Bab and redeployed some of his forces in a tight semi-circle around the capital. But Anderson was under too much pressure elsewhere to exploit the American success at Djedeida. Allied morale was still suffering from local Axis air superiority. Eisenhower was shocked during a tour of American

---

* In the British or American armies a similar formation would have been commanded by at least a major, but captains generally had far more clout in the Wehrmacht, which had fewer field officers than the Allies.

front-line positions over the number of men who told him that the only aircraft they ever saw were 'Heinies'.

As the winter rains started and both sides tried to cope with the mud, the fighting intensified. Nehring's stop-gap force had now been joined by 10th Panzer Division, which had some of the new *Nebelwerfer* multi-barrelled rocket-launchers as well. The Germans were also delighted to find that the newly arrived Italian Superaga Division, which had been shipped over from Sicily with uncharacteristic efficiency, came with an abundance of self-propelled artillery.

Casualties mounted. Britain's newly formed 1st Airborne Division continued to be used as infantry. For three days the 2nd Battalion of the Parachute Regiment under Major John Frost★ became cut off behind Axis lines. Most of the men they were fighting were the same German paratroopers who had arrived with Nehring. Despite their shortage of battle experience, Frost's men had already acquired too high an opinion of themselves to surrender easily. By the time they had fought their way out, they had lost sixteen officers and 250 men killed.

But the brunt of the hill fighting was being borne by the county battalions from the British 78th Division. Like the Americans, most of these soldiers were seeing action for the first time. Those few who had fought in the present war had last done so under Lord Gort in France in 1940. Among the latter was Major Herbert Le Patourel of the Hampshire Regiment, a twenty-six-year-old Sandhurst-trained career officer who came from German-occupied Guernsey in the Channel Islands.† On the afternoon of 3 December 1942, when freezing nights were beginning to add to the misery of rain and mud in the Tunisian highlands, the Hampshires were involved in a struggle for the possession of a hill in the Tebourba area, about twelve miles west of Tunis. Ammunition was running low because behind them a fifty-strong team of German combat engineers under Feldwebel (Sergeant) Peter Arent had severed their brigade's main supply route by establishing a block across one of the River Medjerda's crucial

---

★ The same John Frost and the same battalion who in September 1944 so distinguished themselves on the bridge at Arnhem.

† Following the fall of France, the islands, which are geographically part of the Normandy–Brittany coastline, were the only part of domestic British territory to come under German occupation.

bridges. They had mined it and knocked out two British trucks, and now Arent and his men were holding it against all comers.

Of more immediate concern to Le Patourel was that the enemy had got on to some ground above and to the left of his company. They were beginning to dominate their position with belt-fed MG-42 light machine-guns which fired faster than anything the British or Americans had got. Four men volunteered to accompany Le Patourel in an attack on these Germans and they managed to destroy two of the machine-gun nests, though by then Le Patourel was the only one still on his feet. Clutching a revolver and a grenade, he was last seen by the Hampshires approaching a third machine-gun post and then falling at about the same time as his grenade exploded. Since the Germans ultimately hung on to the position, there was no chance of recovering a body, and the young major was given a 'posthumous' VC. Months later, the International Red Cross confirmed that Le Patourel had been wounded and taken prisoner. He survived the war and retired from the army as a brigadier.

While Le Patourel was being treated by German surgeons, Feldwebel Peter Arent, the man who had begun to starve the Hampshires of ammunition by blocking the bridge, was also being decorated. In Arent's case it was undoubtedly posthumous, and Oberstleutnant Walther Koch, his commanding officer, lay a Knight's Cross on his coffin. The sergeant had survived his stand at the bridge, only to be killed by an artillery shell on returning to his own lines.

Despite Nehring's achievements, Kesselring sacked him for his 'jumpy' withdrawal to Tunis after the American tanks had beaten up Djedeida airfield. He was replaced by Jürgen von Arnim, who had been serving on the Russian front. His command had been given the grandiose title of Fifth Panzer Army. Allied intelligence estimated that at this point it was about 35,000 strong, of whom 10,000 were administrative personnel. Anderson's fighting troops were about 40,000, of whom 20,000 were British, 12,000 American and 7,000 French. Its logistical tail stretched all the way back to Casablanca and was probably at least three times that number, mostly American.

By mid-December the fiercest fighting began to centre on three hills, footstools for the Atlas Mountains, below the northern port of Bizerta. The Allies codenamed these hills Green, Bald and Longstop. The last was a rain-lashed double-crested height of muddy slopes which a British Guards battalion captured and handed over to some

American Rangers, who do not appear to have been properly briefed and lost it in a counter-attack. The Guards retook the hill, only to be ejected from its summit on Christmas Day, 1942; it was an attack that seemed timed to demonstrate that this was a different war from the one which had been fought in the desert. Where was the unspoken truce and the celebratory flares? After that, the Germans called it Christmas Hill and the struggle to possess it was by no means over. Bald and Green also fell, and the Germans claimed to have taken 500 British prisoners.

By now rain was giving way to occasional flurries of snow, and even the wonderful American jeeps, which every army in the theatre wanted more of, were finding the hill tracks impassable. By the end of the year Eisenhower had to accept that Arnim's 5th Panzer Army was solidly established and he had lost the race for Tunisia. Both sides were waiting for the winter weather to relent before they could start their spring campaigns.

At this point it seems that Rommel was deeply demoralized – by some accounts on the edge of a nervous breakdown – after a humiliating visit to Hitler's headquarters in East Prussia. He had gone there on the spur of the moment on 28 November, following a bruising meeting with Kesselring and senior Italian officers at the Arco dei Fileni, Mussolini's hubristic triumphal arch on the boundary between the Libyan provinces of Cyrenaica and Tripolitania. The British called it 'Marble Arch' and it was probably as good a setting as any for the extraordinary decision Rommel reached.

Three weeks after his defeat at El Alamein, this most resilient of generals had decided that the game was up: the Axis had no future in North Africa and should leave. Months before the Anglo-Americans had arrived in French North Africa, Rommel had become increasingly disturbed by evidence of the growing superiority, both in numbers and in the quality of the Allied *matériel*, of which Sherman tanks and six-pounder anti-tank guns were the most glaring examples. Now he had learned that for their landings in North Africa the Americans had achieved the extraordinary logistical feat of shipping an entire corps, about 30,000 men, directly from American ports to land them at Casablanca on Morocco's Atlantic coast. This, above all else, had convinced him that it was pointless to carry on. 'Even if we had overrun the whole of Africa,' he would write later, 'and the Americans had been left with a suitable bridgehead through which they could transport their material, we must eventually have lost the continent.'

Nor could he subscribe to Hitler's view that the German army in North Africa was engaged in a grand example of 'defence in depth' designed to delay or even entirely prevent Allied landings on Sicily. He felt that the only sensible course was to hold the enemy just long enough to enable the Axis to evacuate this last toehold in Africa in an orderly way so that its troops were spared the agony of a Dunkirk or a mass surrender.

Kesselring had agreed with none of this. As far as he was concerned, Rommel's task was to delay the British setting up airfields in western Libya that would enable them to attack Arnim's forces in Tunisia before they could be built up. Rommel could not accept this. The day after the Marble Arch meeting, 28 November 1942, he flew, uninvited, to see Hitler at his headquarters at Rastenburg in East Prussia. It was a quixotic thing to do. It obviously owed much to Rommel's belief that he enjoyed a close rapport with Hitler, based partly on their shared experience as front-line soldiers during the First World War and their shared disdain for the Prussian military hierarchy. The Führer had always listened to him before and Rommel saw no reason why he would not do so again. But the Hitler he encountered at Rastenburg, surrounded by careful Prussian luminaries such as Keitel and Jodl, was a far cry from the comradely figure whose admiration had so furthered his career. Instead, he found a haunted dictator, consumed by the Russian noose visibly tightening around von Paulus's 6th Army at Stalingrad.

Hitler was enraged at this unscheduled appearance of a field marshal who had abandoned his army to fly home and tell him that not only was his battle lost but the campaign was no longer worth fighting. 'How dare you leave your theatre of command without asking my permission?' he bellowed.

Rommel had never before witnessed one of the Führer's temper tantrums (which occurred much more rarely than Allied propaganda made out) and was shocked. There are several accounts of what was said, based mainly on what Rommel told Lucie of the meeting and some of his diary notes. At one point the Führer accused Rommel of being a defeatist and his men of cowardice. Rommel asked whether it was better to lose Tripoli or the Afrika Korps? 'The Afrika Korps didn't matter!' he was told.

Eventually Hitler calmed down and took on the emollient persona
that rarely failed to win over distressed senior officers. (Later in the
war they would call it 'the sun lamp treatment'.) Brigadier Young,
Rommel's first biographer, was told by Lucie that after telling Rommel
to leave, Hitler rushed after him to apologize. 'You must excuse me,
I'm in a very nervous state.'

The Führer explained to Rommel the political as well as the strategic
implications of abandoning Tripolitania and Tunisia. Reichsmarschall
Hermann Goering was summoned and he guaranteed to sort out
Rommel's supply problem with Mussolini. More troops and better
equipment were promised, including the new 41-model dual-purpose
88-mm gun, Tiger tanks and the six-barrelled Nebelwerfer rocket
launchers.

Rommel left Hitler's HQ with Goering, heading south for Rome
in the Reichsmarschall's well-appointed private train which he called
'Asia'. At Munich they stopped to pick up Lucie. Goering's wife
Emmy was already aboard. The head of the Luftwaffe was one of the
most intelligent of the Nazi hierarchy and a First World War fighter
ace – like Rommel he wore the ribbon of the Ordre Pour le Mérite
and in 1918 had taken command of von Richthofen's squadron after
the Red Baron was killed. Also like Rommel he was beginning to
suspect that Germany might well lose the war. But he hid these fears
behind the exterior of a fat fop, bulging out of operatic uniforms and
flaunting a dowager's collection of jewellery. Frau Rommel, who had
firm views on these matters, was particularly appalled when he drew
her attention to an enormous diamond ring he was wearing.

Over dinner in the dining car Goering could easily have opened
up to Rommel or at least talked to him about the things he was most
interested in: fuel, weapons, reinforcements, grand strategy. Instead,
he chose to boast at some length about the art treasures he had looted
from the occupied lands. 'They call me the Maecenas of the Third
Reich.' Rommel, never one of nature's aesthetes, was filled with
despair. When they had a moment alone he told Lucie: 'They just
can't and won't see the danger but it is coming at us with giant strides.
The danger is: defeat.'

In Rome there was a tense meeting with Mussolini. Nor was
Kesselring supportive. He dismissed Rommel's idea: to withdraw all
his forces into Tunisia and then hit out at the Anglo-Americans
coming from the west. On the train, between the paintings and the

pottery, Rommel thought he had sold Goering the idea, but during a gourmet luncheon for senior officers at the superb Hotel Excelsior the mercurial Reichsmarschall rounded on Rommel and repeated Hitler's ranting about 'defeatism'. Rommel was devastated. Another of the luncheon guests, Field Marshal Erhard Milch, described him as 'a nervous wreck', and said that during a long private chat they had afterwards he had burst into tears. '[H]e finally buried his head on my right shoulder and wept for some time. He just couldn't get over Hitler's lack of trust in his leadership.'

Milch kept the awful spectacle of one German field marshal sobbing on the shoulder of another to himself until well after the war had ended. But Rommel's staff knew that the man who returned to Africa the next day was not the one who had flown out four days before.

In London, George Orwell, doing his bit in the propaganda war, gleefully noted in a BBC broadcast that German commentators were straining to explain Rommel's retreat with talk of 'elastic defence' and odd claims that he had 'compelled the British to advance westwards'. But many of the Eighth Army's old sweats predicted that the good times would end once they got to El Agheila. This was as far as O'Connor had reached at the beginning of 1941 and at the end of that year it had also been the high-water mark of the Ritchie–Auchinleck partnership.

One hundred and fifty miles west of Benghazi, almost on the boundary between Libya's Cyrenaica and Tripolitania provinces, El Agheila was a natural defensive line with a desert flank almost as hard to turn as Alamein's. In the south it was bounded by the Wadi Faregh, a deep gorge as good as any man-made anti-tank ditch, while beyond were the same kind of salt marshes and fantastically sculpted dunes as in the Qattara Depression. The British, the Germans and the Italians all expected Rommel to make a stand there.

But by Sunday, 13 December, it was obvious to Captain Alastair Timpson of the Long Range Desert Group, who commanded a road-watching patrol a few miles west of El Agheila, that Rommel intended to do no such thing. On that day, lying on their bellies behind thorn bushes, 200 yards from the Via Balbia, Timpson's team counted a record 3,500 Axis vehicles heading west. Montgomery believed that the enemy was 'windy and starting to pull out'.

Yet if their singing was anything to go by, the enemy's morale

seemed remarkably high. The Germans, Timpson noted, had a preference for 'somewhat outdated jazz numbers', while even the Italians,
packed into the passing lorries, 'sang lustily of Napoli'. By this time
the Panzerarmee was no longer quite the 'shattered remnant' the BBC
had called it immediately after Alamein. Rommel had received some
reinforcements during the retreat. These included two armoured
divisions – one of them a revived Ariete based on a skeleton of officers
and NCOs who had escaped the post-Alamein massacre – and a
couple of thousand German troops. Luftwaffe reinforcements, particularly some new Messerschmitt squadrons, had also begun to reduce
British air superiority.

After El Agheila, Montgomery led from the front, rather like the
old Rommel, and put himself and his tactical headquarters at the
head of 'Pip' Roberts's 22nd Armoured Brigade, ruthlessly urging
his divisional commanders on. Wimberley, whose Highlanders were
along the coast road on the right flank, particularly felt the lash for
'lack of initiative and ginger'.

Rommel fell back on a new defence line, about 150 miles east of
Tripoli, starting at Buerat on the coast and leading southwards along
the Wadi Zem Zem. Here on 15 January the poet Keith Douglas was
wounded when he tripped an S-mine after his Crusader had been hit
during a counter-attack by 15th Panzer. The ball shrapnel Douglas took
in his right foot, leg, arm and shoulder would keep him out of action for
almost four months.★ Four days later John Harding, one of the most
successful commanders 7th Armoured ever had, was badly hurt by an
artillery shell while conferring with Douglas's brigade commander. For
twenty-four hours the loss of Harding had a noticeable effect on the
progress of 7th Armour, who were making the 'left hook' below the
coast. Then Montgomery replaced him with his erstwhile travelling
companion, Brigadier 'Pip' Roberts and the 7th recovered its momentum. At about this time Kesselring noted that the new Rommel always
had enough petrol to retreat but never enough to attack.

Shortly before dawn on 23 January 1943, three months to the day
from the beginning of the Battle of Alamein, armoured cars of the

---

★ Douglas rejoined his regiment during the last days of the Tunisian campaign and
was killed with them in Normandy the following year, a grievous blow to English
letters.

Cherrypickers, the 11th Hussars, entered the streets of Tripoli. The Libyan capital had been vacated by Axis troops the previous day.

The 90th Light's rearguard had bought enough time for Rommel's engineers to sink blockships and blow up as much of the port as possible, and most stores and ammunition had been salvaged. But nothing could detract from the pleasure of capturing Tripoli, the prize that had always eluded the British, however well they started out. Its capture, relatively tame though it turned out to be, marked the end of the desert campaign.

On 3 February, Montgomery staged a victory parade, attended by both Churchill and Brooke. They had flown in from Turkey via Cyprus after the historic conference with Roosevelt at Casablanca at which the Allies' demand for Germany's 'unconditional surrender' was announced. Churchill had then gone on to neutral Turkey but failed to persuade them to join the Allied cause, a favourite hobbyhorse of his.★ As the Highland Division marched through Tripoli to the sound of the pipes that had been played at Alamein, even Brooke began to lose his iron self-control. 'I felt a large lump rise in my throat. I looked round at Winston and saw several tears on his face . . . The depth of these feelings can only be gauged in relation to the utter darkness of those early days of calamities, when no single ray of hope could pierce the depth of gloom . . . I felt no shame that tears should have betrayed my feelings, only a deep relief.'

As Brooke and Churchill shed their glad tears, Rommel was crossing the Tunisian border. Here at last he turned to face his pursuers behind the Mareth line, a chain of sand-filled pre-war French blockhouses, originally built to keep Mussolini at bay but neglected by Vichy once their France was out of the war.

In many ways Rommel's withdrawal so far had been a masterly performance. He made the decision that he would salvage the remains of his Panzerarmee, come what may, and he did so. The longer he retreated – and he retreated for almost 2,000 miles – the more the chances of his army being outflanked diminished.

Montgomery, like all victorious desert commanders, was now at the end of a long main supply-route and finding it hard to fuel his pursuit. Supply problems were compounded by winter gales that had

★ Turkey would eventually declare war on Nazi Germany less than three months before its surrender in order to qualify for membership of the United Nations.

wrecked Benghazi harbour and reduced its intake to less than a third. Tripoli had been a great gift. It took only twelve days for the Royal Navy to clear a passage wide and deep enough through the sunken blockships in the harbour entrance to allow the first supply boats in.

A disgusted Mussolini now wanted to sack the greatest soldier the African campaign had produced, and his intended victim was inclined to agree that he should go. 'I am so depressed that I can hardly do my work,' Rommel wrote to his wife, two days after abandoning Tripoli. 'Maybe someone else can see this situation in a more favourable light and make something of it even now.' This no longer seemed such a fantastic proposition. By now the Axis enclave in Tunisia was far from being what Operation Torch had hoped to find: a battered remnant caught in a nutcracker as its enemies closed in for the kill from west and east. It was a serious fighting force with a ration strength of about 100,000 and growing. In the last days of 1942, German troops expecting to find themselves trying to break the siege around Stalingrad suddenly found to their delight that they would be wintering in the Mediterranean instead.

By the beginning of February 1943, and for the first time in North Africa, German troops outnumbered Italian: 74,000 to 26,000. In infantry alone there were thirty-four German battalions to fourteen Italian holding about 280 miles of front line and 250 miles of coast-line. General Giovanni Messe, probably Mussolini's best general, was transferred to the Tunisian enclave from the Russian front, where he had commanded the Italian expeditionary force fighting alongside the Wehrmacht. The Germans at least were better equipped than they had ever been in Africa. Not only had Allied air supremacy been dented by the greater endurance provided by Tunisian airstrips just behind the front lines, but the aircraft were better, particularly the latest Focke-Wulf fighters, and, as Hitler had promised, the infantry were supported by new *Nebelwerfers*. The British called their 80-pound projectiles 'Moaning Minnies' after the terrible screeching sound they made, and they were as bad for their victims' morale as the first Stuka attacks had been.

Front-line tank strength was just under 300, probably a quarter of the combined Allied strength, but much of Tunisia was too rugged for tanks. Many of the German tanks were the Mark IV Specials with their long-barrelled guns. There were about thirty of the new Tigers, which had first gone into action against the Russians some six months before and which had an 88-mm gun that could outshoot any Allied tank, plus almost impenetrable front and side armour.* Yet for some time it seemed nothing could lift Rommel's depression. Then his spirits miraculously revived. Perhaps it was the sight of Tunisia's green hills, so obviously favouring the defender, embroidered with their amazing carpet of spring flowers. More likely it was because, despite Hitler's tantrums and Mussolini's pleas, he had done exactly what he had wanted to do and withdrawn his army into Tunisia. It may also have had something to do with his competitive juices being roused by the presence of von Arnim, the kind of Prussian aristocrat Rommel always loved to loathe. It was undeniable that the performance of the latter's Fifth Panzer Army during Tunisia's short winter had contrasted painfully with his own retreat from Libya, however skilfully executed.

By now Rommel was supposed to return to Germany and complete the rest cure that had been interrupted by Montgomery's attack at El Alamein. But Berlin, showing a flexibility that made for a complex command structure, had decreed that the date of his departure should be of his own choosing. And Rommel chose to stay on, for he had a new enemy in his sights: the Americans, whose forces to the west of him could cut off his line of retreat should he choose to abandon the Mareth line.

Most of the Americans were in central Tunisia, where the land is dominated by two mountain ranges, spurs of the Atlas. They run south-west and due south like an inverted letter 'Y' and are known as the Western and Eastern Dorsales. The Eastern Dorsale lies about seventy miles from the coast, and between that and its western neighbour is a flat prairie or steppe land.

At the beginning of February, General Lloyd Fredendall's US II Corps held all the passes in the Western Dorsale, among them the Kasserine, about thirty miles from the Algerian border. They also dominated the flat land between the ranges. American troops were concentrated around the date palms of the Gafsa Oasis in the south and the hamlet of Sidi Bou Zid, which is close to the Faid Pass in the Eastern Dorsale. Until a few days before, the pass had been blocked by French colonial troops, until Arnim's Panzers with their Stuka

---

* The Tiger's main drawback was its prodigious fuel consumption. While the Panzer Mark IV had a range of 130 miles before its fuel tank ran dry, the Tiger did well under ninety.

support overwhelmed them, depriving the Americans of this forward screen.★

These were Rommel's intended target. Sharp at 8 a.m. on Friday, 12 February 1943, the second anniversary of Rommel's arrival in Libya, the band of the 8th Panzer Regiment assembled outside the Field Marshal's mobile headquarters and struck up 'Das Panzer Lied'. It was a prelude to a farewell to Africa that would be worthy of the Desert Fox – a piece of tactical ju-jitsu whereby the grand master would attempt to demonstrate how two hulking opponents might be felled by a smaller but nimbler adversary. First he was going to attack Fredendall's US II Corps and then, having disposed of – or at least deterred – one threat, he intended to turn around and do the same to the Eighth Army. Since the two Allied armies were not yet ready to mount a co-ordinated attack, their numerical superiority would be nullified by having to defend themselves against the Axis one at a time.

These were intended to be spoiling operations. They were designed to hurt the Anglo-Americans badly enough to delay their spring offensive, give the Axis the opportunity to strengthen their own defences and, so far as Rommel was concerned, prepare for an orderly evacuation.

The first part of the plan was Operation 'Frühlingswind' ('Spring Breeze'). It was to be a three-pronged tank attack by Arnim's forces on the Americans at Sidi Bou Zid. One prong would come the obvious way, through the recently recaptured Faid Pass, the second a little to the north so that it fell on the Americans' left flank, and the third some thirty miles south of Faid would come north-westwards behind the Americans.

The next day Rommel himself would join in with Operation 'Morgenluft' ('Morning Air'). Although the Panzerarmee had received some reinforcements during its long retreat, it had yet to be properly refitted, and Rommel had at his disposal no more than seventy tanks. Just over half of them were from what was left of 15th Panzer and the rest were Italian from the Centauro Division, which had joined him after El Alamein.

★ It was the last of a series of mini-Blitzkriegs against these neglected trappings of empire, whose ranks included French-officered Arab horsemen. Over 3,000 had been taken prisoner.

While the Americans were distracted by Frühlingswind, Rommel proposed to lead this battle group in a wide north-westwards hook and take first the American base and airfield at Gafsa Oasis and then two other airfields at Feriana and Thelepte near the Western Dorsale. He would then continue northwards until he reached the Kasserine Pass.

Here he expected to meet up with the elements from 10th and 21st Panzer Divisions which had been involved in the three-pronged attack on Sidi Bou Zid. With them he intended to take the pass and capture the logistics centre the Americans had established at the Algerian border town of Tebessa, which was situated on a plateau 3,600 feet above sea level. It had only recently lost its winter snow.

But while 8th Panzer's band reminded Rommel of the days when his biggest gambles had so often paid off, he was told it had been necessary to postpone the attack for forty-eight hours. Heavy rain in the Eastern Dorsale was slowing down 21st Panzer's preparations. The only consolation was that the same rain clouds were also shielding them from Allied air reconnaissance.

As it happened, Eisenhower was expecting an attack on his front, but at the wrong place. Towards the end of January, Ultra decrypts forwarded to First Army from Bletchley Park in England had revealed through the interception of careless Luftwaffe signals that the Axis intended to mount Operation 'Kuckucksei' ('Cuckoo's Egg'), an assault on British positions at Fondouk, some forty miles due north of the Faid Pass. But Kuckucksei was cancelled, to be replaced by Frühlingswind and Morgenluft. Ultra had failed to pick this up.

On St Valentine's Day 1943, the Panzers, supported by Stuka dive-bombers, closed in on Fredendall's men at Sidi Bou Zid. Their success was beyond all expectations. The Americans were facing superior firepower, were locally outnumbered, without adequate air support and very green. In many cases their anti-tank guns were not dug in but merely hitched to the back of their half-tracks.

It started what the Eighth Army, back in its bad old days, called a 'flap'. But this rapidly became something different. The enemy was not a distant dust cloud. Surprise had been complete and soon the German tanks, some of them Tigers, were right among the American infantry. Retreat rapidly became a rout. Real panic set in. Men abandoned their vehicles, discarded their rifles and helmets and ran off in terror across the browning plain where the brief Tunisian spring was already coming to an end.★

Colonel George Drake, the commanding officer of the 168th Infantry Regiment, which had about 3,000 men at Sidi Bou Zid, succeeded in persuading several hundred of them to form a defensive circle. Then a German armoured car flying an enormous white flag drove up and the Americans began to put their hands up. This was more than Drake, a professional soldier in his first major battle, could bear. When a Panzer officer standing in his open turret demanded his own surrender, he told him, 'You go to hell,' and turned his back. In France in 1940 some of Rommel's men had shot dead a French officer who reacted in similar vein. Drake was spared. Eventually he was taken before a German colonel who, apparently without irony, congratulated him on the fight his men had put up. About 500 of the 168th got away. Most of the remaining 2,500 were herded into their own trucks on the first stage of a long journey to PoW camps in Germany. Six months before, many of them had still been civilians in an America slowly coming to terms with being at war.

Next day an attempt was made to stage an armoured counter-attack but this proved a gallant failure. Almost sixty American tanks charged with Custerish élan across the prairie land towards Sidi Bou Zid. But the Germans, unlike their novice enemy, had lost no time in digging in their anti-tank guns and finding those folds in the ground where Panzers might be deployed in hull-down positions. Only four of the American tanks survived.

Fredendall, who was attempting to command from an underground HQ miles to the rear, now ordered his remaining forces to withdraw to the Western Dorsale. In most cases this was superfluous. They were already on their way there.

Rommel's Operation Morgenluft reached Gafsa on the afternoon of 15 February, only to find that the enemy had abandoned the little oasis town, but not before they had blown up an ammunition dump, causing some casualties among the Arab citizens and wrecking some of their property. Now the Arabs stood by the open doorways of their flat-roofed houses shouting 'Hitler!' and 'Rommel!' So far as they

---

★ In places it seems to have resembled the kind of humiliation another American army would, almost half a century later, inflict on the stunned Iraqi conscripts at the Mutla Ridge.

were concerned, these splendid Germans had just liberated them from the French colonialists who had brought these American vandals into their lives. It was a small taste of the adulation Rommel would undoubtedly have received had he ever reached their Cairo brethren.

Among these 'liberators' was the desert veteran, Oberleutnant Heinz-Werner Schmidt, who in 1941 had served on Rommel's original Afrika Korps staff. Schmidt was commanding a mixed force of truck-borne infantry and anti-tank gunners. As they pursued the enemy north out of Gafsa, the morale of his men was high. Among their booty was an intact US truck laden with American cigarettes. The Rommel magic was definitely back.

There was 'a good tar road' and they moved quickly, though they began to encounter some resistance. Twice they came under air attack. Then, as they entered more hilly country, they were subjected to artillery fire, called down by spotters hidden above the winding valley route they were on. Two of the vehicles were destroyed but there were no serious casualties and they drove on. 'We passed a dead American negro lying in the road,' Schmidt recalled. 'He was naked – stripped, you could be certain, by Arabs.'

Their next objective was the village of Feriana. At its outskirts they came under artillery and rifle fire. Unable to make out exactly where the shots were coming from, they hosed down the entire village with heavy machine-guns then entered on foot. At this point their invisible opponents melted away and long columns of black smoke began to rise from what turned out to be hastily torched supply dumps. Groups of excited Arabs emerged from their bullet-pocked homes. Some of them pointed out the freshly turned earth where the retreating Americans had just laid mines.

Leaving a small detachment to salvage what they could from the burning supply dumps before the Arabs got it all, Schmidt pressed on. His scout car was in the lead, with one of the towed anti-tank guns immediately behind him, when they rounded a sharp bend and almost collided with a Sherman.

I jerked the wheel in the driver's hand and the vehicle swerved sharply towards the left bank of the road. The detachment manning the gun immediately behind me were swift in taking their cue. In a matter of seconds they had jumped from their seats, unlimbered, swung and fired their first shell, while the Americans still stood immobile, the muzzle of the tank gun pointing at a hillock half-right from us. Our first shell struck the tank at an angle in the flank. The tank burst into flames.

For an hour Schmidt and the other company in his battalion fought a sharp action with this rearguard, securing high ground off the road on foot and deploying their anti-tank guns. Then a particularly violent explosion indicated that the Americans had blown up one of their own ammunition dumps. Soon the surviving Shermans stopped firing and began to move away.

The Germans reached Thelepte, just below the Western Dorsale and about forty miles from the logistics centre at Tebessa. Here Schmidt procured six American half-tracks intact to replace the vehicles he had lost in action since leaving Gafsa. The best evidence of the success of Morgenluft lay on Thelepte airfield, which was littered with the wrecks of about sixty planes.

At about this time, an Anglo-American wireless intelligence unit, which had hidden its eavesdropping antennae among some tall pines on the Western Dorsale, intercepted and decoded an order which appeared to come from Rommel himself. It was a demand for the immediate delivery of hundreds of new spark plugs; they were needed to start dozens of captured trucks and tanks which the Americans had attempted to immobilize by smashing the plugs.

Rommel was indeed in a jubilant mood. In Feriana on the night of the 17th he did a rare thing and accepted a bottle of champagne one of his staff had acquired. 'I feel like an old warhorse hearing the trumpet,' he informed Lieutenant Berndt. As usual, his Nazi Sancho Panza from Goebbels's Propaganda Ministry was not far from his side. Shortly before the offensive started, Berndt had returned from one of his visits to Hitler with a private message from the Führer. Perhaps Hitler was still trying to make amends for his temper tantrum for, apart from conveying expressions of 'every confidence', Berndt also came back with a firm offer: if Rommel considered his health was up to it, Hitler wished to make him and not Arnim overall commander of Army Group Africa.

Now Rommel began to behave as if he already had the job. Determined to keep up the momentum of his offensive, he proposed taking all three Panzer Divisions – 10th, 21st and 15th – across the border into Algeria and capturing Tebessa. The Americans, he said, lacked experience and it was important to give them 'a severe inferiority complex from the beginning'.

Arnim thought the plan was too risky, and he objected. The Prussian was a military pygmy compared to Rommel, who in any case out-ranked him. But it was a measure of Rommel's fall from grace that Arnim had to be fought first and an appeal lodged with the Comando Supremo in Rome. But while he waited for a reply, Rommel knew that, with every wasted hour, the enemy was recovering his balance.

When the answer came, at midnight at the 18th, it turned out to be a compromise. Yes, Rommel could have the divisions he wanted but he was to make a less ambitious attack. He was not to cross the Tunisian border and attempt to take Tebessa but to go through the Kasserine Pass and turn northwards for the mountain towns of Thala and El Kef.

Throughout history Tunisia's conquerors had to hold El Kef if they were to descend from the mountains and take Tunis itself. Its loss would undoubtedly have been another disaster for the Allies. But Rommel guessed that the enemy would be expecting a thrust in this direction and would deploy most of their considerable reserves there. His sixth sense, his famous *Fingerspitzengefühl*, told him that Tebessa was the way to go, and he was quite right.

Allied resistance began to stiffen and it took Rommel two days to get through the Kasserine Pass. The US official history pays generous tribute to the stubbornness displayed by one scratch British force that found itself under American command. Commanded by Lieutenant-Colonel Albert Gore, it consisted of eleven tanks, four 25-pounder guns and about 100 infantrymen. Not until all the tanks and most of the 25-pounders had been disabled were the Germans able to push them aside.

On the other hand, on the outskirts of Thala, a 600-strong Territorial battalion of the Leicesters, about to put into practice three years' hard training in Britain's Home Army, found themselves surrendering *en masse*. A Panzer battalion had had the bright idea of making their lead tank a captured Valentine. The ploy worked very well; only when the tanks and the Panzer Grenadiers' half-tracks were close enough for conversation and demands for surrender were being made in guttural English did the Leicesters realize the awful truth.

Refused permission to head for Tebessa, and his successes in

Morgenluft notwithstanding, Rommel's enthusiasm was beginning to wane. He railed against the foolishness of those who had doubted his instincts and made him go one way instead of another. Nor were some of his troops capable of thinking on their feet as fast as he would have liked. Unlike Schmidt, most of his officers had not served under him before. Some had come from Russia and already felt they were lucky to be alive. They lacked the dash of the old Afrika Korps. Rommel fretted about the way time had been wasted and the way the enemy had been allowed to deploy his reserve troops in strong hilltop positions. 'Had we attacked Tebessa,' he complained later, 'we would probably have been well advanced before coming up against serious opposition, whereas now we were facing an enemy who was not disorganized after a hurried march to the front.'

Nevertheless, by the evening of 20 February the Germans were through the Kasserine Pass, the final assault being made by five battalions of infantry supported by Nebelwerfers. Through mist, haze and persistent drizzle, the infantry climbed its steep sides, dismaying with a series of surprise attacks the shivering defenders of rocky ridge lines already unnerved by the Nebelwerfers. Among the attackers was a battalion of Bersaglieri, black fighting-cock feathers nodding on their helmets.

Rommel, ever generous to defeated opponents, noted that the Americans had fought 'exceptionally well' and that the losses of the Panzer Grenadier regiment involved had been heavy. Even so, the Axis had captured intact another twenty or so tanks and thirty armoured personnel carriers, 'for the most part having 75-mm anti-tank guns attached'. But the sheer quality of this latest haul of US weaponry plunged Rommel back into depression. 'The Americans were remarkably well equipped. Also we have much to learn from them organizationally. Particularly impressive was the standardization of parts for their armoured equipment. Experience gained from the British had subsequently been put to good use . . .'

By the morning of 22 February he had decided that he could no longer sustain the attack and a phased withdrawal was in order. When he heard this, Kesselring, who had flown in from Rome, was incredulous. He rushed up to the Kasserine, where he found it was raining again and Rommel was keeping dry in his radio van. Smiling Albert radiated his usual optimism and tried to convince Rommel that his men were in a much better position than the Americans and were poised for a major victory. He also made a formal confirmation of Hitler's offer of the overall command of Army Group Africa. Rommel initially declined but then allowed himself to be persuaded. 'Apparently, I am no longer *persona non grata* after the offensive, despite assumed defeatism,' he noted with obvious satisfaction. Nevertheless, his acceptance did not stop him rejecting all Kesselring's arguments for continuing the offensive.

One of the fruits of the Casablanca conference between Roosevelt and Churchill had been an agreement to move Alexander, the British Commander-in-Chief Middle East, from Cairo and make him Eisenhower's deputy. This was a great compliment to the Americans and was accepted as such. Monty might have become Britain's best-known fighting general, but Alexander was its most senior. Since 1939 he had fought in France, Burma and the Middle East. His experience far outweighed that of Eisenhower who, through no fault of his own, had spent twenty-seven years in the US army before hearing his first shots fired in anger in North Africa. All the operational Allied ground forces at the sharp end in North Africa, both the First and Eighth Armies, were now under Alexander's command with his Anglo-American tactical headquarters at El Kef.

On the same day, 22 February, that Rommel had his most recent disagreement with Kesselring, Alexander reinforced his opponent's argument for abandoning the Kasserine offensive by calling on Montgomery to take some of the pressure off the First Army by threatening the enemy's eastern flank. For once Montgomery put aside his fears of being 'unbalanced' and complied, pushing the 7th Armoured Division and Wimberley's 51st Highland Division towards the Mareth line rather faster than he had intended. To a certain extent this deployment seems to have worked. Kesselring bowed to Rommel's determination to return to the Mareth line bunkers and attack the Eighth Army before they attacked him.

Facing the odds that he did, Rommel's decision to withdraw was 'very well judged', in the opinion of Basil Liddell-Hart, the respected British military historian. As a spoiling operation Rommel's first clash with the Americans had been a great success, pocketing over 4,000 prisoners and disabling, destroying or capturing about 200 tanks plus a good many half-tracks, trucks and jeeps. But it was probably much less successful in creating the 'inferiority complex' Rommel so desired to inflict on the newcomers. On the contrary, the Desert Fox's despair at the quality of captured US equipment tells the opposite story. Some of the prisoners also made a good impression. 'I would like to go to Brooklyn,' said Oberleutnant Heinz-Werner Schmidt to a lieutenant of that borough he was practising his English on. 'That can soon be arranged,' said the New Yorker quickly, and they both laughed.

It took some time for General Fredendall to understand that Rommel was retreating, and when he did he failed to get his men moving quickly enough to harry them. About the most serious interference the withdrawing German armour had to contend with came from the raiders of Popski's Private Army. They managed to get behind the enemy lines in their jeeps and lay anti-tank mines in a wadi the Panzers would have to pass through on their way back to Gafsa.

For a while Alexander became very down on the Americans. 'Mentally and physically soft,' he told Montgomery, who was already taking an unholy delight in all First Army failures. '[I]t appears that the Boche does just whatever he likes with the Americans,' the commander of the Eighth Army wrote to Brooke. This sort of unadulterated bitchiness was increasingly to be expected of Montgomery. But then Alexander, whose charm and ability to get a disparate team to work together would be needed more than ever, also wrote a scathing letter to Brooke about the fighting qualities of their Allies. 'They [the Americans] simply do not know their jobs as soldiers and this is the case from the highest to the lowest, from the General to the private soldier. Perhaps the weakest link of all is the junior leader, who just does not lead, with the result that their men do not really fight.'

No doubt there was more than a touch of *Schadenfreude* on the part of the British over the first encounter of their cocky and lavishly equipped Allies with the Nazi war machine. After all the defeats the British had endured during the last three years, it would surely have been almost too much to bear if the 'Doughboys' (to use the 1918 nickname for American soldiers still then preferred by most British generals and newspapermen) had wiped the floor with the Wehrmacht in Round One. They learned quickly enough, as Montgomery, with uncharacteristic generosity, confirmed in the memoirs he published some fifteen years after Sidi Bou Zid and Kasserine. 'It was the old story; lack of proper training allied to no experience of war, and linked with too high a standard of living. They were going through their early days, just as we had to go through ours. We had been at war a long time and our mistakes were mostly behind us . . . It took time but they did it more quickly than we did.'★

By early March, Rommel had disengaged most of his forces from the Americans and was preparing to launch his first attack against Montgomery since his failure at Alam el Halfa, almost six months before. Forewarned by Ultra and its own intelligence, the Eighth Army was desperately trying to shore up its defences in time to meet it. In this they were greatly assisted by Arnim retaining some of the armour Rommel needed for an operation of his own against Allied positions in the north. With Kesselring's encouragement, this attack was enlarged to strike eight different points along a seventy-mile front, manned mainly by French and British units. But after some initial success, Arnim's Panzers were ambushed in a narrow defile by British anti-tank guns and artillery, and about seventy tanks were destroyed or disabled, losses the Axis cause in Tunisia could ill afford.

By the time Rommel was ready to attack, his under-strength Panzer Divisions could muster no more than 160 tanks – rather fewer than the complement of a full-strength division. Montgomery was waiting for him with 600 anti-tank guns, 400 tanks and (as he put it in a letter to Brooke) 'good infantry holding strong pivots; and a great weight of artillery. It is an absolute gift, and the man must be absolutely mad.' For good measure sappers, working around the clock, laid around 70,000 mines.

Expecting an attack along the Mareth–Medenine axis within hours, Montgomery had distributed an eve-of-battle message to his soldiers in the same headmasterly style that had done so much for morale at El Alamein. 'There must be NO WITHDRAWAL anywhere and, of course, NO SURRENDER . . . we will smash the enemy attack and cause him such casualties that it will cripple him; we will in fact give him a very "bloody nose". '

Four days later, the Panzers rolled, shortly after dawn on 6 March. Messe's feint did achieve some tactical surprise. The 90th Light and the Italian La Spezia Divisions hit the Highlanders near the coast with

---

★ At least one of the reasons they did it more quickly was because Eisenhower sacked Fredendall and put General Patton in command of the US II Corps. 'Ole Blood an' Guts' lost no time making clear his own views about the 'pampered youth' who panicked at Kasserine. 'They were like a bunch of bananas,' he said. 'Some's green, some's yaller and some's plain rotten.'

just enough tanks among their infantry to give the British pause for thought. Then the mass of Panzers emerged from the morning haze shrouding the Matmata hills to concentrate their *Schwerpunkt* around the hill of Tajera Khir, seven miles north of Medenine, while 10th Panzer descended on a brigade of Freyberg's New Zealanders who were screening the town itself. But by now it made little difference where the Axis struck. With the Mediterranean on one flank, Montgomery's 600 anti-tank guns were enough to ensure there were no gaps in his defences.

At Tajera Khir the brunt of the attack, with artillery and some Luftwaffe support, fell on the infantry of the 7th Armoured Division. These were three battalions of Guards – Coldstreamers, Grenadiers and Scots – and the Queen's Brigade under Brigadier Lashmer Whistler, who had somehow acquired the nickname 'Bolo'. Since Alamein, Montgomery thought 'Bolo' Whistler 'the best fighting brigadier in the British Army'.

The Queen's and the Guards were targeted by the 15th and 21st Panzer Divisions, in theory the old guard of the Afrika Korps – though by now anybody who had done more than six months was a veteran. As they rumbled forward, tank commanders wedged themselves into their open turrets and tried to hold their field glasses steady enough to scan the innocent-looking ground ahead. The British were well dug in and their guns were deployed with the killing of tanks in mind rather than merely screening the infantry. On the contrary, since Snipe and similar actions, roles had been reversed. The riflemen were there to protect the guns and keep the German infantry at bay. The gun crews held their fire until the Panzers were no more than 400 yards away, and if the crews could not see the white of their enemy's eyes they could certainly make out the white edging around their black crosses. Before long, twenty tanks had been stopped, their crews scrambling clear if they were lucky while Bren gunners and riflemen made another attempt to kill them.

Freed of their fear of tanks, the British infantry seemed to have been gripped with a terrible exhilaration, something like the way the longbow men at Agincourt must have felt when they realized that their arrows were piercing the armour of the French knights. One gun layer who had been blinded in his right eye waved away medical attention and stopped two more tanks, aiming with the eye he normally closed.

As usual, the Panzers rarely caught fire immediately. This led to some being hit several times until the first smoke appeared or until it became obvious that they were stationary hulks. By midday Bolo Whistler's men alone were claiming twenty-seven Panzers. When he felt he was in danger of being overwhelmed, Whistler called on the assistance of a squadron of Shermans, which knocked out seven more without loss to themselves.

'The Marshal has made a balls of it,' Montgomery told Lieutenant-General Oliver Leese when he called at the army commander's caravan to tell him that the battle had started well. 'I shall write letters.' At the end of the day Montgomery reported that the Germans had left fifty-two tanks behind, most of which had been blown up by his sappers to ensure they could not be salvaged. 'Many others were damaged and towed away,' the British commander claimed. 'It was a crippling blow to his tank strength in North Africa.' All but the seven knocked out by the Shermans had been stopped by the anti-tank guns. No British tanks were lost and total Eighth Army casualties, killed or wounded, did not exceed 130. It had been precisely the 'bloody nose' Montgomery had predicted.

The Marshal had indeed made a balls-up of it. It is hard to understand how he expected to do otherwise. Was he so intoxicated by the success of his surprise attack on the Americans that he really expected to do the same thing to Eighth Army veterans who had several days to prepare for him? The interrogation of prisoners from 21st Panzer, who had lots of American cigarettes to share with their captors, suggested that this was the case. 'They said they had been told it would be the same sort of party they had up on the American front,' Monty crowed.

The battle of Medenine lasted one day. As dawn broke on 7 March, and the British demolition teams in their trucks and Bren gun carriers cautiously approached the disabled Panzers, all of Messe's forces that were able to had returned to the Mareth line.

Rommel wanted to go even further back and urged Berlin to allow a withdrawal 200 miles to the north. He wanted the new Axis line to start at the little coastal town of Enfidaville just south of Tunis, 'to gain time so as to bring as many as possible of the battle-tried veterans in safety to Europe'. But Hitler would have no truck with such 'defeatism'. Embittered and frustrated, Rommel decided the time had come to take his long-postponed rest cure and hand the poisoned chalice over to von Arnim.

On 9 March, three days after the Medenine battle, Rommel stood at the airfield at the ancient port of Sfax, once a stronghold of the Barbary pirates, handing out signed photographs to tearful aides before stepping on to the aircraft that was to take him to Rome. Around his neck, covering some unsightly boils and desert sores, was the scarf Trudel had knitted for him. For propaganda reasons Goebbels kept Rommel's departure out of the news bulletins. He never returned to Africa.*

---

* Rommel remained a national hero, but his career had only another sixteen months to run, and his life not much longer. Following Mussolini's overthrow and the Italian Armistice in September 1943, he was in charge of disarming the Italian home army. Transferred to France, he spent six months preparing its most vulnerable coastal areas against Allied invasion. Then, on 17 July 1944, at the height of the Battle of Normandy, his car was strafed by a British fighter and he received a serious head wound among other injuries. Three days later, Hitler escaped with minor injuries when Colonel Klaus von Stauffenberg, who had lost his left eye and his right hand on a mine while serving in Tunisia, planted a bomb at the Führer's headquarters in East Prussia. It was while recovering at home from his Normandy wounds that Rommel was falsely implicated in the failed assassination and given the choice of taking poison or facing a Nazi people's court. On 18 October 1944 he received a field marshal's state funeral at Ulm. Hitler sent condolences, not only for himself but, 'for the entire German people'.

Rommel's departure did not signal the beginning of the end to the fighting in Tunisia. On the contrary, it was about to enter its fiercest phase.

Both sides continued to reinforce. Between them Alexander's Eighth and First Armies now had more divisions than the British had deployed in the field since France in 1940. Arnim's fresh blood included the Hermann Goering Division, the Reichsmarschall and the Führer being the only members of the Nazi hierarchy to have entire divisions named after them.

Among the latest British infantry to arrive was a battalion from Alexander's old regiment, the Irish Guards, of which he was Colonel-in-Chief. As the Guards sailed the 400 miles from Algiers to Bône in a former cross-channel ferry called, appropriately enough, *Royal Ulsterman*, they were attacked by Axis torpedo-bombers and the battalion's Bren gunners added their fire to the ship's anti-aircraft pom-poms.

Lance-Corporal John Kenneally, two days short of his twenty-second birthday, was manning one of the Bren guns in the stern and squeezed off three magazines – although without hitting anything. It was not the first time Kenneally had been in action against low-flying aircraft. He was a deserter from one of the Royal Artillery's light anti-aircraft batteries. During the lull that followed the Battle of Britain he had fallen in with a wild bunch of southern Irish labourers who were earning good money clearing bomb sites and 'blacking out' factories so that they could run night shifts. On the run, his Irish friends had acquired new identity papers for him. Kenneally was not his real name and he had no Irish blood. He was born and brought up in Birmingham, where his mother, the daughter of a Blackpool pharmacist, was, by his own description, 'a fairly high-class whore'. His father, he claimed, had inherited a Jewish textile fortune.* When

---

* Kenneally always insisted that he was the son of Neville Blond, who became chairman of the English Stage Company and married Elaine Marks, heiress to the

his labouring friends, fearing British conscription, returned to neutral Ireland, he had used his new identity to join the Irish Guards.

The Guards arrived in Bône in time to stage a St Patrick's Day (17 March) parade and then did their best to drink the town dry before the military police could muster enough men to stop them. Most of the alcohol available was the red wine the French colonials made, but the Guardsmen drank it like beer. Alexander, mindful of his duties as Colonel of the regiment, managed to procure some approximation of the traditional shamrock for their caps, which he sent with the message, 'Welcome to the Micks! Now we'll get cracking.' For many of these Irish Guardsmen it would be their last St Patrick's Day, and before long a lot more would be heard of Corporal Kenneally. But they did not, as it happened, 'get cracking' straight away. For the moment the big action was going to be in the south, where, two weeks after his victory at Medenine, a confident Montgomery was about to attack the Mareth line.

Between the Eighth Army and Tunis, about 250 miles to the north allowing for the curve of the Golfe de Gabes, the Axis could take advantage of three good natural defensive positions. Each one was a bottleneck where the coastal plain narrowed and the mountains or a salt marsh came close to the sea. The Mareth line was the most southerly of these hurdles. Next, some thirty miles north, came the Gabes Gap, where the Wadi Akarit ran between the coast and the Roumana Hills that adjoined the Chott el Fejaj. This treacherous salt lake depression, good only for gypsum cement powder, had a history of swallowing unwary invaders and their war camels whole. For a mechanized army it was impassable. About eighty miles south of Tunis was the narrowest and therefore the best bottleneck of all, at Enfidaville, though this was so close to the capital that its use was obviously as a last resort.

In an operation codenamed 'Pugilist Gallop', Montgomery intended to smash through the first two hurdles and take the port of Sfax, where Rommel had made his goodbyes. 'Once I loose my army on the night of 20/21 March I am going right through with the business,' Montgomery promised Brooke. 'My soldiers are full of beans and we shall take a lot of stopping.' Montgomery's confidence

---

Marks & Spencer chain-store fortune. Blond always denied he was Kenneally's father. 'I was only one of his mother's many friends,' he once said.

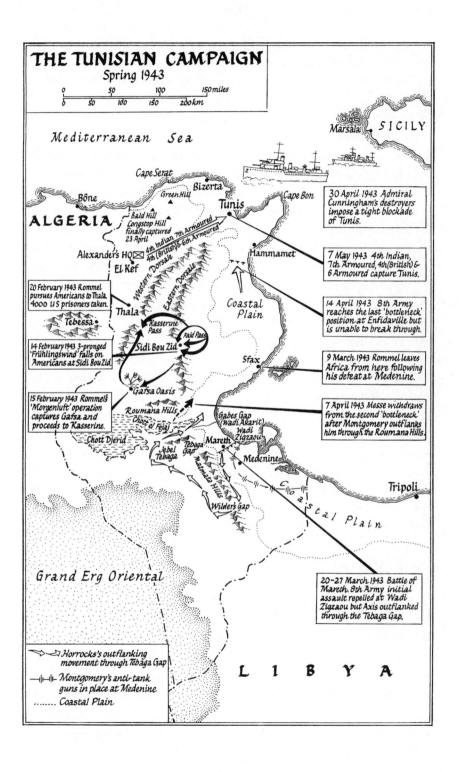

THE TUNISIAN CAMPAIGN
Spring 1943

0 50 100 150 miles
0 50 100 150 200 km

Mediterranean Sea

SICILY

Marsala

Cape Serat

Bizerta

Green Hill

Cape Bon

Tunis

Bône

Bald Hill
Longstop Hill
finally captured
23 April

ALGERIA

Hammamet

Alexander's HQ ⊠
El Kef

4th Indian
4th (British)
7th Armoured
6th Armoured

Western Dorsale

Eastern Dorsale

Coastal Plain

30 April 1943 Admiral
Cunningham's destroyers
impose a tight blockade
of Tunis.

7 May 1943 4th Indian,
7th Armoured, 4th (British) &
6 Armoured capture Tunis.

14 April 1943 8th Army
reaches the last 'bottleneck'
position at Enfidaville but
is unable to break through.

20 February 1943 Rommel
pursues Americans to Thala.
4000 US prisoners taken.

Thala

Kasserine
Pass

Faid Pass

Tebessa

Sidi Bou Zid

Sfax

14 February 1943 3-pronged
'Frühlingswind' falls on
Americans at Sidi Bou Zid.

9 March 1943 Rommel leaves
Africa from here following
his defeat at Medenine.

15 February 1943 Rommel's
'Morgenluft' operation
captures Gafsa and
proceeds to Kasserine.

Gafsa Oasis

Roumana Hills
Chott el Fejaj

Gabes Gap
(Wadi Akarit)
Wadi
Zigzaou

7 April 1943 Messe withdraws
from the second 'bottleneck'
after Montgomery outflanks
him through the Roumana Hills.

Chott Djerid

Tebaga
Gap

Mareth

Jebel
Tebaga

Medenine

Tripoli

Matmata Hills

Wilder's Gap

Coastal Plain

Grand Erg Oriental

20-27 March 1943 Battle of
Mareth. 8th Army initial
assault repelled at Wadi
Zigzaou but Axis outflanked
through the Tebaga Gap.

L I B Y A

↦ Horrocks's outflanking
movement through Tebaga Gap

—‖‖— Montgomery's anti-tank
guns in place at Medenine

.... Coastal Plain

was misplaced. In command of all the Axis forces on this front was the Italian general, Giovanni Messe, whose First Italian Army in fact included most of Rommel's old German formations. Mareth was every bit as well defended by General Messe as Montgomery had prepared Medenine. The line ran south-west for about twenty miles, from the coast to the Matmata hills. Apart from the ferro-concrete bunkers the French had left, much of it was built along a formidable natural anti-tank ditch, the Wadi Zigzaou, which was between sixty and 200 feet wide and twenty feet deep. Unusually heavy spring rains had turned the wadi into a moat in places. And where nature had not been generous enough, German and Italian engineers had steepened and deepened. Before and after the Zigzaou were other obstacles. Behind the wadi the Axis defenders had dug a sheer-sided anti-tank ditch twelve feet wide and eight feet deep. In front of it, up to the shallower Wadi Zeus, they had planted hundreds of Teller anti-tank mines and bouncing S-mines packed with their ghastly steel caviare. After the mines and the booby traps, the line was garrisoned by good infantry bristling with anti-tank guns, and behind them the Panzer Divisions lay in reserve to counter-attack where they were most needed. Some forward strongpoints and listening posts were in the minefields themselves. Four days before the main battle began, some of these minefields decimated a battalion each of the Grenadier and Coldstream Guards who were trying to clear a forward Axis position known as Horseshoe Hill. They were then counter-attacked. The Guards' total casualties out of at most 1,400 men were 512 killed, wounded or captured. Messe, like Montgomery at Medenine, could not be blamed if he thought the Eighth Army's attack was 'a perfect gift'.

The Mareth line was so well defended and the terrain so difficult, there was no question of even attempting to make an initial armoured assault. It would have to be breached Alamein style by the infantry and the armour poured through once a hole had been made. After a heavy barrage, a frontal assault was to be made close to the coast by the 50th Division. This remained very much a north country formation with an entire Durham Light Infantry brigade from around Newcastle-on-Tyne and commanded by Major-General John 'Crasher' Nichols. Supporting the 50th, though they would not take part in the first attack, were Wimberley's 51st Highlanders, with

Tuker's 4th Indian in reserve. Behind them, waiting for the hole to be made, were the tanks of 7th and 1st Armoured Divisions.

But there was more to Montgomery's plan than a frontal assault. A gigantic left hook was to be delivered by Freyberg's New Zealanders. Supporting them was a British armoured brigade, extra artillery and 3,000 Free French colonial troops, Senegalese and Arabs, under the Gaullist officer, Philippe Le Clerc. With the assistance of a Long Range Desert Group liaison team, this French aristocrat had fought his way 1,600 miles through Italian-held southern Libya to meet the Eighth Army at Tripoli and thus changed Montgomery's reluctance to use French troops.★ Freyberg's force was required to advance north along the western side of the Matmata hills until they reached a pass Montgomery's staff called the Tebaga Gap. Here they would turn east towards the coast and threaten to surround Messe's forces by cutting them off from the second bottleneck position at Gabes.

This would put the Italian general in the dilemma of not knowing where to deploy the Panzer Divisions he was holding in reserve. Should they go south to support his infantry on the Mareth line or north to hold Tebaga, which British intelligence reports correctly suggested was weakly held by Italian infantry?

Freyberg's 6,000 vehicles started for Tebaga on 11 March, and it took them eleven days to get there. They took a circuitous, U-shaped route of about 150 miles, travelling first south away from the Mareth line. Once they were through the Matmata hills, taking a pass recently discovered by the Long Range Desert Group, they turned north and met up with the Free French. Le Clerc's men were already west of the Matmata range and on the route, having captured the jagged massif of Ksar Rhilane. A German armoured column which attempted to stop them was caught in the open by a squadron of Hurricane 11Ds (basically a flying anti-tank gun), which inflicted heavy damage.†

By dusk on 20 March Freyberg was camped at the entrance to the

---

★ Rightly or wrongly, at Alamein Montgomery had felt badly let down by General Koenig, the hero of Bir Hacheim, and thereafter resisted attempts to employ French soldiers in the front line. 'I use them to guard aerodromes,' he wrote to Brooke. 'They have no other value.' On 23 August 1944, Eisenhower permitted Le Clerc's French armoured division to be the first Allied troops to enter Paris.

† They destroyed or damaged six tanks, an anti-tank gun, thirteen armoured cars and other vehicles.

Tebaga Pass and could easily have brushed its weak Italian garrison aside with his 20,000 men, 150 tanks, and 136 25-pounder guns. But Freyberg, the lion-hearted First World War VC, wounded for the fifth time in the service of his Empire only the previous summer, was always a cautious general. And only a few weeks before, the New Zealand government had told him that because of the war against Japan reinforcements were not available to replace casualties for the foreseeable future.

One of his brigades made a local attack which enjoyed complete success, but Freyberg declined to follow it up. Before he would venture through the pass and enter the flat lands on the other side, he needed to be certain that Messe had committed his armour to the Mareth line and that it was not lying in wait for him. A wonderful chance was missed to end the Tunisian campaign by cutting off the Axis forces before they could get back to their next natural defence line. As so often when mistakes like this were made for the very best of reasons, the price would be paid in blood.

Shortly before midnight on 20 March the Eighth Army announced their attack on the Mareth line with the biggest barrage they had fired since El Alamein. Reconnaissance had revealed most of the obstacles they faced. Some of 'Crasher' Nichols's north countrymen, like the besiegers of a medieval fortress, were carrying scaling ladders the engineers had made for them in order to climb the far side of the Wadi Zigzaou and then traverse the anti-tank ditch beyond it.

Commanding one of the German battalions opposing them was Oberleutnant Heinz-Werner Schmidt, fresh from his encounter with the Americans at Kasserine. Schmidt was 'delighted' with the protection offered by some of the old French bunkers he had been allotted; they had been lined with armour plate and were, he thought,

practically shell and bomb proof. But among them were bunkers that had been constructed with an eye for cover rather than for field of fire. Others had no loopholes. Then, too, most of them had been planned to house French 25-mm and 47-mm anti-tank guns and were too small for our 50- and 75-mm guns which we had to leave behind the bunker line. There were a number of machine-gun and mortar positions ready in the centre of the trench system – constructed in the sandstone ground.

Schmidt had been standing on top of the bunker he had selected as his headquarters; it was a balmy spring evening with plenty of starlight and he was enjoying the spectacle provided by the slow descent of some parachute flares. Then he noticed the distant flashes that heralded the Eighth Army's opening bombardment, and he leapt into the dark trench below just as the first shells began to cave in the earthworks all around him.

Despite the barrage it rapidly became apparent to the British that it was not going to be easy. When the Green Howards, a Yorkshire battalion, started to go to ground after taking casualties from mortar and machine-gun fire, their commanding officer, Lieutenant-Colonel Derek Seagrim, dashed forward. Revolver in hand, he was the first man to cross the ladder over the anti-tank ditch and start throwing grenades. He was forty years of age and was acting like a subaltern in the war he had just missed as a teenage schoolboy. It was the Somme or the Ypres salient all over again. Later, the lieutenant-colonel was estimated to have killed or captured about twenty Germans single-handed. He seems to have borne a charmed life and, inspired by his example, his men took heart. As the dawn came up, the battalion had driven a wedge in the enemy line and were able to repel the inevitable counter-attack. Time after time Seagrim left cover to rally those places which seemed most threatened.*

Some of the Germans who were fighting along the Mareth line that night were teenage reinforcements who had arrived in Africa the previous day and who had never been in action before. A few, their nerve broken by the shelling perhaps, began giving themselves up, but they were the exception. In the rubble of broken bunkers and the sand heaps of collapsed trenches the Germans got their machine-guns going. Throughout 50th Division's narrow bridgehead, casualties mounted. Seagrim's Green Howards had at least crossed the Wadi Zigzaou; others found they could not even do that. Raw courage was simply not enough.

The British plan called for a regiment of old Valentine infantry tanks to be introduced as soon as the infantry gained a foothold. Only eight of them had the newer six-pounder cannon; the rest still carried

---

* Seagrim received the VC, only to be killed in another action, less than three weeks later. His younger brother Hugh, who served behind enemy lines in Burma, received a rare posthumous George Cross – sometimes referred to as the 'civilian VC'. In order to halt reprisals against Karen villagers who had refused to divulge his whereabouts, he gave himself up to the Japanese, knowing what the probable consequences would be, and was executed by them.

two-pounders which, together with their machine-guns, were considered sufficient for bunker-busting. The expected counter-attack by Messe's Panzers was to be met by anti-tank guns.

Engineers managed to get forty-two of the Valentines across the wadi and over the anti-tank ditch by filling it with fascines: bundles of logs lowered into place from a specially adapted tank. Wheeled transport, including the all-important tows for the anti-tank guns, found it impossible to follow. Attempts to manhandle the six-pounders over while under fire met with little success. One lane was blocked entirely when eighteen tons of Valentine disappeared up to its turret in the sludge on the bed of the Wadi Zigzaou.

Having survived the opening shots of the barrage, Schmidt, like his enemy Seagrim, had an infantry battalion to lead. He began to grope his way around the trench system, trying to rally his men and assess casualties. In some places the hard, sandstone sides of the trenches had already collapsed and he found himself

scrambling over shattered masonry or heaps of rock, even leaping over dud enemy shells. I reached one of the lower bunkers in the centre of the sector on the lip of the Wadi Zigzaou. A number of the detachment there lay dead round their gun. In front of the bunker entrance and a little to one side, in a trench, I came across two soldiers who had been lightly wounded. 'Tanks on the rise immediately ahead of us!' one shouted to me. I did not know him – he must have been one of the replacements. 'The tanks have destroyed our bunker armour with direct hits,' he shouted again. 'It is suicide to remain in the bunker.'

Over the din Schmidt yelled at the men that British infantry were liable to break in at any moment. He ordered them to occupy a weapons pit that had been dug next to their wrecked bunker while he scrambled inside and started dragging out the machine-gun. Shells continued to explode outside. When he emerged with the weapon in his arms, he saw that the men he was going to give the gun to had both been killed. Schmidt who, like Seagrim, seemed that day to be under some divine protection for battalion commanders, managed to get back to his bunker and sent three men, one of them his runner, to man the position he had just left. A few minutes later the runner was back with the news that the Tommies were indeed attacking, 'They are already lying in front of our trench. Now the game was on.

Men raced about the trenches giving the immediate alert: "Infantry attacking – weapons in position!" In a few seconds the machine-guns that the enemy artillery had not blotted out were blazing away criss-cross over the front . . . Belt after belt whipped through the guns.'

Schmidt's most forward company, which was on a slight rise well ahead of their main defensive line, was overrun by Valentines and most of its members taken prisoner or killed. But his battalion held their main position, though small groups of British infantry got into their lines and captured one bunker and some adjacent trenches. Both sides made heavy use of grenades.

In places on the 50th Division front the combatants got even closer. There were those rare episodes of hand-to-hand fighting when brutal collisions occurred in the dark between yelling, frightened men who clubbed, stabbed and hacked at one another with rifle-butts, bayonets and spades. To add to the confusion, 'Crasher' Nichols had lived up to his name and, anxious to see what was holding things up, blundered so far forward that he lost touch with his divisional headquarters.★ It became increasingly obvious to Nichols's harassed and uncertain staff and to the brigadier, a First World War VC left in charge, that Axis resistance was stiffening remarkably well. Panzers were supporting infantry in local counter-attacks and the anti-tank guns meant to stop them were still on the wrong side of the wadi. The undergunned Valentines did their best but it was like the bad old days in the desert when the German tanks were always that much better than the British. The Valentines' commanding officer was killed and they began to take heavy casualties. Shermans were needed, but a Sherman weighed almost twice as much as a Valentine and the lighter tanks had already chewed up the fascines so badly, nothing else could get across.

In Schmidt's sector, his soldiers gradually forced the British infantry out of their lines and began to take a few prisoners. 'Our doctor bandaged a young English lieutenant who had been wounded. "What are you still fighting for?" the Englishman demanded. "We have an overwhelming superiority of men and materials. It is only a question of days or weeks and the war will be over for you anyhow." We refused to believe this and laughed at his optimism.' They were right

---

★ Nichols was forty-six, only six years older than Seagrim, and not an experienced divisional commander.

to mock this cheeky prisoner. Even as he spoke, the 50th Division was preparing to withdraw to its start line on the other side of the Wadi Zigzaou. Worst hit were the Geordies of 151st Brigade, who had lost 600 men. Another casualty of a kind would be 'Crasher' Nichols, fired for allegedly losing his grip on his division. Montgomery was at his most unforgiving: 'He has no brains and is really stupid.'

It was without doubt the worst setback the Eighth Army had suffered under Montgomery, and for a brief moment the imperturbable mask its cocky commander had worn ever since Alam el Halfa began to slip. 'What am I to do, Freddie?' he asked de Guingand as the 50th straggled back under the cover of an artillery barrage. But the battle was far from over. There had been no panic-stricken flight, only reluctant withdrawal by soldiers who were becoming accustomed to winning. Most of the Eighth Army had still not been committed and before long Montgomery knew exactly what he should do. 'I shall now nourish my left hook,' he signalled Alexander. He had decided to switch the main weight of his offensive to an expanded version of Freyberg's outflanking movement at the Tebaga Gap. But Montgomery had had enough of Freyberg's caution. Alongside him and, to all intents and purposes in command, would be Lieutenant-General Brian Horrocks.

The sideshow had now become the main event. Horrocks's forces would include 1st Armoured Division and, in order to compensate for any lack of artillery, further 'nourishment' would come from something the British had never properly tried before. In February, Harry Broadhurst, a Battle of Britain ace and at thirty-seven the RAF's youngest Air Vice-Marshal, had taken command of the Desert Air Force. Broadhurst had long realized that what the army sometimes needed was the kind of Blitzkrieg aerial artillery the Luftwaffe's Stuka crews had so often supplied regardless of risk.* The RAF did not have any dive-bombers as such, but Broadhurst was convinced that the DAF could make a considerable contribution at little cost. As soon as he took over, he had his fighter squadrons training to strafe and bomb on a collection of captured Axis vehicles he had set up outside Tripoli. Montgomery, the ultimate trainer, was delighted. Within the Desert Air Force Broadhurst's enthusiasm was infectious and his pedigree

---

* Some Eighth Army veterans rated the two-man crews of these terrifying if vulnerable gull-winged dive-bombers among their bravest opponents.

impressive. Spitfire purists who objected to the disfigurement of bomb racks were less inclined to argue with one of their own. When de Guingand asked him if he could provide the extra 'artillery' it was thought Horrocks would need, he did not hesitate. 'You will have the whole boiling match,' he replied. 'Bombs and cannon. It will be a real low-flying blitz.'

So Operation 'Pugilist Gallop', which had never even managed a modest trot, was shelved and Operation 'Supercharge Two' was born. This was, of course, the same codename as that used for the breakout at Alamein and was meant to be talismanic.

From their position behind the Wadi Zigzaou, where they had been waiting to exploit the breakthrough that never came, Horrocks took three days to join up with Freyberg. They took a slightly shorter route than the New Zealanders but nevertheless it was a remarkable achievement: three days, compared to eleven.

At the Tebaga Gap all had changed. Despite the successful defence of the Mareth line, Messe was now preparing to abandon it. This had been precipitated by the US II Corps under Patton, who was beginning to revive American morale, moving slowly back towards Gafsa. Arnim was concerned that if the Americans recaptured the oasis and then advanced beyond the Eastern Dorsale, they would cut off the Axis' main supply route from Tunis. He wanted to concentrate his forces behind the next bottleneck, the Wadi Akarit–Gabes line. But to do this it was imperative that the British should not get through the Tebaga Gap and cut Messe off before all his infantry could get back behind the next line.

Freyberg's worst fears had come true. To keep the Tebaga Gap closed, both Panzer formations were waiting for him, plus Major-General Freiherr von Liebenstein's 164th Light Division. Freyberg's only consolation was that he had another armoured division to fight alongside him and the promise of close air support.

Horrocks started the attack late in the afternoon on 26 March, the last of his tank transporters having delivered their loads to the start line some thirty minutes before zero hour. For the first time in almost three years of fighting in North Africa the British attacked from west to east with the setting sun, once firmly allied to Rommel's Panzers, behind them and dazzling the waiting anti-tank crews. At the same time Air Vice-Marshal Broadhurst was as good as his word. While the tanks advanced behind a creeping artillery barrage, low-flying

Hurricanes, Kittyhawks and Bostons roared overhead, picking out targets beyond the shell bursts of the British artillery.

Among the lead tanks was Captain Bill Close's Crusader squadron, with New Zealand infantrymen mounted behind their turrets. The first German gunners they encountered were 'still rather shaken and dazed by the barrage, making no efforts to engage us. [I]n some cases we crushed the guns by running over them. However, shortly after we had bypassed the first defences the German anti-tank gunners came to life, hitting several Shermans which burst into flames . . . I felt a crack on the front of my tank but a reassuring yell from one of my crew confirmed that we had not been penetrated.' Shortly afterwards, standing in his open turret looking for targets, Close spotted a German soldier taking aim at him from a nearby slit-trench. The shot ricocheted off his radio mast and, before the German had a chance to fire again, one of the New Zealanders on the back of the tank hit him with a snap shot. But after that the tank commander's relations with his passengers rapidly deteriorated.

I became rather excited and decided to throw a few hand grenades – we had a box of six in the turret. Not having practised throwing grenades from the turret of a moving tank, I forgot that my gunner had traversed the gun [turned the turret around]. My first grenade dropped among the New Zealand infantrymen on the back of my tank and bounced off. No one was hurt but one of the New Zealanders pointed his Thompson at me, indicating what would happen should I try again.

. By the time darkness had fallen, the British armour was through the Tebaga Gap. The first of what would turn out to be 2,500 German prisoners were beginning to shamble back between the tanks with their hands up, though not everyone was willing to accept defeat. For twenty-four hours, German infantry tried to win back a hill on the side of the gap the British knew as Point 209. The hill was taken and then held against considerable odds by no more than thirty men from the Maori battalion under a Lieutenant Moana Ngarimu. The lieutenant, a Maori aristocrat, broke up the enemy's last attack by leading those still able to stand in a wild, screaming downhill charge, firing his Thompson sub-machine-gun from the hip. According to the citation for his posthumous VC, Ngarimu died 'almost on top of those of the enemy who had fallen to his gun just before he fell to theirs'. He was twenty-five. Elsewhere, a few of 21st Panzer's tanks found themselves isolated and cut off. They tried to shoot their way out by falling on the rear of Horrocks's armour in a surprise attack. None of them got through.

But Horrocks failed to close the trap on the majority of Messe's First Italian Army. A couple of miles south of the town of El Hamma, which is in the central part of the Gabes Gap, German anti-tank gunners stopped the British armour as they came down a narrow defile. At the same time Montgomery's attempt to overrun the rest of Messe's troops as they retreated from the Mareth line was prevented by the skilled rearguard actions that the 90th Light had now honed to perfection since Alamein, including the usual laying of mines and booby traps.

Yet if the majority of Messe's army had got away, they had once again lost men and equipment they could ill afford. And while Montgomery admitted it was 'the toughest fight since Alamein', the brief moment of despair he had known when Crasher Nichols's men had been pushed back across the Wadi Zigzaou was, it seems, entirely forgotten. 'It was the most enjoyable battle,' he exulted in his diary of the campaign. 'Alamein was a slogging match. Mareth gave considerable scope for subtlety and for outwitting the opponent.'

Doubtless Messe and Arnim would have pleaded, 'outnumbered never outwitted'. Nevertheless, tributes poured in. 'Magnificent exploits,' said Alexander. 'Very best congratulations,' said Brooke. Eisenhower flew over from Algiers to pay his respects, as did the French general Henri Giraud, who had replaced the assassinated Admiral Darlan as head of the French military in North Africa.★

Montgomery, petulant as ever, complained that neither of his distinguished guests or their aides had thought to bring any bedding: 'I suppose they think we all live in hotels.' It was his first meeting with Eisenhower, whom he liked, though in his letter to Alexander he added, 'I should say he was good probably on the political line; but he obviously knows nothing whatever about fighting.' Eisenhower was also moved to put pen to paper. He wrote to his friend General

★ Darlan was shot on Christmas Eve by a young French royalist who had connections with the British Special Operations Executive, which supported resistance movements in countries occupied by the Axis. He does not appear to have been acting on SOE's orders.

George Marshall, the US Chief of Staff in Washington, that he found Montgomery 'unquestionably able but very conceited'. Eisenhower thought that Monty had become so proud of his victories he was unwilling to move 'until he was absolutely certain of success'.

Yet what Montgomery did next must have given Eisenhower some pause for thought. By 30 March, the Eighth Army had reached the Gabes Gap, about fifteen miles north of Gabes itself. Montgomery knew that he must not give Messe time to consolidate the already formidable Wadi Akarit position with more mines and barbed wire and turn it into another Mareth line. Yet before he attacked he needed time to organize his troops. It took exactly a week to do this and then Montgomery did something he had never tried before, something almost preposterously at odds with his need to control, his reluctance to take risks. Night attacks had become something of a speciality of the Eighth Army's infantry, and Rommel had admired them for it. But they were always made when there was enough moonlight for people to see what they were doing. Because of this Messe expected he had at least another week's grace, by which time the waxing moon would be almost full. Montgomery guessed this and decided, against all his own staff college teaching, to make a night attack in complete darkness in the hope that the surprise achieved would outweigh the risk of the operation floundering into chaos.

The attack was in two stages. To the west of Wadi Akarit, before the salt marshes, the Axis right flank rested on some rocky highlands, a massif of connected peaks with sharp gullies and good fields of fire. At about 10 p.m. on 6 April 1942, after a six-mile approach march and without the doubled-edged benefit of artillery preparation, two battalions of Gurkhas silently started to climb these hills.

Reports from night patrols of the 1st Royal Sussex (one of the British battalions serving with 4th Indian Division), had convinced Major-General Francis 'Gertie' Tuker that the hills were not quite as impregnable as they looked. The Sussex had observed that the south-facing slope of the flat-topped Djebel Fatnassa was considered so steep that its Italian defenders had confined their sangars on that side to the top of a gully. This was where the Gurkhas were heading.

Tuker, a former Gurkha officer himself and veteran of Gallipoli, had been told that his old battalion, 1st/2nd Gurkhas, was in the lead. Like most ex-Gurkha officers, he retained a deep affection for these loyal and hardy peasants from the highlands of central Nepal. Now he was wondering whether for once he might be asking too much of them. Shortly after midnight, the sounds of machine-gun, artillery and mortar fire told the general that his men had been discovered. Once this had happened and surprise had been lost, they were supposed to get artillery support. But all the radios with the headquarters group of 1st/2nd Gurkhas, including the one used by the gunners' forward observation officer, were wrecked by a well-aimed salvo of mortar bombs which caused several casualties.

About a quarter of a mile further up the hill, at the sharp end of things, was Lalbahadur Thapa, who held the old Indian Army rank of Subedar which, in British army terms, was somewhere between sergeant-major and lieutenant.* Behind Lalbahadur were a dozen or so Gurkhas from the battalion's D company. The Subedar had found a steep, winding path that followed the gully with sangars on top. It was the kind of narrow, twisting goat-track that must, until it was criss-crossed by tracer bullets, have reminded the Gurkhas of home. Above them the darkness was split by artillery flashes, and sometimes a parachute flare would illuminate a patch of slope for a minute at a time. But in the gully it was pitch black; the Gurkhas could hardly see each other.

Crouched behind the loose rock walls of their sangars, the Italians continued to fire into the menacing darkness below. Evidently they knew that the enemy was close, but they had no idea exactly how close and the night had become too noisy to hear the scrabble of boots on loose stones or a seventeen-inch fixed bayonet scraping a rock. Apart from their small arms, all the Gurkhas were carrying their traditional kukri fighting knives, the hacking weapon that is a cross between a machete and a miniature scimitar. They also had grenades – but it is unwise to throw a grenade uphill in the dark.

Once they had made out its waist-high walls in the gloom, Lalbahadur and his men rushed the first sangar. Some were hit by its machine-gun fire, but their leader was among those who got inside intact and began stabbing, hacking and shooting its occupants. When they had finished, determined to keep this uphill charge going, Lalbahadur ran on to the next machine-gun nest, personally killing all four of its occupants with his revolver and kukri.

---

* Indian and Gurkha soldiers were required to salute Subedars. British soldiers were not.

One machine-gun sangar was still firing from the top of the gully, but by now only the Subedar and two other Gurkhas remained on their feet. Why Lalbahadur decided to go ahead alone and charge it, forcing himself up the steepest part of that corkscrew goat-track when he had already done so much, is almost beyond human comprehension. Somehow he got there unscathed, rushed it, killed two of its crew and frightened the others away.

This sangar turned out to be the key position. Once they possessed it, a battalion each of the Sussex and the Punjabis came up the gully and started fanning out. Soon all of Djebel Fatnassa – indeed all the high ground between there and Wadi Akarit – was in the hands of Tuker's division, who began to take a large number of Italian prisoners. It is a rare thing for the outcome of a battle to be so directly influenced by a single act of uncommon valour or, in Lalbahadur's case, several acts. The Subedar was, of course, awarded the Victoria Cross.★

Once Tuker's men had secured the massif, Montgomery started the next stage: the attack on Wadi Akarit itself and the Roumana hills beyond, using Wimberley's 51st Highland Division and a brigade from the 50th Division. The attack started at 4 a.m. when there was still at least an hour and a half of darkness left before dawn.

Among those watching it was Private John Bain, the veteran of Alamein who was now old enough to vote, having celebrated his twenty-first birthday on the day the Eighth Army captured Tripoli. Much to the relief of Bain and his mates, the 5th/7th Gordon Highlanders were being kept in reserve, along with the other two battalions of 153rd Brigade. The night before, the Gordons had taken some casualties from mortar fire as they frantically dug in just below the Roumana hills. But with any luck they would not be needed to take part in the assault itself, which was being made by the other two brigades in their division. Shortly before first light, Bain had watched the Seaforth Highlanders moving 'spectrally in the half light' through their positions, heard the whispered greetings, 'All the best, mate,' and the resigned response, 'It's all right for you, Jimmy.'

★ It was personally pinned to his breast by George VI, India's last King-Emperor, when he visited Tripoli some two months later. Lalbahadur was sent to England, where he brought some colour to the austerity of wartime London, demonstrating kukri technique 'accompanied by blood-curdling shouts' at public lectures organized by a retired field marshal.

Montgomery was understandably proud of the high morale of his army. 'The more the fighting the lower the sick rate, as the men are all eager to be in it,' he bragged in a letter to Brooke. But most of the 180,000 men on the Eighth Army's ration strength were not front-line infantrymen or front-line anything else. They would never know what it was like to climb a hill before dawn, dry-mouthed and sweaty-palmed, knowing that their next step might be their last.

Shortly after the Seaforths had gone through their position, the Gordon Highlanders heard the sound of machine-gun and mortar fire. As the sun came up over the Roumana hills, Bain and his mates could gradually make out something of what was going on. 'Human figures moved insectile and anonymous in little clusters, forming irregular patterns that kept breaking and coming together again. Some of the small individual fragments were left motionless on the hillside. The noise of the machine-guns was irregular, too, coming in quick jabbering bursts which gradually grew less and less frequent.'

When most of the sounds of battle had ebbed away, the Gordons were ordered to follow the Seaforths up the hill, which they did in a long single file. Bain found that the 'steady rhythmic plodding, lack of sleep and too much unrelieved anxiety' produced a trance-like state. Before long they came across the first dead, British and Axis, lying around deserted slit trenches. 'Hughie said, "There's one poor bastard's finished with fuckin'-an-fightin'." The soldier was lying on his stomach, his head turned away from John's regard so his face could not be seen. There was no sign of a wound . . . Already the flesh of the dead soldiers, British and the enemy, was assuming a waxy theatrical look, transformed by the maquillage of dust and sand and the sly beginning of decay.' Bain had seen quite a lot of corpses since Alamein. Yet he found the sight of the Seaforths and their late enemies particularly disturbing, '[I]mmodest yet childlike in their complete surrender to insentience and stillness'.

Now to his horror he watched as the Gordons began to move among the dead, 'sometimes turning them with an indifferent boot,' removing watches, rings and any other valuables they could find from friend and foe alike. 'They seemed to be moving with unnatural slowness, proceeding from one body to another, stooping, reaching each out, methodical and absorbed. Hughie had gone. He must have joined the scavengers.'

Suddenly it was all too much. Although originally a volunteer –

and certainly no coward, for as an army boxing champion he had proved his courage time and again in the ring – Bain had never found reason to be enthusiastic about the military life. Disgusted by the looting of the dead, with his rifle slung and still wearing his tin hat, Bain started to walk slowly back the way he had come. Nobody challenged him. On the contrary, after he had gone a little way an officer from another unit obligingly gave him a lift in his jeep to a rear echelon. Some Gurkhas he met fed him tea and chapattis and he spent the night in an abandoned enemy camp, not realizing he was sharing it with a dead Italian. The next day, Bain hitched a lift in an RAF truck to the outskirts of Tripoli where, about 250 miles from Wadi Akarit and still with his rifle and pack, he was arrested by the military police, who were always on the lookout for deserters.*

The Highland regiments captured all their initial objectives, though most would be bitterly contested by determined counter-attacks. To their left the 50th Division, represented by Lieutenant-Colonel Seagrim's Green Howards and the East Yorkshires, were held up by an anti-tank ditch, behind which were some well-dug-in machine-gun and mortar positions. Seagrim went up to his leading platoons again, as he had done when he won his VC at Mareth. This time his luck ran out. He was hit in the head by shrapnel and died in a field hospital.

Near by, a medic from the East Yorkshires, Private Eric Anderson, also won a VC that day when his battalion was forced back behind a shallow ridge, abandoning several wounded men on its forward slope. The nearest Italian machine-gun nests were no more than 300 yards away. Anderson rescued three of the wounded, staggering back with them across his shoulders one at a time in a fireman's lift despite heavy small-arms fire. Whether up to this point he was just plain lucky or whether his Red Cross arm brassards were being respected is imposs-

---

* Court-martialled for 'deserting in a forward area', a lesser charge than 'deserting in the face of the enemy', Bain was sentenced to three years' imprisonment. He served six months of it in one of the penal hell-holes the British military maintained in Egypt before his sentence was suspended so that he could rejoin the Gordons in time for the D-Day landings. Private Bain's war ended when he was shot in both legs while on night patrol in Normandy. In 1987, by now the poet Vernon Scannell, he published *Argument of Kings*, a moving and highly praised memoir of his soldiering. In the preface he talks of the growing 'feeling of shame' he felt over his desertion, not at the time, but after the war.

ible to say. But whatever was preserving Anderson ran out when he was mortally wounded while preparing to pick up a fourth man. It is unclear how long he took to die. Understandably, nobody else had the cold-blooded nerve to try and get to him to see whether anything could be done; it would have been unusual for one battalion to have produced two Andersons. 'A man of outstanding character, with lofty ideals which he gave his life to uphold,' Captain Clark, the East Yorkshire's doctor, wrote to the young widow in Bradford. Anderson was twenty-seven.

The success of Tuker's Indians on the highlands to their left gradually took the heat off the north country battalions as the Italians were outflanked. But then Messe began to get German reinforcements to the front from elements of 15th Panzer and 90th Light.

For a time it seemed as if, for all the success of Tuker's Gurkhas, it was going to be Wadi Zigzaou all over again, only worse. 'We had on this day the heaviest and most savage fighting we have had since I have commanded the Eighth Army,' Montgomery would write in his campaign diary. 'Certain localities and points changed hands several times.' Bain had witnessed only the beginning of the Seaforths' calvary on the Roumana hills. Twice they and the Cameron Highlanders captured and were driven off the crest until, reinforced by a battalion from the Black Watch, they took it for a third time and finally held it.

East of them, towards the coast, the Argylls tried to hold a vital bridgehead across an anti-tank ditch against tanks and infantry with good artillery support. Luckily for Montgomery, this battalion was commanded by Lieutenant-Colonel Lorne Campbell, who was already something of a legend in the Highland Division. At St Valéry in 1940, when most of the original Territorial Army Division had been cut off and captured by Rommel, Campbell had won a DSO for bringing 200 of them back to Britain, often scouting ahead alone at night for ways to evade the Germans and get to the French coast. Some of those men were with him now.

After the disaster at Wadi Zigzaou all the battalion commanders had been told that they must get their anti-tank guns forward as soon as possible. Campbell had taken this very much to heart. When he discovered that the break the engineers had blasted in the anti-tank ditch did not coincide with their vehicle lane through a minefield, he had personally rushed around in a jeep under heavy machine-gun and mortar fire until he found a new route and got the guns through.

When, towards late afternoon, the Germans made their heaviest attack with armour and infantry, the six-pounders were dug in and ready. Even so, it looked as if the Argylls must be overwhelmed, and one company began to fall back. Campbell ran or jeeped from one hot spot to another, rallying his men and sometimes contributing to the showers of grenades they were exchanging with Panzer Grenadiers who were trying to work around their flanks. By now over half the officers had been killed or wounded, as were many of the Argyll's sergeants and corporals. Campbell himself was hit in the neck by a shell splinter but would not at first even consent to pause long enough to have the ugly-looking gash bandaged, let alone agree to be evacuated. Obviously in some pain, the lieutenant-colonel was still with his dwindling battalion as darkness fell and the German attack slowly spluttered out.*

Montgomery did not know it yet but Messe was about to withdraw. By dusk, 6,000 Italian infantry had been captured and even the Germans were getting towards the end of their endurance. And as at Mareth it was becoming plain that, even if Messe did beat the British off in the south, the Americans might manage to move in from the west and cut his supply route. Once again Montgomery was denied a complete victory. At dawn on 7 April the Eighth Army, about to deliver the kind of co-ordinated armour, air and artillery attack they had laid on at the Tebaga Gap, discovered that the enemy was no longer there. During the night Messe had slipped away, heading towards the last bottleneck at Enfidaville, just below Tunis, as fast as he could.

Some of his rear echelons had no time either to pack or to destroy. 'The booty is very great,' Montgomery reported to Alexander. Among it was a workshop containing forty-two tanks awaiting repair. By 13 April, the ports of Sousse and Sfax were in British hands, and the next day they were on the outskirts of Enfidaville. They had also joined up with Patton's Americans.

Montgomery estimated that his casualties for the one-day battle of

---

* Like Seagrim and Victor Turner at Snipe, Campbell got a VC for 'gallantry and magnificent leadership'. He was undoubtedly very brave, but no single act seems to have compared with Lalbahadur Thapa's berserk charges or Eric Anderson's cold-blooded courage. Campbell's award was for conspicuous and sustained bravery over something like a sixteen-hour period that inspired others and saved the day.

Wadi Akarit were about 2,000; probably 500–600 of these would have been fatalities. This was the Eighth Army's last great battle in North Africa, though some of its divisions still had one great triumph in store for them. By rights it should have been the end of the campaign. Arnim's Army Group Africa was now crushed between Alexander's First Army, including the US II Corps, in the west and the Eighth Army in the south.

Even Kesselring had to admit that the 4,000 square miles or so of north-eastern Tunisia that remained in Axis hands did not have 'sufficient depth' for a plausible defence. Both airfields and ports were increasingly vulnerable to air and sea attack and the supply situation was becoming hopeless. Until February, about 80 per cent of Axis shipping had been getting through to Tunisia. By March, Allied aircraft and the Malta submarines had reduced the supply tonnage to about half the previous monthly total and Italian sailors were calling it 'the death route'. More than half of these sinkings were the work of some newly arrived American squadrons flying twin-engined B-25 Mitchell bombers.

Axis attempts to supplement shipping with an air bridge proved even more costly. The Luftwaffe had long since lost its local tactical superiority, and fighter escorts were hard to find. Allied airfields were now all around them and their own so few that they were so crammed with aircraft and low-level Allied intruders found it impossible to miss them. Kesselring began to withdraw his squadrons to Sicily. As a result, the hapless aircrews of Junkers-52 transports and the mammoth and even more lumbering six-engined Messerschmitt Gigants, a motorized glider, were being slaughtered. When a fleet of twenty-one Gigants, each carrying ten tons of desperately needed fuel, met two South African squadrons of Kittyhawks, sixteen of the glider transports fluttered down into the Mediterranean in flames.

The record kill was the 'Palm Sunday Massacre'. On Sunday, 18 April, one week before Easter 1943, American fighter pilots shot down twenty-four troop-carrying Junkers-52s and caused thirty-five others to crash land on the coast rather than risk staying in the air. RAF Hurricanes then destroyed some of these before they could be salvaged.

By the time Montgomery reached Enfidaville, Arnim's engineers were reduced to trying to distil fuel by boiling off the alcohol content from local wines and liquors. At this point he had about eighty tanks left. But the hills above Tunis and Bizerta were not much good for tanks and, for the moment, Army Group Africa still had enough ammunition to continue their hopeless fight a little longer.

Oberleutnant Schmidt, who had fought in the rearguard during the retreat to Enfidaville, recalls his soldiers' thoughts on their immediate future and the fantasies which kept them going: 'Some thought we should be whirled back to Cape Bon and shipped over to Sicily for a renewed battle. Others believed that Hitler would not give up North Africa, that 'Tiger' Panzers in great numbers and new types of Luftwaffe aircraft would be hurled into action . . . The supply problem would be solved with Siebelfahren ferries which could carry two tanks and were armed with 88-mm flak guns.'

The reality was that by mid-April Army Group Africa claimed a ration strength of 170,000–180,000 men. Of these, about 60,000 were the front-line soldiers from nine German divisions who manned most of about 100 miles of front line which curved down from the northern coast through the mountains to Enfidaville on the east coast. Facing them and their eighty-odd tanks were 300,000 Anglo-Americans and their 1,400 tanks, plus considerable air power. It was not quite the Alamo it sounds. The terrain did favour defence. 'Giant crags and deep gullies in rocky wadis offered excellent protection against artillery and bombing,' Schmidt recalls. Stalingrad had surrendered two months before, but his men's refusal to believe that Hitler would let them down in a similar fashion was probably fairly typical. Little wonder Arnim could continue to resist.

Montgomery would have dearly liked the Eighth Army to conclude its campaign by capturing Tunis before Alexander's Anglo-Americans could get there. But the Enfidaville bottleneck was stoutly defended by Italians and Germans alike. An attempt by Indian and New Zealand troops to repeat the tactics of Wadi Akarit and seize some hills on the Axis right flank was only partially successful despite the heroism of the Maoris and the Rajputs, who won a VC.*

The Geordies and Yorkshiremen of 50th Division captured Enfidaville itself, went a little beyond it and withstood several counter-

---

* The VC was awarded to Havildar-Major (Sergeant-Major) Chhelu Ram of 4th/6th Rajputana Rifles. General Horrocks was 'bitterly disappointed' that another one did not go to Sergeant Manahi of the Maoris who took the peak that was his final objective with eight other men after they had killed forty of the enemy and taken 150 prisoners.

attacks. But it soon became apparent that any breakthrough along the coast would be costly. A few days later, a new and unblooded British division, the 56th, which had come all the way from staid garrison duties in Iraq and Persia, was thrown into the fray with predictable results. '56 Division gave a very bad showing today under heavy shell fire,' complained Montgomery. 'I must accept the fact that this division has little fighting value at present.' By now Montgomery's mind was on other things. He was preparing his plans for Operation 'Husky', the invasion of Sicily. He had already withdrawn the 51st Highlanders to Egypt so they could rest and train for it, and the 50th Division was about to join them.

Eighth Army's thrusts had become a feint to draw Axis troops away from Alexander, who was trying to fight his way to Tunis through the same hills in which Walther Nehring's puny forces had held up the Anglo-Americans four months before. Some of the new Churchill tanks helped British troops take the lower parts of Longstop, or Christmas Hill as the Germans called it, but it was too steep for the Churchills to get up to the next ridge. It was attacked again on 23 April, St George's Day. As the 8th Argylls and their ammunition donkeys wound their way up Longstop, they were observed by an eager audience of well-wishers who had moved into the best seats on the poppy-flecked grass slopes all around it. 'It was like a crowd of spectators watching climbers on the Eiger,' thought Hugh Skillen, a signals officer in a radio intercept unit.

Alexander and his red-tabbed staff officers had gathered in an Alpine meadow with their field glasses to watch Colonel Colin McNabb lead his Argylls up Longstop. Until the previous day McNabb had been one of them, safely manning a desk as General Anderson's Brigadier General Staff – a forty-year-old career officer with an important job. But when he heard that his old battalion had lost its commanding officer during their first attack on Longstop, McNabb had insisted that he be allowed to drop a rank so that he could return to his regiment in its hour of need.★

The Germans were very well dug in and had included in their defences some of the hill's old copper mine workings. Despite the

---

★ McNabb's decision might also have been influenced by a long whispering campaign against him by Montgomery, who accused him of 'bellyaching' and wanted him replaced in Anderson's HQ by a brigadier of his own choice.

artillery bombardment that preceded the attack, the 754 Infantry Regiment was able to unleash a withering fire. At the head of his men McNabb was among the first to die, and Major John Anderson took command. Anderson was twenty-five and one of the Argylls Lorne Campbell had salvaged from the débâcle at St Valéry. The previous month he had led his company through a day's fighting with such dash that many people thought the Distinguished Service Order he received should have been a Victoria Cross.

Anderson managed to rally some of the Argylls and, sometimes screened by smoke shells dropped by 25-pounders, led the storming of three machine-gun nests and a well-protected mortar battery. By this time most of the battalion had decided that the fire was too intense and had gone to ground. Anderson himself had received a leg wound and was limping, but he persuaded four officers and about forty men to stay with him and keep moving forward. Inspired by their example, the rest of the battalion joined them and the Argylls emerged from their final smoke-screen with about 250 prisoners and possession of Longstop Hill. This time Anderson was awarded the VC. He was killed in action at Termoli in Italy the following September. The gallant McNabb, who could have been safely watching it all from the meadow with Alexander and his staff, received only a warm place in the memory of his comrades and friends.

The capture of Longstop, which controlled the Medjerda valley, was a step closer to Tunis for Alexander, but there were still an awful lot of hills to go. If courage alone could open all the gates, some of his British First Army troops seemed to have it in abundance. Most of them were seeing action for the first time in North Africa after three endless years of training in Britain, first waiting to be invaded and then waiting to invade. And if they lacked the experience of the Eighth Army, they also lacked the caution that had sometimes grown with it. Three more Victoria Crosses would be awarded to them. Two went posthumously to officers, one to a twenty-three-year-old lieutenant in the Loyals, an unfashionable Lancashire regiment, and the other to an aristocrat in the Guards.

In a studio portrait taken shortly before his death, Lieutenant Wilwood Clarke, a Lancastrian from Southport, wears a monocle and a clipped Clark Gable moustache, at once defiant and comic, perhaps daring the photographer to laugh at his theatrical rendition of the young British officer. There was nothing comic about his performance on an obscure Tunisian hill named Guirat el Atach, where he seems to have been possessed by the same fury that seized the Gurkha Lalbahadur Thapa. Quite alone, and already wounded in the head, he killed or took prisoner the crews of three machine-gun posts, then died advancing on some snipers who had the temerity to fire at his platoon.

Lieutenant (temporary Captain) Lord Lyell of the Scots Guards, born in Belgravia and married with a four-year-old son, armed himself with a rifle and fixed bayonet, and with four of his men rushed an 88-mm anti-tank gun protected by two heavy machine-guns, one of which Lyell finished with a grenade. Behind him one of his men was killed and two wounded. The others decided to stop and give 'covering fire'. According to Lyell's citation, 'He was a long way in advance of the others . . . So quickly had this officer acted that he was in among the crew with the bayonet before they had time to fire more than one shot. He killed a number of them before being overwhelmed and killed himself.' The surviving members of the gun crew fled and Lyell's company were able to occupy the position.

By now the Irish Guards' battalion were about fourteen miles from Tunis, having suffered heavy casualties capturing a rocky ridgeline known as the Bou. One hundred and seventy-three of them, including five officers, were still on their feet and facing courageous counter-attacks. Both sides were partly fuelled on alcohol. One of the things that kept the Guardsmen going was their discovery that many of the dead German soldiers lying close by were carrying wine or spirits in their water bottles.

Among the defenders of the Bou was the bogus Irishman and deserter Lance-Corporal John Patrick Kenneally (his real name was Jackson) who was about to win the last VC in the North African campaign. Kenneally was alone with a Bren gun at an observation post on the forward slope when the enemy began shelling the top of the ridge behind him. He had already spotted enough German infantry emerging from trucks and armoured vehicles on the lower slope to convince him that another attack was in the offing. When the barrage slackened, the lance-corporal thought he could hear German being spoken close by. About ten yards ahead of him were two large boulders and he ran down to them.

A German voice was very clear now. I left the Bren behind the boulders and crawled through the scrub. The ground fell away into a deep gully and there they were. Most of them were squatting around a German officer. He was holding an 'O' group [orders briefing] and was pointing here and there. Some were lying down taking a breather and they were bunched like a herd of cattle. What an opportunity. I crawled back to the boulders and quickly took off all my equipment – speed was to be the essence of this operation. I put a new magazine in the Bren and one in each pocket. 'Here goes,' I said to myself. I took a deep breath and belted forward, firing from the hip. I achieved complete surprise. I hose-piped them down from the top of the gully. They were being bowled over like ninepins and were diving in all directions. I had time to flip on another magazine and I gave them that too. Enough was enough, and I fled back to the boulders and safety.

The Germans were running in the other direction. Single-handedly Kenneally had broken up their attack before it had even begun. 'Screaming like banshees,' the Guards appeared on the skyline behind him and began picking off the fleeing men as they scrambled down the slope towards their transport. 'Holy Mother of Christ! What have you done?' a sergeant, a pre-war regular, asked young Kenneally as he surveyed the bodies of the German officers and NCOs clustered around their fallen leader in the gully.

This was the beginning of an extraordinary forty-eight hours for Kenneally. Next he played a leading role in wiping out a four-man machine-gun team who were trying to establish themselves in the rear. Then he was instrumental in repelling an attack by three of Arnim's remaining tanks, which backed off after the Guardsmen hurled two anti-tank mines at them which they detonated by taping grenades to them with seven-second fuses and pulling the pin – a unique use of land mines.

The next day, this time accompanied by a Sergeant Salt from the Reconnaissance Regiment who had attached himself to the Guards, Kenneally repeated his performance against fresh German infantry forming up in the same gully. Salt was armed with a Sten and they both emptied a magazine from their automatic weapons at the enemy, in the words of his citation, 'inflicting many casualties'. But as they ran back for cover, the sergeant was killed and Kenneally shot in his right calf by what was probably a Schmeisser bullet. He refused to relinquish his Bren gun and fought for the rest of the day, often under intense mortar and artillery fire, until their opponents finally gave up. Afterwards, according to 1st British Division, about 700 German dead were counted around the Bou. Some eighty Guardsmen out of the original 173 were able to walk off the ridge.*

Alexander was among those who sent congratulations to his 'Micks' for their performance, adding that he was, 'very sorry about your losses'. By now it had become quite obvious that losses would continue to be heavy as long as Alexander persisted in trying to batter his way into Tunis on a broad front through these stubbornly held hills. At the same time, Messe had so effectively stonewalled the Eighth Army at Enfidaville that it was no longer taking any offensive action.

Montgomery and Alexander agreed on a new plan. They would reinforce First Army with the Eighth Army's 7th Armoured and 4th Indian Divisions and then make a concentrated, rapier-like thrust through the Medjez el Bab sector at Tunis.† Meanwhile, all the American forces would be regrouped on the northern coast and push towards the port of Bizerta. Patton had joined the planning team for the invasion of Sicily and the US II Corps was now under General Omar Bradley.

Although they were still bleeding badly from the constant counter-attacks they were having to make in order to keep their lines straight, Arnim's forces still had some fight left in them. A trickle of reinforcements continued to get through by sea and air. At the headquarters of Arnim's Army Group Africa an air of dogged normality prevailed. Oberleutnant Schmidt was summoned there by a mud-spattered messenger who had diligently searched through a dangerous mountain sector for hours before finding him asleep in a shell hole. The weary Schmidt could only imagine it was bad news. But when he arrived, a

---

* Kenneally was wounded again on Italy's Anzio beachhead in March 1944, but after that he was made an instructor in England and survived the war. When he left the army, he returned to the Midlands and ran a garage business but continued to use the name Kenneally. During the immediate post-war years Churchill often declared that any bitterness he felt for the Irish over the often pro-German stance of its wartime leader, Eamonn De Valera, 'dies in my heart when I think of Irish heroes like Kenneally'. Nine years before his death in 2000, Kenneally published his autobiography, *Kenneally VC*, in which he revealed his true origins. Nevertheless, many men from southern Ireland did serve in the Irish Guards and other British formations during the Second World War.

† Montgomery always insisted that it was his plan, 'made in my caravan at my HQ'. But then Alexander did seem to have a knack of getting Monty to suggest what he wanted to hear, and it was a fairly obvious use of available resources.

staff officer shuffled through some papers on his desk and said: 'Over a year ago you applied for permission to get married. Here it is. You are granted fourteen days' immediate special leave.' It was Easter Day 1943 – exactly a week after the Americans' Palm Sunday massacre of the Junkers-52s. That night, Schmidt left Tunisia, 'huddled in an overcrowded transport', and arrived at Catania in Sicily with the dawn. It was the end of his African campaign. Schmidt got married and survived the rest of the war.

The rapier thrust against Tunis was codenamed Operation 'Strike' and Lieutenant-General Brian Horrocks was brought over from Eighth Army, together with the borrowed divisions – 7th Armoured and 4th Indian – to command it.* In all, 'Strike' involved the tanks of 7th and 6th Armoured Divisions and the infantry of 4th Indian and 4th British Division, who had their own 'infantry tank' support, mostly the new Churchills. About 500 tanks were to advance along a narrow front, less than two miles wide, that would have been opened by the infantry divisions.

First Army lacked Eighth Army's confidence about night operations. Nevertheless, 'Gertie' Tuker, who ever since Wadi Akarit had become the prince of darkness with his 4th Indian Division, insisted on a 3 a.m. start on the moonless night of 5/6 May. He also persuaded Horrocks that, instead of a barrage, the supporting artillery should fire localized concentrations on known enemy strongpoints. This technique put down a shell every two yards, five times more intense than an Alamein-style barrage, though greater accuracy was required. Come the dawn, the artillery would be joined by close air support – weather permitting.

Operation Strike worked more or less exactly as planned. Between them the artillery and the infantry made a big enough hole in Arnim's thin crust for the tanks to go through. As usual, a few valiant German anti-tank gunners succeeded in holding some of them up a little longer than perhaps they should have done. But the match was already well into extra time and the scent of victory was in the air. At this point who wanted to risk being the last British tank crew to be 'brewed up' in North Africa? Horrocks's armour did halt for the night, but resumed

---

* It should have been Lieutenant-General John Crocker, whom Alexander rated and who was commander of his IX Corps, but Crocker was badly hurt in an accident at the demonstration of a new mortar.

its advance at first light next day, 7 May, skirmished with a few tanks and guns around a German military cemetery, and by mid-afternoon was within ten miles of Tunis.

Alan Moorehead of the *Daily Express* was among several carloads of American and British war correspondents who caught up with Horrocks at the village of La Mornaghia, where there was a notice up in German warning 'Danger – typhus in village'. Horrocks, obviously feeling pleased with himself, told the journalists that his soldiers had just captured the headquarters of the Hermann Goering Division, along with eighty staff officers. But the general had some even bigger news. He had received word that both his armoured car regiments, the veteran 11th Hussars and their parvenu First Army rivals, the Derbyshire Yeomanry, were in the outskirts of Tunis. If the newsmen wanted to try and catch up with his cavalry, they could do so at their own risk. The reporters, as reporters will, dashed for their cars.

The capture of Tunis, a Mediterranean town that was almost as European as it was Arab, provided the first hint of what might lie in store for Allied troops if they ever liberated Occupied Europe: an exultant sea of weeping, cheering civilians, tossing flowers, cigarettes and even bottles of wine into vehicles. Helmetless and numbed-looking German prisoners in a Bren gun carrier were clutching posies to their breasts that had been thrown to them in the belief that they were British. The crush of the crowd bringing vehicles to a halt; bold young settler women briefly pressing chaste kisses on the more accessible drivers. Surreal scenes in the Rue de Londres where, Moorehead reported, hundreds of off-duty Germans were sitting in the pavement cafés sipping drinks or simply walking the street, 'some with their girl friends'.

No one had warned them the British were near . . . Now, suddenly, like a vision from the sky, appeared these three British armoured cars. The Germans rose from their seats and stared. The Tommies stared back. There was not much they could do. Three armoured cars could not handle all these prisoners. In the hairdressing salon next door more Germans struggled out of their chairs and, with white sheets round their necks and lather on their faces, stood gaping. The three armoured cars turned back for reinforcements.

Tanks and truckloads of infantry were soon on the scene. There were a few apparently unco-ordinated attempts at resistance from snipers and machine-gunners which briefly cleared the streets. Most were quickly dealt with and in some ways only seemed to heighten the party atmosphere. Moorehead watched incredulously as two sergeant photographers, one American and the other British, seized Tommy guns and returned fire with an exuberance 'that seemed madness at first'.

The fall of Tunis split Army Group Africa in two. On the same day the Germans, succumbing to American pressure, withdrew from the port of Bizerta. Its loss sank any faint hope Axis troops might have still entertained of an orderly evacuation supervised by the Italian navy. When the 9th Hussars captured 9,000 men on a beach near Porto Farina, it was discovered that some of them were trying to build rafts. It appears that about 1,500 Axis soldiers tried to escape by sea in a variety of small craft, ranging from yachts to rubber dinghies. Eight hundred were plucked out of the water by Royal Navy destroyers who mercifully were not taking their orders to 'sink, burn and destroy' too literally. According to an Ultra decrypt, 636 officers and men got to Sicily.

At a conservative estimate at least 170,000 Axis soldiers remained in North Africa, of whom a minimum of 100,000 were German. These were divided between the Fifth Panzer Army in the north and Messe's First Italian Army, which was still mainly German.

The first mass surrenders came on the 9th, two days after the fall of Tunis, when General von Vaerst, commander of the Fifth Panzer Army, sent Arnim a message saying: 'Our armour and artillery have been destroyed. Without ammunition and fuel. We shall fight to last.' His men had other ideas, and by nightfall 40,000 of them had joined their general in captivity.

In Messe's sector the battle lasted a little longer. Tanks from the 6th Armoured Division turned south from Tunis and tried to seal off the Cape Bon peninsula. Then at Hamman Lif, where the hills fall almost into the sea and the coastal strip is at its narrowest, they were held up for two days by some 88-mm guns manned by Luftwaffe crews and supported by the remnants of 10th Panzer and the Hermann Goering Divisions. Eventually only a full-scale divisional night attack, which included a squadron of tanks charging along the beach, could overcome them.

The British continued south, dashing through the remaining Axis airfields, workshops, ammunition and fuel dumps. In their wake they left thousands of bewildered enemy troops, still with their personal weapons and adequately fed and watered, who did not seem to know whether to surrender or walk to Cape Bon and try to find a boat. The whole German command system had collapsed.

By the 10th, 6th Armoured had reached the rear areas of the Axis troops confronting the Eighth Army along the Enfidaville line and the first white flags began to appear. It would still be another two days before Arnim surrendered to the Royal Sussex and a ceasefire was agreed. A few hours before the end, Mussolini sent Messe a message promoting him to field marshal. Shortly afterwards Messe gave himself up to Freyberg and the following evening was invited to dine with Montgomery at Eighth Army headquarters at Sousse. They talked of 'various aspects' of the battles they had fought against each other, but it does not seem to have been as lively an occasion as Montgomery's encounter with von Thoma.

Alexander did not invite Arnim to dine at his mess but ordered his Australian aide-de-camp, Captain Rupert Clarke, to look after him and see that he was properly treated. This must have been satisfactory, for on leaving Arnim chose Clarke to be the recipient of his Leica camera and Zeiss binoculars – items that he would not have been allowed to take with him to the PoW camp the British maintained for senior German officers at Latimer in England.

During his first hours in captivity at Alexander's Tactical HQ, the Prussian was anxious to know how his defeat was being depicted on German radio and an operator in the Wireless Intelligence unit was ordered to monitor German news bulletins for him. He must have been relieved to learn that the German High Command had announced that, 'the heroic battle of the German and Italian African units had today reached its honourable conclusion'.

By 13 May 1942 more German soldiers had surrendered in Tunisia than the Russians captured at Stalingrad. Behind Goebbels's back, the Wehrmacht did not talk about an 'honourable conclusion'. They called it 'Tunisgrad'.

The day after Arnim's surrender, one of those incidents occurred which summed up the old desert war and its strange camaraderie between combatants. As men of the 90th Light and 21st Panzer Divisions marched towards a prisoner-of-war holding area, they encountered some of 7th Armoured Division moving in the opposite direction. The Desert Rats were instantly identifiable in their battered and varied sand-coloured transport, each vehicle with its rodent symbol painted in red on the mudguards. The Afrika Korps veterans were cheerful enough. They had acquitted themselves honourably, they had come out alive, and for them the war was now over. So as they marched they sang their favourite song: '*Vor der Kaserne/Bei dem grossen Tor/Stand eine Laterne/Und steht sie noch davor.*' And as they did so, their voices mingled with those of the Desert Rats. The words were different but it was the same song: 'Underneath the lamplight/By the barrack gate/Darling I remember/The way you used to wait.'

Lilli Marlene was fulfilling to the last her role as the shared feminine icon of the desert war.

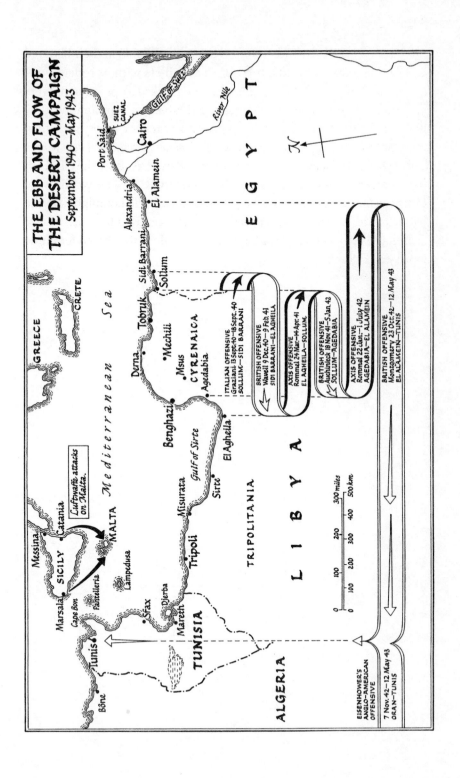

THE EBB AND FLOW OF
THE DESERT CAMPAIGN
September 1940–May 1943

GREECE

CRETE

Messina
SICILY
Catania
Marsala
Cape Bon
Pantelleria
Lampedusa
MALTA

Luftwaffe attacks
on Malta.

M e d i t e r r a n e a n   S e a

Tunis
Bône
TUNISIA
Sfax
Djerba
Mareth
ALGERIA

Misurata
Tripoli
Sirte
Gulf of Sirte
El Agheila

TRIPOLITANIA

Benghazi

Agedabia
Msus
Mechili
CYRENAICA
Derna
Tobruk
Sidi Barrani
Sollum

L   I   B   Y   A

Port Said
Alexandria
El Alamein

Cairo
SUEZ
CANAL
Gulf of Suez
River Nile

E   G   Y   P   T

N

0   100   200   300 miles
0   100   200   300   400   500 km.

ITALIAN OFFENSIVE
Graziani 13 Sept. 40–18 Sept. 40
SOLLUM–SIDI BARRANI

BRITISH OFFENSIVE
Wavell 9 Dec. 40–9 Feb. 41
SIDI BARRANI–EL AGHEILA

AXIS OFFENSIVE
Rommel 24 Mar.–14 Apr. 41
EL AGHEILA–SOLLUM

BRITISH OFFENSIVE
Auchinleck 18 Nov. 41–5 Jan. 43
SOLLUM–AGEDABIA

AXIS OFFENSIVE
Rommel 22 Jan.–1 July 42
AGEDABIA–EL ALAMEIN

BRITISH OFFENSIVE
Montgomery 23 Oct. 42–12 May 43
EL ALAMEIN–TUNIS

EISENHOWER'S
ANGLO-AMERICAN
OFFENSIVE
7 Nov. 42–12 May 43
ORAN–TUNIS

Requiem

El Alamein, Egypt, October 2000

Late October brings the first of the winter rains to the Western Desert, casting sombre clouds over the scene of battle as a scattering of the dwindling band of North African war veterans, augmented by relatives, descendants and dutiful diplomats, arrives to join in the memorial services that are held annually at the three main burial sites.

The British and Commonwealth War Cemetery is strikingly understated. Located in a dip in the mainly featureless desert, half way between the coast and the scruffy little town whose name has been a by-word since 1942, it is laid out so discreetly behind a sandstone wall that it is almost impossible to see from the road.

Once discovered, the ranks of marble headstones mark individual graves, their occupants identified by name, rank and unit where the remains were identifiable, and by the locution 'known unto God' where not. There are disconcertingly many whose shredded bodies, if known to Him, can only have been reassembled in the mind of their Maker.

A few miles west of the British war graves, just off the coast road to Mersa Matruh, the German memorial-cum-mausoleum offers an intriguingly assertive contrast. A massive rough-hewn octagon resembling a medieval castle, it is visible for miles around. Inside, there are no individual graves. The names of the known dead are inscribed collectively on bronze plaques above eight massive, but empty, catafalques while the bones of Rommel's fallen 'Afrikaners' repose in a grim chamber below the paved courtyard.

There is no formal entry to this crypt, but on a quiet day the Arab caretaker will take you down concrete steps into an eternal gloom where a guttering candle reveals a promiscuous tumble of metal containers, each holding a forlorn bundle of German bones.

The Italian memorial and burial site, a few miles further west, is even more conspicuous than the Germans' – a flat-topped, white marble pyramid, designed by the Alamein veteran and architect Paolo Caccia-Dominioni, who spent ten years after the war combing the desert for the forgotten remains of his comrades – and recovered many

Allied dead, too, in the process. His labour of love and remembrance is set on the summit of a modest *tel*, overlooking the sea. A long, ceremonial drive leads up to the pyramid, within which the remains of the dead, known and unknown alike, repose behind inscribed wall panels. As with the British and the Germans, a very large proportion of the Italian dead are 'known only to God'.

Doubtless there are undiscovered places where the bones of long-dead soldiers still shelter in their slit trenches. Like the sea, the desert is reluctant to give up all its secrets.

Reluctant, too, to give up the harvest of death sown there by the belligerents – the 24 million unexploded landmines which the Egyptian government claims still litter the battlefield. In the decades since the war they have killed or injured several thousand Egyptian civilians, mostly Bedouin herdsmen and their families.

Not all the war's detritus is quite so malign, though. In 1994, Egyptian paratroopers on an exercise around the southern flanks of the old El Alamein line came across an intact British three-ton truck, so wonderfully preserved by the arid desert air that, given a new battery, its engine started at the first touch. There were no visible human remains or graves near by.

At the shallow depression which the Rifle Brigade's Colonel Victor Buller Turner decided was the 'Snipe' position, the ground is still littered with the rusted debris of his battalion's stand against the Panzers – pieces of shrapnel, lengths of tank track, unexploded shells, large chunks of armour-piercing solid shot warheads and dozens of S-mines which appear to have been defused.

With dusk about to fall, the temperature drops as fast as the sinking sun. But it's not entirely the cold that makes a visitor shiver; this is a haunted place.

At the Commonwealth cemetery a multi-national service of remembrance is about to begin. Here the headstones of the identified dead bear individual inscriptions, offered by grieving next-of-kin. Some are of a throat-catching simplicity – '*The precious dust of our lovely lad from England is hidden here*', '*Our dear and only son, a constant thought, a glad remembrance*' – while a few reflect the English poetic heritage: '*He was a verray, parfit gentil knight*', '*I could not love thee dear so much, loved I not honour more.*'

A fleet of buses, taxis and diplomatic limousines brings an assortment of surviving desert war veterans, fewer in number year by year and soon to be extinct; a handful of widows still strong enough to make the journey; sons and daughters – now themselves greying – of those who died here; and a gaggle of ambassadors, first secretaries and defence attachés from Cairo's diplomatic corps.

Two Englishwomen, sisters well into their sixties, are making a belated first pilgrimage to the grave of their father, Lieutenant-Colonel John Evatt, officer commanding the 21st Anti-tank Regiment, Royal Artillery, a professional soldier who was killed on the fourth day of the battle. His daughters, Judith and Jancis, were four and six years old respectively at the time; a third daughter, fleetingly conceived during Colonel Evatt's embarkation leave, was yet unborn.

The colonel's widow never remarried. The daughter she was carrying when her husband was killed died earlier this year of cancer. At their father's grave, the surviving sisters use a borrowed hotel spoon to dig an inch or two down into the loose sand. Then, into the shallow depression beneath the headstone they tip the contents of a small casket they have brought from England – the mingled ashes of their mother and their sister. These they cover over, to blend in with desert soil that covers their father.

No tears; the daughters of the bygone Empire do not weep.

The Italians are more demonstrative. There are unashamed tears on the face of Aroldo Conticello, the shoemaker's son from Orvieto, who lost both hands and an eye to a British grenade at Alamein, as he stands to attention in memory of his comrades of the Folgore Parachute Division.

Among the German veterans, widows, sons and daughters, one eighty-five-year-old woman is here to mourn not a countryman but one of the 'enemy' – a young Englishman she met in France during the Munich crisis of 1938 and who, it seems, she can never forget. Wilna Fausten, then a student of modern languages and art history at Heidelberg, and Quentin Drage, reading history at Christ Church, Oxford, were perfecting their French at a summer school in Normandy when they met during the summer of 1938. The following summer, defying the proscriptions of both sets of parents and the imminent prospect of war, they were reunited, became lovers, and vowed to marry. It was too late. Within three weeks of their parting the war broke out. Quentin volunteered for the army and Wilna was directed to translation work by the Nazi *Arbeitsdienst*.

Young Drage was killed while serving as an anti-tank artillery officer with the Eighth Army. Wilna did not discover his fate until after the war. She never married, and now she makes an annual pilgrimage to El Alamein, driven, she says, by love and guilt – 'Love for Quentin and guilt on behalf of the horrible race that started the war he died in.'

Three trumpet calls – the British 'Last Post', the German 'Gute Kamerad' and the Italian 'Silenzio' – conclude the service of commemoration. The mourners disperse, silence once more envelops the cemetery and only the desert wind stirs the sand around the headstones. Soon there will be no veterans of Alamein left alive to make the annual pilgrimage and within twenty years or so even the children of the war dead will be gone. Will any then remember this historic battle?

In the middle of this twenty-first century some backpacker yet unborn may chance upon this place, recall vaguely that it was the scene of 'a famous victory' and wonder, like Old Kaspar after Blenheim, what was the point of it all.

He should know that El Alamein was the place where at last – and even before Stalingrad – the most voraciously effective war-machine in history, and the gangster regime it served, was stopped in its tracks and then turned back.

A war without hate the Desert War might perhaps have been; a war without point it surely was not.

Acknowledgements and Sources

This account of the war in North Africa 1940–43 occupies a border land between historiography and journalism. We make no overweening claims for the former and offer no apologies for the latter.

We have throughout been faithful to the norms and customs of historiography and we have refused to allow the journalism, of which black art we are both experienced and responsible practitioners, to be compromised by chauvinism, exaggeration or ideology (apart from an innate preference for democracy over dictatorship).

While there remained time to do so, we conducted widespread interviews with the ageing veterans of all nationalities who fought in that campaign. Occasionally, but not nearly as often as might be imagined, allowances had to be made for damage inflicted and smoke screens laid by what Abraham Lincoln called, 'the artillery of time'. Wherever possible, veterans' recollections were cross-checked against each other and the written record and confirmed by the more contemporaneous personal recollections of men, since deceased, that we obtained from both published and archival sources in Britain, Germany, Italy, Australia, New Zealand and South Africa.

These bright threads of personal experience – tragic, comic, horrific and sometimes merely banal – were then woven into the big picture of high-level folly, cold *Realpolitik* and bumbling grand strategy to re-create a panoply of mid-twentieth-century warfare, the exact like of which we can mercifully not expect to see again.

To all those who shared their recollections with us, directly or indirectly, the living and the dead, go our special thanks. These individuals are all clearly identified in the text and our source notes, but we may be forgiven for singling out (Major) Sam Bradshaw, chairman of the Eighth Army Veterans' Association, both for his general assistance and for his absorbing personal recollections, and Hans-Gunther Stark, archivist of the Afrika Korps Verband, for access to his extensive files and photographs.

In London, both the Public Record Office and the National Army Museum provided some unexpected trophies. But we are particularly indebted to the Imperial War Museum in London and its Keeper of Documents, Roderick Suddaby, and his staff for their invaluable assistance in research. The IWM is a priceless national resource and, belying the resonances of its name, a long way from being a mere glorification of Britain's martial past.

Thanks also to Vernon Scannell, the best of the surviving Second World War poets, for permission to adapt his 'El Alamein: 50th Anniversary' as an epigraph for this sixtieth anniversary volume, and for other favours; to Willi Dietl for his assistance in covering the Eighth Army/Afrika Korps veterans' reunion; to Gina Pietralunga and the Italian Army generals Guialtieri Stefanon and Giovanni Cerbo for their assistance in textual and photographic research; to Colonel Simon Doughty who, with the aid of a navigational system beyond the wildest dreams of our desert warriors, guided one of us to the position at El Alamein the Rifle Brigade called Snipe; for further guidance to the surviving veterans of that action from Major (retd) K. Gray, the Curator of the Royal Green Jackets' Museum at Peninsular Barracks, Winchester. Our thanks, too, to Alex Berger-Almasy for permission use the photograph of her grand-uncle, László Almásy; to Laurence Pollinger Ltd, and the estate of Alan Moorehead for permission to quote extensively from Moorehead's *African Trilogy* and to Victor Selwyn and the Salamander Oasis Trust for permission to quote from the poetry anthology, *The Voice of War*.

Sources

IWM = Imperial War Museum archive.
PRO = Public Record Office.

Chapter 1

p. 12   Mussolini 'must do something': Wavell to Sir John Dill, CIGS, quoted in Connell, *Wavell, Soldier and Scholar*, p. 229.

pp. 12–13   Flying and spying: King-Clark, *Free for a Blast*, p. 107 et seq.

pp. 13–14   Italian military statistics: *Oxford Companion to the Second World War*.

p. 15   'A few thousand dead': Badoglio, *L'Italia nella seconda guerra mondiale*, p. 58.

p. 16   Missing machine-guns: Leakey/Forty, *Leakey's Luck*, p. 23.

p. 16   The general's mistress: *The Years of Defeat, Regimental History of RA*, p. 122.

p. 17   Cleere's 'mutiny': Cleere memoir, IWM, 67/279/1.

Chapter 2

p. 22   'I increased speed': Bagnold, *Libyan Sands*, pp. 157–8.

p. 22   'too much dash had its penalties': Maclean, *Eastern Approaches*, p. 232.

p. 22   'Never in our peacetime travels': Bagnold, IWM Sound Archive, 9862/3.

p. 23   'What a man!': Bagnold, *Sand, Wind and War*, p. 125.

p. 24   'the strange new life': ibid., p. 129.

p. 24   'we could not travel': IWM, op. cit.

p. 25   'During the next few months': *Sand, Wind and War*, p. 131.

p. 25   'temperatures exceeding 50°': ibid., p. 136.

p. 26   'no longer feeling at my best': ibid., p. 137.

Chapter 3

p. 28   'radiant with joy': Ciano, *Diaries*, p. 45.

p. 28   'We're trying to fight this war': Moorehead, *African Trilogy*, p. 70.

p. 29   'Taro, chinas': Crimp memoir in IWM archives 96/50/1 and PP/MCR 245.

p. 29   'The Germans are bombing': Ranfurly, *To War with Whitaker*, p. 49.

p. 30   'hard-riding, hard-drinking': Verney, *Going to the Wars*, pp. 13–39.

p. 31   'Brindians' et seq.: Mason, *A Matter of Honour*, pp. 458–66.

p. 32   'cowardice of the British': quoted in Moorehead, op. cit., p. 70.

Chapter 4

p. 36   'Even when it had a height advantage': post-war correspondence between Air-Vice Marshal Sir John Lapsley and Col. Rex King-Clark.

p. 37   'in a few weeks the raiders': IWM, SA 1172/E/E.

p. 37   'we bagged one or two': IWM, SA 1160/H/A.

p. 37   'never very accurate': IWM, SA 1161/H/B.

p. 38   'The Italians didn't like it': IWM, 76/26/1.

p. 38   'a big problem for us': IWM, SA 12528/4/2.

p. 39   'He prays aloud': Mountbatten to Sir Robert Neville, 8/5/41, quoted in Ziegler, *Mountbatten*, p. 142 (N.B. Ziegler misreads 'Dobbie' for 'Bobbie').

p. 39   'summoned for prayer': Strickland, IWM, 76/26/1.

p. 40   'outstanding character': Churchill, *The Second World War*, Vol. 3, p. 62.

p. 40   'just my affair': Channon, *Letters*, p. 82.

p. 41   'enjoyable, of course': Coward, *Middle East Diary*, p. 49.

p. 41   'French in spirit': Beaton, *Near East*, pp. 27, 29–30.

p. 41   'a blazing town': Durrell, *Spirit of Place*, pp. 74–5.

p. 46   'five acres of officers': Collier, *The War in the Desert*, p. 28.

p. 47   'a very unpleasant surprise': O'Connor, O'Connor transcript, National Army Museum archives, London, Ref. 6312–29.

p. 47   'The driver was killed': Leakey, *Leakey's Luck*, p. 47.

p. 48   'a small beer barrel': Cleere, IWM, 67/279/1.

p. 48   'A gas mask haversack': Tutt, IWM, 67/324/1.

p. 48   'men from the dockside': Moorehead, *African Trilogy*, p. 87.

p. 48   'laid out with clean sheets': ibid., p. 89.

p. 49   'This is a good war': Bird to father, 24/1/40 (private collection).

p. 49   'couldn't help feeling sorry': ibid., 12/2/41.

p. 49   'a great bit of luck': ibid., 2/3/41.

p. 50   'coming in by the hundreds': Leakey, op. cit., p. 52.

Chapter 5

p. 53   'very daring and skilful': Churchill, op. cit., Vol. 4, p. 69.

p. 54   'Where Rommel is': quoted in Gilbert, *The First World War*, p. 127.

p. 54   'under the spell': 1941 German magazine biography, quoted in Irving, *The Trail of the Fox*, p. 13.

p. 55   Fall of Longarone: ibid., p. 16.

p. 57   broad Schwabian accent: author interview with Willi Utz and Hans-Gunther Stark, October 1999.

p. 57   'a bright fellow': Schmidt, *With Rommel in the Desert*, p. 164.

Chapter 6

p. 59   'we were watching experts': Cunningham, *A Sailor's Odyssey*, p. 303.

p. 60   'a struggle for existence': Lee, IWM, op. cit.

p. 60   'really meant business': Paine, IWM, op. cit.

p. 60   'asphyxiated . . . by dust': Heffernan, IWM, 91/29/1.

p. 61   'sad and disgusting' et seq.: Blois-Brooke, IWM, 95/5/1.

p. 61   'my hands grew cold': Fleming, IWM, 87/23/1.

p. 62   'striding into my office': Strickland, IWM, op. cit.

p. 62   'little excuse': *Times of Malta*, 20–23 Jan. 1941.

p. 62   'a comforting sight': Frank de Domenico, quoted in Jellison, *Besieged*, p. 205.

p. 62   'cheering all over': Paine, IWM, op. cit.

p. 63   'given up counting': Cunningham, op. cit., p. 39.

Chapter 7

p. 65   'no resistance worthy of the name': *Rommel Papers*, p. 94.

p. 66   down to the sea with a bucket: Bowden, IWM, 91/26/1.

p. 66   urinating into the radiators: Cleere memoir, IWM, 67/279/1.

p. 66   'numerous disgraceful incidents': Neame to Morshead, 31/3/41, quoted in Maughan, *Tobruk and El Alamein*, p. 44.

p. 67   His 5th Light Division: all tank figures from ibid., pp. 19–20.

p. 68   'Only then did the penny drop': Schmidt, op. cit., p. 16.

p. 69   'waiting for the tortoise': Churchill, op. cit., Vol. 3, p. 165.

p. 69   'like a field full of lancers': Tutt, IWM, 67/324/1 memoir et seq.

p. 69   'Take this for London': Bowden memoir, IWM, 91/26/1 et seq.

p. 70   'of little military importance': Maughan, op. cit., p. 40.

p. 71   'the rot seemed to set in': Tutt, op. cit.

p. 71   'a ghostly sight': *Die Oase*, Afrika Korps veterans' magazine, Limburg, Germany, 1986

p. 72   'too far to the north': O'Connor transcript, National Army Museum archives, London, Ref. 6312–29.

p. 73   'It was very dark': Ranfurly, op. cit., p. 232.

p. 73   dumps of petrol, food and ammunition: Maughan, op. cit., p. 77.

p. 74   The Rommel–Streich row: Irving, *The Trail of the Fox*, p. 74.

p. 75   'permissible booty': Schmidt, op. cit., p. 38.

Chapter 8

p. 78   'It was pandemonium': Rolf-Werner Völker, author interview, July 2000.

p. 79   'about to open fire on you': quoted in Irving, op. cit., p. 78.

p. 79   'held to the death': Churchill, op. cit., p. 169.

p. 79   'Still he ran on': Maughan, op. cit., p. 148.

p. 80   'quiet, courageous': Ellis memoir, IWM, PP/MCR/388.

p. 80   'the first shot': ibid.

p. 81   'already on fire': Schorm, Joachim, 5th Panzer Regiment. As quoted in Harrison, *Tobruk – the Great Siege Reassessed*.

p. 81   'safe to lie low': McGinley memoir, IWM, 93/11/1 et seq.

p. 82   'We all had dysentery': Youden–author interview, October 1999.

p. 82   'couldn't let your mates down': Lockwood–author interview, October 1999.

p. 82   'We could see the bodies': quoted in Wilmot, *Tobruk*, p. 200.

p. 83   'Hit him between the eyes': Leakey, op. cit., p. 82.

Chapter 9

pp. 91ff. Details of Rommel raid in IWM, 93/17/1.

p. 93   'Geoffrey closed with him': ibid.

p. 93   Corporal Barth's barricade: Carell, *The Foxes of the Desert*, p. 97.

p. 94   Campbell's survival: IWM, file, op. cit.

p. 94   'for the most part ineffective': Laycock, PRO DEF 2/205.

p. 95   'I have a scheme': Ranfurly, op. cit., p. 98.

pp. 95–6 Birth of the SAS: Otway, *British Airborne Forces*, pp. 101–3.

p. 96   'the stormy blackness': Pleydell (aka Malcolm James), *Born of the Desert*, cited in Otway, op. cit., pp. 103–4.

Chapter 10

p. 102   'undreamed-of advantages': Caccia-Dominioni, *Alamein 1933–1962*, p. 209 et seq.

p. 102   'swearing to take vengeance': Bird to mother, 14/1/42 (private collection).

p. 104   'sheer stupidity': Parry memoir, IWM, 83/24/1.

p. 105   Defeat at Bir el Gubi: Liddell-Hart, *History of the Second World War*, p. 186.

p. 106   Startled by 'flamers': H. L. Sykes memoir, IWM, 78/74/1.

p. 107   'moving up to the scarp line': Hall–author interview, October 1999.

p. 107   'a tank commander's battle': CB P108 PRO.

p. 108   'ever decreasing circles': Close, *A View from the Turret*, p. 62.

p. 108   'a sordid cemetery': ibid., p. 66.

p. 108   'could knock us out': Bradshaw–author interviews, October 1999.

p. 109   'sitting on its roof': ibid., June 2000.

p. 109   'Nobody relishes the job': Crimp, IWM, 96/50/1.

p. 110   order had been 'a mistake': Young, *Rommel the Desert Fox*, pp. 163–4.

p. 110   'I drew alongside' et seq.: Bradshaw–author interviews, Oct. 1999, June 2000.

p. 112   'You have the chance': quoted in Young, op. cit., p. 189.

p. 113 'a shoal of mackerel': Moorehead, op. cit., pp. 226–7.

p. 114 'Attack . . . relentlessly': Parkinson, *The Auk*, p. 129.

p. 114 'A rainbow cake': Moorehead, op. cit., p. 229.

p. 114 Some 30,000 vehicles: Fraser, *And We Shall Shock Them*, p. 162.

pp. 114–15 Rommel at clearing station: Young, op. cit., p. 122.

p. 115 'Let sleeping generals lie': ibid., p. 124.

p. 118 'this lush valley': Moorehead, op. cit., p. 242.

p. 118 'Since it was Christmas Eve': Schmidt, *With Rommel in the Desert*, p. 122 et seq.

p. 119 'an almighty bang': Doughty memoir, IWM, 95/12/1.

Chapter 11

p. 121 'Malta completely eliminated': Bekker, *The Luftwaffe Diaries*, p. 7.

p. 121 'Three submarines sunk': Brighton memoir, IWM, 94/6/1.

p. 122 'Constant raids as before': Bates diary, IWM, 90/30/1.

p. 122 'Only five of us airborne': anon. pilot memoir, IWM SO 1163/H/D.

p. 123 'Would you be willing': Churchill, op. cit., p. 231.

p. 123 'one big dogfight': anon. pilot, op. cit.

p. 123 'our red letter day': Lee memoir, IWM, op. cit.

p. 123 'Who says a Wasp can't sting twice?': Churchill, op. cit., p. 255.

p. 124 'stupefying in its openness': Behrend, *Rommel's Intelligence in the Desert Campaign*, p. 146.

p. 124 Black Code theft: Norman, *Secret Warfare*, pp. 123–31.

p. 125 'They went crazy': ibid., p. 125.

p. 126 'instead of being the best': PRO, P20 WO 208/3575.

p. 127 'to inform us so well': Kahn, *Hitler's Spies*, p. 185.

p. 127 'friendship produced the information': Fellers, cable No. 852, US National Military Archives (USNMA), File 201.

p. 127 'an original person': Ranfurly, op. cit., p. 78.

p. 127 'top brass over-confident': ibid., p. 117.

p. 128 'Rommel knew exactly': Norman, op. cit., p. 127.

p. 128 'my position should be made clear': Fellers, cable No. 989, USNMA.

p. 128 'to avoid conflicting activities': Maxwell, cable No. 21, USNMA.

p. 128 'a wealth of information': Strong to Marshall, 28/6/42, USNMA.

p. 128 'not repeat not desired': Marshall to Maxwell, 4/7/42, USNMA.

p. 129 'highly desirable': Strong to Marshall, 9/7/42, USNMA.

p. 129 'all we needed to know': cited in Irving, op. cit., p. 180.

p. 129 'clarity, brevity and accuracy': MIS/I WWC 2177, USNMA.

p. 130 'no friend of mine': Ranfurly, op. cit., p. 202.

Chapter 12

p. 133 'infuriated the forward troops': Messervy, quoted in Barnett, op. cit., p. 131.

p. 133 'it is NOT my intention': Auchinleck to Ritchie, Operational Instruction 110 of 19/1/42, PRO WO 169/3795.

p. 134 'two hours from now': letter cited in Pimlott, *Rommel in His Own Words*, p. 86.

p. 135 thirty battle-worthy Valentines: Mitcham, *Hitler's Commanders*, p. 21.

p. 135 'the British fled madly': von Mellenthin, *Panzer Battles*, p. 119.

p. 135 'We leapfrogged': Schmidt, op. cit., p. 126.

p. 135 'further things from Tommy's supply dump': cited in Forty, *The Afrika Korps at War*, Vol. 2, p. 15.

p. 137 'a very daring and skilful opponent': *Hansard*, 27/1/41.

p. 137 'a land rich in raw materials': Rommel, quoted in Pimlott, op. cit., p. 89.

Chapter 13

p. 140 'the doorbell rang': author–Rabin interview, March 1999.

p. 141 'used for infiltration': Airey to DDO, 1/4/42, PRO WO 201/732.

p. 141 'a sort of Q-ship': Airey to Haselden, 16/3/42, PRO WO201/727.

p. 142 'Don't answer now': author–Shai interview, January 1999.

p. 143 'brilliant, but naïve': author–Carmi interview, January 1999.

p. 143 'tall, handsome, very blond': Rabin, loc. cit.

p. 144 'tired of bully beef': Shai, loc. cit.

p. 145 'Get away fast': ibid.

p. 146 'ill with shame and anger': Tiefenbrunner, *A Long Journey Home*, p. 40.

p. 146 'very upset': Shai, loc. cit.

p. 146 'sick at heart': Carmi, loc. cit.

p. 147 Klager and Korner: PRO WO201/727.

p. 148 Schaedel's account: Norman, *Secret Warfare*, p. 129; also in Kahn, *Hitler's Spies*, pp. 184–5.

Chapter 14

p. 149 'Twenty-one years old and crazy': quoted in Forty, op. cit., Vol. 1, p. 29.

p. 150 'what wonderful things': ibid., p. 30.

p. 151 British soldiers usually thought it quite awful: author interviews with various veterans.

p. 151 'hot ice cream': Ellis, *The Sharp End of the War*, p. 285.

p. 152 'nigger sweat': author interview, Rolf-Werner Völker, July 2000.

p. 152 reverently parcelled up: Mitcham, op. cit., p. 51.

p. 154 Tank figures from Playfair, *History of the Second World War*, Vol. III: *The Mediterranean and the Middle East*, p. 220.

p. 155 'he is NOT snooping!': Greacen, *Chink*, p. 191.

p. 157 '*embarras de Ritchies*': ibid., p. 196.

p. 157 personal prejudices had to be set aside: Dorman-Smith papers, John Rylands Library, Manchester University.

p. 158 'Was it so hot?': Irving, op. cit., p. 103.

p. 159 'didn't speak German properly': author interview, Munninger, July 2000.

Chapter 15

p. 164 'I'm a Cherman': Lt.-Col. Michael Parker, IWM, 88/4/1.

p. 164 'German political refugees': PRO HW1/643.

p. 165 Lost thirty-two tanks: Bergot, *The Afrika Korps*, pp. 133–4.

p. 165 'a cloud of dust': Major D. F. Parry, IWM, 83/24/1.

pp. 166–7 'the whole bloody German army': General Sir John Hackett, IWM Sound Archives 004527/06.

p. 167 'Aren't you a bit old': Maule, *Spearhead General*, p. 179.

p. 168 'Bravo Eighth Army': message cited in Mitcham, op. cit., p. 86.

p. 168 'we cannot go on like this': Young, *Rommel the Desert Fox*, p. 142.

p. 168 Indian prisoners were released: Holmes, *Bir Hacheim*, p. 112.

p. 169 'considerable skill and courage': Pimlott, op. cit., p. 101.

p. 170 'Wave a white flag': Mitcham, op. cit., p. 91.

p. 170 Difference could not have been greater: Sir Edward Tomkins–author interview, October 2000.

p. 170 don't worry, they'll be back': Munninger–author interview, July 2000.

p. 171 'at least four direct hits': Leakey, op. cit., p. 96.

p. 171 'more useless blood': Holmes, op. cit., p. 117.

p. 174 'Shells were falling around us': Travers, *Tomorrow to Be Brave*, p. 178.

p. 176 'realities being faced calmly': cited in Connell, op. cit., p. 563.

p. 176 'with the help of a sandstorm': Foote, IWM Sound Archives 10413/17.

p. 177 'like a naughty child': Völker–author interview, July 2000.

p. 177 'so many dead Englishmen': Munninger, loc. cit.

p. 177 'going very well indeed': quoted in Agar-Hamilton, *Crisis in the Desert*, p. 129.

p. 178 Tobruk 'dominated the tactics': quoted in Parkinson, *The Auk*, p. 184.

p. 178 'Presume there is no question': Churchill, op. cit., p. 340.

p. 180 'not a single professional soldier': preface to Rosmarin, *Inside Story*, p. 3.

p. 181 'We lay on our bellies': Schmidt, op. cit., p. 145.

p. 181 'Never have I seen': Quilter, *No Dishonourable Name*, p. 132.

p. 182 'On we went': cited in Pimlott, op. cit., p. 112.

p. 182 million and a half gallons: Mitcham, op. cit., p. 175.

p. 182 Löwenbräu beer: Forty, op. cit., Vol. 2, p. 46.

p. 182 'Shoot, man, shoot!': Mitcham, op. cit., p. 176.

p. 182 'some of the surgeons': Major A. O. McGinley, IWM, 93/11/1.

p. 183 'My crust is broken!': Colonel F. M. V. Tregear memoir, IWM, 94/78/1.

p. 183 'itching to fight': ibid.

p. 183 'There'll Always Be an England': Gunner W. A. Lewis memoir, IWM, 88/60/1.

pp. 183–4 'They've surrendered?': Mitcham, op. cit., p. 182.

Chapter 16

p. 188 'never trusted [Almasy]': Bagnold, quoted in Gordon, *The Other Desert War*, p. 99.

p. 189 Operation Salaam diary: in Lloyd-Owen Papers, IWM, 15/5/42.

p. 193 'Sandy gasped': Eppler, *Operation Condor*, p. 217.

p. 194 'Sadat was shocked': Sadat, *Revolt on the Nile*, p. 47.

p. 196 'a Hungarian desert enthusiast': Bagnold, *Sand, Wind and War*, p. 155.

p. 196 'a Nazi but a sportsman': *Geographic Journal*, Vol. 117, Jan.–Dec. 1951.

Chapter 17

p. 197 'the last obstacle': Pimlott, op. cit., p. 117.

p. 197 'At all costs': Playfair, op. cit., p. 147.

p. 198 'Advance Rommel': Sadat, op. cit., p. 32.

p. 198 'the attitude was rude': Samwell, *An Infantry Officer with the Eighth Army*, p. 21.

p. 198 'You're just in time': ibid., p. 15.

p. 201 'so contemptible an enemy': Greacen, op. cit., p. 212.

p. 201 'One man . . . wanted to fight': extract from Nell's unpublished memoirs, quoted in anthology *Private Words*, ed. Blythe, pp. 84–5.

p. 202 howling Kiwis: McLeod, *Myth and Reality*, p. 86.

p. 202 'My headquarters were soon surrounded': Pimlott, op. cit., p. 116.

p. 203 'the Boche is flat out': Greacen, op. cit., p. 209.

p. 204 'British shells whistled in': Pimlott, op. cit., p. 120.

p. 205 'The battles . . . are hard': ibid., p. 122.

p. 205 'Dearest Lu' letters: Pimlott, op. cit., pp. 125–7.

p. 206 'Hey, Vic, they're coming in': Keith Murdoch Sound Archive Int. No. S555.

p. 208 'You have done well': Parkinson, *The Auk*, p. 213.

p. 209 'As the [German] tanks closed in': Manghan, op. cit., p. 595.

Chapter 18

p. 213 'inexplicable inertia': Bryant, *The Turn of the Tide*, p. 361.

p. 214 'very tiresome': Churchill, op. cit., Vol. 4, p. 374.

p. 214 'Instead of sitting at home': ibid.

p. 214 'with a wooden box': Bryant, op. cit., p. 364.

p. 215 'Too great a man': IWM, 84/1027 Gott file. Extracted from a letter dated June 1983 Field Marshal Lord Carver wrote to Mr J. A. J. Agar-Hamilton, one of the joint authors of the Official South African history of the campaign.

p. 216 'sitting at tea together': Bryant, op. cit., p. 368.

p. 216 'three months' leave': Churchill, op. cit., p. 376.

p. 217 'full of flies': ibid.

p. 217 'I remember noticing': de Guingand, *Operation Victory*, p. 134.

p. 217 'a gay occasion': Churchill, op. cit., p. 377.

p. 217 'This made my heart race': Bryant, op. cit., p. 369.

p. 219 'absolutely scared to death' et seq.: author interview, May 1999.

p. 220 'the hand of God': Alanbrooke diary, 23 March 1945. Quoted in General David Fraser's *Alanbrooke*, p. 455.

p. 220 'the scene of decisive operations': Churchill, op. cit., p. 383.

p. 221 'it was a backwater': Parkinson, *The Auk*, pp. 224–5.

p. 221 'What else matters?': Churchill, quoting Jacob's diary, op. cit., p. 384.

Chapter 19

p. 223 ten shillings a week: Hamilton, *Monty*, Vol. 1, p. 30.

p. 223 'Disobedience brought swift punishment': Montgomery, *Memoirs*, p. 16.

p. 224 'confronted by a large German': ibid., p. 29.

p. 225 'Clever, energetic, ambitious': Hamilton, op. cit., p. 213.

p. 225 'his little-man walk': Greacen, op. cit., p. 100.

p. 225 'worse than the Great War': Montgomery, op. cit., p. 34.

p. 226 'Cromwell or the Germans': quoted in Hamilton, op. cit., p. 151.

p. 226 'sorry to leave Palestine': Hamilton (Vol. 1) p. 290.

p. 226 'Women never interested me': Montgomery, op. cit., p. 36.

p. 227 'terribly disorganized': Hamilton (Vol. 1), quoting Montgomery's stepson, Richard Carver.

p. 227 'a very good Colonel's lady': Montgomery, op. cit., p. 37.

p. 227 'utterly defeated': ibid., p. 38.

p. 228 'he'll never see action': Hamilton, op. cit., p. 293.

p. 229 'a pathetic sight': Montgomery, op. cit., p. 54.

p. 230 'like a 15-inch shell': letter to Colonel Kit Dawnay, quoted in Hamilton, Vol. 1, p. 452.

p. 230 'our worst enemy': Hamilton, Vol. 1, p. 476.

p. 231 'enough to lower . . . morale': Montgomery, op. cit., p. 86.

p. 232 'stand and fight': PRO cabinet office historical section 106/703.

Chapter 20

p. 233 'amid the sand dunes': Churchill, op. cit., p. 418.

p. 233 'perspiring profusely': Flatow memoir, IWM, 99/16/1.

p. 234 'The corn will be ripe': PRO CAB 106/783.

p. 234 'a scalding broth': Churchill, op. cit., p. 420.

p. 234 'So he sat outside': ibid., p. 420.

p. 234 'what a change there was': ibid., p. 419.

p. 235 'the first of a long series': von Mellenthin, op. cit., p. 142.

p. 236 'peeing in our bags': quoted in Hamilton, op. cit., p. 642.

p. 237 'The swine isn't attacking': ibid., p. 641.

p. 238 'Egypt has been saved': Hamilton, op. cit., Vol. 1, p. 662.

p. 238 'a kind of magician': Parkinson, op. cit., p. 172.

p. 239 'a bit cheesed off': Fraser memoir, IWM, SA 10259/5.

p. 241 'anxiously awaiting': Churchill, op. cit., p. 474.

p. 241 'no ideas of his own': quoted in Fraser, *Alanbrooke*, p. 353.

p. 241 'preparations could not be completed': Montgomery, op. cit., p. 102.

p. 241 'Now, Alex, I won't do it': quoted in Hamilton, op. cit., p. 701.

p. 242 'My stock was high': Montgomery, op. cit., p. 103.

p. 242 'We are in your hands': Churchill, op. cit., p. 474.

p. 242 'they must be worked up': quoted in Hamilton, op. cit., p. 712.

p. 242 'even the padres': de Guingand, op. cit., p. 186.

Chapter 21

p. 243 'low grade elements': PRO WO 201/751.

p. 244 'Lovely dark Syrian heads': Peniakoff, *Popski's Private Army*, p. 194.

p. 244 'Serious Breach of Security': PRO WO 201/49.

p. 244 'Why my force had arrived late': Smith, *Massacre at Tobruk*, p. 11.

p. 244 'much too well informed': Maclean, op. cit., p. 229.

p. 245 'to clearly understand': PRO WO 201/751.

p. 245 'the most hazardous phase': ibid.

p. 246 'take the garrison by surprise': Maclean, op. cit., p. 230.

p. 247 'Minefields had been laid': ibid., p. 235.

p. 247 'A dozen machine-guns': ibid., p. 239.

p. 247 'we headed out of it': Sherwood, IWM, 9783/8.

p. 247 'Haselden came running': Hillman, PRO WO 201/751.

p. 248 'We changed his name' et seq.: Langton, ibid.

Chapter 22

p. 255 'I cannot conceive': Maughan, op. cit., p. 663.

p. 255 Italians had a trick: History of 44 Division, Vol. 2, p. 107, IWM 02 (41) 41.

p. 257 Wounded German officers: McKee, *El Alamein: Ultra and the Three Battles*, p. 120.

p. 258 'the troops of this division': 44 Divn History, Vol. 2, p. 116.

p. 260 'well above average': 44 Divn Intelligence summary, 17 August 1942, Divisional History, IWM 02 (41) 41.

p. 260 'In a matter of seconds': Norris memoir, IWM, 80/18/1.

p. 262 'I had already imported': Montgomery, op. cit., p. 99.

p. 263 'able to have a good look': ibid., p. 95.

p. 263 'a certain tactic': ibid., p. 104.

p. 264 'If I was not careful': ibid., p. 104.

p. 264 'beaten the guts': Brooks, *Montgomery and the Eighth Army*, p. 67.

p. 264 'Our troops must not think': ibid., p. 68.

p. 265 'to take the enemy's tanks apart': author interview with Nino Arena, Folgore Divn Historian.

p. 268 'a size too small for him': Caccia-Dominioni, op. cit., p. 210.

p. 268 'roll call of the Empire': Maughan, op. cit., pp. 664–5.

p. 268 'Technically a "Scientific Instrument"': Miles memoir, IWM, 86/25/1.

p. 269 'wondering rather wistfully': Flatow memoir, IWM, 99/16/1.

p. 269 Private Arthur Kennett: author interview, May 2001.

pp. 269–70 Major Robert Snowdon: *Daily Telegraph* obituary, 1997.

p. 270 'YES DARLING': Cope memoir, IWM, 80/37/1 & 1a.

p. 271 'a spectator for a great event': Samwell, op. cit., p. 28.

p. 272 volunteered 'as a lark': Scannell–author interview, 1999.

pp. 272–3 Lieutenant Keith Douglas: Graham, *Keith Douglas 1920–1944*, p. 161.

p. 274 Pre-battle dental check: Neillands, *The Desert Rats*, p. 153.

p. 274 'in exactly two hours' time': Maughan, op. cit., p. 665.

p. 275 'Zip': Churchill, op. cit., p. 475.

p. 275 'great possibilities and great dangers': Bryant, op. cit., p. 420.

Chapter 23

p. 276 Forty-eight shells a minute: Carver, *El Alamein*, p. 100.

p. 276 'a giant . . . fist': Neillands, op. cit., p. 151.

p. 276 'The . . . stars were shaken': Schmidt, op. cit., p. 175.

p. 276 'one sheet of incandescence': Caccia-Dominioni, op. cit., p. 210.

p. 277 'a real tough guy': Neillands, op. cit., p. 151.

p. 277 'Nothing had been seen like it': IWM Sound Archives 10923/17.

p. 277 beginning to regret it: McKee, op. cit., p. 147.

p. 278 'a wonderful sight': Brooks, op. cit., p. 71.

p. 278 'There was nothing I could do': Montgomery, *Memoirs*, p. 113.

p. 278 'It really got us going': Lunn–author interview, October 1999.

p. 278 school sports days: Scannell–author interview, April 2001.

p. 279 'Keep up there': Samwell, op. cit., p. 30.

p. 279 'as if on exercise': Close, op. cit., p. 82.

p. 279 'the only real soldiers': Sergeant Geordie Reay of 3rd Royal Tank Regiment, as quoted in Patrick Delaforce's *Montgomery's Highlanders*, pp. 54–5.

p. 280 fingers still on the chanter: Fergusson, *The Black Watch*, p. 128.

p. 280 instinct made him jump: Samwell, op. cit., p. 31.

p. 280 'something . . . like "Mardray"': ibid., p. 31.

p. 281 'a sergeant . . . quite close to me': Scannell, *Argument of Kings*, pp. 165–6.

p. 281 For the 26-hour period: all casualty figures from IWM, Montgomery Papers BLM 28/1.

p. 283 'I saw Herbert Lumsden': Montgomery's diary notes, 24/10/42, Army Records Society.

p. 283 'a stoat on a rabbit': quoted in Hamilton, op. cit., p. 744.

p. 284 thought the French had let him down badly: IWM, Montgomery Papers BLM 49/12.

p. 284 'a snake-like procession': Horrocks, *Corps Commander*, p. 82.

p. 284 'once daylight came': Neillands, op. cit., p. 149.

p. 284 'We followed what was left': ibid., p. 153.

p. 285 'emphatic orders': Horrocks, op. cit., p. 84.

p. 285 'an 88-mm, I think': Neillands, op. cit., p. 154.

p. 286 'splendid American academic': Miles memoir, IWM, 86/25/1.

p. 286 'rather sheepishly': Neillands, op. cit., p. 156.

Chapter 24

p. 288 the 15 October prediction: Fraser, op. cit., p. 368.

p. 289 Operation 'Slender': details from CAB106/758 PRO, London, and David Fisher, *The War Magician*, pp. 294–5.

p. 289 Many British sailors . . . mystified: author interview with CPO Ernest Dillingham (rtd), Guernsey, October 1992.

pp. 289–90 'Stumme . . . came under fire': Kühn, *With Rommel in the Desert*, p. 154.

p. 291 'I have taken command': Fraser, op. cit., p. 373.

p. 291 'tremendous limitations': Pimlott, op. cit., p. 136.

p. 291 'Sometimes it is a disadvantage': ibid., p. 139.

p. 292 Three Axis infantry battalions: ibid., p. 138.

p. 292 'actually fell asleep': author interview, April 2001.

p. 292 'I actually saw a shell': author interview, April 2001.

p. 293 'a certain tactical advantage': Pimlott, op. cit., p. 136.

p. 293 'for the first time I swore' et seq.: Samwell, op. cit., pp. 41–7.

p. 295 the advice of medical officers: author interview with Colonel Tim Marten, April 2001.

p. 295 a man on a bicycle: Flatow memoir, IWM, 99/16/1.

p. 296 'Bell loaded with great eagerness': ibid.

p. 297 Montgomery became incensed: Hamilton, op. cit., p. 749.

Chapter 25

Apart from our interviews with four British survivors, the main narrative of the stand the 2nd Battalion of the Rifle Brigade made at 'Snipe' during the battle of El Alamein was put together from three documentary sources. First, a recording in the Sound Archives of the Imperial War Museum of a long public lecture Colonel Victor Buller Turner, VC, gave some years after the war. (The transcript runs to 43 pages.) Second, an account of the 'Snipe' action completed in May 1953 by Lieutenant-Colonel M. E. S. Laws, OBE, MC, RA, for the Historical Section of the Cabinet Office. Although the war had been over for eight years and the six-pounder anti-tank gun was long since obsolete, the British love of secrecy resulted in the cover of Laws's typescript being labelled 'To be kept under lock and key. The information contained in this document is not to be communicated either directly or indirectly to the press or to any other person not authorised to receive it.' It is now available to any interested member of the public who can get to the London suburb of Kew and visit the Public Record Office. The third, and probably the most authoritative, document is an account written for their battalion shortly after the event by Captain (later Colonel) Tim Marten and Major Tom Bird, DSO, MC and bar. Colonel Marten made a copy available to the authors.

p. 298 'what can be done by surprise': G. H. Mills and R. F. Nixon, *The Annals of the King's Royal Rifle Corps*, Vol. VI, p. 304.

p. 299 'on the backs of the shells': Colonel Victor Buller Turner VC, IWM Sound Archives 13023/4.

p. 299 'We were like a family': Swann–author interview, May 2001.

p. 299 'they had long experience': Marten–author interview, May 2001.

p. 300 'Here we are': ibid.

p. 301 Bird always considered Chard: Tom Bird–author interview, February 2001.

p. 301 'like a massive car park': Swann, ibid.

p. 303 '"Aye," said one voice': Flatow memoir, IWM, 99/16/1.

p. 304 'Ducks in a . . . barrel': Blacker–author interview, April 2001.

p. 305 'We . . . pulled off the ammunition': Turner, IWM Sound Archives 13023/4.

p. 305 'self-propelled funeral pyres': Caccia-Dominioni, op. cit., p. 215.

p. 306 'Hat trick!': Calistan, in his account in the *Rifle Brigade Chronicle* 26–27 Oct. 1942, p. 152, Green Jackets' Museum, Winchester.

p. 306 'Sink that destroyer!': Marten interview.

p. 306 'During an unpleasant day': 2RB Report, Sheet 7. Copy given to authors by Colonel Marten.

p. 307 got to within 100 yards: Marten-Bird written account.

p. 308 Hine held his fire: ibid.

p. 309 'He's got him!': Marten interview.

p. 309 'nicely silhouetted': 2RB Report, Sheet 8.

p. 309 'I . . . kissed my gun': Calistan, ibid.

p. 310 'some weird swaying figures': Flatow, IWM, op. cit.

p. 310 'lost all my officers': Bird interview.

Chapter 26

p. 313 'rotten Pommy bastards': Main memoir, IWM, 87/35/1.

p. 313 'roaring drunk': Caccia-Dominioni, op. cit., p. 219.

p. 313 'distinct smell of liquor': Ranft–author interview, May 2001.

p. 314 'one more attempt': Liddell-Hart, op. cit., p. 293.

p. 315 'The courage of these men': Maughan, op. cit., p. 722.

p. 315 'I like you, sir': Douglas, *Alamein to Zem Zem*, p. 17.

p. 315 'blazed like a beacon': ibid., p. 42.

p. 316 'When we've destroyed': ibid., p. 46.

p. 316 'What . . . was my Monty doing': Bryant, op. cit., pp. 421–2.

p. 316 'shaken his confidence': Fraser, op. cit., p. 272.

p. 317 'I had my own doubts': Bryant, op. cit., p. 423.

p. 319 'If you do': de Guingand, op. cit., p. 295.

p. 319 'I haven't much hope left': Pimlott, op. cit., p. 142.

p. 320 The ammunition ship *Tergestea*: McKee, op. cit., pp. 122–3.

p. 320 'This was the master plan': Montgomery, *Memoirs*, p. 117.

Chapter 27

p. 322   'doubts in high places': Montgomery, *Memoirs*, p. 121.

p. 322   'If everything goes really well': Montgomery, letter to Brooke dated 1 November 1942, Alanbrooke Papers, Liddell-Hart Centre for Military Archives, King's College, London, published by Army Records Society, *Montgomery and the Eighth Army*, p. 78.

p. 323   'They thought Africa would be easier': Völker—author interview, July 2000.

p. 323   'I thought I was dreaming': ibid.

p. 323   'figures with their arms up': Watson memoir, IWM Sound Archives, 15012/7.

p. 325   'They could not avoid the tanks': Diath, *The Royal Wiltshire Yeomanry*, p. 205.

p. 325   'the battlefield was thick with smoke': Bolitho, *The Galloping Third*, p. 278.

p. 326   'If the British armour owed any debt': Montgomery in *The Sunday Times*, 22 October 1967.

p. 327   'Sleepy Axis guards sat rubbing': Pitt-Rivers, *The Story of the Royal Dragoons 1938–1945*, p. 60.

p. 327   'to take advantage': Wiltshires regimental history, p. 145.

p. 328   He had only twenty-four 88-mm guns left: Pimlott, op. cit., p. 141.

p. 328   'extricate the remnants': Fraser, op. cit., p. 272.

p. 328   'treading on air': Bryant, op. cit., p. 425.

p. 328   'The Führer must be crazy': Irving, op. cit., p. 213.

p. 329   'disproportionate . . . disapproval': PRO INF 1/284.

p. 330   'Typical of the army': Völker—author interview, July 2000.

p. 331   'I am Burckhardt': Household Cavalry regimental history, p. 86.

p. 331   'The British were good to us': Neumaier interview for German TV, 1982.

p. 331   'by 3rd or 4th of November': Calio—author interview, March 2001.

p. 332   'The paratroopers shouted "Folgore!"': Caccia-Dominioni, op. cit., p. 242.

p. 332   'twenty Italians at a time': Kennett—author interview, May 2001.

p. 333   'Do you know the Italian': Greenfield, *Chasing the Beast*, p. 204.

p. 334   'The German glanced casually': Douglas, op. cit., p. 64.

p. 334   'We have a new experience': Carver, op. cit., p. 188.

p. 334 'Did you hear them': *Chronicle of the 20th Century*, Longman, 1989, p. 575.

p. 334 Eighth Army casualties: PRO CAB 106/792.

Chapter 28

p. 339 'an awed disquiet': PRO INF 1/284.

p. 339 'the strain . . . was intense': Bryant, op. cit., p. 317.

p. 339 'scared shitless': author interview Guernsey, 1992.

p. 340 'dead to blame': Jellison, op. cit., p. 164.

p. 340 'did not . . . accept what I was told': Churchill, op. cit., p. 256.

p. 341 'What do you mean': Strickland, op. cit., IWM.

p. 342 'the necessary fighting spirit': Bekker, *Hitler's Naval War*, pp. 253–4.

p. 342 'pressed to the last gasp': Churchill, op. cit., p. 254.

p. 343 'some people smoked bamboo': Strickland, op. cit., IWM.

p. 344 'three thin sausages': Lee, op. cit., IWM.

p. 344 'more than could be borne': Churchill, op. cit., p. 255.

pp. 344ff. War of the convoys: Operation Pedestal, supplement to the *London Gazette*, 10 May 1948; official log of SS *Ohio*; Cunningham, op. cit.; et al.

Chapter 29

p. 348 'Having miraculously survived': Carver, op. cit., p. 188.

p. 353 demolishing rooftop machine-gun positions: Kühn, *With Rommel in the Desert*, p. 170.

p. 353 when seventeen American-manned: Liddell-Hart, op. cit., p. 338.

p. 354 Ammuntion was running low because: Kühn, op. cit., p. 180.

p. 355 lay a Knight's Cross: Kühn, op. cit., p. 180.

p. 355 Allied intelligence estimated: Liddell-Hart, op. cit., p. 341.

p. 356 'Even if we had overrun': *Rommel Papers*, as quoted by Young, op. cit., p. 307.

p. 357 'How dare you': Irving, op. cit., p. 224.

p. 358 'You must excuse me': Young, op. cit., p. 193.

p. 358 an enormous diamond ring: Moseley, *The Reich Marshal*, p. 293.

p. 358 'They call me': ibid.

p. 358 'They just can't and won't see': Irving, op. cit., p. 226.

p. 359 '[he] finally buried his head': ibid., p. 227.

p. 359 'windy and starting to': Army Records Society, p. 97.

p. 360 'outdated jazz numbers': Timpson, *In Rommel's Backyard*, p. 159.

p. 361 'a large lump': Bryant, op. cit., pp. 474–5.

p. 362 'I am so depressed': Pimlott, op. cit., pp. 157–8.

p. 366 'You go to hell': Blummerson, *Kasserine*, pp. 82–4.

p. 366 shouting 'Hitler!' and 'Rommel!': Fraser, *Knight's Cross*, p. 405.

p. 367 'We passed a dead American negro': Schmidt, op. cit., p. 199.

p. 367 'I jerked the wheel': Schmidt, ibid., p. 200.

p. 368 At about this time, an Anglo-American wireless intelligence unit: Skillen, *Spies of the Airwaves*, p. 274.

p. 368 'I feel like an old warhorse': IWM, EAP 21-X-14/9.

p. 368 apart from conveying expessions of: Irving, op. cit., pp. 235–6.

p. 369 'a severe inferiority': Pimlott, op. cit., p. 158.

p. 369 hold El Kef: Clarke, *With Alex at War*, p. 85.

p. 369 The US official history: Howe, *The Mediterranean Theatre of Operations: Northwest Africa: Seizing the Initiative in the West*, p. 456.

p. 370 'The Americans were remarkably well equipped': Pimlott, op. cit., pp. 159–60.

p. 371 'Apparently, I am no longer *persona non grata*': ibid., p. 159.

p. 371 'very well judged': Liddell-Hart, op. cit., p. 410.

p. 372 'I would like to go to Brooklyn': Schmidt, op. cit., pp. 208–10.

p. 372 'It appears that the Boche': *Montgomery and the Eighth Army*, Army Records Society, p. 153.

p. 372 'They simply do not know their jobs': Clarke, op. cit., p. 84.

p. 372 'It was the old story': Montgomery, op. cit., p. 141.

p. 373 about seventy tanks were destroyed: Liddell-Hart, op. cit., p. 412.

p. 373 'good infantry holding strong pivots': letter to General Sir Alan Brooke, March 1943, *Montgomery and the Eighth Army*, Army Records Society, p. 172.

p. 373 'There must be NO WITHDRAWAL': ibid., p. 159.

p. 373 'They were like a bunch': Millard, *Patton the Commander*, p. 66.

p. 375 'The Marshal has made a balls of it': Hamilton, *Monty*, Vol. 2, p. 172.

p. 375 'Many others were damaged and towed away': Army Records Society, p. 172.

p. 375 'to gain time': *Rommel Papers*, as quoted by Young, op. cit., p. 307.

p. 376 handing out signed photographs: Fraser, *Knight's Cross*, p. 413.

Chapter 30

p. 377 'On the run, his Irish friends': Kenneally, *Kenneally VC*, p. 33.

p. 378 'Welcome to the Micks!': Clarke, op. cit., p. 87.

p. 378 'Once I loose my Army': letter from Montgomery to Brooke, 17.3.43, Army Records Society, p. 176.

p. 378 'I was only one of his mother's': *Daily Telegraph* obituary of John Patrick Kenneally, 28 September 2000.

p. 381 'They destroyed or damaged': Stewart, *Eighth Army's Greatest Victories*, p. 165.

p. 382 But Freyberg . . . was always a cautious general: McLeod, op. cit., pp. 179–82.

p. 382 'practically shell and bomb proof': Schmidt, op. cit., p. 222.

p. 383 Revolver in hand: Laffin, *British VCs of World War Two*, pp. 90–91.

p. 383 Some of the Germans: Schmidt, op. cit., p. 223.

p. 384 Engineers managed: Stewart, op. cit., pp. 171–2.

p. 384 One lane was blocked: Stewart, ibid., p. 172, quoting Jackson, General Sir William, *The North African Campaign 1940–43*, Batsford, London, 1975.

p. 384 'scrambling over shattered masonry': Schmidt, op. cit., p. 224.

p. 384 'Now the game was on': ibid., p. 225.

p. 385 'Our doctor bandaged': ibid., p. 226.

p. 386 'He has no brains': Hamilton, op. cit., Vol. 2, p. 212.

p. 386 'I shall now nourish': hand-written note to Alexander dated 23 March 1943, Army Record Society, p. 180.

p. 387 'the whole boiling match': Stewart, op. cit., p. 180.

p. 388 'still rather shaken and dazed': Close, op. cit., p. 93.

p. 388 'I became rather excited': ibid., p. 94.

p. 389 'toughest fight since Alamein': Montgomery diary notes 20–28 March 1943, Army Records Society, p. 184.

p. 389 'It was the most': ibid., p. 185.

p. 389 'I suppose they think': ibid., p. 191.

p. 390 Reports from night patrols of the 1st Royal Sussex: Stewart, op. cit., p. 186.

pp. 390–1 Now he was wondering: Farwell, *The Gurkhas*, p. 187.

p. 390 all the radios with the headquarters: ibid., p. 188.

p. 392 killed two of its crew: ibid., p. 189.

p. 392 'spectrally in the half light': Scannell, op. cit., p. 20.

p. 392 'All the best, mate': ibid.

p. 392 It was personally pinned to his breast: Farwell, p. 189.

p. 393 'The more the fighting': letter to Sir Alan Brooke, 15 April 1943, Army Records Society, p. 210.

p. 393 'Human figures moved insectile': Scannell, op. cit., p. 21.

p. 393 'Hughie said, "There's one poor"': ibid., p. 22.

p. 393 '[I]mmodest yet childlike': ibid., p. 27.

p. 393 'They seemed to be': ibid., p. 23.

p. 395 'A man of outstanding': Laffin, op. cit., p. 94.

p. 395 'We had on this day': Army Records Society, p. 198.

p. 398 'Some thought we should be': Schmidt, op. cit., p. 237.

p. 398 'Giant crags and deep gullies': ibid.

p. 398 The VC was awarded: Stewart, op. cit., p. 199.

p. 399 '56 Division gave a very bad': Army Records Society, p. 220.

p. 399 'It was like a crowd of spectators': Skillen, op. cit., p. 328.

p. 402 'A German voice': Kenneally, op. cit., p. 82.

p. 402 'Holy Mother of Christ!': ibid., p. 83.

p. 403 'dies in my heart': *Daily Telegraph* obituary, 28 September 2000.

p. 403 'made in my caravan': Army Records Society, p. 266.

p. 404 'Over a year ago': Schmidt, op. cit., p. 238.

p. 404 'huddled in an overcrowded': ibid.

p. 404 First Army lacked: Liddell-Hart, op. cit., p. 428.

p. 405 'No one had warned them': Moorehead, op. cit., p. 563

p. 406 'that seemed madness': ibid.

p. 407 During his first hours: Skillen, op. cit., p. 335.

p. 407 They called it 'Tunisgrad': Kühn, op. cit., p. 205.

Chronology

10 June 1940	Mussolini declares war, Italian bombers raid Malta.
13 September 1940	Italian forces invade Egypt from Cyrenaica, advance as far as Sidi Barrani.
9 December 1940	British open counter-offensive, Italians go reeling back.
5 January 1941	Australians capture Bardia, taking 40,000 Italian prisoners.
7 February 1941	Retreating Italian Tenth Army cut off and most of it captured at Beda Fomm. Total of prisoners in two-month campaign: 130,000.
12 February 1941	Rommel arrives with advance party of Afrika Korps.
31 March 1941	Rommel launches his first offensive, driving back British forces depleted by sending battle-hardened troops to help Greece.
13 April 1941	Afrika Korps begin siege of the vital port of Tobruk.
27 April 1941	All British forces, except the besieged Tobruk garrison, withdraw across border into Egypt.
15 June 1941	British launch Operation Battleaxe in vain bid to relieve Tobruk. Germans throw them back to start line.
5 July 1941	Churchill sacks Wavell, replacing him as C-in-C Middle East by Auchinleck.
17/18 November 1941	British attempt to assassinate Rommel with raid on a rear HQ, but he is elsewhere.
18 November 1941	Auchinleck launches Operation Crusader to retake Cyrenaica and relieve Tobruk.

19–22 November 1941	Bloody and confused armoured battles around Sidi Rezegh leave Rommel with tactical advantage. Cunningham begins to crack and Auchinleck leaves Cairo to take personal command. Ritchie succeeds Cunningham.
7 December 1941	Tobruk relieved after 242-day siege, but victory is eclipsed by news of Japanese attack on Pearl Harbor.
30 December 1941	Rommel completes withdrawal in good order, clearing out of Cyrenaica and digging in at Mersa el Brega. Auchinleck's command depleted by need to send reinforcements to fight Japanese in Far East.
21 January 1942	Rommel launches new offensive from Mersa el Brega line, lunging forward at great speed.
29 January 1942	Benghazi falls to Axis forces.
7 February 1942	British stop Rommel at Gazala line; three months' lull follows.
26 May 1942	Rommel strikes again, catching British by surprise and outflanking them. 'Cauldron' battles follow.
21 June 1942	Tobruk falls to whirlwind German attack; 33,000 British and South African troops captured with vast stockpile of supplies and equipment.
25 June 1942	Auchinleck sacks Ritchie, and takes direct command of Eighth Army.
1 July 1942	British fall back to El Alamein, where they first repulse Axis attacks, then launch series of counter-attacks.
22 July 1942	First Battle of Alamein ends in deadlock
5 August 1942	Churchill, on visit to Egypt, decides to sack Auchinleck, replacing him as C-in-C with Alexander and choosing Gott to command Eighth Army, despite Sir Alan Brooke's misgivings.

7 August 1942	Gott shot down and killed while flying to Cairo to take command. Montgomery chosen to take his place.
13 August 1942	Montgomery assumes command.
30 August 1942	Rommel tries to outflank British again in desperate bid to reach Nile Delta, sixty miles away, but is stopped by Montgomery at Alam el Halfa Ridge.
September–October 1942	Both sides build up for decisive next round, Montgomery refusing Churchill's demands for attack until he is quite ready.
23 October 1942	The second Battle of Alamein opens with a colossal British artillery barrage, but after a week of hard fighting by the infantry the British armour has still not broken through.
1–2 November 1942	As the Australians draw away most of Rommel's armour, Montgomery renews his offensive by launching Operation Supercharge, just south of the Australian sector.
4 November 1942	British tanks break through at last and Rommel's Panzerarmee Afrika begins to retire in good order.
8 November 1942	Operation Torch, the Anglo-American invasion of French North Africa, is successfully launched.
4 February 1943	Last Axis forces cleared out of Libya; Eighth Army continues advance into Tunisia.
12 May 1943	Germans and Italians surrender at Tunis; 275,000 Axis prisoners taken. End of war in North Africa.

Bibliography

Agar-Hamilton, J. A. I., and L. C. F. Turner *Crisis in the Desert*, OUP, Oxford, 1950

Arena, Nino *Folgore: Storia del Paracadutism Militare Italiano*, Centro Editoriale, Rome, 1966

Badoglio, Pietro *Italy in the Second World War*, Greenwood Press, Westport, Connecticut, 1976

Bagnold, R. A. *Sand, Wind and War: Memoirs of a Desert Explorer*, University of Arizona Press, Tucson, 1990; *Libyan Sands, Travels in a Dead World*, Hodder and Stoughton, London, 1935; *The Physics of Blown Sand*, Morrow, New York, 1941

Beaton, Cecil *Near East*, Batsford, London, 1943

Behrend, Hans-Otto *Rommel's Intelligence in the Desert Campaign*, William Kimber, London, 1985

Bekker, Cajus *Hitler's Naval War*, MacDonald, London 1974; *The Luftwaffe Diaries*, MacDonald, London, 1967

Bennett, Ralph *Ultra and Mediterranean Strategy*, Hamish Hamilton, London, 1989

Bergot, Erwan *The Afrika Korps*, W. H. Allen, New York, 1975

Blummerson, M. *Kasserine*, Dell Publishing, New York, 1963

Blythe, Ronald (ed.) *Private Words, Letters and Diaries from the Second World War*, Penguin, 1993

Bolitho, Hector *The Galloping Third*, John Murray, London, 1963

Brooks, Stephen (ed.) *Montgomery and the Eighth Army*, Bodley Head (for the Army Records Society), London, 1991

Bryant, Sir Arthur *The Turn of the Tide 1939–1943*, Collins, London, 1958

Caccia-Dominioni, Paolo (trans. Dennis Chamberlain) *Alamein 1933–1962: An Italian Story*, Allen and Unwin, London, 1966

Calder, Angus *The Myth of the Blitz*, Pimlico, London, 1992

Carell, Paul *The Foxes of the Desert*, MacDonald, London, 1953

Carver, Field Marshal Lord *El Alamein*, Wordsworth Edition, Ware, Hertfordshire, 2000

Channon, Sir Charles *Letters*, Weidenfeld & Nicolson, London, 1967

Churchill, Winston *The Second World War*, Vols 3 and 4, Cassell, London, 1951

Ciano, Galeazzo *Diary, 1939–43*, William Heinemann, London, 1947

Clarke, Rupert *With Alex at War*, Leo Cooper, Barnsley, 2000

Close, Bill *A View from the Turret*, Dell and Breden, Tewkesbury, Glos, 1998

Collier, Richard *The War in the Desert*, Time Life Books, Alexandria, VA, 1979

Connell, John *Wavell, Soldier and Scholar*, Collins, London, 1964

Cooper, Artemis *Cairo in the War 1939–1945*, Penguin, London, 1995

Coward, Noël *Middle East Diary*, Heinemann, London, 1944

Cowles, Virginia *The Phantom Major*, Collins, London, 1958

Crimp, R. L. *Diary of a Desert Rat*, Leo Cooper, London, 1971

Cruickshank, Charles *Deception in World War Two*, Oxford University Press, 1979; *Greece 1940–41*, Davis-Poynter Ltd, London, 1976

Cunningham, Admiral Sir Andrew *A Sailor's Odyssey*, Dutton, New York, 1951

Dahl, Roald *Over to You*, Penguin, London, 1986

Dear, I. C. B. and Foot, M. R. D. (Eds) *The Oxford Companion to the Second World War*, Oxford, 1995

Deighton, Len *Blitzkrieg*, Jonathan Cape, London, 1979

Delaforce, Patrick *Montgomery's Highlanders*, Tom Donovan Publishing, 1997

Diath, J. R. I. *The Royal Wiltshire Yeomanry*, Garnstone Press, London, 1972

Dobbie, William *A Very Present Help*, Marshall, Morgan and Scott, London, 1945

Doronzo, Rafael *Folgore! Diario di un Paracantista*, Gruppa Murcia, Milan, 1995

Douglas, Keith *Alamein to Zem Zem*, Faber & Faber, London, 1992; *The Complete Poems*, OUP, Oxford and NY, 3rd edn, 1998

Du Preez, Laurie *Inside the Cage*, C. Struik (Pty) Ltd, Cape Town, 1973

Durrell, Lawrence *Spirit of Place*, Faber & Faber, London, 1969

Ellis, John *The Sharp End of the War*, Corgi, London, 1982

Eppler, John *Operation Condor: Rommel's Spy*, Futura, London, 1978

Essame, H. *Patton – The Commander*, Purnell Book Services, London, 1974

Farndale, Martin *History of the Royal Regiment of Artillery, The Years of Defeat 1939–41*, Brassey's, London, 1996

Farwell, Byron *The Gurkhas*, Penguin, London, 1985

Fergusson, Bernard *The Black Watch and the King's Enemies*, Collins, London, 1950

Fisher, David *The War Magician*, Putnam Publishing Group, New York, 1983; Corgi, London, 1985

Forty, George *The Afrika Korps at War* (two vols), Ian Allan Publishing, Littlehampton, 1979

Fraser, David *And We Shall Shock Them*, Cassell Military Paperbacks, London, 1999; *Knight's Cross: A Life of Field Marshal Rommel*, HarperCollins, London, 1993; *Alanbrooke*, HarperCollins, London, 1982

Fussell, Paul *Wartime: Understanding and Behaviour in the Second World War*, Oxford, 1989

Gilbert, Adrian (ed.) *The Imperial War Museum Book of the Desert War, 1940–42*, Sidgwick and Jackson, London, 1992

Gilbert, Martin *The First World War*, Weidenfeld & Nicolson, London, 1994

Gordon, John W. *The Other Desert War*, Greenwood Press, Westport, Conn., 1987

Graham, Desmond *Keith Douglas, a Biography*, OUP, Oxford, 1988

Gravina, Igino *Le Tre Battaglie di Alamein*, Longaresi, Milan, 1971

Greacen, Lavinia *Chink*, Macmillan, London, 1989

Greenfield, George *Chasing the Beast*, Richard Cohen Books, London, 1999

de Guingand, General Sir Francis *Operation Victory*, Hodder & Stoughton, London, 1947; *From Brass Hat to Bowler Hat*, Hodder & Stoughton, 1979

Hamilton, Nigel *Monty* (Vols 1,2,3) Hamish Hamilton, London, 1981, 1983, 1986

Harrison, Frank *Tobruk, the Great Siege Reassessed*, Arms and Armour Press, London, 1996

Hibbert, Christopher *Benito Mussolini*, Penguin, London, 1975

Hinsley, F. H. and Stripp, Alan (eds) *Code Breakers: The Inside Story of Bletchley Park*, OUP, Oxford, 1993

Hoe, Alan *David Stirling*, Little, Brown, London, 1992

Holmes, Richard *Bir Hacheim, Desert Citadel*, Ballantine, NY, 1971

Horrocks, Sir Brian *A Full Life*, Collins, London, 1960

Howe, George F. *The Mediterranean Theatre of Operations: Northwest Africa: Seizing the Initiative in the West*, Office of the Chief of Military History, US Army, Washington, DC, 1955

Irving, David *The Trail of the Fox: the Life of Field Marshal Erwin Rommel*, Weidenfeld & Nicolson, London, 1977

James, Lawrence *Warrior Race*, Little, Brown, 2001

James, Malcolm (aka Malcolm Pleydell) *Born of the Desert, With the SAS in North Africa*, Greenhill Books, London, 1991

Jellison, Charles A. *Besieged: The World War II Ordeal of Malta, 1940–42*, University Press of New England, 1984

Johnson, J. E. *Full Circle: the Story of Air Fighting*, Chatto & Windus, London, 1964

Kahn, David *Hitler's Spies*, Hodder & Stoughton, London, 1978

Keegan, John *The Second World War*, Pimlico, London, 1997; *The Mask of Command*, Penguin, London, 1988

Kenneally, John Patrick *Kenneally VC*, Kenwood, Huddersfield, 1991

Kennedy-Shaw, W. B. *The LRDG*, Greenhill Books, London, 1989

King-Clark, Rex *Free for a Blast*, Grenville Publishing, London, 1988

Klein, Harry *Springboks in Armour*, Purnell & Sons, Cape Town, undated.

Kühn, Volkmar *With Rommel in the Desert. Victories and Defeat of the Afrika Korps 1941–43*, Schiffer Publishing, West Chester, Pennsylvania, 1991 (originally *Mit Rommel in der Wüste*, Motorbuch Verlag, Stuttgart).

Laffin, John *British VCs of World War Two*, Sutton Publishing, Stroud, Glos, 1997

Leakey, Rea (with George Forty) *Leakey's Luck*, Sutton Publishing, Stroud, Glos, 1999

Lebucois, Jean *Notre Première Victoire: La 1ere IDF à Bir Hacheim*, Editions Colbert, Paris, 1945

Liddell-Hart, B. H. *History of the Second World War*, Cassell, London, 1970

Lindsay, T. M. *Sherwood Rangers*, Burrup, Mathieson & Co., London, 1952

Lively, Penelope *Oleander, Jacaranda*, Penguin, London, 1995

Lucas, James *Rommel's Year of Victory*, Greenhill Books, London, 1998; *War in the Desert – the Eighth Army at El Alamein*, Arms and Armour Press, London, 1982

Lucas-Phillips, C. E. *Alamein*, Heinemann, London, 1962

Maclean, Fitzroy *Eastern Approaches*, Jonathan Cape, London, 1949; Penguin, 1991

Manning, Olivia *The Levant Trilogy*, Penguin, London, 1982

Mason, Philip *A Matter of Honour*, Jonathan Cape, London, 1974

Mather, Carol *When the Grass Stops Growing*, Leo Cooper, Barnsley, 1999

Maughan, Barton *Tobruk and El Alamein: Australia in the War of 1939–45*, Australian War Memorial, Canberra, 1966

Maule, Henry *Spearhead General: the Epic Story of Sir Francis Messervy*, Odhams, London, 1961

McGuirk, Dal *Afrika Korps Self Portrait*, Airlife Publishing, Shrewsbury, England, 1992

McKee, Alexander *El Alamein: Ultra and the Three Battles*, Souvenir Press, London, 1991

McLeod, John *Myth and Reality – The New Zealand Soldier in World War Two*, Heinemann Reed, Auckland, New Zealand, 1986

Mellenthin, F. W. von *Panzer Battles: A Study of Employment of Armor during the Second World War*, Ballantine Books, NY, 1976

Messenger, Charles *The Middle East Commandos*, William Kimber, London, 1988

Millard, Harmon *Patton the Commander*, Purnell Book Services, London, 1974

Mitcham, Samuel, and Mueller, Gene *Hitler's Commanders*, Scarborough Books, Maryland, 1993

Montgomery, Bernard Law *The Memoirs of Field Marshal The Viscount Montgomery of Alamein, K.G.*, New American Library, New York, 1959

Moorehead, Alan *African Trilogy*, Hamish Hamilton, London, 1944; *A Late Education*, Penguin, London, 1976

Moseley, Leonard *Gideon Goes to War*, Arthur Barker, London, 1955; *The Reich Marshal*, Weidenfeld & Nicolson, 1974

Mure, David *Master of Deception*, William Kimber, London, 1980

Neillands, Robin *The Desert Rats*, Orion, London, 1997

Norman, Bruce *Secret Warfare: The Battle of Codes and Ciphers*, David and Charles, Newton Abbot, 1973

Otway, T. B. H. *British Airborne Forces*, IWM Facsimile Reprint, London, 1990

Page, Martin *Kiss Me Goodnight Sergeant-Major*, Granada, London, 1973; *For Gawdsake Don't Take Me*, Granada, London, 1977

Parkinson, Roger *The Auk, Victor at Alamein*, Granada, London, 1977

Peniakoff, Vladimir *Popski's Private Army*, Jonathan Cape, London, 1950

Phillips, Cecil *El Alamein*, Heinemann, London, 1962

Pimlott, John (ed.) *Rommel in His Own Words*, Greenhill Books, London, 1994

Pitt-Rivers, J. A. *The Story of the Royal Dragoons 1938–1945*, Wm Clowes & Son, London, undated

Playfair, ISO *History of the Second World War, The Mediterranean and the Middle East*, HMSO, 1966

Quilter, D. C. *No Dishonoured Name: The 2nd and 3rd Battalions Coldstream Guards, 1939–46*, William Clowes & Sons, London, 1947

Ranfurly, Countess of *To War with Whitaker, The Wartime Diaries of the Countess of Ranfurly, 1939–45*, Mandarin, London, 1995

Robinson, Derek *A Good Clean Fight*, HarperCollins, London, 1994

Rommel, Field Marshal Erwin *Infantry Attacks*, The English Book Depot, Dehra Dun, India, 1967

Rosmarin, Ike *Inside Story*, Flesch, Capetown, 1990

Sadat, Anwar el *In Search of Identity: an Autobiography*, Harper & Row, New York, 1977; *Revolt on the Nile*, Allan Wingate, London, 1957

Samwell, H. P. *An Infantry Officer with the Eighth Army*, Blackwood, London, 1945

Sansom, A. E. W. *I Spied Spies*, Harrap, London, 1965

Scannell, Vernon *Argument of Kings*, Futura, London, 1989

Schmidt, Heinz-Werner *With Rommel in the Desert*, Constable, London, 1997

Seton-Watson, Christopher *Letters and Diaries of an Artilleryman 1939–45*, Buckland Publications, London, 1993

Shankland, Peter and Hunter, Anthony *Malta Convoy*, Collins, London, 1961

Skillen, Hugh *Spies of the Airwaves*, privately published by Hugh Skillen, 56 St Thomas Drive, Pinner, Middlesex HA5 4SS, 1989

Smith, Peter C. *Pedestal: the Malta Convoy of August 1942*, William Kimber, London, 1970; *Massacre at Tobruk*, William Kimber, London, 1987

Stewart, Adrian *Eighth Army's Greatest Victories – Alam Halfa to Tunis 1942–1943*, Leo Cooper, Barnsley, 1999

Thompson, Julian *War Behind Enemy Lines*, Imperial War Museum/Sidgwick and Jackson, London, 1998

Timpson, Alastair, with Gibson-Watt, Andrew *In Rommel's Backyard*, Leo Cooper, Barnsley, 2000

Travers, Susan *Tomorrow to Be Brave*, Bantam Press, London, 2000

Tute, Warren *The North African War*, Sidgwick and Jackson, London, 1976

Verney, John *Going to the Wars*, Collins, London, 1955

Warner, Philip *The Special Air Service*, William Kimber, London, 1971

Wilmot, Chester *Tobruk*, Angus & Robertson, Sydney, 1945

Winston, John *Cunningham, the Greatest Admiral Since Nelson*, John Murray, London, 1998

Young, Desmond *Rommel the Desert Fox*, Fontana, London, 1955

Ziegler, Philip *Mountbatten*, Knopf, New York, 1985

Index